Public Policy

Public Policy
A Concise Introduction

Sara R. Rinfret
University of Montana

Denise Scheberle
University of Colorado, Denver

Michelle C. Pautz
University of Dayton

FOR INFORMATION:

CQ Press

An Imprint of SAGE Publications, Inc.

2455 Teller Road

Thousand Oaks, California 91320

E-mail: order@sagepub.com

SAGE Publications Ltd.

1 Oliver's Yard

55 City Road

London, EC1Y 1SP

United Kingdom

SAGE Publications India Pvt. Ltd.

B 1/I 1 Mohan Cooperative Industrial Area

Mathura Road, New Delhi 110 044

India

SAGE Publications Asia-Pacific Pte. Ltd.

3 Church Street

#10-04 Samsung Hub

Singapore 049483

Acquisitions Editor: Scott Greenan

Editorial Assistant: Sarah Christensen

Content Development Editor: Anna Villarruel

Production Editor: Tracy Buyan

Copy Editor: Talia Greenberg

Typesetter: Cenveo

Proofreader: Eleni-Maria Georgiou

Indexer: May Hasso

Cover Designer: Dally Verghese

Marketing Manager: Jennifer Jones

Printed in the United States of America

Library of Congress Cataloging-in-Publication Data

Names: Rinfret, Sara R., author. | Scheberle, Denise, author. | Pautz, Michelle C., author.

Title: Public policy : a concise introduction / Sara Rinfret, Denise Scheberle, Michelle C. Pautz.

Description: Thousand Oaks, California : CQ Press, 2018. | Includes bibliographical references and index.

Identifiers: LCCN 2018006959 | ISBN 9781506329710 (pbk.) Subjects: LCSH: Political planning–United States. | Public administration–United States.

Classification: LCC JK468.P64 R56 2018 | DDC 320.60973–dc23 LC record available at https://lccn.loc.gov/2018006959

This book is printed on acid-free paper.

19 20 21 22 10 9 8 7 6 5 4 3 2

Brief Contents

LIST OF FIGURES AND TABLES   xvi

PREFACE   xviii

ACKNOWLEDGMENTS   xxi

ABOUT THE AUTHORS   xxiii

SECTION I   DEFINING U.S. PUBLIC POLICYMAKING

CHAPTER 1   The Foundation   1

CHAPTER 2   The Policy Process and Policy Theories   19

SECTION II   THE PRACTICE OF PUBLIC POLICY

CHAPTER 3   Federalism and Intergovernmental Relations   45

CHAPTER 4   Rulemaking and Regulations   71

SECTION III   UNDERSTANDING KEY PUBLIC POLICY ISSUES

CHAPTER 5   Economic Policy and Public Budgeting   95

CHAPTER 6   Crime and Public Policy   126

CHAPTER 7   Education Policy   154

CHAPTER 8   Civil Rights and Immigration Policy   177

CHAPTER 9   Social Welfare and Health Care Policy   205

CHAPTER 10 **Environmental and Energy Policy**   235

CONCLUSION   268

GLOSSARY   279

REFERENCES   284

INDEX   300

Detailed Contents

LIST OF FIGURES AND TABLES   xvi

PREFACE   xviii

ACKNOWLEDGMENTS   xxi

ABOUT THE AUTHORS   xxiii

SECTION I   DEFINING U.S. PUBLIC POLICYMAKING

CHAPTER 1   **The Foundation**   1

LEARNING OBJECTIVES   1

OPENING VIGNETTE: PUBLIC POLICY AND OUR EVERYDAY LIVES   1

STARTING WITH A DEFINITION   2

Power and Politics   3

A Federal System   3

Categories of Public Policy   4

THE PROCESS   5

A MOTLEY CREW: INSTITUTIONAL AND NONINSTITUTIONAL ACTORS   7

The Three Branches of Government   7

The Implementers   9

The Media, Interest Groups, and Us   10

Shaping Policy   11

What about Us?   12

POLICY ANALYSIS   12

Policy Evaluation   13

WHY STUDYING PUBLIC POLICY MATTERS   13

PLAN OF THE BOOK   14

CONCLUDING THOUGHTS   17

GLOSSARY TERMS   17

DISCUSSION QUESTIONS   17

SUGGESTED RESOURCES   18

NOTES   18

CHAPTER 2   **The Policy Process and Policy Theories**   19

LEARNING OBJECTIVES   19

OPENING VIGNETTE: POLICY RHETORIC AND REALITY   19

WHAT REALLY IS POLICY?   20

UNDERSTANDING THE CONTEXT OF PUBLIC POLICY   21
  The Political Environment   21
  The Economic Environment   22
  The Social and Cultural Environment   23
  The Administrative Environment   23

THE QUEST FOR PUBLIC POLICY THEORY   24

THE STAGES HEURISTIC MODEL OF PUBLIC POLICYMAKING   26
  Sugary Drinks   27
  Stage 1: Problem Identification and Definition   27
  Stage 2: Agenda Setting   28
  Stage 3: Policy Formulation   30
  Stage 4: Policy Legitimation   33
  Stage 5: Policy Implementation   33
  Stage 6: Policy Evaluation   35
  Assessing the Stages Model   37

ALTERNATIVE POLICY PROCESS MODELS   38
  Multiple Streams Framework   38
  Pros and Cons of the MSF   39
  Punctuated Equilibrium   40

ACTORS IN THE POLICY PROCESS   41

CONCLUDING THOUGHTS   42

GLOSSARY TERMS   43

DISCUSSION QUESTIONS   43

SUGGESTED RESOURCES   43

SECTION II   THE PRACTICE OF PUBLIC POLICY

CHAPTER 3   Federalism and Intergovernmental Relations   45

LEARNING OBJECTIVES   45

OPENING VIGNETTE: UP IN SMOKE: FEDERAL AND STATE
MARIJUANA POLICIES COLLIDE   45

TELLING STORIES WITH DATA: USING GALLUP POLLING
DATA TO DETECT TRENDS   47

OVERVIEW OF FEDERALISM AND INTERGOVERNMENTAL
RELATIONS   48
  National Policymaking Constrained under the Articles of
  Confederation   48
  Constitutional Foundation of Federalism   49
  Intergovernmental Relations   50

FEDERALISM AND INTERGOVERNMENTAL RELATIONS
EVOLVE   51
  Dual Federalism   52
  Cooperative Federalism   53
  Creative Federalism   54

FEDERALISM AND INTERGOVERNMENTAL RELATIONS
TODAY 56

  Underfunded and Unfunded Mandates 56

  Building Picket Fences 58

  Increasing Capacity of State and Local Governments 60

  Differences in State Cultures, Politics, Economies,
    and Events 62

ENDURING VIRTUES OF A FEDERAL SYSTEM 66

  Safeguards Individual Rights and Democracy 66

  Promotes Responsibility 66

  Stimulates Innovation 67

  Increases Efficiency and Effectiveness in Policy
  Implementation 67

EVERYDAY CITIZEN CONNECTION 67

CONCLUDING THOUGHTS 68

GLOSSARY TERMS 69

DISCUSSION QUESTIONS 69

SUGGESTED RESOURCES 70

CHAPTER 4 **Rulemaking and Regulations** **71**

LEARNING OBJECTIVES 71

OPENING VIGNETTE: FROM PEANUTS ON A PLANE TO
  THE FUTURE OF E-CIGARETTES 71

UNDERSTANDING THE CONTEXT OF U.S. REGULATIONS 73

  Defining Regulatory Policy 74

  Delegation of Authority 76

  Why Delegate? 76

  Congress and Accountability 77

  The President and Accountability 78

  The Supreme Court and Accountability 79

UNDERSTANDING REGULATORY PROCESSES 79

  State Rulemaking 81

INFLUENCE AND PARTICIPATION 83

AFTER A RULE BECOMES A LAW 85

  Regulating Your Local Dry Cleaner 86

THE GOOD, THE BAD, AND THE UGLY 87

THE FUTURE OF REGULATORY POLICY 90

EVERYDAY CITIZEN CONNECTION 92

CONCLUDING THOUGHTS 92

GLOSSARY TERMS 93

DISCUSSION QUESTIONS 93

SUGGESTED RESOURCES 94

NOTES 94

SECTION III UNDERSTANDING KEY PUBLIC POLICY ISSUES

CHAPTER 5 **Economic Policy and Public Budgeting** 95

LEARNING OBJECTIVES 95

OPENING VIGNETTE: *GREEN EGGS AND HAM*
AND THE FEDERAL GOVERNMENT SHUTDOWN
IN 2013 95

OVERVIEW OF ECONOMIC POLICY AND PUBLIC
BUDGETING 96
    Types of Economies and Economic Policy Definition 97
    Economic Theories 97

SIZE AND SCOPE OF THE U.S. ECONOMY 98
    Public Opinion and the Economy 100

TELLING STORIES WITH DATA: USING THE BUREAU OF
LABOR STATISTICS TO EXPLORE REGIONAL
ECONOMIC DATA 102
    Monetary and Fiscal Policy 103

THE FEDERAL BUDGET 104
    Budget Process 105
    Government Revenues and Expenditures 107
    Revenues 107
    Expenditures 108
    Debt and Deficit 109

HISTORY AND DEVELOPMENT OF ECONOMIC POLICY 110
    Founding Period 111
    Growth of Government Spending 111
    Great Recession and Government Response 113

MAJOR ECONOMIC POLICY AND BUDGETING STATUTES 115

MAJOR ACTORS IN ECONOMIC POLICY 116
    Congress 116
    President 117
    Government Agencies 117

ISSUES AND CHALLENGES 119
    Political Polarization 119
    Debts and Deficits 119
    Global Markets and Free Trade 120

EVERYDAY CITIZEN CONNECTION 120

CONCLUDING THOUGHTS 121

POLICY CHOICES: THE FEDERAL TAX SYSTEM 122

POLICY CHOICES: FEDERAL TAX POLICY 123

GLOSSARY TERMS 124

DISCUSSION QUESTIONS 124

SUGGESTED RESOURCES 124

CHAPTER 6 **Crime and Public Policy**   126

LEARNING OBJECTIVES   126

OPENING VIGNETTE: GUNS ON CAMPUS: SAFETY OR RISK?   126

OVERVIEW OF CRIME IN AMERICA   128

     Types of Crime   128

     The U.S. Crime Rate   130

     Explaining Decreases in the U.S. Crime Rate   130

     Public Perceptions about Crime   134

     The U.S. Incarceration Rate   135

HISTORY AND DEVELOPMENT   137

     Federalizing Crime   137

     Public Attitudes about the Incidence of Crime   138

     Media and Crime   139

ACTORS IN CRIMINAL JUSTICE POLICY   140

     Federal Law Enforcement Agencies   140

     State and Local Law Enforcement Agencies   140

     Federal and State Courts   141

     Crime Victims   141

     Probation Officers and Parole Officers   142

MAJOR U.S. CRIMINAL JUSTICE AND CRIME POLICY STATUTES   142

     Capital Punishment   143

ISSUES AND CHALLENGES   144

     Deterrence and Recidivism   144

TELLING STORIES WITH DATA: THE DEATH PENALTY   145

     Crime and Race   146

     Juvenile Crime   147

     Mass Shootings   148

EVERYDAY CITIZEN CONNECTION   149

POLICY CHOICES: GUN CONTROL   150

CONCLUDING THOUGHTS   151

GLOSSARY TERMS   152

DISCUSSION QUESTIONS   152

SUGGESTED RESOURCES   152

CHAPTER 7 **Education Policy**   154

LEARNING OBJECTIVES   154

OPENING VIGNETTE: BEHIND THE CURTAIN OF A PUBLIC EDUCATION   154

OVERVIEW OF U.S. EDUCATION POLICY   155

     Understanding the Structure of a U.S. Education   155

     Status and Scope   157

TELLING STORIES WITH DATA: USING MAPS TO EXPLORE EDUCATION FUNDING   158

HISTORY AND DEVELOPMENT OF THE U.S.
EDUCATION SYSTEM   159
   Colonialism and Mann   159
   Challenges and Change   160
   Choice and a Digital Revolution   161
MAJOR EDUCATION POLICY STATUTES   162
   Major U.S. Education Laws   162
MAJOR ACTORS IN U.S. EDUCATION POLICY   163
   President   163
   Congress   164
   Courts   164
   Bureaucracy   165
STATE ACTORS AND VESTED INTERESTS   166
   Governors and State Legislatures   166
   State Expertise   166
   Mayors, Superintendents, and Teachers   167
   Interest Groups   168
   What's for Lunch?   170
ISSUES AND CHALLENGES   171
   Paradigm Shift   171
   Curriculum and Technology   171
   Connecting the Dots   172
   New Narrative   172
EVERYDAY CITIZEN CONNECTION   173
CONCLUDING THOUGHTS   173
POLICY CHOICES: STUDENT EVALUATION   174
GLOSSARY TERMS   175
DISCUSSION QUESTIONS   176
SUGGESTED RESOURCES   176

CHAPTER 8   Civil Rights and Immigration Policy   177

LEARNING OBJECTIVES   177
OPENING VIGNETTE: THE DESERT AND AN ELUSIVE CAT   177
OVERVIEW OF CIVIL RIGHTS   178
   Civil Rights and Immigration   181
   Status and Scope   183
   Longitudinal Trends   183
   Public Opinion Research   184
   Immigration Sentiments   184
TELLING STORIES WITH DATA: USING GALLUP POLLING
DATA TO DETECT TRENDS   185
HISTORY AND DEVELOPMENT OF U.S.
IMMIGRATION POLICY   187
   National Origin Quotas   187
   Civil Rights, Amnesty, and Enforcement   188
   9/11, Dreamers, and Deportation   189

MAJOR U.S. IMMIGRATION POLICY STATUTES   189
    Select Major U.S. Immigration Laws   189
THE ACTORS IN IMMIGRATION POLICY   192
    President   192
    Congress   194
    Courts   194
    Bureaucracy   195
UNOFFICIAL ACTORS IN IMMIGRATION POLICY   196
    States   197
    The Immigration Posse and the ACLU   199
ISSUES AND CHALLENGES   199
    Security and Crime   200
    Sanctuary Cities and Refugees   200
    Small Town USA   200
EVERYDAY CITIZEN CONNECTION   201
CONCLUDING THOUGHTS   201
POLICY CHOICES: IMMIGRATION REFORM   202
GLOSSARY TERMS   203
DISCUSSION QUESTIONS   203
SUGGESTED RESOURCES   204
NOTES   204

CHAPTER 9   **Social Welfare and Health Care Policy**   205

LEARNING OBJECTIVES   205
OPENING VIGNETTE: LIVING ON $2 A DAY   205
OVERVIEW OF SOCIAL WELFARE POLICY   207
    Defining Poverty   207
    Who Is Poor?   208
TELLING STORIES WITH DATA: USING CENSUS DATA   209
    Public Values and Types of Social Welfare Programs   210
    Public Support for Social Welfare Programs   211
HISTORY AND DEVELOPMENT OF U.S. SOCIAL
WELFARE POLICY   213
    Poor Houses and "Outdoor Relief"   213
    The New Deal and Social Security   214
    Unemployment Insurance and AFDC   215
    The Great Society and Connecting Health Care to
      Social Welfare   216
    Welfare Reform through TANF   218
OVERVIEW OF HEALTH CARE POLICY   218
    Government-Run Insurance Programs: Medicare,
      Medicaid, and CHIP   219
    The Affordable Care Act and Beyond   220
    Key Provisions of the ACA   220

HISTORY AND DEVELOPMENT OF U.S. HEALTH CARE POLICY   222
Early Efforts to Establish Health Care   223
Health Reform Efforts after the Great Depression   223
The 1960s through 2017: Government Steps In   224
ACA Repeal Attempts under President Trump   225

MAJOR U.S. SOCIAL WELFARE AND HEALTH CARE STATUTES   225
Select Major U.S. Social Welfare and Health Care Laws   225

MAJOR ACTORS IN SOCIAL WELFARE AND HEALTH
CARE POLICY   226
The President   227
Congress   227
Courts   227
Federal Bureaucracies   227
State Governments   228
Unofficial Actors   228

ISSUES AND CHALLENGES   228
Income Inequality   228
The High Health Cost of Being Poor   229
Universal Health Care Coverage and Single-Payer Health Care   229

EVERYDAY CITIZEN CONNECTION   230

CONCLUDING THOUGHTS   230

POLICY CHOICES: SOCIAL AND WELFARE POLICY—FAMILY LEAVE   231

GLOSSARY TERMS   233

DISCUSSION QUESTIONS   233

SUGGESTED RESOURCES   233

CHAPTER 10   **Environmental and Energy Policy**   **235**

LEARNING OBJECTIVES   235

OPENING VIGNETTE: A WEB OF ACTORS WHEN DISASTER
STRIKES   235

OVERVIEW OF ENVIRONMENTAL AND ENERGY POLICY   237
Understanding U.S. Environmental Policy   237
Status and Scope   238

TELLING STORIES WITH DATA: USING U.S. EPA AIR QUALITY
TRENDS DATA   239

HISTORY AND DEVELOPMENT OF ENVIRONMENTAL POLICY   239
Birth of the Modern Environmental Movement
(1960s and 1970s)   240
Changing Course (1980s)   241
Diffused Attention in the 1990s and Early 2000s   242
Executive Action in the 2010s   243

UNDERSTANDING U.S. ENERGY POLICY   245
Status and Scope   245

HISTORY AND DEVELOPMENT OF ENERGY POLICY   248
Crisis in the 1970s   248
Deregulation in the 1980s   249

Toward a Comprehensive Energy Policy in the 1990s 249
Energy and National Security Concerns in the 2000s 250
MAJOR ENVIRONMENTAL AND ENERGY POLICY STATUTES 251
MAJOR ACTORS IN ENVIRONMENTAL AND ENERGY POLICY 254
Congress 254
President 254
Federal Courts 256
Executive Agencies 257
Interest Groups and Lobbyists 258
Greenhouse Gases Go to Court 259
ISSUES AND CHALLENGES 260
Lack of a Coherent, Cohesive Policy 260
Politicization 261
Role of Science in Policy Debates 261
Trade-offs between the Environment and the Economy 262
The Commons 262
EVERYDAY CITIZEN CONNECTION 263
CONCLUDING THOUGHTS 264
POLICY CHOICES: NONPOINT SOURCE POLLUTION 264
POLICY CHOICES REFLECTION QUESTIONS 264
POLICY CHOICES: NONPOINT SOURCE WATER POLLUTION 265
GLOSSARY TERMS 266
DISCUSSION QUESTIONS 266
SUGGESTED RESOURCES 266

CONCLUSION **Public Policy: A Concise Introduction** 268
LEARNING OBJECTIVES 268
OPENING VIGNETTE: ON THE FRONT LINES 268
PUTTING THE PIECES TOGETHER 269
A Dynamic Enterprise 270
WHY PUBLIC POLICY MATTERS 271
Public Problems and Solutions 271
Finding the Facts 272
Consensus and Public Policy 275
CONCLUDING THOUGHTS 277
GLOSSARY TERMS 277
DISCUSSION QUESTIONS 277
SUGGESTED RESOURCES 278

GLOSSARY 279
REFERENCES 284
INDEX 300

List of Figures and Tables

Figure 1.1	Levels of Government	4
Figure 1.2	Policy Typologies	4
Figure 1.3	Policymaking Process	5
Figure 2.1	The Policymaking Process	26
Figure 2.2	Multiple Streams Framework	38
Figure 3.1	Public Support for Legalizing Marijuana, 1969–2017	47
Figure 3.2	Federal Grants to State and Local Governments, 1980–2010	56
Figure 3.3	Picket Fence Federalism: A Schematic Representation	59
Figure 3.4	Trifectas in State Governments in 2018	65
Figure 4.1	Public Perceptions	73
Figure 4.2	Mechanisms of Accountability	77
Figure 4.3	Stages of Federal Rulemaking	79
Figure 4.4	Sample Final Rule	82
Figure 4.5	Rulemaking and Influence	84
Figure 4.6	Enforcement Style	88
Figure 5.1	Growth and Contraction of the U.S. Economy, 1930–2016	101
Figure 5.2	Bureau of Labor Statistics	102
Figure 5.3	Overview of the Federal Budget Process	106
Figure 5.4	Federal Government Revenues, 2016	107
Figure 5.5	Federal Government Spending, 2016	109
Figure 5.6	U.S. Government Outlays, 1914–1978	113
Figure 5.7	U.S. Government Outlays, 1980–2016	114
Figure 6.1	Types of Cases Heard in State Courts, 2015	129
Figure 6.2	U.S. Violent Crime Rate, 1960–2014	131
Figure 6.3	U.S. Murder Rate, 1960–2014	131
Figure 6.4	National Crime Victimization Survey Crime Rates, 1976–2012	132
Figure 6.5	UCR Violent Crime, Including Homicide, and Motor Vehicle Theft Rates per 100,000 Population, 1960–2012	133
Figure 6.6	International Rates of Incarceration per 100,000	136
Figure 6.7	Public Support for Capital Punishment, 1936–2016	145
Figure 7.1	A Tangled Web of Actors	170
Figure 8.1	Sample Literacy Test	180
Figure 8.2	Experiences of Religious Discrimination, 2011	182
Figure 8.3	Levels of Government	185
Figure 8.4	E-Verify States	186
Figure 8.5	Benefits per State, 2016: 1	198
Figure 8.6	Benefits per State, 2016: 2	198
Figure 9.1	Official U.S. Poverty Rates in 1968, 1990, and 2015, by Age and Racial Group	209
Figure 9.2	Public Support for Budget Cuts, 2017	212
Figure 9.3	National Health Expenditures per Capita, 1960–2010	221

Figure 10.1	U.S. Energy Production, 2016	246
Figure 10.2	U.S. Energy Consumption, 1950–2014	247
Figure C.1	Pieces of the Policy Puzzle	270
Figure C.2	Where We Get Our News, by Age, 2016	273

Table 1.1	Actors and Involvement in Process	8
Table 1.2	Follow the Money	12
Table 3.1	State Political Cultures as Described by Elazar, 1966	63
Table 3.2	Top- and Bottom-Ranked States in the Camelot Index	64
Table 4.1	Examples of U.S. Federal Agencies	75
Table 4.2	Examples of Stage Agencies	75
Table 5.1	U.S. Annual Unemployment Rates, 1995–2016	99
Table 5.2	U.S. Consumer Price Index, 1990–2010	100
Table 5.3	Federal Income Tax Brackets, 2016	108
Table 7.1	Local, State, and Federal Roles	156
Table 7.2	Examples of Federal Education Agencies	169
Table 8.1	President Trump and Executive Orders	193
Table 8.2	Agency Actors	195
Table 8.3	Sample of Unofficial Actors	197
Table 9.1	Opinions about Welfare Responsibility	211
Table 9.2	Key Provisions of the Affordable Care Act	222
Table 10.1	Select Major U.S. Environmental Laws	241
Table 10.2	Congressional Committees and Subcommittees in the 115th Congress with Jurisdiction over Environmental and Energy Policy Issues	255

Preface

The study and practice of public policy are multifaceted and transcend disciplines. As a result, *Public Policy: A Concise Introduction* is a succinct, student-friendly public policy textbook that connects responsible citizens to the public policy world. We cover the fundamentals of American public policy in an engaging manner by incorporating the historical development with a contemporary examination of various policy areas. Additionally, we place a particular emphasis on giving readers an understanding of how policy works and the role those individuals on the front lines play in translating vague legislation into actionable regulations to achieve policy goals. In short, our focus is on the "doing" side of public policy and the role that citizens play in shaping it.

This book will give you some of the background, analytical, and practical skills you need in order to understand complex problems and craft concrete solutions to the most important policy questions in the governance arena today. Recent policy questions include how to shape the country's health care system, to what extent national and state governments should address climate change, how to address issues of immigration and what those issues are, how to address income inequality, whether or not to lower taxes and who should benefit, how to grow the economy, how to address increases in costs of tuition, and whether or not transgendered men and women can serve in the military—just to name a few. Education, energy, environment, social welfare, health care, civil rights, and immigration are large policy areas, and will likely touch each of us at some point in our lives. These are *public* policies, in that they involve issues that affect the common good, our common good as Americans. It is up to us to let policymakers know how we feel about the scope and nature of policy solutions that address these public concerns.

WHY *CONCISE*?

This book addresses the large field of public policy in a clear and concise way. Although there are a number of public policy textbooks on the market, current offerings lack a brief, but comprehensive, overview that is essential for students. This introduction is meant to get us thinking about the way public policy develops, is implemented, and who the major actors are that influence various policy areas. Other courses will dive into greater depth on these issues, and we encourage you to take additional classes in the public policy fields that interest you.

After all, policy wonks are not made without knowing the necessary basics that this textbook provides. Introductory public policy courses do not enroll just political science students; indeed, most public policy students are nonmajors who are taking the course as part of a public administration, business administration, communication studies, sociology, or criminal justice program, for example. Our textbook is designed to be approachable to readers with a wide range of interests and reasons for engaging in the study of policy.

ORGANIZATION

While this textbook incorporates many facets of traditional approaches to public policy, we pay particular attention to the implementation of policy by focusing on the administration of policy—rulemaking, in particular. Accordingly, we designed this book to introduce students to what happens after a bill becomes a law and focus on policy implementation, how to research and design public policy, and how to be informed participants of the policymaking process.

Additionally, we consider several topics that are not often included in introductory public policy texts. We offer chapters on federalism and regulatory policy, and explore connections between civil rights and immigration, and the relationship between health care and social welfare policy. At the same time, we include the basics that everyone needs—an introductory chapter that defines terms; a chapter on the policymaking process, along with policy analysis—before shifting to the various public policies described above. This foundation gives students the grounding they need to explore substantive policy areas, including environment, crime and justice, immigration, and education policy. The essential elements of these foundation chapters are demonstrated in these chapters detailing specific policy areas.

Ultimately, we believe this book makes public policy worthwhile for a range of readers who come to the study of public policy for a host of reasons. Each of the substantive policy chapters follows a similar format: an opening story or vignette, an overview of the issue area, an exploration of its status and scope, its history, a review of major statutes, a look at major institutional and noninstitutional actors, and a concluding section enumerating challenges and possibilities for the future. We are confident our readers will come to understand the complexities of public policy while being able to engage in a richer debate about issues as they will understand that policy is far more complex than the binary choices that seem to be traditionally presented.

FEATURES

Our volume serves to enrich a student's learning experiences with an applied approach. For example, each chapter begins with a series of **Learning Objectives** in order to understand the key points to learn in completing each chapter. **Opening Vignettes** let us consider current examples of public policy in action. For example, we consider what life is like living on less than $2 a day in America; we look at the legalization of marijuana by several states, and how that plays into the constitutional notion of federalism; we explore gun violence through the lens of shifting policies on campuses regarding concealed-carry gun policies. In addition, each chapter includes a **Telling Stories with Data** section that invites students to evaluate data in order to decipher their impact on a particular policy issue or dilemma.

Also, this policy text includes in its chapters on various policy areas sections devoted to **Policy Choices** that make students think about the policy alternatives available—beyond the simplistic "for or against" approach so often conveyed in the media and public dialogue. These "policy choices" sections provide more than discussion questions—they are policy choices designed to make students think about and discuss the potential remedies to important policy questions and the consequences of those choices.

We also emphasize how our readers can engage in policy issues that matter to them in an effort to encourage political efficacy among the next generations of citizens and public servants. We accomplish this feat through **Everyday Citizen Connections** in each chapter to illustrate how people are affected by public policy. This is just a sampling of the ways in which we can engage in conversation about current, and real, policy dilemmas.

DIGITAL RESOURCES

SAGE edge content is open access and available on demand at **http://edge.sagepub. com/rinfret**.

SAGE edge for Students provides a personalized approach to help students accomplish their coursework goals in an easy-to-use learning environment.

- Mobile-friendly **eFlashcards** strengthen understanding of key terms and concepts.

- Mobile-friendly practice **quizzes** allow for independent assessment by students of their mastery of course material.

- Access to full-text **SAGE journal articles** that have been carefully selected to support and expand on the concepts presented in each chapter is included.

- **Multimedia content** includes web links and third-party videos that appeal to diverse learners.

SAGE edge for Instructors, supports your teaching by making it easy to integrate quality content and create a rich learning environment for students.

- **Test banks** provide a diverse range of pre-written options as well as the opportunity to edit any question and/or insert your own personalized questions to effectively assess students' progress and understanding.

- Editable, chapter-specific **PowerPoint® slides** offer complete flexibility for creating a multimedia presentation for your course.

- **Lecture notes** summarize key concepts by chapter to help you prepare for lectures and class discussions.

- **Sample course syllabi** for semester and quarter courses provide suggested models for structuring your courses.

- **Chapter-specific discussion questions** help launch classroom interaction by prompting students to engage with the material and by reinforcing important content.

- Lively and stimulating **chapter activities** that can be used in class to reinforce active learning. The activities apply to individual or group projects.

- Access to full-text **SAGE journal articles** that have been carefully selected to support and expand on the concepts presented in each chapter is included.

- **Multimedia content** includes web links and third-party videos that appeal to diverse learners.

Acknowledgments

The origins of this book date back to 2008 in Green Bay, Wisconsin. Sara Rinfret's first academic position was at the University of Wisconsin–Green Bay, serving under the direction and guidance of Denise Scheberle, her chair of the Department of Public and Environmental Affairs. Within this capacity, Sara attended the annual Midwest Political Science Conference in 2010 and met Michelle. We are fortunate that our paths crossed because the three of us share two common interests: (1) advancing understanding of the practical side of public policy and its significance, and (2) deep commitments to teaching and learning. The following pages of this book would not be possible without the help of our students, who are our inspiration and the reason why we do what we do.

First, we want to acknowledge our respective institutions, the University of Montana, the University of Dayton, and the University of Colorado–Denver. We thank Jeffrey Greene for encouraging us to write this book. And we owe a great deal of gratitude to students in the University of Montana's Master of Public Administration Program—Christina Barsky, Sam Scott, and Marci Lewandowski. Christina and Sam spent an entire year engaged in independent research projects that informed much of the background research for many of the chapters. Marci spent countless hours during a semester constructing and designing several of the public policy choices sections. We are indebted to her for this work, and the credit is all hers. These students are exceptional graduate students, and we admire their ongoing commitment to the public service profession. Moreover, students in Sara Rinfret's Political Science 468: Public Policy and the Climate course read drafts of each chapter and provided invaluable feedback, including the observation that this is "Finally a book that we can apply to our own experiences and can comprehend because of its accessible style." Additionally, the expertise of Emily Kaylor was essential to drafting Chapter 5. After completing her undergraduate degree at the University of Dayton, Emily earned her Master of Public Administration degree at Indiana University and has gone on to a very successful career in Ohio state government. Her command of public budgeting and finance is outstanding, and we are grateful to have her help in this area. She continues to have a bright future, and we are excited to see it unfold.

Michelle owes tremendous gratitude to her students, coauthors, colleagues, and family. Her students inspire her daily with their curiosity and desire to make the world a better place. In particular, those students who strive to serve the public in a variety of capacities despite the multitude of challenges that beset the public sector, cultivate deep respect and admiration. The passion and commitment of Sara and Denise leave Michelle energized and wishing to follow their example. Several colleagues at the University of Dayton merit specific mention, including Grant Neeley, who is an outstanding department chair and an incredibly supportive mentor, and Deb Bickford, associate provost and director of the Ryan C. Harris Learning Teaching Center, whose leadership and commitment to learning inspire all those around her daily. The love and support of Michelle's family are the foundation of all she does. If it were not for Steven's steadfast patience, unwavering support, love, and encouragement, much would not be possible. It takes a special individual to love and support the kind of academic Michelle aspires to be, and he provides the essential foundation. Three special and amazing dogs—Emma, Sydney, and Victoria—have to be mentioned, as their assistance in this project was invaluable. Their supportive tail wags and simple presence did much to facilitate these pages.

Denise believes that college students are the "spark plugs" who energize conversations about the common good, how to engage in public service, and what direction public policy should take to better serve future generations. Her students have inspired her with their grace, enthusiasm, and dedication, for which she is very thankful. She is also grateful to Sara and Michelle, who encouraged her to be a third author on this text, and to expand her own intellectual horizons in researching and writing this book. It's been a terrific journey, and you couldn't ask for better traveling companions.

Additionally, we want to publicly recognize Anna Villarruel, content development editor for SAGE Publishing and CQ Press, whose help was unwavering and enthusiasm contagious. Scott Greenan, acquisitions editor, also provided much help along the way. Indeed, the entire SAGE/CQ Press staff have been a wonderful team, and we thank them all, with special thanks to Talia Greenberg for her sharp eye in copyediting the manuscript, and Tracy Buyan for her skillful shepherding of the production of the manuscript. We would also like to thank the following reviewers, who offered their feedback throughout the process of writing this book:

Kwame Antwi-Boasiako, Stephen F. Austin State University

John Aughenbaugh, Virginia Commonwealth University–Monroe Park

Rev. Mary D. Bruce

Dorothy Dillard, Delaware State University

Laura Fidelie, Midwestern State University

Don Gardiner, Lewis University

Matthew Hale, Seton Hall University

Alton Jelks, California State University, East Bay

Martha Kropf, University of North Carolina, Charlotte

John Mandeville, University of North Carolina, Chapel Hill

Lisa K. Parshall, Daemen College

Jay Ryu, Ohio University

Carlene Thornton, University of West Florida

Linda M. Trautman, Ohio University

William Wallis, California State University, Northridge

Mary Eleanor Wickersham, College of Coastal Georgia

Indeed, we have tremendous debts of gratitude toward all the individuals who supported our efforts here. Any and all mistakes are entirely our own.

Sara Rinfret
Michelle Pautz
Denise Scheberle
January 2018

About the Authors

Sara R. Rinfret is an associate professor at the University of Montana, where she directs the Master of Public Administration Program and codirects the Social Science Research Laboratory. Her main area of research is environmental regulations. More specifically, she is interested in the interactions between agencies and interest groups during the stages of environmental rulemaking at the federal and state level. To date, her work has been published in *Society and Natural Resources, Environmental Politics, Review of Policy Research, Journal of Environmental Studies and Sciences, PS: Political Science and Politics, Public Administration Quarterly,* and the *Oxford Handbook of U.S. Environmental Policy.* She has coauthored *The Lilliputians of Environmental Regulation: The Perspective of State Regulators,* and *U.S. Environmental Policy: A Practical Approach to Understanding Implementation* (cowritten with Michelle Pautz). She is a Fulbright Specialist Program Scholar in public administration and has studied with the University of Aarhus (Denmark) in 2016.

Denise Scheberle is a clinical teaching professor for the School of Public Affairs at the University of Colorado–Denver. She is Professor Emerita from the University of Wisconsin–Green Bay, where she served as the Herbert Fisk Johnson Professor in Environmental Studies and professor and chair of the Department of Public and Environmental Affairs. She is the recipient of national, state, and campus teaching awards, including the American Political Science Association's (APSA) Distinguished Teaching Award and University of Wisconsin Regents Teaching Excellence Award. She is the author of *Industrial Disasters and Environmental Policy: Stories of Villains, Heroes, and the Rest of Us* and *Federalism and Environmental Policy: Trust and the Politics of Administration,* as well as numerous articles. Her research focuses on environmental policy, public service, and intergovernmental relations. She holds a PhD in political science from Colorado State University and an MPA from the University of Wyoming.

(Continued)

(Continued)

Michelle C. Pautz is an associate professor of political science and assistant provost of the Common Academic Program at the University of Dayton. Her research has appeared in *Administration & Society, Administrative Theory & Praxis, Journal of Political Science Education, Journal of Environmental Studies & Sciences, Journal of Public Affairs Education, Policy Studies Journal, PS: Political Science & Politics, Public Voices,* and the *Review of Policy Research,* among others. She is the author of *Civil Servants on the Silver Screen: Hollywood's Depiction of Government and Bureaucrats;* coauthor of *The Lilliputians of Environmental Regulation: The Perspective of State Regulators* and *U.S. Environmental Policy in Action: Practice & Implementation;* and coeditor of *The Intersection of Food and Public Health: Current Policy Challenges and Solutions.* She holds a PhD in public administration and an MPA from Virginia Tech. She earned a BA in economics, political science, and public administration from Elon University.

The Foundation

PUBLIC POLICY AND OUR EVERYDAY LIVES

A personal experience can be the starting point to understand public policy. Think about the glass of milk you drank with your breakfast or your alarm clock—both are guided by U.S. public policies. The following stories—Professor Rinfret, Amish politics; Professor Scheberle, wool and banking; and Professor Pautz, marine mammals—demonstrate how our experiences can shape public policy.

Professor Rinfret: Amish Politics

I grew up in a rural, small town in northeast Ohio—population: 3,000. When I was ten, my father ran for county prosecutor. As a result, I spent my evenings and weekends knocking on doors and stating, "Please vote for my dad." In addition to nightly door knocking, I attended local meetings and pancake breakfasts with my dad. I still remember one rainy evening; we drove up to a local township building within the heart of our Amish community. Yes, I grew up in one of the largest Amish counties in the United States. I got out of our family minivan, but my dad stopped me and said, "Hey, you need to sit in the car tonight and work on your homework." I did not complain, but on the car ride home I remember asking, "Why wasn't I allowed to go inside tonight?" My dad's response: "Because you are a girl. Women do not attend Amish community meetings." This response invoked constant dinner conversations with my family about politics and continuous questions to my parents, teachers, and friends.

Professor Scheberle: Wool and Banking

As an undergraduate majoring in journalism, with a marketing emphasis, my first two jobs were eye-opening

LEARNING OBJECTIVES

Readers of this chapter will be able to:

1. Understand how personal stories shape our understanding of public policymaking

2. Identify the variety of institutional and noninstitutional actors who drive how and why policies are adopted

3. Comprehend that the public policymaking process is devised by a series of stages more complex than "how a bill becomes a law"

4. Explore how public policy is a profession driven by expertise

experiences. My first "real" job was to write the monthly newsletter and press releases for the Wool Growers Association, an organization that represents the interests of sheep ranchers or farmers. The organization took strong positions on public policy matters. For example, the organization opposed the listing of the gray wolf as an endangered species, as sheep herders argued that wolves were attacking the sheep. After I received my bachelor's degree, my second job was as an officer of the bank. Officers were strongly encouraged to contribute to the American Bankers Association Political Action Committee (PAC), an organization pressing hard for deregulation of banks. The CEO would come to every officer's desk and collect contributions. He was an imposing 6'3" man, and when he leaned over my desk, it got my attention! Regardless, these experiences increased my awareness that organizations try to sway policymakers' actions on policies designed to protect their perceived interests.

Professor Pautz: Marine Mammals

In middle school, I was fascinated by politics because I watched the nightly news; yet I did not think politics would be a viable career path for me. I entered college a declared economics major. It was not until the fall of my sophomore year, when I took environmental economics and environmental policy, that I began to change my perspective. These topics were of interest to me because I grew up in the coastal city of Portsmouth, New Hampshire, where marine animals were common. Needless to say, I was mortified by the images from the *Exxon Valdez* disaster. It upset me to see how the oil spill damaged the ecosystem and habitat for wildlife such as whales. Because of my own appreciation for marine mammals and the heartbreak caused by *Exxon Valdez*, my environmental classes enabled me to understand the role of public policy and politics in these issues.

Our own stories present policy questions: Should women be unallowed to attend a local meeting? What is the role of organizations in influencing policy? Who should protect wildlife from an oil spill? Answering such questions is not easily done and can engender controversy. Furthermore, how do you answer these questions through a **value-neutral** lens instead of **value-laden** fashion? More specifically, how do you present solutions to such questions that do not incorporate a person's own biases (value-neutral)? Is this even possible? Or are all policy decisions driven with biased responses driven by personal opinions (value-laden)?

The purpose of *Public Policy: A Concise Introduction* is simple—to provide students with the necessary skills and tools to understand how and why public policy is created. Our goal is to provide connections between our own everyday experiences with the "doing" side of policy: **implementation**. This approach allows the reader to merge theory and practice. This chapter sets the tone as we define public policy, the process, key actors, theories involved, and how it all applies to you.

STARTING WITH A DEFINITION

The word **public** encompasses ordinary people, or community. **Policy** is a course of action adopted or created by the government[1] in response to public problems. When the terms are put together, public policy is a "confusing game of players, dynamics, processes, and stages" (Theodoulou and Kofinis 2004). Public policy is "a relatively stable, purposive course of action followed by government in dealing with some problem or matter of concern" (Anderson 2003, 3). Reading these definitions of public policy serves as a reminder that "Every day the intended and unintended consequences of public policy intimately touch the lives of everyone within the United States" (Theodoulou and Kofinis 2004, 2). Public policy is government action to solve a public problem.

Power and Politics

Related to government action to solve a problem are power and politics. **Power** represents the ability to alter or influence a course of action (Theodoulou and Kofinis 2004, 3). Power is a person or group's ability to persuade or alter perceptions. For instance, when former governor Howard Dean (Democrat of Vermont) ran for president in 2004, the Republicans used the powerful footage of him exclaiming *Yippee!* at a campaign rally to weaken support for his campaign. The image of Dean yelping was played on news outlets to demonstrate his inability to govern. Therefore, the media were able to influence our perceptions of a candidate and change a person's mind on whether or not to vote for him for president.

Politics, as Lasswell (1958) describes, is "who gets what, when, and how." However, politics is a broad concept—it defines the communication between branches of government and levels of government. Moreover, "Politics, at its essence, captures the competitive communication, exchange, discussions, and debate that emerge between competing ideas and groups within a state" (Theodoulou and Kofinis 2004, 8). Politics is part of policymaking and allows us to have a discussion and debate the merits of solutions to public problems.

As we define public policy and discuss the roles power and politics play within this definition, who in society controls policymaking? Pluralism and elitism help us to understand this question. **Pluralism** is the notion that we all have equal access to influence policymaking (Dahl 1961; Truman 1951). However, **elitism** suggests only a select few, the elite, have the power to influence policymaking in a Democratic society (Mills 1956). Although these two conceptualizations offer different theories, "In general, each perspective helps to identify that the concept of power should not be measured solely as an explicit consequence, but as a complex interrelationship between the ability of certain actors to influence what actions are taken" (Theodoulou and Kofinis 2004, 4).

With this in mind, public policy is not created by one person; nor does it happen overnight. There are a myriad of actors involved. Each year hundreds of laws and ordinances are created at the national, state, and local level. More specifically, U.S. public policy is guided by a system of **federalism** in which power is divided between national government and the states.

A Federal System

Figure 1.1 illustrates a brief overview of our federal system, and Chapter 3 delves into the details more fully. For foundational purposes, each level of government has separate and overlapping functions to execute public policy. For example, the federal government is responsible for overseeing relationships with other countries, deciding whether or not to go to war, or creating money. Under the Tenth Amendment, anything not specified in the U.S. Constitution is within the scope of state governments, such as public schools. Within this federal

FIGURE 1.1

Levels of Government

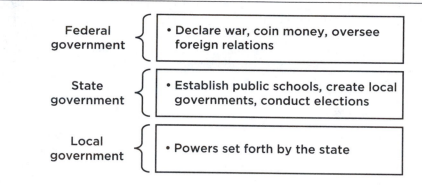

Federal government	• Declare war, coin money, oversee foreign relations
State government	• Establish public schools, create local governments, conduct elections
Local government	• Powers set forth by the state

system, there is a lot of overlap, or shared responsibility, in carrying out policy. For instance, public education standards are created by the federal government and carried out by state and local governments. Nonetheless, policy spans across governments and topics ranging from pollution control, business regulation, energy, welfare, and transportation, to name a few.

Categories of Public Policy

Scholars have attempted to categorize public policy into three broad categories. As Anderson (2003) suggests, "These typologies will prove much more useful in distinguishing among and generalizing about policies that have some of the more traditional and widely used categorization schemes, such as by issue area ..." (10). Figure 1.2 defines the three categories of public policy.

Distributive public policy involves the allocation of resources to individuals, groups, corporations, or communities. This type of policy benefits a segment of the population. An example of a distributive public policy is a farm subsidy. In this example, the federal government provides financial support each year to farmers to manage their crops (e.g., cotton, corn, rice, soybeans) because of inconsistencies due to weather or disease.

FIGURE 1.2

Policy Typologies

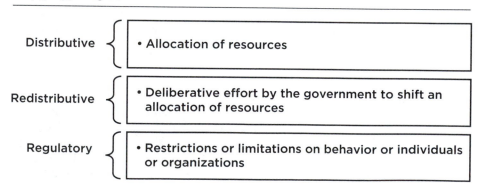

Distributive	• Allocation of resources
Redistributive	• Deliberative effort by the government to shift an allocation of resources
Regulatory	• Restrictions or limitations on behavior or individuals or organizations

The purpose of a redistributive public policy is to promote equality, or occurs when the government allocates support from one group to another through social programs. The financial aid you receive to attend college is an example of a redistributive public policy. It is based on your parents' annual earnings.

Regulatory policy imposes restrictions on the behaviors of individuals or organizations. This type of policy is exemplary of U.S. environmental policy because regulatory policy limits the behaviors of businesses or organizations. For instance, a coal-burning power plant is allowed to produce a set limit of pollution into the air because of the Clean Air Act. If a company exceeds its limits, a fine ensues. Although there are different categories of public policy, how does a policy come to fruition? Who are the actors involved? Is public policy made through the "how a bill becomes a law" steps you learned in your high school government class?

THE PROCESS

The public policymaking process, coined as the **stages heuristic approach**, helps address the aforementioned questions. U.S. public policymaking occurs across a variety of stages and includes several actors. Figure 1.3 provides a brief explanation and foundation of this process, with Chapter 2 delving deeper into specifics.

Stage One: Problem Identification and Definition The first phase of the policymaking process is to determine that there is a problem. This is not an easy endeavor. A problem or an issue can be defined by the public or lawmakers. For example, Black Lives Matter, an activist movement, has argued that violence against black people in the United

FIGURE 1.3
Policymaking Process

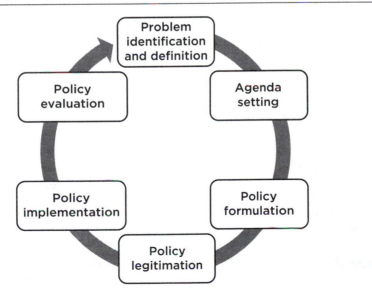

States needs to end. Although a problem has been identified by Black Lives Matter, the question then becomes how to define the problem. Many within the Black Lives Matter movement claim the problem is due in part to unwarranted police brutality against blacks. However, the police force defines the problem differently—lack of training of police officers. As such, problem identification and definition are inherently political. This stage can be driven by value-laden (biased) perspectives shaped by our own experiences. In this case, a member of the Black Lives Matter movement uses statistical evidence in which blacks are targeted more than whites and video footage of police brutality to demonstrate this problem needs to be addressed by lawmakers. Police officers define the problem as a lack of resources to properly train employees (Chapter 6 provides much more detail).

Stage Two: Agenda Setting After determining a problem exists, the second phase is how to place the problem on lawmakers' agenda. This can also be a difficult endeavor. Focusing events and policy entrepreneurs are two explanatory factors to determine what gets placed on their agenda. First, a focusing event is a sudden event that can reshape the nation's attention. An example of a focusing event is 9/11. Combating terrorism was placed on lawmakers' agenda post-9/11.

Second, a policy entrepreneur could be a congressperson, governor, member of an interest group, or legislative champion. This person fixates on a problem and calls for action. An example of a policy entrepreneur is former vice president Al Gore. His quest is to address climate change in the United States. Throughout the 1990s, early 2000s, and even today, Vice President Gore ardently supports legislative efforts to combat global climate change, documented through his film *An Inconvenient Truth*, and now in the Climate Reality Project, to pressure lawmakers into action.

Stage Three: Policy Formulation Once a problem has been recognized or reached the agenda of lawmakers, policy formulation or design occurs. As Schneider and Ingram (1997) suggest, "Policy design is inherently a purposeful and normative enterprise though which elements of policy are warranted to serve particular values, purposes, and interests" (3). It is at this juncture that lawmakers consider the pros and cons of a particular policy and potential solutions. For example, for health care policy, lawmakers would consider the benefits and drawbacks for the public, hospitals, doctors, and insurance companies. The views of different groups allow for policymakers to determine a viable pathway moving forward.

Stage Four: Policy Legitimation This stage is the one with which we are most familiar, or "how a bill becomes a law." For the sake of brevity, Congress (U.S. House of Representatives or U.S. Senate) assigns a piece of legislation to a committee. The committee determines if the bill should move to the floor for deliberation, debate, and a vote. If the vote passes both chambers of Congress the president can sign or veto the legislation. If the president signs the bill it becomes law. As Chapter 9 presents with an examination of the Affordable Care Act, legislative lawmaking is a complex and arduous process. For instance, in 2015, approximately 561 out of 6,845 bills introduced became law.

Stage Five: Policy Implementation The fifth stage of the process is important, yet often overlooked. This stage addresses: What happens after a law goes into effect? Do members of Congress carry out every piece of legislation? There is no way for members of Congress to implement all of the policies it creates due to lack of time, expertise, and resources. This stage is where the "doing side" of policy occurs via implementation by administrative agencies. For example, the doers or implementers of public policy in Professor Pautz's vignette are agency officials who work for the U.S. Environmental Protection Agency or the U.S. Fish and Wildlife Service. These agencies were created by Congress to carry out laws that not only protect the public's health, but also species. This is often where a lot of the excitement or real policy occurs, and why we focus Chapter 4 entirely on this stage in the process.

Stage Six: Policy Evaluation Policymaking would not be complete without the final stage: evaluation. Within this phase, **policy evaluators** measure and assess the effectiveness of programs and policies. For example, a policy evaluator will determine if the Affordable Care Act has increased health benefits for the public. A policy evaluator researches the intended outcomes of programs and policies, and provides recommendations to members of Congress. Such recommendations could include that Congress provides more funding for a program or that a program should be eliminated. The goal is for a policy evaluator to use data-driven evaluations (value-neutral) in their assessment, not their personal opinion (value-laden) to document the viable options moving forward.

This description of the policy process model provides a brief introduction to how policy is made in the United States. Inevitably, there are flaws to this model. A policy might not occur in a linear fashion as described or does not make it all the way through each of the stages. Despite these shortcomings, Chapter 2 addresses these concerns and offers additional policy models for exploration. Regardless, each of the aforementioned steps is the foundation to understand the creation of public policy, from start to finish. Our theme that connects each chapter is how public policy implementation determines whether the goals of the public policy created are realized. This is where the rubber meets the road, or as we define it, the **doing side of policy**.

A MOTLEY CREW: INSTITUTIONAL AND NONINSTITUTIONAL ACTORS

The policymaking process would not occur without the work and involvement of policy actors—institutional and noninstitutional. Table 1.1 highlights how the institutional actors—the three branches of government, the bureaucracy—and the noninstitutional actors—the media, interest groups, and us—are all drivers in U.S. public policymaking processes.

The Three Branches of Government

Congress, the president, and the Supreme Court are all involved in U.S. public policymaking. Article I, Section I, of the U.S. Constitution clearly notes that Congress has the lawmaking authority to create or develop legislation. A total of 535 elected individuals comprise Congress: 435 for the U.S. House of Representatives and 100 for the U.S. Senate. Members of Congress determine what reaches the policymaking agenda and how these policies are formulated and adopted.

TABLE 1.1

Actors and Involvement in Process

Actor	Role within Policymaking Process
Congress	Agenda setting, policy formulation, policy legitimation
President	Agenda setting, policy formulation, policy legitimation
Courts	Policy evaluation
Bureaucracy	Policy implementation, policy evaluation
Interest groups	Agenda setting, policy formulation
Media	Agenda setting
Us	All stages of the process

Specifically, within the stages of how a bill becomes a law, a policy can move forward or cease to exist within a committee. The committee determines which bills are heard and make it to the floor for deliberation for a vote. For example, in 2009, climate change made it to the policymaking agenda. The House of Representatives passed the American Clean Energy and Security Act (also known as Waxman-Markey legislation) to address climate change. This legislation did not become law because it did not make it out of committee in the U.S. Senate; therefore, this legislation died and did not become law. Remember, even if you reach the policymaking agenda and out of committee, it needs to be passed in both the House and Senate. Nonetheless, Congress is a powerful power broker in setting the tone for U.S. policymaking (Mayhew 2004).

This is not to say that the president does not play a role in policymaking. The president can and does shape public policy. Presidents are elected every four years and can serve two consecutive four-year terms. Popular presidents can use the **bully pulpit**—speeches, radio addresses, YouTube videos, Twitter, or forums to engender public support for a position. For instance, in 2016, President Barack Obama's approval ratings were approximately 50 percent (Gallup 2016). Put simply, 50 percent of the population thought President Obama was doing a good job. Because of this, President Obama used public support to push for his policy directives to take shape. The idea is that popular presidents can use speeches to engender support from the public to then call their congressperson to pressure for action on a public problem.

One such example is paid parental leave for parents. In speeches to the public and the 2016 State of the Union address, President Obama stressed that the United States should pass legislation to provide six weeks of paid parental leave for all federal employees as part of the 2017 budget (Lunney 2016). As Lunney suggests, "Obama's push for paid parental leave is part of a larger agenda to strengthen the middle class by giving families more work–life flexibility." Although Congress has yet to adopt this policy, there is growing backing among members due to President Obama's and the public's support for the endeavor.

The U.S. Supreme Court is not an active participant in public policymaking like Congress or the president. The courts are reactive. Simply put, the courts do not initiate public policy, yet their decisions have public policy implications. We have a dual court system in the United States, guided by three types of law: public, criminal, and civil.

Public law deals with constitutional and administrative questions related to government actions, **criminal law** regulates the conduct of individuals, and **civil law** deals with disputes between individuals or organizations. Also, there are differences between federal and state courts. For instance, the entry point for all federal criminal cases (such as robbing a bank) or civil cases (disputes between states or individuals, such as divorce) is the U.S. district court. If convicted at the U.S. district court level, the accused have the right to appeal the case. If the appeal is heard, this would take place at the U.S. court of appeals (thirteen total, eleven geographically located, and two specialty circuits for bankruptcy and patents). If again convicted, cases can be appealed to the U.S. Supreme Court. However, on average, the U.S. Supreme Court hears about seventy to eighty cases per year; this is about 1–5 percent of all cases appealed to the Court.

The U.S. Supreme Court typically includes nine justices who are appointed by the president and confirmed by the Senate. The justices can serve for life, providing "good behavior."[2] The Court impacts policy by how the justices choose to interpret the law. If a business decides to sue the government because the business believes the Affordable Care Act placed unwarranted economic burdens on it, then the Court would need to interpret the intent of the law.

The Affordable Care Act was challenged by the arts-and-crafts chain Hobby Lobby in 2013. Hobby Lobby executives did not think they should have to cover restrictive contraception options for female employees, such as Plan B, also known as the morning-after pill. Company founders believed that life begins after conception, and therefore Hobby Lobby did not want to provide coverage for female employees. Hobby Lobby noted that its religious preferences were protected under the Religious Freedom Restoration Act as the rationale for the suit. In *Burrell v. Hobby Lobby Stores, Inc.,* the Court found in favor of Hobby Lobby and concluded that for-profit companies do not have to provide employees restrictive contraception coverage due to religious reasons. However, the company would still have to provide less restrictive coverage, such as birth control pills, for its employees. This case demonstrates how the Supreme Court impacts public policy, or how the Affordable Care Act is interpreted, which affects the lives of individuals who work for organizations like Hobby Lobby (Oyez 2016).

The Implementers

We often forget about the heavy lifters in the process: bureaucrats or the bureaucracy. There are a variety of ways scholars have defined "bureaucracy."[3] According to William Niskanen (1971), "the original use of the term, I understand, referred to cloth covering the desk (bureau) of eighteenth century French officials" (23). The bureaucracy, as defined by James Q. Wilson (1991), is "a complex and varied phenomenon, not a simple category or political epithet" (10). Armies, schools, and prisons, as Wilson (1991) notes, are all bureaucracies. The seminal approach to define the bureaucracy originates from the work of Max Weber (1947). For Weber, the bureaucracy is synonymous with defining all large organizations.

However, when bureaucracy is mentioned, pejorative terms come to mind—lazy, incompetent employees, or paper pushers. This should not be the case, as Anthony Downs's *Inside Bureaucracy* (1964) reminds us:

It is ironic that the bureaucracy is still primarily a term of scorn, even though bureaus are among the most important institutions in every nation in the world. Not only do bureaus provide employment for a very significant fraction of the world's population, but also they make critical decisions which shape the economic, political, social, and even moral lives of nearly everyone on earth. (130)

The bureaucracy and a bureaucrat's role in society are much more than the common stereotypes. These individuals are your next-door neighbors and ensure you have clean drinking water or protect the whales from oil spills in Professor Pautz's vignette. Yet are these individuals allowed to do this? Are bureaucrats doing Congress's job?

The bureaucracy was created by Congress to translate vague congressional statutes and to implement public policies. It is the people within the bureaucracy, the bureaucrats or civil servants—police officers, teachers, or environmental inspectors—who carry out legislation on a daily basis (Niskanen 1971). The bureaucrats are the individuals who work within the bureaucracy to implement public policy. Put succinctly, policy implementation "[r]epresents the state where government executes an adopted policy as specified legislation or policy action" (Theodoulou and Kofinis 2004, 166–167). The bureaucracy was created to implement public policy in the United States because members of Congress do not have the time or expertise to carry out the laws they pass.

Thus, agencies, including the Human Resources and Services Administration (HRSA), Environmental Protection Agency (EPA), and U.S. Fish and Wildlife Service (USFWS), to name a few, fulfill an essential role in ensuring that landmark legislation such as the Clean Air Act, the Endangered Species Act, or the Affordable Care Act are carried out and implemented. The HRSA determines what contraceptive plans should be covered for women under the Affordable Care Act. The EPA protects the public's health by making sure the air we breathe and the water in which we swim is clean. And the USFWS ensures that species like whales are protected from oil spills. This introduction on the bureaucracy sets the tone for bureaucratic decision-making discussions in Chapters 2 and 4.

Although the aforementioned examples for Congress, president, Supreme Court, and bureaucracy are not exhaustive, the point is to begin to understand how each affects public policy. The remaining chapters of our text fill in the details.

The Media, Interest Groups, and Us

Noninstitutional actors—the media, interest groups, and us—play a pivotal role in public policymaking. There are three ways to classify media in the United States—**broadcast**, **print**, and the Internet. Broadcast media include radio and television, print encompasses newspapers and magazines, and the Internet is an online resource that incorporates cyber versions of the more traditional media sources (Ginsburg et al. 2013). Interest groups are organized groups of individuals who fight for a cause.

There are several types of interest groups in the United States, ranging from businesses and professional associations to public interest and ideological interest groups. A **business interest group** wants to protect economic interests and includes groups such as chambers of commerce, which represent small and large businesses in the United States. **Professional interest groups** include organizations such as the American Bar Association (lawyers) or the American Medical Association (medical professionals). Public interest groups include organizations that advocate for causes, such as consumer or environmental protection. One such example is the Wool Growers Association from Professor Scheberle's vignette.

The Wool Growers Association wants to advocate for policies that protect livestock or the economic interests of ranchers. This group would be in contrast with another public interest group—the Sierra Club, a large environmental organization that advocates for environmental and species protection. In this case, the Sierra Club would promote the protection of species like wolves to counter the arguments of the Wool Growers Association.

The final type of interest group, ideological groups, provides individuals with an organization to promote their broader political perspectives or government ideologies. For instance, individuals from a religious perspective might be attracted to the Christian Coalition. The purpose of the Christian Coalition is to allow individuals of faith a pathway to be involved in policymaking.

Shaping Policy

The media and interest groups can and do shape public policy. For example, the media coverage about a topic can impact Americans' perceptions about public problems. Journalists interpret or frame the story to the public. Framing is a powerful mechanism because it shapes a person's preferences regarding policy priorities. Moreover, framing can and does set the policymaking agenda (Guber and Bosso 2013) because when a journalist uses images (e.g., photos or video), priming occurs. For instance, think about how the image below (Photo 1.1) after the *Exxon Valdez* oil spill might have impacted individuals like Professor Pautz. Images like this stick in the minds of the American public, and interest groups use them to support their causes and pressure lawmakers to pass policy.

More specifically, each type of interest group attempts to advocate for positions to set the agenda for members of Congress. Interest group advocacy occurs through the act of **lobbying**. A lobbyist is a person who is hired by an organization to meet with congressional representatives to persuade them to pass policies to benefit their interests. Interest group advocacy is achievable because we are members of interest groups. Members of Congress listen to interest groups because they represent us, who elect them into office. Also, professional interest groups such as the American Medical Association can offer research on topics—for instance, the effectiveness of programs like Medicaid use per hospital in the United States.

In addition to lobbying, interest groups provide financial support for campaigns. Table 1.2 demonstrates the amount of money provided to members of Congress for 2015–2016. The idea is that if you donate money to a congressional candidate this helps to pass policies on your group's behalf. The top financial contributors to Congress for 2015–2016 were professional interests within the areas of finance, insurance, and real estate. Regardless, millions of dollars are spent to pressure lawmakers to act, and the question becomes if we can play a role in this process.

PHOTO 1.1
Exxon Valdez oil spill

AP Photo/John Gaps III

TABLE 1.2

Follow the Money

Rank	Interests Represented	Amount Provided to Members of Congress
1	Financial, insurance, real estate	$258,721,966
2	Ideology or single issue	$165,602,084
3	Lawyers	$118,145,140
4	Health	$115,681,393
5	Communications or electronics	$103,060,671

Source: Center for Responsive Politics, https://www.opensecrets.org/industries/. Accessed February 17, 2018.

What about Us?

Although the media and interest groups can affect our own perceptions about public policy or a policymaker, how can the normal, everyday citizen make an impact on U.S. public policymaking? You can run for office, and if elected, shape the design or formulation of policy. But at the federal level, this only includes 535 individuals within Congress. There are over 300 million individuals living in the United States.

More realistically, you can make more of an impact as a member of an interest group, as a journalist, or as an implementer. If you are interested in pay equity, we might suggest you join the League of Women Voters to understand why men and women are paid different wages for the same type of position. You could major in journalism and interpret and present policy facts for us to digest. Or you could major in political science, wildlife biology, sociology, or forestry and work for a state or federal agency and implement public policy. Through these examples, we can and do shape the public policymaking process more broadly.

But you cannot forget that beyond understanding the process and the actors involved, you consume public policy every day. As you check Snapchat, Facebook, Twitter, LinkedIn, BuzzFeed, or Instagram, in what ways did you consume public policy today? Did you just skim the headlines that span across your Facebook feed? As you consume public policy, it impacts your judgments about what should or should not be done. However, are judgments and daily consumption driven by value-laden or value-neutral research?

POLICY ANALYSIS

One of the best ways we can become involved in public policymaking is to understand the profession of policy analysis. We consume information, but how do we know if a policy is efficient and effective? Policy evaluators regularly assess the effectiveness of all major laws to ensure they are achieving their goals. An entire field—policy analysis—has been dedicated to the evaluation of policy (Dunn 2008; Quade 1989). We suggest policy evaluation is "deconstructing an object of study—that is, breaking it down into basic elements to understand it better" (Kraft and Furlong 2015, 8).

Policy Evaluation

Policy evaluation, stage six of the policymaking process, is conducted by policy analysts or program evaluators. These individuals have varying skills, expertise, and educational backgrounds depending upon the policy they study (Bardach 2004). Policy analysts may have backgrounds in biology, ecology, political science, engineering, or economics, to name a few. More specifically, a policy analyst is not supposed to inject her values or beliefs into the analysis. Therefore, the evaluator can provide an evidence-based policy analysis that includes all of the relevant factors so policymakers can make changes or modifications based upon that objective information (Dunn 2008).

However, the act of policy evaluation is not this simple (Dunn 2008; Weimer and Vining 2011). Policy analysts do not have unlimited resources to acquire data regarding every single policy problem (Weimer and Vining 2011). Also, how an evaluator structures analyses may elevate some priorities over others, based upon necessity (Dunn 2008). The supporter of the evaluation (the person funding the project) may also sway the overall outcome of the analysis based upon their own values (Bardach 2004; Weimer and Vining 2011). For instance, if a member of Congress does not agree with charter schools, he can pay a private firm in his home district to conduct an evaluation to provide evidence that aligns with his stance.

Since we are all consumers of policy, what sources have been evaluated in a value-neutral fashion? The U.S. Government Accountability Office (GAO) and the National Academy of Sciences (NAS) assessments of policy are sources of unbiased and accurate analyses, but these are not the only entities that provide policy evaluation (Kraft and Furlong 2015). There are a whole host of other federal agencies, think tanks, trade associations, environmental interests, and other entities that provide policy evaluations, but their assumptions and evaluative criteria (the way a group evaluates a program) can vary greatly, which Chapter 2 delves into more deeply.

WHY STUDYING PUBLIC POLICY MATTERS

Public policy is complex, with a variety of actors involved and models to understand how and why policies are made. Without our participation in the policy process, we may get policies we do not agree with because someone from a different viewpoint may press policymakers much more strongly. For example, Chapter 6 explores the power of the National Rifle Association (NRA) to maintain limited gun control in the United States, even though many Americans favor additional controls. As such, understanding the study and practice of public policy is important for you because (1) it helps our communities address problems, (2) it follows a systematic process to provide solutions, and (3) it is designed and implemented by countless practitioners.

Public Policy and Community Understanding public policy is important because "Public policy is about communities trying to achieve something as communities" (Stone 2012, 20). More specifically, community can be a political or cultural community.

As Stone (2012) succinctly remarks, "A political community is a group of people who live under the same rules and structure of governance. A cultural community is a group of people who share a culture and draw their identities from shared language, history and traditions" (21). It is within these communities that we define public problems or dilemmas. Simply put, our community defines our own experiences.

Our opening vignettes presented how different communities identify and grapple with public problems. Professor Rinfret's small, rural community allowed her to question more broadly what role women can, and should, play in society. Professor Scheberle's experiences are defined by her work community—whether or not to donate money to policymakers who favor the deregulation of the banking industry. Professor Pautz explained how her college community or the classroom demonstrated that solutions are available to protect whales from a public problem—oil spills. These experiences identify that where we live or with whom we interact shapes how we define what a problem is.

Public Policy and Solutions To address public problems, public policy is also the practice of a rigorous, systematic process. Answering our questions warrants "designated policy study" (Anderson 2003, 1). Specifically, the policymaking process is a method that is inspired by a series of steps on how public policy develops to tackle public problems. In this chapter we have discussed the stages heuristic approach, but more approaches will be discussed in Chapter 2.

The notion is that most public problems, if they reach the agenda, are addressed through a framework to provide solutions. The stages heuristic approach is invaluable for students of public policy to understand the evolution of the process. As Theodoulou and Kofinis (2004) conclude:

By focusing on each of these phases, and the various additional stages, students may come to understand how policies originate, develop, and grow in a step-by-step process. Although no method is perfect, the policy cycle approach offers students a solid, practical tool with which to understand the dynamics and structure of American policy making. (34)

Public Policy: A Profession We could not understand public policy without studying the doing side of public policy. In particular, public policy is a profession guided by experts in specific fields (e.g., health, education, civil rights, environment, energy). These individuals not only translate vague legislation into programs to address public problems and evaluate its effectiveness, but they ensure we have clean water to drink or fresh air to breathe. Nevertheless, public policy is multifaceted and messy: it is affected and shaped by our communities; addressed through processes; and designed and implemented by public servants in agencies, nonprofits, or volunteers in local government.

PLAN OF THE BOOK

Public Policy: A Concise Introduction includes three sections, totaling eleven chapters. Section I (Defining U.S. Public Policymaking) of the textbook introduces students to how and why policy is made in the United States. Section II (The Practice of Public Policy) focuses on connecting theory to practice through an exploration of federalism and how rules and regulations are crafted in a federal structure that includes state and local governments. Section III (Understanding Key Public Policy Issues) covers specific policy topics ranging from economics to immigration, civil rights, education, health care, criminal justice, and environmental and energy policy. Unique to this textbook is the everyday citizen connection and the policy choice sections of each of the topical policy chapters. Chapters 5–10 conclude with policy choice sections, which demonstrate policy dilemmas with several arguments for or against to engender meaningful classroom discussions. The policy choices are not painted as pro and con; instead, they offer several options to demonstrate that public policy is multifaceted and involves the consideration of multiple solutions before a problem can be addressed.

Chapter 2: The Policy Process and Policy Theories. Chapter 2 focuses on how policy is made and evaluated. One of the predominant theories of public policymaking, the stages approach, is discussed in great detail to give readers a foundation and vocabulary to discuss public policymaking, notably at the federal level. The chapter moves onto a discussion of other dominant policy theories (e.g., rational choice, issues networks, punctuated equilibrium, multiple streams approach) to more accurately represent policymaking.

In Section II: The Practice of Public Policy, we include Chapters 3 and 4. Put succinctly, Chapters 3 and 4 are necessary to understand to contextualize the theme of our textbook—the doing side of policy. To make this case clear, Chapters 3 and 4 utilize everyday citizen connections to connect theory to practice.

Chapter 3: Federalism and Intergovernmental Relations. This chapter describes the evolution of federalism and explains how policy is affected by agencies at the federal, state, and local levels of government. Special attention is given to how interactions occur among state, local, and federal implementers of policy, and how policies connect across state lines. The chapter ends by unpacking how and why it is imperative for federal, state, and local governments to work together in order to tackle large-scale policy issues such as medical or recreational marijuana. We document through our everyday citizen connections that cooperation among levels of government has waned over the last decade and the future appears to present a new form of federalism—competitive federalism.

Chapter 4: Rulemaking and Regulations. Chapter 4 illustrates how vague policy language, often in the form of congressional legislation, is translated into rules and regulations for organizations and individuals to follow. We begin this chapter with an overview of the federal and state rulemaking processes. Accordingly, the lawmaking processes, or rulemaking stages, are overviewed in this chapter from the pre-proposal stage to rule finalization in the *Federal Register*. The second part of the chapter explains what happens after a rule goes into effect or how state inspectors ensure compliance with rules or laws. Chapter 4 concludes with the everyday citizen connection and evaluation of how technology could possibly change how individuals participate in rulemaking processes in the United States.

The final section of the textbook, Section III: Understanding Key Public Policy Issues, focuses on substantive public policy areas, with each chapter concluding with policy choices to provoke fruitful classroom discussions and debate.

Chapter 5: Economic Policy and Public Budgeting. This chapter covers a varied array of the major factors that affect economic policy, ranging from fiscal policy (the taxing and spending policies of the federal government) and the Federal Reserve, which controls monetary policy (the supply of money and interest rates), to the types of taxes used, who pays them, and what difference it makes. As this is one of our chapters on substantive public policy, we conclude it with three policy choices for the future and to drive classroom discussion. This discussion centers on revamping the federal tax system.

Chapter 6: Crime and Public Policy. Despite lower overall crime rates than in the past, violent and serious crimes remain higher in the United States than in any other industrialized nation. Experts concede that the nation still has too much crime. Thus, in Chapter 6, we cover the major policy areas for crime and criminal justice, ranging from the causes of crime, to policies designed to combat or prevent crime, to prisons and capital punishment. The chapter is also concept driven, containing both theoretical frameworks such as theories on the causes of crime and practical examples of crime policy (e.g., drug-related crime). The chapter ends with three policy choices for the future that center on the future of guns in the United States.

Chapter 7: Education Policy. Schools have remained one of the public's top concerns for decades. This chapter examines public education policy ranging from school funding to school performance, the roles various policymakers play, the impact of court decisions, innovations that have been implemented by states and local school districts, federal programs such as No Child Left Behind and Common Core, and alternative policies such as the voucher system and charter schools. The chapter concludes with three alternative policy choices for the direction of K–12 student evaluation criteria.

Chapter 8: Civil Rights and Immigration Policy. This chapter begins by briefly defining civil rights in the United States. This definition serves as a framework for addressing one of the most pressing and controversial policy issues of the twenty-first century—immigration policy. Following is a discussion of how U.S. immigration policy has evolved over the last decade. In particular, this chapter examines how immigration policy has been shaped by societal events and also differing state viewpoints on immigration (e.g., Arizona, New York). As such, this chapter identifies how perceptions about immigration policy shifted post-9/11. The chapter concludes with an overview of choices for a pathway toward U.S. citizenship.

Chapter 9: Social Welfare Policy and Health Care Policy. This chapter centers on the role and importance of social and welfare policy in the United States. The goal of this chapter is to document how the U.S. social welfare and health care system developed to provide a solid understanding of "how we got to where we are today." The chapter's concluding policy choices spotlight using market forces to bring down costs and increase coverage, expand the current system to include and cover more people, and ultimately to consider a truly universal health care system.

Chapter 10: Environmental and Energy Policy. This chapter begins by briefly contextualizing environmental and energy issues today in their broader historical evolution. Following is a discussion of how American society approaches scientifically and technically complex issues to enable a better understanding of the challenges of solving—or at least ameliorating—these challenges. Included here is a review of the major environmental laws that provide the structure for executing environmental and energy policy today. The chapter concludes with an overview of the choices that surround nonpoint source pollution.

The Conclusion. In our final chapter, we return to the importance of the "doing side" of public policy and revisit how it helps us to understand policies that range from regulation to federalism, civil rights, immigration, education, crime and guns, welfare and health care, and environmental and energy concerns. We conclude the text with a discussion about the future, noting the importance not only of the role of the doing side of policy, but the importance of policy facts and consensus-building.

CONCLUDING THOUGHTS

Public policy is driven by our own experiences, but it is often messy due to the actors involved or the roles that power and politics play. Remember that the work of public policy is a process and does not end with its creation or inception, but continues with the doing side of public policy—implementation and evaluation.

Also, we cannot forget the important recognition of *value-neutral* and *value-laden*. We are consumers of public policy each and every day, and this consumption is defined by our communities, which can lead to value-laden decisions. Public policy experts across specialized fields are trained to make value-neutral solutions to address public problems.

In short, this chapter presented a variety of concepts to provide insights into why the field of public policy is far-reaching and essential. This chapter serves as a guidepost for what is to follow. And, by the time you complete this textbook at the end of your semester, you will have the skills necessary to engage in the process.

GLOSSARY TERMS

broadcast   10
bully pulpit   8
business interest group   10
civil law   9
criminal law   9
doing side of policy   7
elitism   3
federalism   3

implementation   2
lobbying   11
pluralism   3
policy   2
policy evaluators   7
politics   3
power   3
print   10

professional interest groups   10
public   2
public law   9
stages heuristic approach   5
value-laden   2
value-neutral   2

DISCUSSION QUESTIONS

1. The chapter begins with our own, personal stories. What personal experiences have you had that raise a policy question?

2. A variety of policy actors are involved in the policymaking process. Yet many Americans do not involve themselves in this process. What suggestions would you present to your friends and family about how to get involved in policymaking?

3. From the list of categories to public policy (distributive, redistributed, regulatory), what

are the strengths and weaknesses of each category? Which category, in your opinion, best represents public policymaking in the twenty-first century?

4. Policymaking can be controversial. Select a current public policy you define as controversial and explain why the concepts of value-neutral and value-laden are important in these conversations.

SUGGESTED RESOURCES

Suggested Websites

GovTrack, https://www.govtrack.us/congress/committees/

Oyez, https://www.oyez.org/

U.S. Congress, https://www.congress.gov/

U.S. Supreme Court, http://www.supremecourt.gov/

White House, http://www.whitehouse.gov

Suggested Books or Articles

Bachrach, Peter, and Morton S. Baratz. 1962. "Two Faces of Power." *The American Political Science Review* 56, no. 4: 947–52.

Dahl, Robert A. 1961. *Who Governs? Democracy and Power in an American City.* New Haven, CT: Yale University Press.

Kraft, Michael, and Scott Furlong. 2015. *Public Policy: Politics, Analysis, and Alternatives.* Washington, DC: CQ Press.

Lukes, Steven. (1974) 2005. *Power: A Radical View* (vol. 1). London: Macmillan.

Suggested Films

All the Way, DVD, directed by Jay Roach (2016: United States), http://www.imdb.com/title/tt3791216/

Confirmation, DVD, directed by Rick Famuyiwa (2016: United States), http://www.imdb.com/title/tt4608402/

Iron Jawed Angels, DVD, directed by Katja von Garnier (2004: United States), www.imdb.com/title/tt0338139/

Mr. Smith Goes to Washington, DVD, directed by Frank Capra (1939: United States), http://www.imdb.com/title/tt0031679/

The Suffragette, DVD, directed by Sarah Gavron (2015: United States), http://www.imdb.com/title/tt3077214/

NOTES

1. Institutions (e.g., Congress) and process by which policy choices are made or determined.

2. The U.S. Constitution grants Congress the authority to determine the size of the U.S. Supreme Court. The 1789 Judiciary Act set the number of justices at six, which fluctuated until 1869, when Congress set the number to nine justices; this has remained the same till today.

3. A federal agency is representative of the bureaucracy.

for CQ Press

Sharpen your skills with SAGE edge at **http://edge.sagepub.com/rinfret.** **SAGE edge for students** provides a personalized approach to help you accomplish your coursework goals in an easy-to-use learning environment.

The Policy Process and Policy Theories

POLICY RHETORIC AND REALITY

It is logical to approach the study of public policy thinking that policy is about two choices: for or against a particular issue, since that is so often how policy choices are framed. Indeed, we are taught from a young age that you are either for something or against it. Think about other, long-standing policy issues, such as capital punishment. It would seem that one is either for it or against it. As is often the case, though, reality is far more complicated than policy rhetoric might lead you to believe. After all, consider your own view on capital punishment. Some of you might have clear-cut positions that are absolute; however, you likely find yourself among the majority of Americans whose views on these issues are far more complex or nuanced. For instance, you might think the death penalty may be an appropriate punishment in certain circumstances, but you may still express trepidation about how it is carried out or the disproportionate representation of minorities there are on death row.

In the 115th Congress, Republicans took control of both chambers with a promise to fulfill a long-standing quest to repeal and replace Obamacare. However, multiple efforts have tried and failed, prompting President Donald Trump to grow impatient with a Congress that promised to have a bill to sign repealing Obamacare waiting for him on day one of his administration. Even within the Republican Party, the policy issue of health care is far more complicated than merely being for or against something—in this case, Obamacare. Numerous Republican senators expressed concern over repealing and replacing Obamacare for a variety of reasons, from the replacement legislation, such as the Graham-Cassidy bill, still costing too much money, to the risks that the replacement might allow states to deny coverage or make it prohibitively expensive for those individuals with preexisting conditions. The point is that while it may

LEARNING OBJECTIVES

Readers of this chapter will be able to:

1. Offer a definition of public policy

2. Discuss the context of public policy and the challenges that environment presents for achieving goals

3. Explain the desire for a coherent, universal theory of public policy

4. Apply the six steps of the stages heuristic model of public policy to a policy issue

5. Articulate strengths and weaknesses of competing public policy models

seem like policy issues result in a binary choice—being for or against something—policy issues are far more complicated in reality than the rhetoric might imply.

WHAT REALLY IS POLICY?

The term *public policy* is ubiquitous. Whether it is the discussion of public policy that comes with the arrival of new presidents, such as Donald Trump, to the White House or the circumstances that ushered in Franklin Delano Roosevelt's administration in the midst of the Great Depression, conversations about public policy abound. In particular, discussions of new policy directions and initiatives range from political circles, elected officials, the news media, to the classroom. But what really is public policy? Is it simply new leadership at the federal level in Washington, D.C., or in a state capital? Is it the process of how a bill becomes a law? Is it a new regulation? Quite simply, public policy is all of this and much more.

Public policy, as introduced in the last chapter, is a course of action adopted or created by the government in response to public problems. As we will see in the coming pages, public problems are those issues identified by the public and elected leaders as worthy of a coordinated response from the government. A response could entail the passage of laws or may involve an executive, such as the president or a governor, directing a government agency to do something. Just as problems often beget action, it is important to recognize that public policy is just as much what government decides to do as it is what government decides not to do. Ultimately, public policy is all about choices.

Government policies are not always easy to spot. Of course, public policy includes the laws passed by legislative bodies, whether they are statutes or local government ordinances, including the Patient Protection and Affordable Care Act, better known as Obamacare (see Chapter 8 for a discussion of health policy). But policy is much more. Policy also encompasses the regulations promulgated by executive agencies that translate the often vague statutes into actionable steps, which is discussed in more detail in Chapter 4. More broadly, policy is also the priorities of government entities, since policy is just as much about what government does not do as what it does. Public policy was manifested in the U.S. Department of Agriculture's MyPlate, or in the U.S. Forest Service's campaign to prevent forest fires with Smokey the Bear.

In this chapter, we introduce the process of government initiating action around public problems and supporting theories. The foundation here is instrumental for the remainder of the textbook and your ability to apply the core concepts from this chapter to various areas of public policy, such as education policy and criminal justice policy. We begin by focusing on the context for policymaking before delving into the realm of policy theories and efforts to explain the often convoluted process that produces public policy. The most common policy theory, the stages model, is discussed, along with some alternative theories to understand policymaking. Finally, the chapter ends with an assessment of whether or not policy theory helps advance our comprehension of policymaking.

UNDERSTANDING THE CONTEXT OF PUBLIC POLICY

Before delving into the policy theories that offer insight into the policy process, it is essential to point out that public policy does not happen in a vacuum—it does not happen in isolation. Whether it is health care policy or reforms to the tax code, public policy happens in a broader context with other concerns, priorities, and issues swirling about. Even though our subsequent chapters deal with particular areas of policy seemingly independent of other areas, this is not how policy exists in real life. What happens in immigration policy, for example, has implications for health care policy and education policy, and vice versa. Policy areas are all interrelated. As a result, policy action on a particular, even seemingly unrelated issue may be competing with action on another issue. Just as you can only deal with a certain number of courses each semester, government can only handle a certain number of policy options at any given time. What this exact number is varies and is ill-defined, but the point is that all sorts of policies compete with one another to become priorities of government. Not every issue can be the government—or society's—top priority.

PHOTO 2.1
Transportation Security Administration in action
REUTERS/Rick Wilking

Additionally, the priorities of government can change rapidly and dramatically with focusing events. **Focusing events** are significant episodes or experiences that catapult particular issues to prominence on the public's agenda. One classic example is the terrorist attacks of September 11, 2001. Airport security and the threat of terrorism were issues prior to the attacks, but the prominence of those concerns changed decisively afterward, prompting new security measures and a new agency, the Transportation Security Administration (TSA).

More recently, mass shootings at Sandy Hook Elementary School in Connecticut, the Pulse nightclub in Florida, the Route 91 Harvest Festival in Nevada, and Marjory Stoneman Douglas High School in Florida have renewed debates about gun control. The 2010 explosion and sinking of the *Deepwater Horizon* drilling rig in the Gulf of Mexico precipitated conversation about offshore drilling and environmental protection. Sometimes, focusing events have significant staying power in the national consciousness and result in policy action, such as the terrorist attacks, and other times, there are too many competing priorities and the nation's attention does not stay focused enough to compel action, as has been the case with the latest mass shootings. It is very difficult to determine whether or not a focusing event will bring about policy change in the moment, but retrospectively, looking for focusing events can help us understand movement on public policy issues.

With a realization of competing priorities and focusing events, we discuss four factors that affect the context of policymaking: (1) the political environment, (2) the economic environment, (3) the social and cultural environment, and (4) the administrative environment. We unpack what each of these contexts means for creating policy.

The Political Environment

One of the first factors that might influence policymaking that comes to mind is likely the political environment, or the politics of it all. In an increasingly polarized political climate, the role of politics is significant. More specifically, the priorities of political parties and elected officials do much to shape the policymaking agenda. For example, at the start of Donald Trump's administration in 2017, a stated policy priority was to repeal the Affordable Care Act, better known as Obamacare, which was enacted in 2009. Republican leaders in Congress pursued these objectives and scheduled a vote. This vote was pulled on the day it was scheduled, however, as it became clear the bill would not pass.

This example brings up another dimension of the political environment—the cycle of elections. Politicians coming up on reelection can be more reluctant to take a position on controversial issues that their challengers in the race might use against them. Also, after an election, the new party in control—and particularly if that political party controls multiple branches of government—will try to work quickly to action many of the priorities its members campaigned on during the election season. The issues that are particularly salient to the electorate, as well, are likely to help shape the priorities of elected officials and influence the policy options that are pursued. Again, consider the presidential election of 2016, in which salient issues for candidate Trump's supporters were immigration policy reform and building a wall on the United States' southern border. The new administration is already taking policy steps to solicit proposals for building the wall, and its pursuit of these efforts is driven, as the public's support for a candidate is an implicit endorsement of the candidate's policy positions. As Chapter 8 explores, the public opinion data do not support the construction of the wall, but only time will tell the outcomes of these policy efforts.

The Economic Environment

The politics of the moment are only a piece of the policy environment, however, as economics is also a major driver. After all, we all understand that money plays a large role in many situations. The health and overall well-being of both the American economy and the global economy can also have a significant effect on policy. When the economy is not performing well, Americans and their elected leaders are often focused on "fixing" the economy, and any other policy priorities are likely to be secondary.

These circumstances were evident during the Great Depression, which saw Franklin Delano Roosevelt's administration propel policies under the New Deal designed to stimulate the economy. Another example is the Great Recession of 2008 and 2009, when the downward spiral of the automotive industry and the housing crisis brought sweeping policy actions to save major car manufacturers and bolster the financial markets—the explanation being that the health of the economy is paramount. During these times, policy conversations about other issues, such as environmental efforts or education policies, were pushed aside.

On the flipside, when the economy is performing well, the nation is willing to engage in other policy issues that may be construed as being more "quality of life." For example, environmental or social policies are likely to gain more traction when the economy is robust because the thought is that these policies might cost money—regardless of the accuracy of these perceptions—and the public is more willing to entertain such action. Remember, much of the economy is based on faith and perceptions, just like the value of money. If people perceive that the economy is doing well, then it will be a self-reinforcing cycle and the economy will do well (for more on the contours of economic policy, see Chapter 5). But if people are worried that the economy is trending downward, they will be less inclined to spend money. These realities contribute toward a third aspect of the policy environment.

The Social and Cultural Environment

Another component of the policy context is social and cultural values. The norms of a society and what is culturally acceptable drive policymaking. Who we are as a country helps set the boundaries of what types of policies are likely to be enacted and successfully implemented. Consider the following scenario to illustrate this point. Perhaps scientists and engineers in the next year determine that in order to protect the planet from carbon emissions the most efficient and effective course of action would be for all Americans to drive Toyota Priuses. Accordingly, Congress takes up a bill to mandate that all other cars and trucks on the road nationwide have to be phased out over the next five years and replaced with Priuses. Let us also stipulate that Americans are desperate for action to curb emissions and politicians also support such steps. Would a policy like this one ever pass? In a word, no. And this conclusion is grounded in an understanding of Americans' culture and social values.

Since the creation of the interstate highway system during President Dwight D. Eisenhower's time in office, Americans' love affair with their cars has only grown. Moreover, nostalgia surrounds the freedom of the open road and even driving Route 66 across much of the nation. Additionally, fundamental to our identities as Americans is a belief in freedom and the free market. Therefore, when it comes to consumption, we value choice. We do not want to be told what kind of car to drive. Among your own friends and families, it is probably safe to assume that there are divergent opinions about the preferred style of car, much less the color selection. Some of us prefer American-made cars; others will only drive foreign cars. Still others like small, compact cars, while others want cars capable of hauling lots of people and their stuff. These realities about who we are as Americans and our preferences lead to the conclusion that there is no scenario—at least not at the present time—that can be envisioned in which Congress stipulates we all drive Priuses. It should be noted that values can and do change over time.

The Administrative Environment

The final environmental dimension of the policymaking context has to do with the practical, administrative side of policies. Put succinctly, the administrative environment concerns who in government (or the broader public sector, for that matter) will implement the policy; what level of government will be responsible for it? Many of these administrative and implementation details play an important role in public policy. It might be easy to argue at this juncture that these nitty-gritty details are of less significance, but we should remember the rollout of the Obamacare website, healthcare.gov, in October 2013. By almost every measure, the implementation of the nationwide marketplace website for health care exchanges was atrocious. The website crashed repeatedly, frustrating many on all sides of the issue. The implementation challenges were steep, considering that the website had to work with various state websites that had created their own exchanges. The website also had to work with the Internal Revenue Service's systems, as income and tax information for potential enrollees was required. And unlike the norms of the information technology industry, healthcare.gov was not phased in in pieces or tested in certain markets the way other internet retailers, such as Amazon.com, might do; rather, the website went live nationwide all at once.

Although these seemingly less important details are not as pervasive in public debate about a particular policy issue, they are extremely significant as policy ideas are being offered to solve a public problem. Sometimes the debate is less about government doing something and more about what level of government should do about something. A large portion

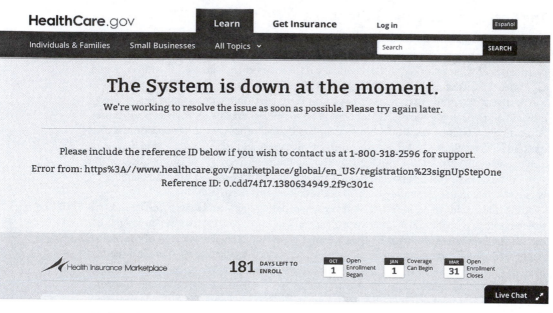

PHOTO 2.2
Healthcare.gov error screen
Courtesy of Healthcare.gov

of Americans would concede that much needs to be done about public education in this country, so the policy conversation becomes less about whether something should be done and instead more about who should take action. A particular area of that divide concerns the role of the federal government and fifty state governments in education. Depending on one's viewpoint about which level of government should be at the forefront of education, policy reforms will drive discussions about policy actions. Oftentimes there is consensus that action is needed on a particular issue, but the challenge becomes how something should be done; therefore, this context of policymaking is significant, even if it is a bit less glamorous.

The key idea to take away from this discussion of the policymaking context is that policy action does not happen in isolation—many factors affect a particular policy idea that may have little to do with the merit or validity of a policy. At any given time, multiple policies in different areas are always competing with one another for the attention of people and their lawmakers; the politics of the moment are likely to play a role, just as the economic conditions will as well. Finally, questions about the administration of a policy solution are also intertwined with social and cultural values. It is essential to keep these points in mind as we turn our attention to the path a particular policy idea must travel to be created and implemented.

THE QUEST FOR PUBLIC POLICY THEORY

With the complexities of the policy environment, it is unsurprising that there is a desire to produce theories that explain when policies will or will not move forward. Indeed, this quest for public policy theories drives many scholars and practitioners throughout their careers. But before we delve into the work of these scholars, we should start at the beginning: What is a theory? According to Google, a theory is "a supposition or a system of ideas intended to explain something, especially one based on general principles independent of the thing to be explained." Theories help us understand phenomena, conditions, and events that seem to escape explanation. Even with just our brief discussion of what policy is in both this chapter and the last, it is already apparent that public policy is something that craves explanation. Moreover, since public policy can and does have significant effects on our day-to-day lives, it is unsurprising that we want theories to explain it.

More formally, Professor Paul Sabatier (2007) maintains there are five reasons why we seek theories of public policy. First, there are a great deal of people and organizations who are involved in public policy issues. Within this complex array of actors, individuals have various interests, values, perceptions, and preferences that can and do have tremendous effects on the creation and implementation of public policy. After all, if some actors do not even perceive an issue as being a problem, there are significant ramifications to any effort to enact policy to solve that problem. With this complexity, policy theories should help us better grasp the multitude of actors involved and what their impact might be on policy.

Second, policymaking encompasses significant time spans, so theories can help us grasp the timeline for policies. Think about some of the policy issues that have already been mentioned, including health care and air pollution. Neither of these issues is likely to be addressed quickly, and the existing policies about these topics go back decades. Arguably, the role of government in health care dates back to at least the 1930s, and the federal government has been involved in environmental policy since the 1950s and 1960s. Policy theory can help us account for the timelines of these policy issues.

As is evident in the brief examples in the previous paragraph, health care and environmental concerns are not encapsulated in just one policy. Instead, there are multiple policies and programs that may or may not align well with one another. It is not just the Affordable Care Act from 2009; there are numerous laws dealing with the creation of Social Security, Medicare and Medicaid, the Consolidated Omnibus Budget Reconciliation Act (creating COBRA), the Health Insurance Portability and Accountability Act, the State Children's Health Insurance Program, or the Medicare Prescription Drug Act. The point here is that there are lots and lots of policies and theories that can help us understand how they fit together.

A fourth reason why theories are helpful is they account for all the different ways public problems are approached and understood. At first glance, it may be fairly simple for you to think about a public issue and what should be done about it. But as you reflect on that topic, you realize that your ideas about that problem are *your* ideas and others are likely to understand the problem differently, think about the problem differently, and offer a range of other solutions. And this leads to the final reason Sabatier offers about the value of policy theory: theories can help us understand and consider what government should and should not be doing. The debates surrounding public policy are rooted in our varying ideas about the role of government in society, how the government should fulfill that role, and what resources it takes to accomplish its objectives. To put it more succinctly, "understanding the policy process requires knowledge of the goals and perceptions of hundreds of actors throughout the country involving possibly very technical scientific and legal issues over periods of a decade or more while most of those actors are actively seeking to propagate their specific 'spin' on events" (Sabatier 2007, 4).

Of course, it may be appealing just to apply common sense or take an ad hoc approach to a policy, but that is limited in that you are unable to extrapolate from one particular policy topic at one particular time to any other instance of policymaking. Accordingly, numerous policy scholars have sought theories to explain policy in more than just one case. Theories can help us identify similarities and patterns across multiple cases that enable us to understand what is happening presently and perhaps even predict what might happen in the future. They provide an organizing framework and a vocabulary in which we can talk about policy. So with that in mind, we introduce next some specific policy theories, starting with the most common: the stages heuristic model. After a robust discussion of this pervasive policy theory, we also introduce several other theories that have gained traction in the policy community more recently.

THE STAGES HEURISTIC MODEL OF PUBLIC POLICYMAKING

The stages heuristic model of public policymaking, as described in Chapter 1, is without doubt the most common theory that endeavors to explain policy. It is worth pointing out that theories to describe policymaking are relatively new, as studying public policy in a formal, academic setting only began in the middle part of the twentieth century. Granted, this may not seem new to readers of this text, but keep in mind that biologists and theologians have been hard at work in their fields for centuries. Political scientist Harold Lasswell was the first scholar to describe a "decision process" for public policy and articulate "policy sciences" (Lasswell 1951, 1956). Although the language used to describe the steps of the policymaking process have evolved over the intervening decades, the steps of making public policy can be thought of in the following terms (as introduced in the last chapter): (1) problem identification and definition, (2) agenda setting, (3) policy formulation, (4) policy legitimation, (5) policy implementation, and (6) policy evaluation (see also Figure 2.1).

FIGURE 2.1

The Policymaking Process

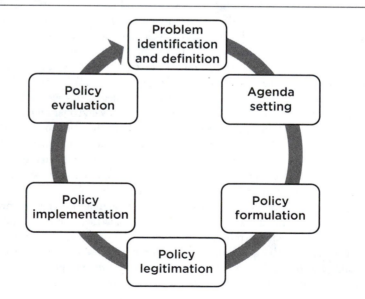

Sugary Drinks

As we consider each of these six steps, it is helpful to have an example to walk through each stage of the process. For our purposes, we have selected a fictitious and somewhat ridiculous example, but it is based in real life. In 2013, New York City mayor Michael Bloomberg led an effort to limit the size of drinks sold in the city that were sweetened. The Sugary Drinks Portion Cap Rule, promulgated in 2013 for New York City, limited the size of drinks that were sweetened (e.g., sodas) to no more than 16 ounces. The thought was that by limiting the size of drinks with added sugar that people could buy, the intake of sugar would decrease.

Ultimately, the attempts were unsuccessful, as New York state courts ruled that the city exceeded its authority in instituting the limits. Nevertheless, let us use this as a foundation to employ an example that helps us understand the policy process.

PHOTO 2.3

Mayor Michael Bloomberg and the Sugary Drinks Portion Cap Rule effort

Bloomberg Philanthropies

Stage 1: Problem Identification and Definition

You have likely heard the old adage, "The first step in solving a problem is recognizing there is one." This is absolutely essential to policymaking. The first stage of the policy process is to figure out what the problem is and to define it. A key component of figuring out the problem is determining a public problem. Just because you think an issue may be a problem does not necessarily make it a public problem. For instance, not having enough movie theaters nearby or figuring out which pair of shoes to wear might be a problem for you, but it does not rise to the level of a public problem. Therefore, public problems are what constitute policymaking efforts. For example, public problems might include the rise of opioid abuse nationwide or concerns about the proper disposal of batteries and outdated technology. Of course, it bears remembering that just because you think any of these aforementioned challenges are public problems does not mean there is widespread agreement among others that they are problems. A particular region of the country or a state might champion a particular issue, but that may not capture the attention of the nation, for instance.

Over time, issues gain traction and become public problems through a variety of ways including through the media, advocacy organizations, politicians, and even average citizens. There are many ways we come to understand public problems through these channels. Sometimes it is a new research study that documents the growing abuse of opioids in the country, or perhaps it is cell phone footage capturing police officers using deadly force. Other times a natural disaster, such as Hurricane Sandy, can galvanize attention on storm readiness and needed revisions to construction requirements. And in other instances, it may be a handful of policy entrepreneurs who focus all of their efforts on a particular issue and compel others to address the problem.

Once problems are raised by society, we have to define them. After all, we have to have a common understanding of the problem so we can figure out how to solve it. On the surface, this seems simple enough, but this is where the challenge begins. How you understand a challenge or a problem may be different than how your roommate comprehends it. Returning to the example of opioid abuse, you might think the problem is a function of physicians too readily prescribing painkillers for people who then become addicted because the medical professional should have better controlled access to the substance. Your roommate, however, may think that it is not the medical community's fault because people just need to "toughen up" and cope with pain from an injury or a chronic condition. Of course, the issue is far more complicated, but our understanding of the problem and how we define it could be expressed in these underlying terms. The point is that how we think of a problem and define the contours of that problem can often be a social construction (see Berger and Luckman 1966 for the theoretical underpinnings).

Simply put, our ideas about problems come from our own experiences, our own perceptions of situations and institutions, and this affects our approach and attitude about public problems (Schneider and Ingram 1997). Given the variability in constructing and defining public problems, it is unsurprising that we end up with many competing definitions of a problem; and with these different conceptions, there are very significant implications for the remaining five steps of the policymaking process.

To see the complexities associated with this very first step of the policy process, let us return to the Sugary Drinks Portion Cap Rule example. In our efforts to understand more fully this part of the policymaking process, let us take this real-life example and go further with it. What actually is the problem with soda and other sugary drinks, and concern over Americans' health? One way to look at the issue of extra-large sodas might be that Americans are always thirsty and can never get enough to drink, so portion sizes have to increase. Another way to consider the issue might be that Americans have a sweet tooth and prefer beverages that have added sugar, like soda. Perhaps government should not care whether Americans drink soda. And who cares what is in soda, whether it is sugar or some poisonous chemical. Or maybe there is concern that Americans' health is declining while obesity rates are climbing, and the major culprit is sugar—and soda is one of the primary ways Americans absorb extra sugar in their diets. There are not a lot of national public data on the topic, but back in 2013 Gallup found that 69 percent of respondents disapproved of laws limiting sodas over 16 ounces (Gallup 2013).

These comments vary in their plausibility; nevertheless, the point is that there are lots of different directions from which a discussion of soda portions can be defined. Accordingly, this is where the importance of definition comes into focus. If we can agree that obesity is linked to sugary sodas (which, of course, is a stretch, but let us continue with this intellectual exercise), what should be done? Should sodas be banned, for public health concerns? Should there just be limits to the size of sodas that can be purchased? Should Americans be better educated about their beverage choices? Should the government place warning labels on sodas, as it does for many other products, and let consumers decide for themselves? Should nutritional guidance and labels on sodas be changed? Should Americans be able to drink whatever they want, since freedom in consumption is a basic tenet of U.S. society? What you should be gathering from this fictitious example are the complexities associated with even a basic understanding of the public problem. With all these questions, the remaining five steps of the policy process appear all the more daunting.

Stage 2: Agenda Setting

Once a problem has been identified and definitions offered, it moves to the agenda of government for action. Or maybe not. It is at this stage of the policymaking process where most policy options never get any further. After all, just because a problem has been acknowledged and defined does not mean anything will get done about it. The problem has to captivate the attention of the government and the public to compel action. And the government only has so much bandwidth in which to consider a problem. Just like you are unlikely to take twelve classes in a particular semester, government can only handle so much on its agenda.

A variety of circumstances can bring a particular public problem to the attention of government. Focusing events are those often discrete incidents that captivate the attention of citizens and policymakers alike. For example, a focusing event might be a mass shooting, such as the one at Marjory Stoneman Douglas High School in Parkland, Florida, on Valentine's Day 2018 or the often-cited example of the terrorist attacks of September 11, 2001. Focusing events do not always galvanize action around a particular topic. To date, there has not been policy action around guns, and access to them, that is directly attributable to the event, but the terrorist attacks in 2001 brought widespread and dramatic change to everything from how security for commercial air travel is conducted to the creation of new government agencies.

Dramatic and often terrible acts of violence are not the only kinds of focusing events, however. Public problems can also come to the forefront and demand attention because the public demands action or has had enough of a particular circumstance. Interest from citizens may also be accentuated, or even driven, by the work of interest groups and other **policy entrepreneurs** who make it their professional objective to get the public and their policymakers to focus on addressing a particular public problem. It is worth noting that a multitude of actors can and do involve themselves in the policy process. Obviously, our elected political leaders are the individuals who make decisions about public problems, but lobbyists who work for interest groups, advocacy groups, the media, and the general public also can and do call attention to public problems. Additionally, the results of researchers and scientists often help society understand issues that need to be addressed as well.

Oftentimes it is a combination of many of these factors, and perhaps even a little bit of serendipity, that brings a problem to the agenda of government. Sometimes it is easy to understand why a problem is now the focus of government, and other times it is less clear. Regardless of how an issue gets to the agenda, it must get to the agenda and exhibit staying power to progress through the policy process.

Public policy scholar Thomas Birkland (2016) points out that there are different levels of the policy agenda that help us understand how and why some issues do not stay in the public spotlight while others work their way through the layers of the agenda and make it further in the policy process. At the most macro level, Birkland discusses an agenda universe in which all the ideas about all the public problems are discussed in the political arena. Some issues, such as Social Security reform or tax code modifications, often persist at this level and find it difficult to progress to the systematic agenda. This second layer of the agenda constitutes those public problems that policymakers are actually willing to consider as part of their reach and issues that could potentially be addressed. The boundary between the agenda universe and systemic universe is porous, and policy issues flow back and forth.

Beyond the agenda universe is the institutional agenda, which comprises all the policy problems and possible policy options that are being considered and might reasonably stand a chance of action. For the last several presidential administrations, environmentalists have been anxious for Congress to take up legislation to address climate change at a national level. But in recent years, the issue has made little further progress toward the final level of agenda: the decision agenda. The decision agenda—as the name indicates—describes those problems for which government is actively debating a solution and taking specific actions and making decisions, like taking a vote. So far, it could easily seem that defining a problem is the harder of the two steps of the policy process covered, but you can start to see that just because a problem has been identified and is being discussed does not mean it is gaining the attention of policymakers, either.

Returning to our example of sugary drinks helps us further understand the importance of this stage of the policy process. While the health risks of overconsumption of sugar have been well established, and soda has long been a staple of Americans' diets, what might compel the government to discuss action about the issue? With the recognition of the obesity crisis in the United States, pretend that Congress has decided to take action to get Americans to reduce their intake of sugary drinks such as soda. The belief is that if Americans drink less soda, then the obesity crisis will be mitigated. These discussions may come about from a variety of sources. Professionals in the health community, including government scientists, may release reports that document rising rates of not only adult obesity, but childhood obesity as well.

Additionally, there may be a new docudrama on reality television that depicts a family's decision to drink nothing but soda for six months to see what happens (much like how real-life filmmaker Morgan Spurlock decided to eat nothing but McDonald's food for thirty days to see what happened to his health for the 2004 film *Super Size Me*). There could also be ongoing efforts by juice manufacturers to promote their products over soda as a less sugary option. Or perhaps one state bans soda and sees dramatic improvements in a range of health outcomes. Any of these scenarios are plausible ways that the concern over soda and its increasing portion sizes is making its way to the agenda of government. The challenges associated with both problem identification and agenda setting may already seem daunting in bringing about policy action, but keep in mind: these are only the first two steps of six in the policy process.

Stage 3: Policy Formulation

The third step of the policy process, policy formulation, entails devising ways to solve—or at least ameliorate—public problems. Once the government's attention is adequately piqued, work is focused on crafting the solution to the public problem. This is the stage of the policymaking process where specific, concrete actions about how to address an issue are brainstormed, discussed, and debated. For very technical matters, such as building safety in areas prone to natural disasters like earthquakes, hurricanes, or floods, this is the stage of the process where experts come together to discuss what the government can and cannot mandate and what those building standards might look like.

In other areas of policy, such as prevention of terrorist attacks on airplanes, the technical aspects of policy options have to move forward alongside debates surrounding what levels of invasion Americans are willing to contend with regarding their privacy. For example, recently, the Transportation Security Administration (TSA) introduced body scanners to be used at airports nationwide that could more effectively screen passengers to see if they were attempting to carry prohibited items on board a commercial aircraft. Critics charged body scanners, which captured images of passengers beneath their clothing, were too invasive. This controversy ignited debate about the need to maintain safety while also protecting a person's privacy. The point here is that just because there is a technical solution to an issue—we need to screen passengers for weapons more easily and effectively—that does not always mean the options are viable. After all, the best way to prevent destruction from hurricanes is not to build structures anywhere near where hurricanes might strike; but what is the likelihood that all construction near beaches ceases? This demonstrates that policy formulation is far more than technical solutions to problems; it also involves reconciling competing goals and values, not to mention specific choices among policy tools.

As indicated in the previous examples, devising a solution to a public problem involves a variety of goals and values that are often in competition with one another. Consider the values of American society that political scientist Deborah Stone (2012) articulates: equity, efficiency, welfare, liberty, and security. It is reasonable to conclude that Americans widely hold these values, but can all of these values be held to their highest ideals at the same time and for each policy issue? Returning to the issue of safety in commercial air travel and body scanners: How are we to reconcile our desire for security with our desires for efficiency in screening processes as well as our liberty not to have our privacy invaded? Can we be completely safe and completely free at the same time? If not, as the answer likely is, what balance between safety and liberty are we willing to accept? On one hand, these might seem existential questions more appropriate in political theory and philosophy classrooms, but they are just as relevant questions for policymakers trying to take action surrounding issues facing the general public.

In addition to these questions, policy formulation also entails selection among policy tools to address problems. The government uses a variety of tools and techniques to compel action from individuals and organizations, and we turn to political scientist B. Guy Peters's (1999) useful typology of those tools. Peters offers six broad categories of policy tools at the disposal of government: laws, services, money, taxes, other economic instruments, and suasion.

Laws encompass acts of legislative bodies, like Congress, as well as regulations promulgated by executive agencies. These decrees tell individuals and organizations what they can and cannot do. For instance, the amount of effluent that can be released into a stream from a manufacturing company is the result of the Clean Water Act and subsequent regulations that implement the law.

The government can also provide services as a way to coax behavior. For example, the government ensures the safety of the skies by providing air traffic control and monitors weather through the National Weather Service in the Department of Commerce.

Money is a third tool available to policymakers. All levels of government—federal, state, and local governments—provide money to citizens and organizations through transfer payments, such as via the Supplemental Nutrition Assistance Program (SNAP) or Social Security payments to those individuals retired or unable to work due to injury or medical condition, grants to researchers, other governmental entities to study and solve a problem, or through contracting out. Increasingly, the government pays other firms to provide services on behalf of government. For example, contracting out includes everything from your local municipality paying a large waste management company to collect your trash and recyclables, to some states paying privately run prison companies to incarcerate those individuals convicted of crimes. With this policy tool, governments use money to address public problems.

A related fourth tool policymakers have is the power to tax. Taxes are used in myriad instances where government wants to change the behavior of people and organizations without expressly telling them what to do. A case in point is cigarette taxes. The evidence is clear that smoking cigarettes can be hazardous to one's health, and in aggregate, a public health problem as well. But instead of governments forbidding citizens from smoking, many governments add taxes to the price of cigarettes to discourage people from smoking.

Another category of tools identified by Peters and related to money are assorted economic instruments. There are other ways governments employ funds to affect policy outcomes, including the use of loans and subsidies. Perhaps you are furthering your education with the assistance of federal government student loans. Here the government is encouraging people to advance their education by making money readily available, and traditionally at lower interest rates, for students to take loans. Subsidies are also used by the government, including for farmers, to keep the nation engaged in agriculture and keep prices affordable.

A final category of tools is more nebulous: the use of suasion. This category of tools refers to all the indirect means the government might employ to encourage behaviors of individuals and organizations it wants and discourage behaviors it does not. For example, we are all familiar with public service announcements (PSAs) that encourage citizens if they "see something, say something" in an effort to prevent violence and attacks and other announcements about the perils of drug abuse. These are some of the broad categories of tools that are available for policymakers to consider when endeavoring to craft a solution to a public problem. As is evident from this discussion list of tools, there are many different ways to go about compelling action in response to public challenges. And how a particular issue is defined and how it comes to government's agenda will go a long way in helping us understand the tools that are selected to address the problem.

It should become increasingly clear that the policy process (at least in this model) is sequential and one step builds on another; therefore, the previous steps impact future steps. Returning to our example of sugary sodas, think about how a policy could be designed. One option could be for the government to curb consumption of sodas by doing what New York City endeavored to do—limit the size of sodas available for purchase. So a proposal might employ laws and regulations that ban the sale of any soda larger than 12 ounces, thereby making large fountain sodas, liters, and so forth illegal. Of course, this does not preclude someone from buying eight sodas every morning, but instead of carrying one extra-large cup, an individual might have to carry eight now. This policy option would be indicative of a problem definition centered around the notion that people consume too much soda because the portion sizes available to them are too large, so if the size is curtailed, so will the intake of soda.

Another policy option might be to allow individuals to buy whatever size soda they want but to use taxes as a means of discouraging behavior. This policy option might be the addition of a $5 per soda tax on any and all sodas bought in the United States. Such an option would be predicated on the idea that people buy and consume soda because it is cheap and therefore if it is made to be more expensive, people will consume less of it. Still another policy option might be to launch a widespread education campaign and encourage people to limit their consumption of soda through persuasive techniques. This approach is based on the problem definition that people consume as much soda as they do because they do not fully understand the risks of drinking so much soda. Therefore, in addition to the creation of an anti–soda drinking mascot, new labels might adorn soda cups and cans that show people who have become obese because they drank too much soda. The point of these examples is that the way the public problem is constructed and how it comes to the agenda will likely affect the kinds of policies that are designed and the tools that are called upon to address the problem. It is becoming increasingly evident just how complicated the policy process is, we are only at step three, and nothing has actually been enacted.

Stage 4: Policy Legitimation

The fourth step of the policy process, policy legitimation, is probably the step of the policy process you best understand, as this is the point at which a policy is decided and enacted. In other words, this is the step in which a bill becomes a law. At the federal level, policy legitimation occurs when Congress passes a bill; at the state level, policy legitimation occurs when a state legislature passes a bill; and at the local level, policy legitimation occurs when a local legislative body, such as a city council, passes an ordinance. For a brief refresher about the lawmaking process: a bill has to be drafted, introduced into one chamber (House or Senate at the federal level), referred to committee, and then usually referred to a subcommittee for hearings and investigation. Then those committees make changes to the bill before voting on whether to refer it to the entire chamber. From there, the entire legislative chamber debates a bill and votes. If all of these pieces fall into place, the process starts in the other chamber. And then, if the entire legislative body supports the bill, the bill moves the executive (president or governor, for instance) for signature or a veto. Only after both legislative and executive branch involvement does a bill actually become a law and a policy legitimated. It is worth pausing for a moment and thinking about the difficulties associated with passing legislation, particularly at the federal level, in recent years. The policy process is incumbent on decisions being made at this stage of the process.

With our example of government intervention surrounding soda consumption, what would it take to get Congress to pass one of the policy options discussed in the last section? Congress might take up a bill entitled the No Extra-Large Sodas Bill. Recall that this option would ban the sale of sodas above a certain size. Even if the best health and scientific information aligns to support this bill, there are going to be lots of actors who would mobilize to challenge the bill. For instance, the soda and beverage industry would likely lobby members of Congress to thwart such a bill. And it is likely that representatives of other similar industries, like the candy industry, would rally to support the soda lobbyists because if Congress limits sodas, it might seek to curb candy bar sizes next. An alternative may be banning soda outright; perhaps Congress would draft legislation to outlaw soda. An argument could be made that Americans are not in a position to make the best choices about what kinds of beverages to drink, so Congress should make those decisions for them. While this may seem extreme, remember that it was not that long ago that the United States endeavored to outlaw alcohol through constitutional amendment. A range of other options exist to limit Americans' consumption of soda, from bans, to size or portion limits, to taxes and other means of persuasion. Whatever policy options are offered, though, they must make it through the process of becoming legitimized by the decisions of our political leaders. At this juncture, the policy process seems daunting, but remember: this is not the end of the process.

Stage 5: Policy Implementation

Oftentimes, widespread attention to public problems and corresponding policy options stops by this stage of the process. The news media are usually focused on the process of identifying issues and the path to devising options to address those challenges. And the politics associated with how a bill becomes a law in step four makes for good news stories. Policy implementation, the fifth stage of the policy process, is the doing of policy, the executing of decisions to bring about change to address a public problem. After a policy has been decided on, the general presumption is the implementation just happens and is far less interesting. However, anyone who studies public policy at all knows that policy implementation, which is the process of carrying out policies, accomplishing the actual policy is often far more intriguing and indicative of the overall success or failure of a policy. Policy scholars Jeffrey Pressman and Aaron Wildavsky note that common perceptions hold that policy "implementation should be easy; [people] are therefore upset when expected events do not occur or turn out badly" (Pressman and Wildavsky 1973, xi–xvii).

There are many factors that make policy implementation just as complex as each of the preceding steps in the policy process. Although we devote an entire chapter to rulemaking (Chapter 4), here we provide an overview of the basics of implementation. Recall where we were in the policy process: a legislative body made a decision and chose among many competing policy options to address a problem. Typically, when bodies, such as Congress, pass a law, those laws are vague and rather general. For example, the 1972 Clean Water Act addresses water pollution in the nation's waterways by mandating the U.S. Environmental Protection Agency (EPA) make those waterways "swimmable" and "fishable." This might seem a great description of how we want our bodies of water in the United States, but what does it mean to make a river or a lake "swimmable"? Your definition of what makes something swimmable may vary dramatically from the person next to you in class. Policy implementation becomes about operationalizing terms like these. You might be thinking, Why did Congress not get more specific about what makes a waterway swimmable? But remember, it takes a lot of consensus building to pass legislation, and the product of those negotiations typically has to be somewhat vague or more general in nature in order to gain enough votes to pass. Moreover, members of Congress, in this case, are not necessarily experts in water quality, as most of them are highly trained lawyers rather than ecologists and environmental engineers. As a result, Congress leaves the specifics to the experts who work at government agencies such as the EPA.

To implement policy decisions, various government agencies get involved in translating statutory language into actionable regulations that achieve the policy objectives in the legislation. This is called rulemaking and conducted by the civil servants who are employed by government agencies. These individuals are the experts who work for the government, who are not given jobs due to political affiliation but because they demonstrate competence in a particular area. While one agency is often given the primary task of implementing a policy, that agency often has to work with a host of other agencies, and many times, those agencies may be at the federal, state, and local level. Already you can see that implementation is not as simple as decreeing that the nation's waterways should be cleaned up. Lots of agencies at the federal level, agencies from the fifty states, and all the organizations that might discharge into waterways or otherwise use the nation's water bodies become involved.

As we have in the previous steps of the policy process, let us incorporate our ongoing example about sugary drinks. For the purposes of this example, remember that Congress decided to pass the No Extra-Large Sodas (NELS) Act despite strong opposition from the soda industry and convenience stores nationwide. Public opinion is split, with many Americans supportive of the efforts to improve the health of their fellow citizens and a large portion annoyed that government is overreaching and trying to control their lives. With these political currents in the background, Congress, through the NELS Act, told the U.S. Department of Health and Human Services (HHS) to work with the U.S. Department of Commerce to determine exactly what size soda constituted "extra-large" (e.g., number of ounces) and then to develop a plan to phase it out. While the media and news pundits may be less interested now that the law has passed, the work is just beginning. HHS and Commerce, tasked with two very different missions (one concerning public health and welfare and the other, job creation and economic growth), now have to come together to figure out the threshold for extra-large sodas. Many convenience stores sell (and have trademarked) their extra-large soda sizes, which range from 20 ounces to 50 ounces. What information should be used or be considered to decide what is too big? Should it be a universal declaration, or should what is too big be dependent on how old you are or your physical health? And once—or if—a decision can be made about the cup size, how do you make it happen? Should it be a phased-in ban—perhaps making super-sized cups collectors' items that sell for lots of money on eBay? Or should it be mandated effective January 1 of a given year? And what happens if people bring their own cup to fill a fountain drink at their favorite snack shop? What are the consequences? And what is to stop someone from buying three drinks to equal the size of the drink cup that was banned? Does this policy option really address the underlying problem as conceived originally? All these questions, and many others, demonstrate the challenges associated with policy implementation. And these issues only comprise the fifth step of a six-step policy process.

Stage 6: Policy Evaluation

The final step in the policy process is policy evaluation. Assessing whether or not a policy is successful is critical, as the entire policy process strives to address, and perhaps even solve, public problems. But just as we have seen in the other stages of this process, this step is highly complex and riddled with challenges. Policy evaluation, simply put, is figuring out if the policy is working. Yet what does it mean to be "working"? As we have seen regarding the importance of defining a problem in the initial stages of policymaking, defining "working" is critical in this stage. Politicians and members of the news media often leave our heads spinning, as they all have different assessments of whether the same policy is working. The reason why they can all have different conclusions about a policy is their definitions of "working" vary. Along these lines, conceptions of "success," "effectiveness," and even "efficiency" have to be defined. Just as we saw with step one of the policy process, arriving at common definitions can be a challenging process.

Despite the complexities of policies, we all seem to quickly decide whether a policy is working or not. For example, conclusions were reached almost immediately about whether or not the Affordable Care Act was successful. But on what would you base your assessment about Obamacare? Is it having more people insured who did not previously have health insurance? Is it driving down costs of health insurance plans over time? Or is it better health outcomes for people to make for a healthier citizenry? Your focal question will likely result in different answers about the success of the law. Furthermore, when the health care exchange website, administered by the federal government, was unveiled in October 2013, there were quick conclusions that Obamacare was a failure because the website crashed repeatedly. The point is that evaluating policy options that strive to solve complex policy problems is not as simple as the yes and no assessments we frequently hear attached to policies.

Beyond definitional complexities, systematically consider how policy evaluation is conducted and the problems inherent in it. Much like the problem definition stage of the policy process, policy evaluation requires an articulation of what about the policy is going to be assessed. Then, policy evaluation typically involves a multitude of actors to gather data;

find out about how the policy is being implemented on the front lines; and analyze how the policy is working across time, cases, individuals, or even water bodies. Then, analysis of the data has to be conducted, findings summarized, and conclusions reached. Just as you have learned in your research methods courses, decisions have to be made in each phase of the investigation, and there are implications to those decisions. And sometimes data may not be readily available, particularly for interested parties. Even though Obamacare passed in 2010, that did not stop politicians from running in the 2012 midterm elections declaring whether or not it was a success or failure. You can already see from our discussion of questions around what aspect of Obamacare we might be evaluating, there is little chance that any answer to those questions could be readily available in 2012, but that did not stop candidates for office from claiming otherwise.

Regarding data, there are additional challenges obtaining them as well. Cost-benefit analysis is routinely employed to figure out if a policy is worthwhile. But the challenge lies in figuring out costs and calculating benefits. For example, if a new food safety policy details safety practices for processing dairy products, reasonable questions might be, "How much would these new requirements for farmers and producers cost?" and "What are the benefits?" If new equipment is required for farmers and producers of milk, cheese, and so forth, we can figure out how much they cost and add it up. But what about figuring out the benefits to compare against the costs to see if the new policy is a good idea? How do you figure out in a comparable unit—likely dollars in this case—what the benefit is for people who do not get sick from dairy products? Do you estimate health care costs? Do you also add in time at work people may miss because they got sick from contaminated dairy products?

These questions bring up another critical aspect of evaluation: **risk assessment**. In determining costs and benefits, questions usually arise surrounding how much risk we are willing to accept. Risk refers to the likelihood that an adverse situation will occur and evaluating its magnitude. In our case of the dairy products and new safety mechanisms, should the government create policy that guarantees no one will get sick from dairy products, indicating a zero tolerance for risk? Or is it reasonable to go with 98 percent of people will not get sick? It might be reasonable to mandate regulations where there is only a 2 percent risk of getting sick, but if you are one of the 2 percent, you are unlikely to agree.

Numerous other problems present themselves during policy evaluation, but that does not mean evaluation is not important. Lots of resources, time, and energy are expended implementing policy and we want policies to solve problems, so evaluation is crucial. Consider a handful of additional challenges in the evaluation process. First, as we have seen, uncertainty over goals and definitions is a perennial challenge in evaluation. Ambiguity around what is being assessed and the evaluative criteria create problems for evaluation from the start. Second, if clear criteria can be established it is very difficult in social science research to isolate all of the factors that could be influencing a policy. And isolating causation is often integral to assessing whether or not a policy is working. For instance, if a determination is trying to be made about whether or not taxes on tobacco products are discouraging tobacco use, it is impossible to rule out any other reasons besides the tax alone that might be contributing to declining rates of tobacco use. While the taxes may be higher on tobacco products, perhaps the primary driver for declines in tobacco product consumption have to do with bans on advertising these items and not the increased taxes. A third factor is that isolating the effects, positive or negative, of a particular policy might be diffuse and intertwined with other policies. This challenge points out that some policy options have unintended consequences. Fourth, evaluations of policy are contingent on data and sometimes data are far harder to gather than one might think.

Finally, policy evaluations, as do all good social science research, take time. However, time is often not in ready supply when citizens and their elected leaders want answers about whether or not a problem is actually being solved. Moreover, credible evaluations often need data that span over many years, and that may not always be feasible. These are just some of the many issues that arise in trying to assess whether a policy that has made it through the entire policy process is working.

Returning to our example of the NELS Act, think about the aforementioned challenges of evaluation in this scenario. With congressional action limiting the size of sodas available to purchase, a reasonable assessment of this policy might be if rates of obesity among Americans are falling. So data could be gathered that track obesity rates pre- and postimplementation of the policy. But this evaluation is challenging because rates of obesity might have little to do with consuming sodas. And since Americans would no longer be able to buy large sodas, could they still be drinking the same amount of soda, just buying more cups? This increased consumption of smaller containers may have implications for solid waste as well. Furthermore, consumption patterns of soda may have changed because new, groundbreaking research proves that drinking coffee is the healthiest beverage for you and coffee producers have responded by making all sorts of palate-appealing coffee flavors for reluctant coffee drinkers. Additionally, making determinations about whether a policy is working often involves calculations around costs and benefits. How do we put a dollar figure on the costs associated with obesity so we can compare the costs associated with the benefits of the law? How do we calculate the lost soda sales convenience stores might experience—along with the bag of chips bought with a large soda—if this law takes effect? The point is, evaluating the success of our policy option is hard.

Assessing the Stages Model

The stages model of public policymaking is very common owing to a variety of advantages that will be discussed shortly; but at the conclusion of this overview of the six steps, it should also be evident that there are flaws in this particular policy theory. Pause and consider the pros and cons of this approach.

There are numerous advantages to this model, as evidenced by its continued use in policy studies and by the many pages spent discussing it here. In particular, this model offers a linear, methodical introduction to the complexities of policymaking. It provides a vocabulary to help discuss and comprehend policy, and its neatly divided stages of the policy process help foster understanding for those new to policy studies. After all, there is something to be said for a simple explanation of a complicated process.

However, there are drawbacks to this approach. While it could be argued that a simple model is helpful, perhaps this model is too simple and does not adequately account for the reality of public policy. The model offers steps that appear discrete and sequential, but many times various steps occur simultaneously and even out of order during real-life policymaking. Additionally, the six steps of the model would make it seem that each step takes a similar amount of time; however, that is not the case, and it varies wildly from policy to policy. The model does little to account for the web of actors who play a role in the policy process and provides no predictive value as well in helping forecast when and if a policy will make it to the next stage of the process. Finally, this model can lead to the conclusion that policymaking is methodical and rational when, in reality, government action is often not intentional and perhaps irrational.

Regardless of the pros and cons associated with this model, this approach does have staying power and few other models are as widely studied and used as this one—perhaps it is the best policy model we can hope for, as we are unlikely to find a perfect model (Smith and Larimer 2009, 35). Although this model is the foundation to understanding policy, in the next section we explore some alternative models that have been developed in response to the critiques offered about the stages heuristic model: the **Multiple Streams Framework** and Punctuated Equilibrium.

ALTERNATIVE POLICY PROCESS MODELS

In the final pages of this chapter, we introduce two alternative policy models that have been advanced in an effort to address some of the disadvantages of the stages model. John Kingdon's Multiple Streams Framework is an effort to account for the lack of sequential order of public policymaking; **Punctuated Equilibrium Theory**, advanced by Frank Baumgartner and Bryan Jones, speaks to how policymaking is often described in periods of stability and incrementalism while at other times it can be described in rapid and massive change.

Multiple Streams Framework

The Multiple Streams Framework (MSF) of policymaking speaks to the messy nature of the policy process and how policy is not often made in a neat, orderly fashion. Working in the 1970s and early 1980s, John Kingdon was studying health care and transportation policy at the federal level, and through these investigations he sought an understanding of the agenda setting process, or step two as discussed earlier (see Kingdon 1984, 2010). But what he ultimately crafted in the MSF is a theory of policymaking in its own right. This model is built on three different "streams" that can converge in a "policy window," which is where policymaking can occur. Consider each of the three streams and how they all may coalesce with a policy opening (see Figure 2.2).

FIGURE 2.2

Multiple Streams Framework

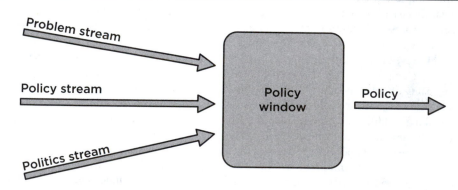

Think of a flowing stream. In the *problem stream* of the MSF, all sorts of public problems, issues, and challenges are flowing, mixing, and circulating. Some of the problems rise up to the surface of the stream; others sink toward the bottom. Actors in the policy process become cognizant of problems through indicators, or data and statistics about an issue, focusing events, and feedback on existing problems. Different problems captivate the attention of different policy actors, but all the problems exist together in the problem stream. The problem stream helps describe the mixing of problems that exist simultaneously and account for the interconnected problems.

Another flowing stream exists alongside the problem stream; this is the *policy stream*. This stream, which Kingdon referred to as the "policy primeval soup," is the mix of ideas and solutions that vie to win traction and acceptance by policymakers in response to a particular problem. In other words, these are all the different ways any particular public problem might be addressed. These policy options may be in search of a particular problem or they may be in direct response to a given problem. These ideas come in all shapes and sizes from everywhere you can imagine. They originate in hearings, the presentations and publications of researchers, or the ideas of policy actors. Some of the ideas evolve a lot in the stream, while other ideas exist in the stream in a more static manner.

The third stream running beside the other two streams is the *politics stream*. This is the stream that deals with all of the political aspects and considerations of policymaking. For example, this stream encapsulates the nation's mood—what the citizens want or have the willingness to embrace. Additionally, this stream incorporates campaign and election cycles, which political party is in power, and the politics of the political institutions. Here is where all the considerations surrounding politics come into play in the policy process. As in the other streams, different political facets surround different issues, and some rise to the top while others do not.

Each of the three streams described previously exists independently of one another in the MSF. Figure 2.2 provides a visual representation of these streams. But these streams can and do come together, and this coupling of the streams results in a *policy window* opening. When the streams converge—and it is difficult to predict or know what it will take for the streams to come together surrounding a particular issue—policy gets created. You can think of this as when all the stars—or streams, if you will—align and something happens. How long the policy window opens is uncertain, but it happens. If two streams come together, though, policymaking does not happen, according to this model. All three streams have to come together to result in a policy window.

Pros and Cons of the MSF

Kingdon's MSF is a policy model that is frequently presented in contrast to the stages heuristic model. Consider some of the advantages of this particular model over the stages approach. With the MSF, the unpredictability that is lacking in the stages model is (somewhat) addressed. Here, policymaking happens in a less orderly, more ad hoc manner. Furthermore, this model demonstrates that efforts surrounding problems, policy options, and politics happen simultaneously and may or may not be connected to one another. For some, this model is far more descriptive of policymaking in the real world. And the concept of the streams in this approach helps account for the ebbing and flowing of ideas and approaches that may not fit nicely into the six steps of the stages model. Yet, much like the stages model, the MSF does not help us predict when policy windows may open and policy gets made. In other words, there is little predictive value associated with this model as well. Perhaps a strength *and* a weakness of this model is that the MSF conveys that policymaking is messy and often hard to describe.

Punctuated Equilibrium

Around the same time that the previous model was being developed, Frank Baumgartner and Bryan Jones sought to account for why policymaking often seems stable, while at other times rather dramatic. Before we get into their Punctuated Equilibrium Theory (PET) outright, we need to start with the theoretical underpinnings of this approach. During the middle part of the twentieth century, the work of two scholars endeavored to explain decisions and action in government. Charles Lindblom advanced the idea of "muddling through," or **incrementalism**, arguing that decision making and governmental action are governed by small, incremental steps (Lindblom 1959). Paul Schulman responded to Lindblom, arguing that incrementalism is not a universal explanation for government action (Schulman 1975). Instead, Schulman contended that "**nonincrementalism**" is more a way to understand. In his explanations, he pointed to the National Aeronautics and Space Administration during the 1960s in its quest for a moon landing as evidence that swift and significant action is possible. PET endeavors to incorporate both perspectives on government decision making and actions.

First published in 1993, *Agendas and Instability in American Politics* is the foundation for PET. Baumgartner and Jones argue that periods of stability (drawing on Lindblom) are periods of "equilibria" in policymaking. And periods of instability (drawing on Schulman) are periods of "punctuations." Equilibrium is the most common. During these times, policymaking can and does happen, but it happens beneath the surface, if you will, often among policy subsystems. **Policy subsystems**, sometimes called issue networks, refer to the networks of actors working to achieve policy goals. Typically, these actors include representatives from interest groups, congressional staffers, and even those individuals working in government agencies. This type of policy work could be thought of as steady work among low-profile actors. Examples abound of policymaking during equilibrium, ranging from the next generation of airbags for passenger cars to updates on nutrition labels on food packages. While these issues undoubtedly garner attention from relevant industry sectors, government agencies, and even some politicians, the issues are worked on beneath the surface, and rarely do the debates boil up to the surface commanding national attention.

By contrast, policymaking during periods of punctuations is characterized by high-profile and dramatic action—or at least more dramatic than "business as usual." During punctuations, which are typically far shorter and less common than periods of equilibria, a particular public problem or issue has galvanized attention from high-profile actors and commands national attention. Large-scale change happens during these periods at the macro-political level. A classic example of a punctuation is the period after the Great Depression when the nation's attention and energies were fixated on economics (c.f. Kettl 2013). Additional examples include efforts to replace Obamacare, particularly with the election of Donald Trump, and Republican control of Congress might be judged over time to be another period of punctuation. This leads to an important point about PET. Knowing how or when a punctuation will occur is very difficult, and it is typically only after a punctuation and significant policy change that a period of punctuation can be defined. In other words, it is hard to know when we are in a period of punctuation until after it is over.

Much like Kingdon's MSF endeavored to address the less orderly process of policymaking, PET strives to explain why most of the time policymaking is incremental and moves along gradually, while during other times massive change can and does occur. Both theories stand in contrast to the stages heuristic model we spent the bulk of our time discussing. And these models are not the only alternative theories, either. The point is that policy studies has come a long way in trying to make sense out of the policymaking process in the United States, but it is also far from complete in that we do not have a definitive public policy theory. We have a variety of theories that do a credible job explaining how policy happens in some instances, but we lack one with universal applicability. At this juncture, the struggle policy scholars have with making sense of the policy process is understandable. Perhaps you will come up with a policy model in the near future that replaces all of these models!

ACTORS IN THE POLICY PROCESS

Part of the challenge in devising public policy models has to do with the sheer number of actors, or individuals, who are involved in the creation and implementation of public policy. The remaining section of this chapter introduces the major categories of policy actors. In the subsequent chapters that focus on specific areas of public policy, those actors and their roles will be examined in greater detail. Think for a moment about all the individuals and organizations that might be involved in passenger cars and their safety features, like seat belts and airbags. Who might be on that list? Of course, there are the car manufacturers, the companies that make the safety equipment that car manufacturers install, there are drivers, there are auto repair mechanics, police officers, first responders (including paramedics and fire fighters who respond to traffic accidents), the National Highway Traffic Safety Administration, Insurance Institute for Highway Safety, Center for Auto Safety, Safe Kids Worldwide, *Consumer Reports*, Advocates for Highway and Auto Safety, the Alliance of Automobile Manufacturers, Automobile Manufacturers Association, the American Automobile Association, and the list goes on and on. The point is, there are far more actors involved than you might initially think, and we did not even include elected leaders, other government agencies, researchers, and even the media.

In an effort to ease our understanding of all the actors involved in policy, we start by introducing two broad categories of actors: official and unofficial. **Official actors** are those individuals and organizations in the policy process that have a constitutionally defined role in creating legislation. This category of actor includes legislative bodies, including Congress and state legislatures; executives, including the president, governors, and executive agencies; and the courts. This group of actors is responsible for passing laws, implementing laws, and evaluating the legality of those laws.

During the 1960s, public pressure mounted on lawmakers to make cars and the nation's highways safer, and Congress responded. In 1966, Congress passed laws requiring seat belts in cars and created the Department of Transportation. Then, in 1970, the Highway Safety Act was passed, which, among other things, created the National Highway Traffic Safety Administration within the Department of Transportation. These steps required the action from Congress and the president. Since their passage, executive agencies have gone to work implementing these policies and the courts have reviewed the government's work.

The category of **unofficial actors** refers to all the other people involved in policymaking, ranging from citizens, state legislatures, governors, and the media to lobbyists and representatives of a variety of organizations. Actors in this category may be the experts in a particular area, like automotive safety, and do extensive research about the latest safety methods and standards. Researchers in universities or "think tanks" may spend a good deal of time understanding the complexities of problems and coming up with possible solutions to those problems. Interest groups are very common, such as the American Automobile Association, better known as AAA; in addition to its efforts to provide services such as roadside assistance to stranded drivers, and educate the public about various subjects, it also lobbies lawmakers to take action on particular issues. Automobile manufacturers also have interests to represent, and they band together with other companies and lobby lawmakers as well. These actors were involved in the passage of the legislation mentioned above and continue to be active calling attention to safety concerns and the needs of drivers, auto manufacturers, and insurance companies, among others.

CONCLUDING THOUGHTS

This chapter has provided the foundation and the language we need to talk about public policymaking in the United States. It should be evident how complex the process is to create policy, as it is far more complicated than the legislative work of a bill becoming a law. To help us understand the intricacies of this process, we looked at the stages model of policymaking that is encapsulated in six steps: (1) problem identification and definition, (2) agenda setting, (3) policy formulation, (4) policy legitimation, (5) policy implementation, and (6) policy evaluation. We recognize policymaking is not entirely explained by this model, as it has strengths and weaknesses; therefore, we considered two alternative models: the Multiple Streams Framework and Punctuated Equilibrium Theory. While none of the models is perfect, they do provide us a means of talking about and analyzing policymaking, which are necessary for understanding the substantive policy chapters within this text. Part of the complexities of policy creation has to do with the number of actors—both official and unofficial—involved in the process. These discussions provide a foundation for us to explore in greater detail the nature of policymaking *after* a legislative body creates a law. The next chapter brings our attention to the multiple layers of government at work in public policy in our federal structure. Then, Chapter 4 details how legislative language is translated into actionable regulations.

GLOSSARY TERMS

focusing events   21
incrementalism   40
Multiple Streams
   Framework   38
nonincrementalism   40

official actors   41
policy entrepreneurs   29
policy subsystems   40
public policy   20

Punctuated Equilibrium
   Theory   38
risk assessment   36
unofficial actors   42

DISCUSSION QUESTIONS

1. Of the six steps outlined in the stages heuristic model of public policymaking, which is the most complicated and likely step where a policy might fail? Why? Which step is likely the easiest for a policy working its way through the process?

2. The stages heuristic model of public policymaking persists as arguably the most common model of policymaking. What are the advantages of this model? Where does this model fall short? In light of that evaluation, should this model continue to be used to introduce the policy process?

3. There are many public policy models that strive to explain policymaking, but a universally accepted one remains elusive. What are the essential elements of a policymaking model? Which elements are more important to include versus other elements?

4. One of the challenges of policymaking is the multitude of actors involved in the process. Which actors do you think are the most influential and why? Which actors are the least? Does the level of influence vary depending upon the policy issue? Which actors are likely to be the most vocal in the example of sugary drinks?

5. With your understanding of the policy process and actors involved, what types of careers might you pursue if you want to play a role in policymaking?

SUGGESTED RESOURCES

Suggested Websites

Congressional Bill Tracker, http://www.congress.gov

Government Accountability Office, http://www.gao.gov

National Conference of State Legislatures, http://www.ncsl.org

Pew Research Center, http://www.pewresearch.org

Suggested Books or Articles

Bardach, Eugene, and Eric M. Patashnik. 2015. *Practical Guide for Policy Analysis: The Eightfold Path to More Effective Problem Solving*. 5th ed. Washington, DC: CQ Press.

Baumgartner, Frank R., and Bryan D. Jones. 1993. *Agendas and Instability in American Politics*. Chicago, IL: University of Chicago Press.

Birkland, Thomas A. 2016. *An Introduction to the Policy Process: Theories, Concepts, and Models of Public Policy Making.* 4th ed. New York: Routledge.

Kingdon, John. 2010. *Agendas, Alternatives, and Public Policies.* Updated 2nd ed. New York: Pearson.

Schultz, David. 2017. "What Is a Fact? The Scientific versus Political Definition." *The Hill.* March 11. http://thehill.com/blogs/pundits-blog/energy-environment/323464-what-is-a-fact-the-scientific-versus-political. Accessed October 30, 2017.

Stone, Deborah A. 2012. *Policy Paradox: The Art of Political Decision Making.* 3rd ed. New York: W. W. Norton & Company.

Suggested Films

I'm Just a Bill (Schoolhouse Rock!), Disney (1973, United States), https://www.youtube.com/watch?v=tyeJ55o3El0

Super Size Me, DVD, directed by Morgan Spurlock (2004: United States), http://www.imdb.com/title/tt0390521/

for CQ Press

Sharpen your skills with SAGE edge at **http://edge.sagepub.com/rinfret. SAGE edge for students** provides a personalized approach to help you accomplish your coursework goals in an easy-to-use learning environment.

Federalism and Intergovernmental Relations

UP IN SMOKE: FEDERAL AND STATE MARIJUANA POLICIES COLLIDE

When one thinks of policymaking it is easy to picture the national government, but public policy also comes from state and local governments. These different sources of policy create some of the country's most interesting dilemmas. One example is legalizing marijuana for medicinal or recreational use by state governments. In 2017, twenty-nine states and the District of Columbia had laws legalizing marijuana for one or both uses, and marijuana policies were under consideration in other states. At the same time, the nation's top law enforcement officer, U.S. attorney general Jeff Sessions, signaled that federal prohibitions on marijuana would be enforced, creating a sticky public policy dilemma and pitting long-standing federal policy against the marijuana policies of over two dozen states. It started with a major federal law passed in 1970.

Congress passed the Controlled Substances Act (CSA) to address what was viewed as a dangerous and growing drug problem. The law combined existing drug laws and expanded the ability of the federal government to prosecute drug-related crimes. It also created a tiered classification system for drugs, depending on a drug's perceived dangers. Marijuana is a Schedule 1 drug, along with heroin, LSD, and Ecstasy. These are considered the most harmful substances because they have a high potential for abuse, no accepted medical uses, and the potential to create severe psychological and/or physical dependence. (Cocaine and morphine, by contrast, were listed as Schedule 2 substances because they had medical uses.) Anyone found possessing, manufacturing, cultivating, using, or distributing a Schedule 1 drug potentially faces large criminal penalties and jail time.

The Drug Enforcement Administration (DEA), established by President Richard Nixon in 1973, was tasked with

LEARNING OBJECTIVES

Readers of this chapter will be able to:

1. Define federalism and its constitutional basis

2. Discuss how federalism has evolved from the founding of the country until today

3. Understand the role of state and local governments in developing and implementing public policies, and the importance of intergovernmental relations

4. Explore the virtues of the federal system for U.S. public policy

regulating the use of these controlled substances. But the federal government could not do it alone. States were expected to help enforce the CSA inside their borders, and to create drug policies in concert with those of the national government. With support from the DEA, state and local governments investigated drug-related crimes and created their own drug policies reflecting the CSA.

Fast-forward to 1996. California became the first state to remove state-level penalties for the use, possession, and cultivation of marijuana by patients whose doctors recommended they would benefit from using marijuana to treat debilitating illnesses such as AIDS, cancer, multiple sclerosis, glaucoma, or chronic pain. Medical marijuana dispensaries were quickly established in California, and in 1998, Oregon, Washington, and Alaska passed similar medicinal marijuana laws. State policy was evolving in response to citizen demands to access marijuana for medicinal purposes.

The passage of medical marijuana laws created a schism between state and national government policies. The national government (still operating under the CSA) was in a tough spot. While legally bound to decades-old policy that labeled marijuana a Schedule 1 drug, the DEA could scarcely act against the tide of citizens who wanted access to marijuana to assist them with various illnesses. Faced with this policy divergence, the U.S. Department of Justice (DOJ) indicated that the federal government would rely on state and local law enforcement to address medical marijuana activity through state-level narcotics laws. However, the DOJ would act to prevent the distribution of marijuana to minors; revenue from marijuana sales from going to criminal enterprises, gangs, and cartels; and marijuana from crossing state lines.

At first glance, it would appear that the federal and state governments had addressed these policy differences. However, the story is not over. In 2012, two states (Colorado and Washington) legalized marijuana for *recreational* use. If you are twenty-one years old in these states, you can buy and possess up to an ounce of marijuana. As of 2017, eight states and the District of Columbia permitted the use of marijuana—not just for those who are ill as a therapeutic drug, but for anyone over the age of twenty-one who wanted to use it just for fun. The DOJ, under the Obama administration and led by U.S. attorney general Eric Holder, indicated it would not enforce federal penalties against recreational marijuana users in states where such use was legal, unless its enforcement priorities (described above) were violated.

The Trump administration, however, advocated a return to a stronger enforcement of federal prohibitions against marijuana use, and signaled it would act against state governments with recreational or medicinal marijuana policies in place, pitting it against states where over 200 million citizens reside. In 2017, over 71 percent of Americans felt the U.S. government should not intervene in states where marijuana use is legal (Chilkoti 2017), and 64 percent said marijuana should be legal (McCarthy 2017; see Figure 3.1). U.S. attorney general Sessions, however, considers marijuana a gateway drug, linking it to the rise in opioid use in the country, and efforts to change the CSA not to regulate marijuana as a Class 1 substance are not on the national policy agenda. Therefore, the chasm between state and federal policies will likely continue.

The cases of medical and recreational marijuana offer examples of national and state governments at odds in the development and implementation of public policy. Understanding how local, state, and the national governments interact in legal,

Box 3.1: Telling Stories with Data

Using Gallup Polling Data to Detect Trends

When you visit Gallup's website—http://news.gallup.com/poll/221018/record-high-support-legalizing-marijuana.aspx—you can explore historical trends about support for legalizing marijuana in the United States. Polling data show that 64 percent of Americans supported legalizing marijuana in 2017, up from just 13 percent in 1969, as indicated in Figure 3.1 below.

What do you think?

Take a look at these trend data showing increasing levels of support for legalizing marijuana over time, then decide what actions or steps you would take as a staff adviser to a U.S. congressional representative. Would you advise him or her to change the law currently listing marijuana as a controlled substance? Why or why not? What role should public opinion play in developing policy? Do you expect public support for legalizing marijuana to continue to increase? Why or why not?

FIGURE 3.1

Public Support for Legalizing Marijuana, 1969–2017

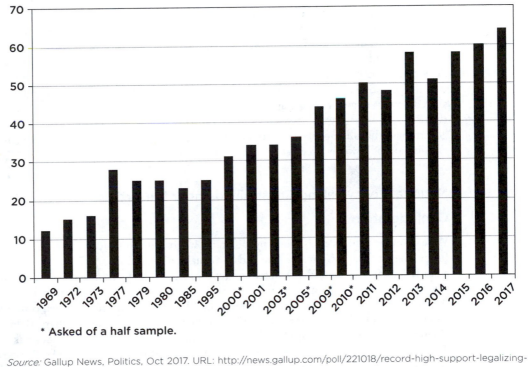

* Asked of a half sample.

Source: Gallup News, Politics, Oct 2017. URL: http://news.gallup.com/poll/221018/record-high-support-legalizing-marijuana.aspx.

economic, and political ways is important to understanding how public policy comes to be. Indeed, it is very important, since most public policies are implemented by subnational governments, given that the national government lacks the resources to put policies into action within state borders. At the same time, as illustrated by shifting marijuana laws, local and state governments create policies unique to their jurisdictions, opening up the possibility that the national government will eventually change existing policy to fit with state policies.

In this chapter, we'll define what federalism and intergovernmental relations (IGR) mean historically, constitutionally, and today. Next, we explore how federalism and IGR evolved. The chapter illustrates the enduring values of our federal system. We close the chapter with an example of differing policies among states that prompted a change in national government policy: same-sex marriage. Our goal with this chapter is to engage public policy students in a conversation about why federalism and IGR are essential to how public policy is formulated, evaluated, and implemented in the United States.

....

OVERVIEW OF FEDERALISM AND INTERGOVERNMENTAL RELATIONS

Chapter 1 described public policy as a course of action adopted or created by the government in response to public problems. Citizens expect government to address their concerns about a wide range of issues. However, which government (national, state, or local) or combination of governments should create and put those policies into action is a subject of debate today, as it was at the founding of the country. Chapter 1 offered a brief introduction to the U.S. system of government, noting that the system is one of both unique and shared powers among national and state governments. More broadly defined, federalism is the allocation of powers between a central or national government, and other levels of government that share control over the same geographic region. In the United States, it is the division of power between states and the national government.

National Policymaking Constrained under the Articles of Confederation

We can understand federalism best by looking at its constitutional roots. The first constitution, the Articles of Confederation and Perpetual Union, ratified in 1781, was based on a **confederation, or confederal system of government**, where states were sovereign and the national government had only the powers granted it by the states. Article III of the Articles declared that the states entered into a "firm league of friendship" for their common defense, to secure their liberties, and provide for their mutual and general welfare. But this "friendship" had many shortcomings, both for governing the country and for policymaking. The Articles lacked any way to compel states to honor national policies, and citizens lacked any direct way to influence the national government. Thus, national policies were not only hard to enact, they were hard to implement through the states. The Articles provided for no executive branch, and created a limited legislative branch. Congress could enter into treaties, declare war, and resolve disputes between states—but only as a last resort.

It could not levy taxes or regulate commerce; nor could it effectively protect the country, as the nation's army was composed of state militias. Representatives were chosen by state legislatures and each state had one vote in matters before Congress. To pass a law, which we learned in the last chapter represents national policy, Congress needed an extraordinary majority (nine votes), and changes to the Articles themselves required the unanimous consent of all states. Had delegates to the Constitutional Convention not met in 1787 to create a new constitution, we might have very little to say about national policies. But they did meet, and they fashioned a more powerful national government–but with safeguards to limit abuses of that power. The result is our unique federal system.

Constitutional Foundation of Federalism

The U.S. Constitution that we know today was not a league of friendship among states, but a document that drew power from citizens—"we the people." It established a federal system of government where power is divided between state and national governments. **Sovereignty** is retained by both governments, but the national government was given the ability to act in traditional state policy domains, provided that such action is in accordance with constitutional authority. Article VI, Section II, of the Constitution, referred to as the "national supremacy clause," stipulates that national laws take preeminence over state laws whenever such action is viewed as legitimate and within the scope of constitutional authority. This has come into play as laws passed by Congress and subsequent federal regulations have displaced previous state law and regulations, such as in the field of environmental policy described in Chapter 10. Sometimes, however, states create policy opposite that of the national government, as shown in the marijuana example that opened the chapter, prompting constitutional questions about the scope of state and national authority.

Article I of the Constitution established Congress and gave it listed, or enumerated, powers. These powers include the power to tax, borrow money, regulate commerce with other countries and between states (known as interstate commerce), coin money, declare war, and raise and support an army and navy, among others. Myriad public policies have been established as a result. Under Article I, Section 8—often called the "elastic clause"—Congress could make laws "necessary and proper" to exercise its enumerated powers and provide for the general welfare. Thus, the framers of the Constitution provided powers that were implied as well as listed. While the framers thought that listing powers would act to limit Congress, federal legislation has dealt with many policy matters that had traditionally been managed by the states. The use of the necessary and proper clause, as well as the commerce clause, has expanded the role of Congress, as discussed in the next part of the chapter.

Article IV of the Constitution provides for **horizontal federalism**, where states recognize the actions of other states. The first section contains the full faith and credit principle, which established a legal system for states to honor the actions of other states. So, for example, if you drive your car to another state, that state recognizes the driver's license from your home state as valid. This proved challenging in the area of same-sex marriage, when some states had given marriage licenses to gay and lesbian couples, while others had not. Congress passed the Defense of Marriage Act in 1996, prohibiting federal recognition of same-sex marriages, but thirty-six states went on to allow same-sex marriages. The matter went to the U.S. Supreme Court in 2015, which ruled that all states must grant marriage licenses to same-sex couples and recognize same-sex marriages already in place in other states. The Court's decision was cause for celebration for many same-sex couples, and brought federal and varying state policies together. This topic is explored in the everyday citizen connection later in this chapter.

PHOTO 3.1
Hundreds gather outside the U.S. Supreme Court to celebrate the marriage equality ruling on June 26, 2015.

Michael Hernandez/ Anadolu Agency/Getty Images

The second section guarantees that citizens of each state shall be entitled to "all privileges and immunities of citizens of the several states." In this, the framers hoped to protect the rights of citizens, creating a national citizenship and prohibiting states from enacting policies that are prejudicial to people from other states. Think, for example, if you were robbed while visiting another state, but when you contacted the police were told, "Sorry, our policy is that we only protect our state's citizens." Not affording all citizens equal treatment not only runs contrary to democracy, it also creates an unworkable federal system. Extradition, or the return of someone accused of a crime to the state where the crime was committed to face trial, is another kind of horizontal federalism.

State sovereignty is protected, in part, by the Tenth Amendment to the Constitution, which holds that powers not given expressly to the national government are reserved for the state governments and the people. These **reserved powers**, most notably the police power, gave states authority to establish policies that regulate citizen behavior, protect property, and ensure public safety, health, and welfare. Constitutional guarantees to the states also include a republican form of government, equal representation in the Senate, a role in selecting the U.S. president through the Electoral College, and the power to ratify constitutional amendments or petition Congress to call a constitutional convention. Thus, this was not a confederation; the framers made clear that this would be a federal system.

In sum, federalism is best understood as a system of constitutionally derived and apportioned authority where state and national governments retain sovereignty and the ability to create policy independently. At the same time, the actions of the national government will take precedence over those of state governments, as long as those actions are deemed within the purview of the Constitution.

Intergovernmental Relations

Federalism describes a constitutional arrangement between states and the national government acting in a federal system. By contrast, **intergovernmental relations** (IGR) is the interaction among national, state, and local governments. IGR is a broad term that concerns how all governments work together in the daily business of solving public problems. The term originated in the 1930s with the advent of President Franklin Delano Roosevelt's New Deal programs, the set of policies that addressed the social and economic conditions of the Great Depression (described in the next section, and also in Chapter 9). This was a watershed period, when the federal government worked with state and local governments to help a struggling nation.

Today, national, state, and local governments are inextricably linked in most policy situations. Take, for example, public safety. Most of us think of our cities and towns, instead of the national government, when we think of public safety policies. Local governments establish policies, such as speed limits, and provide the police force who patrol the streets, thus assuming the major responsibility for public safety. Communities may have neighborhood watch programs or engage in public safety in other ways. In turn, they may work with state troopers or federal agency personnel, such as in the Federal Bureau of Investigation, in fighting crime. How these governmental units interact is but one example of IGR in action.

Local governments do not have the constitutionally derived sovereignty that state governments do. Instead, local governments are created by state governments and exercise powers given them through state constitutions and state laws. States vary in the amount of policymaking autonomy they grant to local governments. Thirty-nine states are described by the National League of Cities as "Dillon's Rule" states, named after Judge John Dillion of Iowa, who wrote in an 1868 court decision that local governments were "mere tenants at will of the legislature" whose origin, powers, and rights were given to them by the states (*City of Clinton v. Cedar Rapids and Missouri River Railroad Co.,* 24 Iowa 455). This decision, later affirmed by the U.S. Supreme Court, reinforced a strict and narrow construction of the authority of local governments (National League of Cities 2016a).

In some states, local governments may be granted home rule authority, which gives these local governments broad control over the policies within their jurisdiction. Local governments that have been granted home rule charters may pass local laws, or ordinances, that are desired by citizens, provided that those ordinances abide by state laws and constitutions. Just as national and state government may have policy disagreements, local governments and state governments don't always agree over policy. For example, local governments have acted to ban plastic bags at grocery and retail stores, raise minimum wages, or ban hydraulic fracturing, only to have these ordinances nullified by state legislatures. Local officials may feel that the state has acted unfairly in barring local policy, but they have little legal recourse. Nonetheless, local governments play critically important roles in implementing public policies. Local governments provide safe drinking water; offer police and fire protection; establish local schools; are the first responders in emergencies and disasters; establish building codes, zoning, and land-use requirements; and provide parks and recreation opportunities, just to name a few. Each of these public services requires local public policymaking and local governments to implement the policy.

It's also worth noting that local governments include not only city governments, but also counties, villages, towns, school districts, and special districts. The 2012 *U.S. Census Report* records over 89,000 local governments, and most of them make policy decisions. You'll learn, for example, more about the role of school districts in developing policy in Chapter 7. Thus, while it is tempting to focus on actions taken at the national or state level, local governments assist in implementing many state and national programs and are indispensable actors in their own right in developing and implementing policy.

In short, both IGR and federalism are essential to understanding how American public policy works. As President Nixon observed in 1969, "We can no longer have effective government at any level unless we have it at all levels. There is too much to be done for the cities to do it alone, or for Washington to do it alone, or for the states to do it alone" (quoted in Wright 1982, 4). The next section describes the evolution of federalism and IGR in public policy.

FEDERALISM AND INTERGOVERNMENTAL RELATIONS EVOLVE

As noted in the previous section, the framers of the Constitution wanted at once to create a national government capable of governing while also preserving the sovereignty of state governments. Efficient government was not the goal; limited government was the goal. Consider for a moment if we had only a sovereign national government, where state governments had to conform to national policies. This would be a **unitary system of government**, the most common system of government in the world. On the one hand, it might make putting national policies into place easier because states would all have to do the same thing—there could be no state challenge to the federal drug law, for example. On the other hand, we would be reliant solely on the wisdom of the U.S. Congress and the president to find the best solutions, or policies, to address public concerns. By creating two sovereign entities (the national and the state governments), the framers established a check on the power of the national government. They also created a system where policymaking would not be confined to one government, but many governments. This is the messy, contentious, sometimes cooperative system that we have today. But it is also a system that has evolved over time. Let's explore some major changes.

Dual Federalism

The early history of the country has been described as **dual federalism**, where national and state governments were viewed as equal partners with clearly defined spheres of authority (Boyd and Fauntroy 2000). State and local governments made policies for public education, safety, welfare, health, and social services; the national government established policies in areas prescribed by the Constitution, such as in national defense or interstate commerce. This kind of federalism was described using the metaphor of a layer cake, which suggested that the policymaking functions of state and national governments were separate and distinct.

The parameters of national and state policymaking were tested during this dual federalism period, sometimes in the courts. In 1816, Congress established a national bank and located it in Maryland. Congress reasoned that creating a national bank was within its policymaking authority to regulate commerce. Two years later, Maryland passed legislation to impose taxes on the bank, reasoning that it was good policy to tax businesses in the state. The issue came to the U.S. Supreme Court in 1819 in *McCulloch v. Maryland*. The justices faced two constitutional questions. First, could Congress create a bank? The Constitution did not provide Congress with direct authority to create a bank, just to coin money and regulate commerce. Second, did a state (Maryland) have the right to tax a national bank? Chief Justice John Marshall, speaking for a unanimous Court, found that the power to create a national bank could be implied from the "necessary and proper clause" of the Constitution. Moreover, the Court found that Maryland's effort to tax the Bank of the United States was unconstitutional, as "the power to tax involves the power to destroy." The Court's decision opened a window for additional policymaking by Congress and strengthened the ability of Congress to regulate commerce.

A much bigger test of our federal system was the Civil War. Beginning in 1860, the conflict addressed whether or not the country would continue with the federalism principles of the Constitution. Reminiscent of the Articles of Confederation, Southern states argued they could nullify federal laws or, barring that, secede from the Union. Others reasoned the source of power both for states and the national government came from the people, who make up a nation. As Daniel Webster had eloquently put it, "It is ... the people's Constitution, the people's government, made for the people, made by the people, and answerable to the people" (cited in Benedict 1988, 11).

While the conclusion of the war saw an expanded national government, most federalism scholars suggest that the period of dual federalism remained largely in place until Franklin Roosevelt's presidency. The Great Depression, which began after the stock market crash of 1929, devastated the lives of many Americans and reverberated around the world. It was the largest and most significant economic depression the country had ever faced. The U.S. economy declined, banks failed, and the unemployment rate skyrocketed; by 1933, nearly 25 percent of the labor force was unemployed.

Roosevelt, who won a landslide election in 1932, campaigned on the promise of a "new deal" for the American people, which embodied a host of national policies including banking reform, emergency relief aid to people who were hungry and homeless, and putting unemployed citizens back to work. His New Deal programs included the Civil Works Administration, the Federal Housing Administration, the Work Projects Administration, the Public Works Administration, and the Civil Conservation Corps. The photo above shows a worker receiving his first paycheck from the Work Projects Administration (WPA) in 1939. The WPA employed Americans to complete a range of public projects, such as roads, bridges, and buildings. The message for public policy was clear: addressing social and economic needs required national, state, and local governments working together.

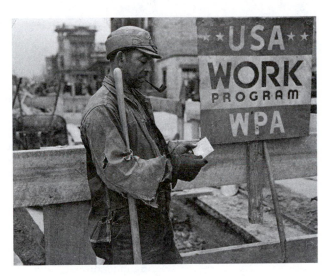

PHOTO 3.2
A WPA worker receives a paycheck, January 1939. Part of the New Deal efforts addressing unemployment, priority employment in the WPA went to those in need of relief.

Records of the Work Projects Administration, 1922–1944

Cooperative Federalism

The enormity of the Great Depression was the catalyst for a new kind of relationship between national, state, and local governments. State and local governments alone could not handle the social welfare problems caused by economic disruption of the magnitude of a depression. It was incumbent that governments at all levels work collaboratively and cooperatively to solve public problems. The new era of **cooperative federalism** brought governments at all levels together. Federalism scholar Morton Grodzins (1960) believed that the shift to cooperative federalism as a result of the New Deal not only prompted the development of IGR, but it blurred the lines between governmental functions, making it hard to distinguish where the national government ended and state and local governments began. Using the metaphor of a marble cake, Grodzins saw that a far more accurate image of federalism after the 1930s was "the rainbow of a marble cake, characterized by an inseparable mingling of differently colored ingredients, the colors appearing in vertical and diagonal strands and unexpected whirls" (quoted in Wright 1982, 50).

If collaboration provided flavor to the marble cake, the leavening for it was fiscal, in the form of grants. More than a dozen **grants-in-aid**, or federal money distributed to state and local governments to carry out a public purpose, were enacted during the Depression. The national government had given a limited number of grants to states before the 1930s, but the need to provide for citizens demanded a much greater presence of the national government. By 1937, 85 percent of all grants-in-aid were given to programs in social welfare, health, and security, and 13 percent for transportation and communication (Maxwell 1952, 6). Federal grants-in-aid increased from $100 million in 1930 to $967 million by 1940 (Dilger 2015, 5). By the end of 1940, Congress had doubled the number of federal grants to state and local governments. The number of grants would continue to increase in the 1940s and 1950s (Dilger 2015, 11).

While these grants were designed to support policy implementation at the state and local level, and encourage cooperation, they also were a form of federal influence on state and local government programs. This financial relationship, often called **fiscal federalism**, shaped state and local policies by transferring funds from the national government to recipient governments. The governments that received the "carrot" of funding would also have to participate in the implementing of a federally driven policy. Requirements, or conditions of aid, were attached to federal dollars—requirements state and local governments had to satisfy in order to continue to receive funding. For example, many grants required state or local governments to provide part of the funding for the programs paid for by the grants, so-called "matching" requirements. Money allocated by a recipient government to meet the matching requirement cannot be spent on other programs.

Sometimes, conditions on the receipt of intergovernmental grants required policy changes on the part of state governments. Perhaps you've wondered why all across the country the minimum drinking age is twenty-one years of age. The policy is not a result of a minimum drinking age law passed by Congress. Instead, states are required to set a minimum drinking age of twenty-one or risk losing federal highway grant funds. In 1987, South Dakota sued the national government, arguing that this amounted to a kind of federal blackmail over state policy (South Dakota at the time permitted eighteen-year-olds to drink 3.2 percent beer). The Supreme Court, in deciding *South Dakota v. Dole*, upheld the constitutionality of Congress setting this funding condition on highway grants, reasoning that states are free to decline funding. But what state wants to lose highway funding? Many federally funded highway grants pay for 80 percent of the cost of the project; with states or local governments picking up just the remaining 20 percent (Congressional Budget Office 2013, 18). The increase in grants to deal with the Great Depression opened a door to a new kind of federalism and IGR that has never closed.

After the 1930s, the era of dual federalism was clearly over, replaced by cooperative efforts of state, local, and national actors in public policy. Slowly, but inexorably, intergovernmental actions among governments became increasingly important components of public policymaking and implementation. The 1960s would greatly escalate intergovernmental fiscal relationships, during an era sometimes called "creative federalism."

Creative Federalism

When John F. Kennedy became president in 1961, over 130 categorical grants, or grants given by the national government to state or local governments for a specific purpose, were in operation. This represented a considerable increase over the programs established as part of the New Deal. However, the five years that Lyndon Johnson was president (he served the last year of Kennedy's term and was elected to an additional four-year term) were remarkable for the sheer number of grant programs added, and the expansion of the national government in domestic affairs. Johnson used the slogan "creative federalism" to describe his intention to address poverty, urban decay, and civil rights abuses. He called on the nation to create a system that would move not only toward equality, but one that would move upward to end poverty and racial injustice—a Great Society (Miller Center, n.d.).

The aftershock of Kennedy's assassination, coupled with a strong Democratic Congress, provided an opportunity for Johnson to make these dramatic changes in domestic policies. And dramatic they were. In just three years (1965–1968), government funding devoted to addressing the needs of the poor doubled from $6 billion to $12 billion (Miller Center n.d.). It would double again by 1974. National programs reached other policy areas that had previously been in the realm of state and local governments, including education, police and fire protection, infant health care, urban renewal, and public transit.

Working with Congress, Johnson pushed for the Civil Rights Act and the Economic Opportunity Act designed to end discrimination and attack the roots of poverty in America. Both passed in 1964. Other programs, including Head Start and the Volunteers in Service to America (VISTA), were designed to help struggling communities with low literacy levels by funding preschool programs and putting volunteer teachers into public schools. The Voting Rights Act was passed in 1965. That same year, President Johnson signed the Social Security Amendments, which established Medicare, a health care program for people over age sixty-five, and Medicaid, a health care program for low-income and disabled persons. While Medicare was a national program, Medicaid relied on states to voluntarily implement the program. Medicaid offered federal matching payments, provided that the state agreed to cover mandatory populations with necessary services (Kaiser Family Foundation n.d.). These are but a few examples, each discussed in more detail in Chapter 9.

When Johnson left office in 1969, fiscal federalism had mushroomed in the number of grants, the type of grants, and the amount of funding provided to state and local governments. Federal grants jumped from $7 billion in 1960 to $24 billion in 1970 (White House n.d., 271). Over four hundred specific authorizations for funding were in place, with seventy of those going directly from the national government to local governments (Wright 1982, 57). Grants given to local governments, instead of to state governments, worked to weaken the role of states in the federal system. Moreover, it greatly increased the number of intergovernmental actors in public policy implementation. By 1970, nearly 25 percent of the money spent by state and local governments came as a result of federal grants. The proliferation of grants, and their attendant requirements, gave rise to the term *coercive federalism*, as states objected to what they saw as an intrusion by the national government pushing policies based on its superior funding resources.

Grants have grown in both number and size. In fiscal year 2011, the federal government gave over $607 billion in grants to state and local governments (Congressional Budget Office 2013). Funding was distributed in more than two hundred intergovernmental grant programs that were administered by thirty federal departments and agencies. As shown in Figure 3.2, this represented nearly 17 percent of federal outlays and roughly 4 percent of our gross domestic product (GDP). Federal grants for health programs, primarily Medicaid, have grown rapidly, and they now account for roughly half ($293 billion) of total federal grant dollars (Congressional Budget Office 2013, 5).

In sum, the Great Society policies would prove to be the largest social improvement agenda since the New Deal and would change the landscape of federalism and IGR forever. While the national government has remained a major force in domestic policy, federalism and IGR have continued to evolve since the 1960s. Relationships between local, national, and state governments have variously been described as "coercive," "creative," "cooperative," "regulatory," "contentious," and dozens of other adjectives. The reality is that federalism and IGR can be described in many ways, but that national, state, and local governments are at the core of public policy. The next section provides an overview of the key themes of federalism and IGR today.

FIGURE 3.2

Federal Grants to State and Local Governments, 1980–2010

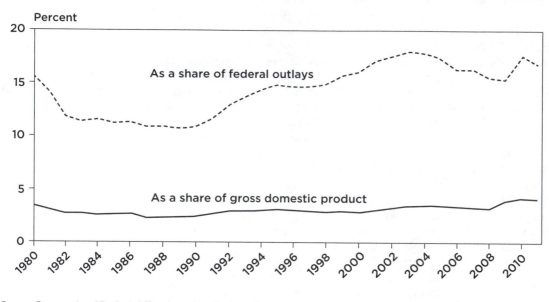

Source: Congressional Budget Office, based on *Budget of the United States Government, Fiscal Year 2013*: Historical Tables, Table 12.1.

FEDERALISM AND INTERGOVERNMENTAL RELATIONS TODAY

Federalism and intergovernmental relations after 1970 can be characterized by four over-arching themes. First, state and local governments have faced increased regulatory require-ments and unfunded or partially funded mandates from the national government. Second, government policies have increasingly been organized around function, where national, state, and local specialists manage policy implementation. Third, state and local govern-ments, while still reliant on grants-in-aid, have increased their capacity and innovated in key policy arenas, such as environmental policy. Finally, states have responded to new issues in different ways, depending on their unique cultural, economic, and political characteris-tics. Each will be described in turn.

Underfunded and Unfunded Mandates

As described in the previous sections, a key historical observation that can be made about the evolution of federalism is the continued, and stronger, presence of the national gov-ernment in policy areas that originally were thought to be the domain of state or local governments. Federalism scholar Paul Posner observed that it appeared national senti-ment was that state and local governments were "stumbling blocks to achieving goals and services valued by an increasingly cohesive national community" (Posner 1998, 1). As the national government has acted in areas such as health care, education, or social welfare, it frequently offered the "carrot" of a grant-in-aid to state or local governments as a way of gaining their cooperation in implementing public policy developed at the national level. This funding relationship, labeled earlier as "fiscal federalism," varies among programs and over time. Many of these programs with funding "carrots" are voluntary. States can choose to accept funding, which they typically do, or decline to participate in the grant. Choosing not to participate may be hard, especially if the terms for a matching requirement given by the national government are favorable, such as in the highway funding example mentioned earlier.

However, sometimes Congress passes a law addressing a public problem, and, just like the old Nike ad, tells states and local governments to "just do it." States are mandated, or required, to perform certain actions to implement the policy. Mandates include provisions in laws or regulations that impose an enforceable duty on state, local, or tribal governments (United States General Accounting Office 2004). Along with the mandate, Congress may offer states funding to run the program, or it may choose to impose standards and requirements on state and local governments without providing any funding at all. When the proffered funding is insufficient to address the problem, creating a fiscal gap that must be picked up by state or local governments, it results in an underfunded mandate. When no funding is provided at all for the imposed requirement or national standard, it results in an unfunded mandate.

Before the 1970s, financial incentives were often provided to assist state and local governments, but as the federal government's budget condition worsened and its involvement in social programs increased, fewer dollars were available to give to recipient governments. The result was that unfunded mandates increased, threatening to undermine the vitality of state and local governments (Posner 1998).

Between 1960 and 1993, over sixty new federal mandates were enacted, including twenty-seven new federal laws between 1981 and 1990 alone (United States General Accounting Office 1994, 2). The Americans with Disabilities Act of 1990, which established national standards to prohibit discrimination in public services and accommodations and promote access to public buildings and transportation for disabled individuals, was one example. Other mandates came from the field of environmental protection, including unfunded or underfunded requirements under, for example, the Clean Air Act, Safe Drinking Water Act and Clean Water Act, and the Asbestos Hazards and Emergency Response Act.

Chafing at what they viewed as unfunded responsibilities that they would have to bear, local government officials organized the first "National Unfunded Mandates Day" on October 27, 1993, calling for relief from federal mandates that threatened the intergovernmental partnership. The Unfunded Mandates Reform Act, signed by President Bill Clinton on March 22, 1995, signaled that politicians in Washington recognized the concerns of state and local governments about the increased cost of complying with new federal requirements. The law, however, did not prohibit Congress from imposing unfunded mandates. Instead, it required that Congress identify any mandate that exceeded an annual cost of $50 million annually to recipient governments and, if so, permit a legislative point of order to be called. Dubbed a "stop, look, and listen" requirement for members of Congress, it forced congresspersons to own up to their imposition of a mandate on state and local governments. Initial research suggested that the Unfunded Mandates law did little to decrease federal mandates or costs to state and local governments (United States General Accounting Office 2004).

Thus, the era of unfunded and underfunded mandates continues to weave a thread through the fabric of IGR and federalism. What this means for public policy is twofold. On the one hand, national standards help to set a nationwide threshold for solving public problems. In other words, we see more uniform policies from states and local governments. As demonstrated in several of the subsequent chapters of the book, history shows that some states have been reluctant to act to protect the environment, protect workplaces, or provide for the poor. Mandates are meant to force governments to act on a problem. On the other hand, they sharpen the push and pull of the federal system, prompting contentious relationships among governmental actors. They also often decrease the ability of state and local governments to develop policy in other areas, since they must abide by the mandates.

Money put toward achieving a national standard, to the extent that the national government does not fully compensate that government, is money that cannot be put to other pressing public problems in the state.

Building Picket Fences

As the number and size of grants-in-aid increased, Congress wrestled with how best to deliver the funds and maintain effective oversight of recipient governments. The solution was largely to offer targeted grants for specific purposes, or categories (which give categorical grants their name) and then assign that grant to a particular agency. In turn, a federal oversight agency official would work closely with her or his counterpart in the state agency running the program. Often, local government staff were involved as well in implementing policy at the ground level. The result is what the Advisory Commission on Intergovernmental Relations termed "vertical functional autocracies," where policies connect federal, state, and local officials who will then implement them. The key actors were not the politicians, but rather the men and women who worked in government agencies.

NOW IT COMES WITH A LIST OF INGREDIENTS.

What's in your tap water besides water? A short new report from your water supplier will tell you where your water comes from, what's in it, and how safe it is. Look for the report in your mail, and read it. Because when it comes to understanding your drinking water, the most important ingredient is you.

♣EPA   <u>DRINKING WATER. KNOW WHAT'S IN IT FOR YOU.</u>
Call your water supplier or the Safe Drinking Water Hotline at 1-800-426-4791. Or visit www.epa.gov/safewater/

PHOTO 3.3
EPA public service announcement promoting regulatory requirements for public disclosure of drinking water quality

EPA

One example is evident when we drink water from our faucets. Here, the U.S. Environmental Protection Agency staff set safe drinking-water standards and work with environmental or public health departments of the various states to implement the program. State staff, in turn, rely on local public water supply systems to deliver clean water. The EPA's public service announcement shown in the image illustrates this relationship.

The close relationships developed among intergovernmental actors within a particular program is also called **picket fence federalism** (see Figure 3.3). Imagine a picket fence with three rails. Each rail represents one level of government (national, state, or local). The pickets represent policy arenas (say, for example, agriculture, education, environment,

FIGURE 3.3

Picket Fence Federalism: A Schematic Representation

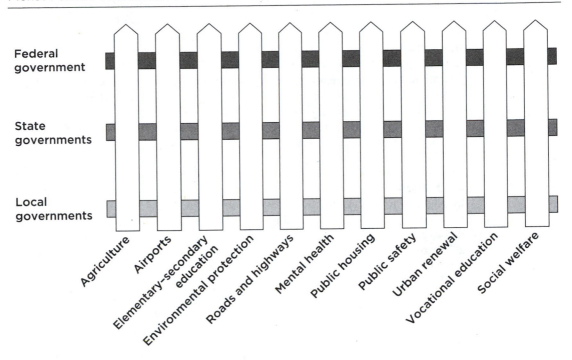

Source: Michael E. Milakovich and George J. Gordon (2013), "Public Administration in America," Figure 3-4, page 119. Wadsworth and Brooks/Cole Publishing.

welfare, health care, emergency management, etc.). Specialists in each policy interact closely with specialists at other levels, developing close administrative ties over time. Thus, government policies have increasingly been organized around function, where national, state, and local specialists manage policy implementation.

This is important for public policy development and implementation for two reasons. First, these specialists care about their program and attendant policy goals. They are paying attention to new developments, improvements, or innovations in their area. As a result, they may feel closer to their counterparts on the "picket" than the rail (the governmental level) they occupy, and seek to preserve their program over others. Second, specialists along the picket of one policy arena are the experts that help shape future policies. They know the policy and program well, and often influence the way policy changes. These bureaucratic officials may not always agree on the direction of oversight, procedures, or funding, but "the responsibility for formulating many basic policies and for resolving many of the conflicts that arise rests largely—and often exclusively—within the discretion of these functional groupings" (Milakovich and Gordon 2009,130).

Increasing Capacity of State and Local Governments

If you've read the discussion in the chapter so far, you may be feeling that state governments have become minor players in our federal system, with state-level policies making way for national ones. While it is true that the national government does more now than the framers had imagined, it is not the case that state and local governments are unimportant in public policy. Far from it. States play a major role in public education, and in higher education, as demonstrated in Chapter 7. It is likely that you are attending a university that is overseen by state governments. The vast majority of all criminal trials are heard by state courts. States and local governments have policies on elections, registration requirements, marriage, divorce, licensing requirements, smoking, traffic control, welfare, health services—the list is long and filled with policies that affect us every day.

Over the last four decades, state and local governments have increased their capacity and innovated in many key policy arenas. Adapting a definition offered by Hanson and Sigman (2013), healthy capacity in state and local governments is characterized by plentiful resources, the ability to effectively raise revenue, skilled administration, innovative and active policymaking that promotes a strong economy, the ability to deliver services, and manage complex affairs. In short, state capacity reflects a state's ability to effectively develop, implement, and maintain the policies and programs that serve its citizens.

Thirty years ago, political scientists Ann O'M Bowman and Richard Kearney (1986) identified several factors that made state and local governments "resurgent" and central to the policymaking process. They argued that a lack of public confidence in the national government had given states greater power in politics. Public opinion polls consistently show that Americans trust state and local governments more than they trust the national government. Over 70 percent of Americans polled by Gallup trust local governments to solve local problems; over 60 percent trust state governments to handle state problems (McCarthy 2016). In contrast, just one in three Americans express confidence in the U.S. Congress in polling conducted by Gallup (Saad 2016).

National politicians have reinforced and capitalized on this public perception, arguing that the national government is too big and acting beyond its constitutional powers. In his 1981 inaugural address, President Ronald Reagan proclaimed that "government is not the solution to our problem; government is the problem." Reagan then slowed the growth of the national government, cutting budgets of federal agencies. His administration also made cuts to intergovernmental aid, in part by consolidating categorical grants into large block grants. These block grants, as the name implies, were designed to give more discretion and flexibility to the recipient governments within one broadly defined policy area. At the same time, however, funding to state and local governments was cut.

Also important to state and local government resurgence is the rise of intergovernmental lobbying. Organizations such as the National Governors Association, the Council of State Governments, the National League of Cities, and the U.S. Conference of Mayors pressure the national government to act in ways that advantage their constituents. The goal of federal advocacy for the National League of Cities, for example, is to "serve as the voice for America's cities and towns in Washington … protecting municipal interests, seeking federal support for local investments, and influencing the outcome of federal policy debates affecting local governments" (National League of Cities 2016b). As the National League of Cities example shows, these organizations not only lobby the national government for more funding, fewer mandates, and greater autonomy in implementing policy, they also push for policies to be adopted at the national level.

State administrative capacity has grown as well. Professionals within state and local agencies are better educated and able to address public policies than they were a few decades ago. Take, for example, environmental policies. After the passage of national environmental laws in the 1970s, states had the opportunity to run the programs that would protect our air, water, and land, provided the states created programs that were at least as stringent as those of the national government. Chapter 10 overviews environmental policy. Over time, these state agencies have assumed responsibility for over 96 percent of the federal environmental programs that are delegable to them (Environmental Council of the States 2010, 2). While still reliant on federal funds to operate these programs, state-level sources of funding pay the lion's share of the costs, with only one-fourth of the costs of environmental programs paid for by the national government. It was left to the states to create professional programs and new funding sources. The lack of increasing funding for environmental programs, along with what many state officials viewed as micromanagement of state activities by their federal counterparts, created a contentious relationship that required the hard work of both state and national officials to reestablish a partnership in implementing environmental policy (Scheberle 2004).

States have long been considered innovators of new policies, or laboratories of democracy. U.S. Supreme Court justice Louis Brandeis famously quipped, "a single courageous state may, if its citizens choose, serve as a laboratory and try novel social and economic experiments without risk to the rest of the country" (*New State Ice v. Liebmann* 1932). As such, these fifty laboratories can become the testing grounds for innovative policies that can be replicated by other states, or even by the national government. Welfare reform, education standards, and the Affordable Care Act are examples of state initiatives that have served as models for national policy change. Moreover, states may act in the face of a recalcitrant Congress—as shown in the marijuana example that opened the chapter.

Another example of state–national policy divergence is the declaration by President Donald Trump in 2017 that the United States

would pull out of the Paris Climate Accord, the international agreement addressing climate change, leaving the United States the only country not participating. After his announcement, over a dozen states defied that declaration by saying the national commitments to reducing greenhouse gasses would be accomplished at the state and local government level, if not at the national level. Thirteen states formed the U.S. Climate Alliance, led by the governors of California, New York, and Washington.

Sharp differences in climate change policy resulted in California and New York emerging as the nation's de facto leaders in global warming initiatives. As Governor Jerry Brown sharply remarked, "The President has already said climate change is a hoax, which is the exact opposite of virtually all scientific and worldwide opinion. I don't believe fighting reality is a good strategy—not for America, not for anybody. If the President is going to be AWOL in this profoundly important human endeavor, then California and other states will step up" (U.S. Climate Alliance 2017). An unprecedented series of hurricanes, coupled with wildfires in western states (as shown in the photo), notably California and Montana, put a punctuation mark on the dedication of many states to shift to renewable energy as soon as possible. Whether states opt to be these laboratories of innovation responding to citizen needs or demands is in part related to each state's unique political, cultural, and economic setting, the topic of the next section.

Differences in State Cultures, Politics, Economies, and Events

So far, state and local governments have largely been grouped together as one actor in public policymaking. However, it is important to understand that individual states have responded to emerging issues in different ways, depending on their unique cultural, economic, and political characteristics. Let's begin with culture.

Daniel Elazar recognized the importance of understanding the political culture of states and local governments in 1966. He saw that a state's ethnic and religious values established certain political cultures, which he defined as "the particular pattern of orientation to political action in which each political system is embedded" (Elazar 1966, 78). Political culture, in turn, helped to explain state policy development. It defined the parameters of the purpose of politics and permissible actions, as well as set the stage for public involvement in the policymaking process.

Elazar saw three political subcultures in American states: individualistic, moralistic, and traditionalistic. States with traditionalistic cultures seek to preserve the status quo and maintain benefits to the politically powerful, or wealthy elite. In contrast, states with a moralistic culture value public participation and collective action, as well as policies that improve the welfare of communities. Individualistic cultures promote a give-and-take system where private concerns are presented in a "marketplace of competing individual interests" (Leckrone 2013). To the extent that Elazar was right about culture, we would expect to see innovative public policies that advance the common good (rather than policies that advantage particular interests) in states with moralistic cultures (see Table 3.1). States with traditionalistic political cultures would be less interested in creating policies that advance public welfare.

Political cultures as described by Elazar nearly five decades ago have changed, as people have moved around the country and out of rural areas. Still, political cultures, however defined, help explain different views on public policy among states. A new political culture has developed showing differences in urban and rural communities, bringing in economic and demographic factors associated with a more mobile population. The new political culture is defined by cities that are socially diverse, with more educated citizens who see social issues such as gay rights or abortion as important when compared with long-standing issues of economic development or public safety. Understanding the degree to which a community or state has a homogeneous culture helps us understand the nature of policies that develop.

Another way of comparing states is to look at characteristics of the state on a per capita basis. One example is the Camelot Index. Developed by Hal Hovey, the founding editor of *State Policy Reports*, the index ranks states on six "quality of life" measures: economy, health, crime, education, society, and state government (*State Policy Reports* 2016, 1). An ideal, or "Camelot-like," state would have a strong economy, low poverty rates,

TABLE 3.1

State Political Cultures as Described by Elazar, 1966

Moralistic	Individualistic	Traditionalistic
California	Connecticut	Alabama
Colorado	Delaware	Arizona
Idaho	Illinois	Arkansas
Iowa	Indiana	Florida
Kansas	Nebraska	Georgia
Maine	Nevada	Kentucky
Michigan	Maryland	Louisiana
Minnesota	Massachusetts	Mississippi
Montana	Missouri	New Mexico
New Hampshire	New Jersey	North Carolina
North Dakota	New York	Oklahoma
Oregon	Ohio	South Carolina
South Dakota	Pennsylvania	Tennessee
Utah	Rhode Island	Texas
Vermont	Wyoming	Virginia
Washington		West Virginia
Wisconsin		

Source: Elazar, Daniel J. 1966. *American Federalism: A View from the States.* New York: Thomas Y. Crowell Company.

high incomes, and healthy and well-educated residents, with little crime and a light tax burden. The government would be well managed and responsive to the need to create and maintain policies. Table 3.2 shows the highest- and lowest-ranked states by category in the Camelot Index for 2016. Sometimes, states shine in one area, but not in others. In 2017, the Index of State Economic Momentum ranked Nevada at the top for its economic vitality, though the state occupied the bottom position for its social measures in the Camelot Index.

Yet another ranking of states is conducted by 24/7 Wall St. Using data from the U.S. Census Bureau, this organization rates states on median household income, population, 2015 unemployment rate, and poverty rate (Frohlich et al. 2016). According to this analysis, Mississippi was the poorest state, with the highest poverty rate in the nation at 22 percent, and a median household income of $40,593; Maryland was the richest state, with a 9.7 percent poverty rate, the second-lowest in the nation, and median household income of $75,847.

TABLE 3.2

Top- and Bottom-Ranked States in the Camelot Index

The top-ranked states in 2016 for each of the six measures are as follows:
- Economy: Massachusetts
- Health: Massachusetts
- Crime: Vermont
- Education: Nebraska
- Society: Minnesota
- Government: South Dakota

The bottom-ranked for each of the measures are:
- Economy: West Virginia
- Health: Mississippi
- Crime: New Mexico
- Education: Michigan
- Society: Nevada
- Government: Illinois

Source: State Policy Reports, "The 2016 Camelot Index" 34, no 7 (April 2016): Federal Funds Information for States.

What are the implications of these characteristics for public policies at the state level? For one thing, states that score high on the rankings share certain social and economic characteristics. States with the highest incomes tend to have better education levels, with more residents having a college degree. It also seems likely that states with stronger economies will be more likely to innovate and diversify; states with a less educated workforce, higher rates of crime, or less effective government may be less capable of addressing public needs through policy development. These studies are also suggestive of the kinds of issues that need to be addressed. So the state of Mississippi, with the lowest health ranking on the Camelot Index and the most people living in poverty, might well have an interest in health-related policies as well as be concerned with diversifying and strengthening its economy; the state of New Mexico may want to better understand the factors causing a high crime rate.

Also important to understanding how and which policies develop at the state level is the extent to which one political party controls the legislature and the governor's office, sometimes referred to as a "trifecta." The concept of a trifecta is important to policymaking because it is likely that one party's agenda can succeed, as it has the support of both houses of the legislature and the governor. The 2018 state legislative sessions started with twenty-six Republican trifectas and eight Democratic trifectas. The other sixteen states had divided governments, where one party controlled the legislature and another controlled the governorship (Ballotpedia 2018; see Figure 3.4). If you were to look into your crystal ball, you'd predict that policy positions favored by Republicans would be more likely to pass in Texas, Alabama, or Georgia, while policies favored by Democrats would find more success in California or Hawaii. You'd also predict that more policies favored by the Republican Party will be adopted by state governments, given the predominance of Republican trifectas.

Here's a case in point. Kansas, a Republican trifecta state, became the first state in the country to pass a law banning a second-trimester abortion procedure, narrowing the window in which a woman in the state could choose to have an abortion. Unsurprisingly, this

FIGURE 3.4

Trifectas in State Governments in 2018

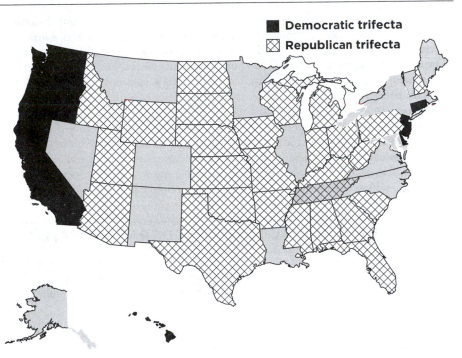

■ **Democratic trifecta**
⊠ **Republican trifecta**

Source: Courtesy of Ballotpedia, https://ballotpedia.org/State_government_trifectas.

bill was supported by Governor Sam Brownback (a Republican), since limiting or banning abortions has been a long-standing Republican issue. (The law was blocked by the courts in 2015, three months after it was passed.) On the other hand, a bill limiting abortion rights would be unlikely in a state like California, where Democrats hold a trifecta and support a woman's right to choose.

Finally, the force of events can change policy at the state and local level. You may be aware that triggering events often prompt changes in national policy, as these events focus the attention of the public, the media, and politicians on the issue. You may have heard about the *Exxon Valdez* oil spill in 1989. Just six months later, Congress passed the Oil Pollution Act establishing additional regulations on oil tankers. That is the power of a focusing, or triggering, event. The same is true for state and local government policymaking.

One example of a focusing event at the state level was the high level of lead found in the drinking water in Flint, Michigan. In 2014, an emergency manager appointed by Governor Rick Snyder to address budget shortfalls of the city changed the city's water source in an effort to save money. That effort failed miserably when the new source, the Flint River, was left untreated, leaving the residents of Flint exposed to dangerous levels of lead and bacteria. The result was a public health emergency, the resignation of several public officials, criminal charges brought for several state and local officials, and the state considering new policies for appointing emergency managers (Fehr and Murphy 2016). While the state of Michigan will likely change more than one policy in the aftermath of Flint, this triggering event has also focused attention on lead pipes throughout the country. Another example in 2018 was the shooting at Stoneman Douglas High School in Parkland, Florida. In response to the mass shooting that killed seventeen people and injured fourteen others, teenagers at the high school started a #NeverAgain movement against gun violence and demanded that the state of Florida as well as the national government act on gun control. Students met with Florida's legislative leaders, staged vigils, walked out of school, and organized a nationwide march mandating new policies on gun control.

In sum, when looking at policies at state and local levels, considering the political composition of the state, unique cultures, demographic characteristics, and economic conditions is essential. State and local governments don't always act in concert; instead, they advance the policies that represent the values and needs of their communities. The next section explores the benefits of our federal system for public policy.

ENDURING VIRTUES OF A FEDERAL SYSTEM

Federalism scholar David B. Robertson in *Federalism and the Making of America* (2011) observed that federalism has many virtues in keeping the government resilient. These virtues help explain why our federal system is an essential element in U.S. public policy development. Let's briefly look at four virtues.

Safeguards Individual Rights and Democracy

James Madison, one of the authors of *The Federalist Papers* in 1787, noted that federalism provides double security for the rights of the people. In *Federalist* no. 51, he argued that "The different governments will control each other, at the same time each will be controlled by itself." If a citizen judges an action of a state government or private organization to be against his or her civil rights, that citizen can seek redress through national laws such as the Civil Rights Act of 1964, as well as applicable state laws. During the civil rights movement in the 1960s, it was the national government that advanced protections for Americans regardless of race or ethnicity when many states had adopted discriminatory practices and policies. If, on the other hand, the national government is perceived to be obstructing rights, such as in the case of same-sex marriage described in the everyday citizen connection later in this chapter, citizens can seek shelter in state laws, which may be more protective than the national government.

Promotes Responsibility

As discussed in an earlier section, citizens trust their local governments more than they do the state government, and the state government more than they do the national government. Governments closest to the people are most likely to understand citizen needs and create policies and programs in an attempt to meet those needs. The framers believed that people would be most attached to local and state governments, as those would be the governments that were familiar to them and most likely to deal with citizens directly. If you think about the services you receive from government, most of them come from local and state agencies.

Stimulates Innovation

Earlier in the chapter, the term *laboratories of democracy* was used to explain the innovation that occurs in policies at state and local levels. These subnational governments can innovate, and try novel approaches to solving public problems. These innovations, then, can be adopted across states and local governments, and also evolve into federal government policy. Noted federalism scholar Richard Nathan observed that states were essential to policy innovation, and it was in state programs that policies were "tested, refined, debugged, and often diffused across the country" (quoted in Robertson 2011, 9).

Increases Efficiency and Effectiveness in Policy Implementation

This virtue may, at first glance, seem counterintuitive. After all, we've seen many policy arenas where states arrive at quite different policies, such as climate change, same-sex marriage, or marijuana use. As a result, we see a policy patchwork throughout the country. This does not seem efficient at all. However, our decentralized system suggests that a lot of trial and error happens at subnational levels. So, before major policies are developed at the national level, they are vetted by states and municipalities. Federalism scholar Aaron Wildavsky observed that states discover sooner than federal government when a policy is unpopular or unworkable. What he described as a "crazy-quilt pattern of interaction" helps to generate information about citizen preferences earlier on in the policy process before significant resources are committed (Wildavsky 2018, 152).

In sum, federalism offers a useful way to bring state governments together with the national government to achieve larger policy goals, while at the same time providing many points of access into the policy process and room for experimentation on policy approaches. Local, state, and national governments manage public policy together.

Everyday Citizen Connection

Perhaps no public policy is more reflective of the power of federalism than same-sex marriage. The evolution of American public policy toward same-sex marriage began in 1972, when the U.S. Supreme Court dismissed a case filed by a same-sex couple in Minnesota who wanted to marry, "for want of a substantial federal question." At the time, no state sanctioned same-sex marriage and gay couples had few legal rights. Twenty-one years later, the Hawaii Supreme Court would rule that denying marriage to same-sex couples was a violation of the equal protection clause of Hawaii's constitution.

This 1993 ruling prompted political outcry in state legislatures throughout the country, and in Congress, which passed the Defense of Marriage Act (DOMA) in 1996. DOMA denied federal benefits to married same-sex couples. Just three months after President Clinton signed DOMA, a judge in Hawaii would uphold the right of same-sex couples to marry. But the people of Hawaii did not approve of the court's interpretation, and they changed the state constitution to ban same-sex marriage. The federalism stage was set: the national government did not support policies protecting the rights of same-sex couples to marry; the courts of one state (Hawaii) saw this as an equal protection issue, but a majority of Hawaiians did not agree. The issue would now move to various states, and ultimately again to the U.S. Supreme Court.

Just one year after Hawaiians approved a constitutional amendment banning same-sex marriage

(1999), California became the first state to pass a domestic partnership law. Vermont followed suit the following year. But the state of Massachusetts took it a step further. The Massachusetts Supreme Court legalized same-sex marriage in 2003, prompting eighteen states to pass constitutional amendments denying same-sex marriage in the next four years. Between 2008 and 2010, some states (Iowa, Vermont, New Hampshire, the District of Columbia, and Connecticut) legalized same-sex marriage; other states moved to overturn same-sex marriage decisions in state courts.

It would be the courts that would settle the federalism question. First, in 2010, a federal district court ruled that part of DOMA was unconstitutional; later that year, California's Proposition 8 that banned same-sex marriage was declared unconstitutional in federal district court. In 2011, U.S. attorney general Holder said that the Obama administration would no longer defend DOMA, and in 2012, President Barack Obama became the first sitting president to announce his support for same-sex marriage. The U.S. Supreme Court would strike down a key section of DOMA in 2013, and dismiss the challenge to the Proposition 8 ruling in California—effectively making same-sex marriage legal once again in that state. Meanwhile, states operated on vastly different policies—thirty-seven states had legalized same-sex marriage; thirteen had specifically denied it (Liebelson and Terkel 2015). In 2015, the U.S. Supreme Court, in a 5–4 ruling in *Obergefell v. Hodges*, legalized same-sex marriage throughout the country, finding that states must issue marriage licenses to same-sex couples and recognize same-sex unions performed in other states. However, the issue wasn't settled. Kim Davis, a county clerk in Kentucky, refused to issue marriage licenses to gay couples the day after the Court's decision. Though religious conservatives hailed her as courageous, she was held in contempt of court. Other local officials also refused to issue marriage licenses to gay couples. The U.S. Supreme Court would once again weigh in on the issue, this time to reject Davis's argument that she could refuse to issue marriage licenses to gay couples due to her religious beliefs.

Discovery Question:

Look at the interactive history of gay marriage in the *New York Times* article by Haeyoun Park, "Gay Marriage State by State: From a Few States to the Whole Nation" (http://nyti.ms/1yvzRYT). How did our federal system both help and hinder the issue of same-sex marriage?

CONCLUDING THOUGHTS

Federalism is so deeply rooted in our everyday experience that few of us appreciate how much it shapes our daily lives. It is likely that intergovernmental relations is not a topic of conversation around your dinner table; perhaps you had not even considered its importance before reading this chapter. Nonetheless, as Thomas Anton suggested, the "interrelationships among levels of government are the defining characteristics of American public policies" (Anton, 1989, v). Federalism scholar Dale Krane agreed with the critical connection between federalism and IGR and policy formulation and development, arguing that "policymaking can be understood *only* from an intergovernmental perspective" (Krane, 1993, 186). He saw American federalism as a matrix of reciprocal power relationships shaping public policy at all levels of government. This matrix of federalism is unlikely to go away anytime soon. Instead, it will continuously be adapting to changing political, economic, and social events (Scheberle 2005).

Federalism is at the heart of political conflicts, as the national government has expanded the areas in which it makes policy, such as in the fields of education, environment, criminal justice, and social welfare. Often, the national government develops policies and then encourages state and local governments to implement the policies through grants-in-aid, such as actions that gave rise to the New Deal and Great Society programs. National policies can be mandatory for state and local governments as well, prompting cries of coercive and regulatory federalism predicated on unfunded or underfunded mandates. The Constitution created this unique system where all state governments are equal and national and state governments sovereign, but where national actions can trump state actions through the national supremacy clause. At the same time, states produce different policies that may result in changes at the national level, as we have recounted in this chapter. State governments are not impassive players in public policy—they are active and often innovative players. The constitutional constructs of federalism create a frustrating, sometimes contentious intergovernmental system, but one that is at the center of policymaking and implementation. Virtually every major domestic policy is based on the working of the federal system, and depends on state and local governments, as we shall see in subsequent chapters.

GLOSSARY TERMS

confederation or confederal
   system of government   48
cooperative federalism   53
dual federalism   52
fiscal federalism   54
grants-in-aid   53

horizontal federalism   49
intergovernmental relations   50
picket fence federalism   58
reserved powers   50
sovereignty   49

unitary system of
   government   52

DISCUSSION QUESTIONS

1. What distinctions do you see between federalism and intergovernmental relations, and how have they evolved over the history of our country? What historic events served as a catalyst for the entrance of the national government into what had been traditionally state policy arenas?

2. How do grants-in-aid to state and local governments influence the implementation of national policy? In what other ways (other than fiscal) does the federal government influence state and local governments to develop and implement policy?

3. Despite the growth of the federal government into what historically has been policy areas

of the states, the national government cannot do everything it wants. How is it constrained by the Constitution, by the courts, and by the public?

4. What characteristics influence state-level policymaking? How do states act as innovators in public policy? What types of public policies do you think should remain as primarily local and/or state government responsibilities? How about the national government?

5. Which of these adjectives do you think best describes federalism in public policymaking today: cooperative, creative, confrontational, fiscal, or dual?—or choose one of your own. Explain.

SUGGESTED RESOURCES

Suggested Websites

Council of State Governments, http://www.csg.org/pubs/capitolideas/index.aspx

National Association of Counties, http://www.naco.org

National Conference of State Legislatures, http://www.ncsl.org/

National Governors Association, http://www.nga.org/cms/home.html

National League of Cities, http://www.nlc.org/

Nelson A. Rockefeller Institute of Government, http://rockinst.org/

Pew Center on the States and Stateline, http://bit.ly/1kTjbmt

U.S. Conference of Mayors http://usmayors.org/

Suggested Books or Articles

Conlan, Timothy, and Paul Posner. 2008. *Intergovernmental Management for the 21st Century*. Washington, DC: Brookings.

Grodzins, Morton. 1966. *The American System: A New View of Government in the United States*. Chicago: Rand McNally.

Kincaid, John. 1990. "From Cooperative to Coercive Federalism." *Annals of the American Academy of Political and Social Science* 509 (May): 139–52.

Nathan, Richard. 2008. "Updating Theories of American Federalism." In *Intergovernmental Management for*

the 21st Century, edited by Timothy Conlan and Paul Posner. Washington, DC: Brookings.

Posner, Paul L. 2005. "The Politics of Preemption: Prospects for the States." *PS: Political Science and Politics* 38 (July): 371–74. http://dx.doi.org/10.1017/S1049096505050043

Publius: The Journal of Federalism. Peruse this journal, published quarterly by the Oxford University Press, to learn about issues in federalism and IGR.

Robertson, David Brian. 2011. *Federalism and the Making of America*. New York: Routledge.

Wright, Deil S. 1982. *Understanding Intergovernmental Relations*. Monterey, CA: Brooks/Cole.

Zimmerman, Joseph F. 1992. *Contemporary American Federalism: The Growth of National Power*. New York: SUNY Press.

_____. 2001. "National–State Relations: Cooperative Federalism in the Twentieth Century." *Publius* 31 (Spring): 15–30.

Suggested Films

The Pot Republic, DVD, PBS (2011: United States), http://www.pbs.org/wgbh/pages/frontline/the-pot-republic/

The Storm, DVD, PBS (2005: United States), http://www.pbs.org/wgbh/pages/frontline/storm/

Sharpen your skills with SAGE edge at **http://edge.sagepub.com/rinfret. SAGE edge for students** provides a personalized approach to help you accomplish your coursework goals in an easy-to-use learning environment.

Rulemaking and Regulations

FROM PEANUTS ON A PLANE TO THE FUTURE OF E-CIGARETTES

Imagine that as you embark on a holiday vacation, you encounter two out of the ordinary travel situations. First, as you wait your turn at the Transportation Security Administration (TSA) checkpoint, you cannot help but notice the person in front of you is getting a pat-down and an extensive bag check. Next, you notice an airport security official pull an e-cigarette from this person's purse. The TSA officer appears befuddled, asking his coworker, "What's the regulation on these?" Since this situation does not involve your own luggage, you move on to your gate, awaiting your departure.

Eventually, you board your plane and depart on time. As your plane reaches a cruising altitude, the airline attendant seems overly attentive to the passenger in front of you. Suddenly, the airline attendant is on the intercom asking if anyone has an EpiPen. Unfortunately, the nearby passenger was allergic to the free airline peanuts. Although these two encounters may seem out of the ordinary, they both involve government regulation and are explainable.

One of the perks of flying in the United States today is that you receive free peanuts and a drink. But, in 2011, the U.S. Department of Transportation (DOT), under agency rulemaking processes, proposed a rule in the *Federal Register* (a daily publication of the federal government detailing new or changing rules and regulations) to ban airlines from serving peanuts on a plane due to growing concerns surrounding allergic reactions. Based upon extensive research and the fear of airline lawsuits, the DOT provided the public three options for consideration in its proposed rule: (1) complete ban; (2) ban when a passenger requests

LEARNING OBJECTIVES

Readers of this chapter will be able to:

1. Understand how rules and regulations are far-reaching and impact our everyday lives

2. Identify the differences between regulatory processes and compliance

3. Comprehend what occurs once a rule becomes law and the individuals involved carry out regulatory policy

4. Explore how technology is shaping the future of regulatory policy

a peanut-free flight; or (3) offer a peanut-free buffer zone (sit where you can't be in contact with peanuts). After careful consideration of the law and input from the public, the DOT determined peanuts could stay (Anjarwalla 2010; *Federal Register* 2011).

While peanuts on the plane are not regulated by the DOT, what about the use of e-cigarettes? Most people are well aware that smoking regular cigarettes is not allowed on an airplane, but an e-cigarette is a battery-operated vaporizer that allows a person to simulate the effects of smoking without the smoke. Although the impacts of e-cigarettes are still being examined by the Food and Drug Administration (FDA) for minors, the Pipeline and Hazardous Safety Administration (part of the DOT) made a determination about their use during air travel. If traveling by airplane, a person is not allowed to have an e-cigarette in their checked bag or charge the battery while sitting in their seat during flight. The concern is that the batteries could catch fire during flight. A person is, however, allowed to bring their e-cigarette in their carry-on bag if it is turned off during the duration of the flight (Gilliard 2015).

Inevitably, we might not spend a lot of our time thinking about peanuts on a plane or e-cigarettes, but federal agencies like the DOT or FDA do, from which we benefit. To better understand how and why agencies are able to create regulations, this chapter introduces you to an often overlooked aspect of decision making.

....

The focus of Chapter 4 is to examine the *process* and *implementation* of U.S. regulations. Specifically, the goal of this chapter is to unpack how and why U.S. regulations are made, and what happens after a regulation goes into effect. To provide context, we begin the chapter with a definition of regulation. With this definition, we use the concept of delegation of authority to illustrate that regulatory policymaking cannot occur until *after* Congress creates a law. With this foundation, we introduce students to agency policymaking (also known as rulemaking) with a step-by-step guide about the process, using federal and state examples. Inevitably, this process can encounter some controversy along the way, and we use the protection of the polar bear to illustrate this point.

To answer our second question—what happens after a regulation goes into effect?—we examine the actors involved with the implementation of U.S. regulations (e.g., regulators or businesses). In order to understand this aspect of the regulatory arena, we use the example of a dry-cleaning business to document how a regulator will conduct a site visit to ensure compliance with a law. This example also allows us to investigate how the relationships between regulators and the regulated community (e.g., businesses) can impact the implementation of public policy.

After our whirlwind tour of U.S. regulations, we close the chapter with innovative solutions for the future and our everyday citizen connection section. We use examples from Cornell University's Regulation Room to suggest how students can become better versed in the rulemaking jargon to participate in processes. Our everyday citizen section will entice the tech-savvy student, or those of us who aspire to become regulatory policy wonks. Our goal with this chapter is to engage public policy students in a conversation about U.S. regulations—how and why they are created.

UNDERSTANDING THE CONTEXT OF U.S. REGULATIONS

Negative connotations often arise when we think of the term *regulation.* For example, take the USDA's efforts to regulate the size of the hole in Swiss cheese. In the United States, Americans prefer smaller-sized holes because we like to use our cheese for sandwiches. However, Europeans prefer larger-sized holes because they demonstrate a high-quality cheese. Also, U.S. cheese manufacturers do not want larger-sized holes because the slicer required for this type of cheese is expensive (Skrzycki 2003).

Common phrases that come to mind when considering the term *regulation* include, but are not limited to, "bad for business," "waste of taxpayer dollars," or "inefficient." To illustrate some of these arguments, we use examples from the Republican primary debates for the 2016 election and public opinion data from Gallup. During the Republican primary debates, several candidates repeatedly noted that regulation is bad for business. In particular, presidential candidate John Kasich (Republican governor of Ohio) argued that if elected president, he would freeze all major government regulations for an entire year because they cost the taxpayer too much money. To examine this point, Figure 4.1 suggests that since 2001, Americans have perceived there is too much government regulation on business and industry.

FIGURE 4.1

Public Perceptions

In general, do you think there is too much, too little, or about the right amount of government regulation of business and industry?

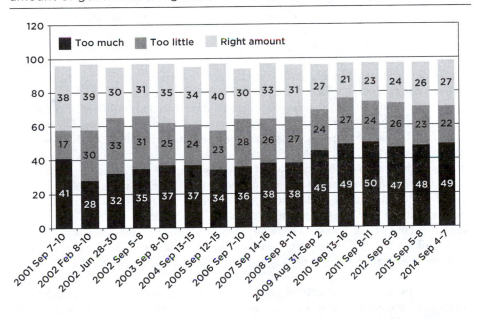

Source: GALLUP News, Politics, Sept 2014. http://news.gallup.com/poll/176015/few-americans-gov-regulation-business.aspx.

To counter these sentiments, Charles Goodsell (2004) suggests we should not allow these negative perceptions about U.S. regulation to overshadow the essential work of those who create government regulations—bureaucrats who work for U.S. agencies. Put succinctly, "The more Americans believe that bureaucracies are bad, the more likely they are to agree with efforts to slash taxes and gut government programs. That is why it is increasingly important that we begin to see that most of the criticisms of government bureaucracy are based more on myth than reality, and that these administrative agencies play a central role in promoting the important missions of a modern democratic government" (Amy 2007). Although the sentiments for and against government regulation exist, it is important to begin with a clear definition.

Defining Regulatory Policy

As noted in Chapter 1, U.S. regulations are a subset of public policies. **Regulation**, as defined by Meier (1985), is an "attempt by government to control the behavior of citizens, corporations, and subgovernments" (1). By way of comparison, Eisner, Worsham, and Ringquist (2006) suggest that regulation is an "array of public policies explicitly designed to govern economic activity and its consequences at the level of the industry, the firm, or individual unit of activity" (3). Nonetheless, U.S. regulations are important to understand because they: (1) attempt to promote public interest, (2) try to prevent or compensate for market failures, and (3) respond to the demands demonstrated by elected officials or the American people (Eisner et al. 2006).

In order to move beyond definitions, it is important to remember that regulations do not occur in a vacuum and that they involve a variety of actors and steps. Simply put, regulations are defined by congressional law (i.e., statutory law).[1] **Statutory law**, by definition, is the outcome of the congressional lawmaking process. The congressional lawmaking process includes: members of Congress drafting legislation; committee actions; floor debate; and votes, by both houses of Congress—and, if successful, approval by the president. The Defense of Marriage Act, the Clean Air Act, and the Endangered Species Act are all examples of statutory law. The resulting statutes are the guidelines that set the direction for the policy actions that follow—regulations by specific agencies.

Due to the breadth of U.S. public policy, agencies at the federal and state level often focus on a specific area. Table 4.1 provides examples of federal agencies and their purposes. The examples range from the FDA, which ensures that what we eat or consume is safe, to the U.S. Department of Homeland Security (DHS), which focuses on securing our nation from potential threats. The goal here is not to provide an exhaustive list of every state and federal agency that exists in the United States, but a snapshot into the scope of policy work taken on by agencies.

Much like the federal level, states also have agencies to help carry out policy. These agencies vary by state, and to demonstrate these differences, Table 4.2 provides some state examples. For instance, Montana has a Department of Livestock that attempts to "control and eradicate animal diseases,"[2] whereas Wisconsin's Department of Natural Resources oversees areas such as hunting, fishing, and clean air and water quality for their respective states.

While the aforementioned briefly defines the U.S. regulations, there is still much more to the story. For instance, how is it possible for both Congress *and* agencies to create public policy? Recall congressional statutes provide the general direction for an agency to create a regulation, which in turn allows for policymaking to occur in both entities. Regulations

TABLE 4.1

Examples of U.S. Federal Agencies

Federal Agency	Purpose of Agency
Department of Education (DOEd)	Promote student achievement and preparation for global competitiveness by fostering educational excellence and ensuring equal access.
Department of Homeland Security (DHS)	Secure the nation from the many threats we face.
Department of Transportation (DOT)	Ensure safe, fast, efficient, accessible, and convenient transportation system.
Environmental Protection Agency (EPA)	Protect human health and the environment.
Food and Drug Administration (FDA)	Protect public health, speed innovations to create medicines, regulate manufacturing and distribution of tobacco, ensure the safety of human and veterinary drugs, and ensure the security of the U.S. food supply.

TABLE 4.2

Examples of State Agencies

State Agency	Purpose of Agency
Arizona (AZ) Department of Administration	Provide benefits for public employees.
Montana (MT) Department of Livestock	Control and eradicate animal diseases, prevent the transmission of animal diseases to humans, and protect the livestock industry from theft and predatory animals.
New York (NY) Department of Corrections and Community Supervision	Provide treatment services in safe facilities for individuals to prepare for reentry into society.
Ohio (OH) Department of Commerce	Assist businesses in operating lawfully.
Wisconsin (WI) Department of Natural Resources	Manage fish, wildlife, forests, parks, air, and water resources, while promoting a healthy, sustainable environment and a full range of outdoor opportunities.

are designed by federal and state agencies through a set process known as rulemaking (which we discuss later in the chapter). Rulemaking is undertaken by agency rule-writers who are charged by Congress to implement congressional statutes (Rinfret and Furlong 2013) by writing rules, which become regulation (law). Once a rule has been written, state and federal regulators and businesses ensure and monitor implementation. However, why would Congress give up its lawmaking authority to an agency? The concept of delegation of authority is necessary to decipher why Congress delegates its lawmaking authority to federal and state agencies.

Delegation of Authority

Delegation of authority is the term to describe when Congress grants policymaking power to agencies. Although seemingly simplistic, reasons why delegation of authority occurs warrant explanation because it includes a variety of actors across U.S. branches of government and raises questions about accountability (e.g., who holds unelected officials— agency officials—accountable for creating policy). We begin by explaining why Congress delegates its lawmaking authority to agencies before turning to how the president and the courts serve as checks on this delegation of policymaking to address concerns surrounding the role of accountability.

Why Delegate?

Congress delegates its lawmaking authority for a number of reasons. First, according to Davis (1969), delegation occurs because programs are necessary and no one (meaning Congress) is willing to set specific guidelines. Members of Congress do not want to specify particular details about programs in legislation because it could be detrimental for reelection efforts or standing with their political party. For instance, if members of Congress stated explicit details in federal legislation that airlines could not have peanuts on a plane, the effects could be negative. To illustrate this point, consider that a peanut company could be within a congressional member's district. The peanut ban might lead to layoffs, which could lead to fewer votes for this member of Congress. Therefore, Congress tries to keep the language of legislation vague, leaving it up to agencies to clarify, interpret, and implement.

This leads us onto another reason for congressional delegation of authority: the theory, **shift of responsibility** (Fiorina 1982). Simply put, this theory presumes that members of Congress shift their decision making to agencies because they can shift the focus, or even blame, to agencies. To illustrate this point, we return to our peanuts on the plane example. Instead of passing legislation that could ban peanuts on a plane, the FDA can research and consider the potential implications for consumers. If a ban is implemented, angry airline companies or passengers would blame the FDA for making this decision, therefore shifting the blame from Congress to the agency.

A final example of why Congress delegates its authority surrounds the role of expertise. Presumably, federal and state agencies are comprised of experts in specific policy areas and therefore have the knowledge to create the necessary details to carry out a policy. For example, a congressional member may not have the expertise to determine how many acres would be necessary to ensure the leatherback sea turtle does not become extinct. Instead, experts within the U.S. Fish and Wildlife Service (FWS) determine what is necessary for the survival of the leatherback sea turtle because their staff have the expertise to study and investigate critical habitat for the species.

Although these examples demonstrate reasons why Congress delegates its authority to agencies to make policy, an overarching concern is that the decisions made by agencies are gone unchecked by unelected bureaucrats. More specifically, the question becomes: How can unelected officials (bureaucrats) within an agency create policy? To address this concern, we document how Congress, the president, and the courts hold agency decisions accountable.

Congress and Accountability

Each branch of government—Congress, the president, and the federal courts—serve as checks on agency decision making. As Figure 4.2 illustrates, Congress, the president, and the U.S. Supreme Court have a variety of mechanisms to ensure that the federal bureaucracy is held accountable. We examine each in turn.

Congress has three dominant mechanisms to oversee agency decision making—the Administrative Procedure Act, budgets, and legislation. For instance, Congress created the **Administrative Procedure Act (APA) of 1946.** The APA was adopted in 1946 as an oversight and accountability tool for the rapidly expanding government under President Franklin D. Roosevelt's New Deal that attempted to bring the United States out of the Great Depression. The APA requires agencies to follow its administrative rulemaking guidelines so government entities could carry out congressional statutes through the creation of rules. According to the APA, a **rule** "means the whole or part of an agency statement of general or particular applicability and future effect designed to implement, interpret, or prescribe law or policy" (Administrative Procedure Act 1946, Section 551). A rule created by an agency could then carry the same legal force as a law. Administrative rulemaking consists of the stages or processes by which an agency creates and implements a rule. The description of the rulemaking stages later defined in this chapter identify that the APA requirement of public participation during the notice/comment portion of the rulemaking processes allows for significant public involvement in policymaking.

Congress can also check agency decisions through two additional measures. Congress controls agency budgets. The U.S. Senate Appropriations Committee determines how much money an agency has for specific programs. If members of Congress are upset with the policy direction of an agency, the agency's budget can be decreased. This occurred with the Supplemental Nutrition Assistance Program. Under this USDA program, families below the poverty line receive food stamps. With decreased funding, the agency may have to decrease the amount of support provided to families.

Another important oversight function Congress provides is that its members can write legislation to overturn an agency rule (Kerwin and Furlong 2011). This approach is

FIGURE 4.2

Mechanisms of Accountability

Congressional Accountability Mechanisms	Presidential Accountability Mechanisms	Supreme Court Accountability Mechanisms
Administrative Procedure Act	Appointment power	Litigation to overturn agency decisions
Budgets	OIRA review	
Legislation	Executive orders	
Hearing		

used less frequently because it takes a great deal of effort to create and pass congressional legislation. However, in 2015, the U.S. House of Representatives passed legislation to prevent the U.S. EPA from updating regulations under the Clean Water Act that focus on creating new regulations to protect U.S. streams and wetlands. At the time of this writing, the U.S. Senate had yet to consider this legislation; therefore, the final outcome was not available.

Congress can also conduct oversight hearings of an agency. For example, Congress could be concerned about the FDA program to evaluate peanuts on a plane due to constituent complaints. During a congressional hearing, members of Congress could ask FDA employees to provide testimony about what approaches the agency is taking to ensure individuals are not having allergic reactions on an airplane.

The President and Accountability

The president also has oversight authority over agency decision making. For the purposes of this chapter, we use appointment power and the Office of Management and Budget's Office of Information and Regulatory Affairs (OIRA) as illustrations. Presidents have the power to appoint (with Senate confirmation) who serves as the head of an agency. An agency head (the person at the top of the agency or organization) can determine the policy direction of an agency, which is often within the same political perspective of a president. For example, the 2015 head of the Department of Justice, Loretta Lynch, noted that her agency, in concert with statements made by President Barack Obama, would not investigate states that allowed for the recreational or medicinal use of marijuana, even though it was a violation of federal law.

The other powerful tool that a president can use is OIRA review. OIRA's role is to review the costs and benefits associated with agency regulations that may be economically burdensome for business (over $100 million). Specifically, under President Ronald Reagan's Executive Order 12291, the OMB director is authorized to "review any draft proposed or final rule or regulatory impact analysis from a covered agency" (Copeland 2013, 10). Or, as Tomkin (1998) stresses, "Under the order, federal agencies would be required to conduct cost-benefit analysis, known as the Regulatory Impact Analysis of proposals for new regulations as well as for final regulations" (206). Presidents have the authority to issue executive orders to provide policy directives for agencies to implement.

Since President Reagan, subsequent presidents, regardless of party, have continued the practice of OIRA review (Copeland 2013). The goal of OIRA review is to ensure regulations do not have an undue impact on business, and if a president is concerned with an agency regulation, he can direct OIRA staff to review the rule. Within this review process, OIRA invites anyone to meet with their staff to express concerns with an agency rule and also conducts economic evaluations weighing the costs and benefits of an agency rule. Agencies are also invited to these review meetings. If OIRA does not believe an agency has done its due diligence in justifying costs of a rule, it can return the rule back to the agency for more research. Until OIRA approves an agency rule, a rule cannot move forward. Scholars have scrutinized this review process, noting that it allows business groups to dominate conversations with OIRA, impacting agency policymaking (Copeland 2013).

The Supreme Court and Accountability

A final oversight mechanism for agency decision making is the role of the U.S. Supreme Court. As Kerwin and Furlong (2011) remind us, "No institution of government has been as persistent in its oversight of rulemaking for a longer period of time than the federal judiciary" (247). Often, individuals or organizations will use the courts to sue because they are unhappy with the outcome of an agency decision. For example, many states such as Ohio and West Virginia are upset about the guidelines enacted by the EPA's Clean Power Plan Rule. Under this regulation, current and future coal-burning power plants have to decrease carbon dioxide emission levels 30 percent by 2030. Therefore, some states are suing the EPA to prevent this rule from becoming law. Inevitably, the courts can determine "whether an agency has performed its rulemaking task in a legally permissible manner" (Kerwin and Furlong 2011, 256).

UNDERSTANDING REGULATORY PROCESSES

Although checks and balances are in place, federal and state agencies do have the authority to create policy through rulemaking because Congress has delegated them the ability to do so. In order to unpack the rulemaking process, Figure 4.3 illustrates the stages of the federal rulemaking process, which we describe in detail.

The APA of 1946 defines the stages by which a rule-writer promulgates a rule. These stages, as Figure 1 indicates, are: (1) pre-rule; (2) Notice of Proposed Rulemaking (NPRM); and (3) final rule. The pre-rule phase (stage 1) is where informal communication occurs between interest groups and agency personnel. This stage is used by an agency to acquire additional research or to discuss a rule with affected entities. For instance, the FDA would use this stage of the process to discuss with tobacco companies and public health organizations their perspectives about e-cigarettes. These conversations inform the agency about potential concerns or areas of research that should be included in a rule.

These informal interactions lead to stage 2, when an agency publishes a Notice of Proposed Rulemaking (NPRM) in the *Federal Register*. The *Federal Register* is a daily publication of U.S. federal agency regulations. Recall that agencies are required by the APA of 1946 to publish and provide notice to the public about a rule. As Photo 4.1 illustrates, the *Federal Register* can be accessed through the Internet by visiting www.federalregister.gov.

FIGURE 4.3
Stages of Federal Rulemaking

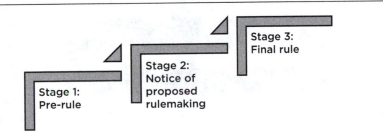

Stage 1:
Pre-rule

Stage 2:
Notice of
proposed
rulemaking

Stage 3:
Final rule

PHOTO 4.1

Federal Register

Courtesy of Federal Register

Each day the government is operating, the *Federal Register* is published and updates the rulemaking activities of all federal agencies. For instance, on Friday, November 20, 2015, the *Federal Register* had seventeen proposed rules. These proposed rules cross agencies, and anyone can search through this information to determine agency activity.

The APA also requires, under stage 2, that the public is provided a window of opportunity to comment on a proposed rule. Congress provided a public comment period to ensure agencies considered public input, creating a mechanism for citizen participation in agency decision making. This comment period is typically open for thirty to sixty days, so that any person can submit a comment to a rule. However, if the agency believes more time is needed for public participation, the comment period can be reopened. This recently occurred with the Bureau of Land Management's (BLM) hydraulic fracturing rule. The public wanted additional time to consider the rule; therefore, the BLM lengthened the time to submit public comments. Any member of the public can go to www.regulations.gov (the online portal that publishes all rulemaking actions of federal agencies), find the proposed rule, and submit a formal/written comment (see Photo 4.2). A person is also able to view what other comments have been submitted for a particular rule.

PHOTO 4.2

Regulations.gov

Courtesy of Regulations.gov

Ultimately, public comments provide opinions about the rule, for or against. After the comment period ends, agency personnel are required by the APA of 1946 to review the comments and respond to commenters. After examining the comments, the agency uses this information to determine the language and substance of the final rule. On average, it can take an agency one to two years to review public comments. This length of time depends on the volume or amount of public comments, as well as staff available to review and provide feedback for commenters (Kerwin and Furlong 2011; Rinfret 2011a, b). If a person or group is upset with the final rule, litigation or the court system can be used to challenge the final actions of an agency. Depending on the outcome of a court case, a rule cannot be finalized until a judicial decision is made. Nonetheless, once an agency moves through the stages of the process, a final rule is published in the *Federal Register*. Although final rules are published electronically in the *Federal Register*, each rule can be downloaded to your computer or laptop. Figure 4.4 provides an example of the first page of a final rule.

State Rulemaking

The federal rulemaking process is extensive, containing three main stages, but what about state processes? By way of comparison, state rulemaking was designed by the Model States Administrative Procedure Act as a guideline for state rule-writers to follow (Renfrow and Houston 1987). Although the state process is very similar to that of federal rulemaking, each state may have a unique or different step, such as the governor's role in the process or involvement of members of the state assembly. Instead of detailing each of the fifty state processes, which would take up the remaining pages of this textbook, we use New York as an example to explore what a state rulemaking process entails. If you are interested in the process of your own respective state, we suggest using www.uniformlaws.org, which provides state-specific procedures for promulgating rules.

The New York process follows a three-step approach much like federal rulemaking. More specifically, New York must follow the State Administrative Procedure Act (SAPA). SAPA sets state-specific guidelines for New York rulemaking, such as requiring public comment and the role of other branches of state government, which we examine next.

Stage 1 of New York's rulemaking process begins with an internal agency review. This review helps to determine if rulemaking is the best or most appropriate action to address a particular problem. For instance, the New York Department of Health decided internally a rule would be necessary to create a program for medical marijuana. More specifically, agency staff would discuss the statutory guidelines for medical marijuana use and determine if their agency had the authority to move forward with a rule. If the agency decides to move forward, agency staff discuss and prepare a proposed rule (NPRM). Often at this stage, agency staff will also reach out to stakeholder groups to receive input on the issue. For the medical marijuana example, an agency may meet with doctors, hospitals, health professionals, and businesses.

Stage 2 of the state process unfolds when the agency submits a formal proposed rulemaking in the *New York State Register*. Photo 4.3 provides an illustration of the *New York State Register*. This is where a person can search for information about rules proposed by New York state agencies.

FIGURE 4.4

Sample Final Rule

75636 **Federal Register**/Vol. 80, No. 232/Thursday, December 3, 2015/Rules and Regulations

---

9A004 Space Launch Vehicles and "Spacecraft," "Spacecraft Buses," "Spacecraft Payloads," "Spacecraft" On-board Systems or Equipment, and Terrestrial Equipment, as Follows (see List of Items Controlled).

License Requirements

*   *   *   *   *

License Requirements Note: *9A004.b through .f are controlled under ECCN 9A515.*

*   *   *   *   *

List of Items Controlled

Related Controls*** (3) See USML Categories IV for the space launch vehicles and XV for other spacecraft that are "subject to the ITAR" (see 22 CFR parts 120 through 130).

*   *   *   *   *

■ 12. In Supplement No. 1 to part 774, Category 9, ECCN 9A010 is amended by:
■ a. Revising the Heading; and
■ b. Adding a Related Controls Note to the List of Items Controlled Section, to read as follows:

9A010 "Specially Designed" "Parts," "Components," Systems and Structures, for Launch Vehicles, Launch Vehicle Propulsion Systems or "Spacecraft". (See Related Controls paragraph.)

List of Items Controlled

Related Controls: (1) See USML Category IV of the International Traffic in Arms Regulations (ITAR) (22 CFR parts 120 through 130) and ECCN 9A604 for paragraphs 9A010.a, .b and .d. (2) See USML Category XV of the ITAR and ECCN 9A515 for paragraph 9A010.c. (3) See Supplement No. 4 to part 774, Order of Review for guidance on the process for determining classification of items.

*   *   *   *   *

Dated: November 23, 2015.

Kevin J. Wolf,

Assistant Secretary for Export Administration.

[FR Doc. 2015–30253 Filed 12–2–15; 8:45 am]

Avenue Bridge across the English Kills, mile 3.4, at New York City, New York. This deviation is necessary to perform operating machinery installation. This deviation allows the bridge to remain in the closed position for approximately 3 days.

DATES: This deviation is effective from 6 a.m. on December 7, 2015 to 5 p.m. on December 10, 2015.

ADDRESSES: The docket for this deviation, [USCG–2015–1019] is available at *http://www.regulations.gov.*

FOR FURTHER INFORMATION CONTACT: If you have questions on this temporary deviation, call or email Ms. Judy K. Leung-Yee, Project Officer, First Coast Guard District, telephone (212) 514–4330, email *judy.k.leung-yee@uscg.mil.*

SUPPLEMENTARY INFORMATION: New York City DOT requested this temporary deviation from the normal operating schedule to perform operating machinery installation.

The Metropolitan Avenue Bridge, mile 3.4, across the English Kills has a vertical clearance in the closed position of 10 feet at mean high water and 15 feet at mean low water. The existing bridge operating regulations are found at 33 CFR 117.801(e).

The waterway has one commercial facility located upstream of the bridge.

Under this temporary deviation, the Metropolitan Avenue Bridge may remain in the closed position from 6 a.m. on December 7, 2015 through 5 p.m. on December 10, 2015.

Vessels able to pass through the bridge in the closed positions may do so at any time. The bridge will not be able to open for emergencies and there is no immediate alternate route for vessel to pass.

ENVIRONMENTAL PROTECTION AGENCY

40 CFR Part 52

[EPA–R06–OAR–2012–0400; FRL–9939–47–Region 6]

Approval and Promulgation of Implementation Plans; New Mexico; Albuquerque-Bernalillo County; Infrastructure and Interstate Transport State Implementation Plan for the 2008 Lead National Ambient Air Quality Standards

AGENCY: Environmental Protection Agency (EPA).

ACTION: Final rule.

SUMMARY: EPA is approving a State Implementation Plan (SIP) submission from the Governor of New Mexico for the City of Albuquerque-Bernalillo County for the 2008 Lead (Pb) National Ambient Air Quality Standards (NAAQS). The submittal addresses how the existing SIP provides for implementation, maintenance, and enforcement of the 2008 Pb NAAQS (infrastructure SIP or i-SIP). This i-SIP ensures that the State's SIP for Albuquerque-Bernalillo County is adequate to meet the state's responsibilities under the Federal Clean Air Act (CAA or Act), including the four CAA requirements for interstate transport of Pb emissions.

DATES: This final rule is effective on January 4, 2016.

ADDRESSES: EPA has established a docket for this action under Docket ID No. EPA–R06–OAR–2012–0400. All documents in the docket are listed on the *http://www.regulations.gov* Web site. Although listed in the index, some information is not publicly available, *e.g.,* Confidential Business Information or other information whose disclosure is

---

After the agency publishes the notice of proposed rulemaking, the public comment period begins. Public comments must be sent via e-mail or regular mail to the respective agency. The *New York State Register* does not allow information to be submitted to a central location as does the federal government, via Regulations.gov. One reason why a person has to submit a comment via e-mail or regular mail is that it can be costly to maintain a central location for state rules. Due to how comments are submitted, however, a New York agency

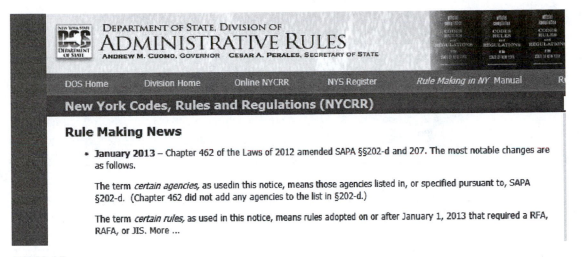

has 180 days to review and respond to public comments, as well as to determine what action to take on a rule. An agency can ask for an extension to review public comments, but on average, New York agencies must respond within 180 days.

Stage 3 of the rulemaking process begins when an agency provides a complete text of the rule being finalized to the governor, the president of the Senate, the Speaker of the Assembly, and the Administrative Regulations Reviews Commission (within the New York State Senate). Therefore, at this stage, the filing of the final terms of the rule is published in the *New York State Register*.

In summary, federal and state rulemaking provide a set process for agencies to turn vague congressional legislation into policy. Agencies at the federal and state levels provide ways for us to participate in these processes. At the federal level, the public can participate by submitting public comments to Regulations.gov; however, at the state level a person typically has to submit comments via e-mail or regular mail.

Unfortunately, not many Americans are aware of rulemaking processes unless they directly impact their day-to-day lives, such as peanuts on a plane or e-cigarettes. Although we might not think about agency rules, many groups or organizations across the United States do pay attention. Specific groups (e.g., interest groups that represent an interest, such as the environment, public health, or car manufacturers) try to use this process to influence agency outcomes, which warrants an explanation.

INFLUENCE AND PARTICIPATION

We know interest groups lobby members of Congress to influence how congressional policy is made. What about agency policymaking—do groups lobby agency officials to create rules? As noted, an agency can and does meet with groups informally during stage 1 of the rulemaking process. But interest group influence on agency decision making is

FIGURE 4.5

Rulemaking and Influence

Rulemaking Stage	Mechanisms of Interest Group Influence
Stage 1: Pre-rule	• Meet with agency rule-writer • Provide research to agency rule-writer
Stage 2: Notice and comment	• Write a substantive public comment and submit to agency
Stage 3: Final rule	• Sue agency, challenging language of the final rule

not as clear-cut. Interest group influence has been investigated over the last two decades by scholars trying to decipher how and at what stage of the rulemaking process groups try to impact agency decision making (see Figure 4.5 for examples).

Specifically, scholars (Kerwin and Furlong 2011; Rinfret 2011a, b; Rinfret and Furlong 2013; Yackee 2012) have examined at what stage in the process groups can make an impact. One would presume the best mechanism to influence an agency rule would be to submit a public comment. And what scholars have found is the groups that are going to be impacted by a rule—usually businesses—dominate the public comment phase, which can impact the language of a rule finalized by an agency (Golden 1998). In particular, Marissa Golden compared comments submitted by groups with the actual language of a final rule. With this comparison, her research documented that business group comments or their language could be found in a final rule.

Although submitting a public comment is important to document your voice to an agency about a given rule, we are increasingly seeing a variety of groups that are trying to meet with an agency rule-writer during stage 1 to provide positions (Rinfret 2011a, b). For example, Rinfret (2011) has extensively studied this stage of the process and found that groups try to meet with an agency during stage 1. These meetings can often impact what language is placed in an NPRM (stage 2). Although qualitative research suggests agencies and groups note the importance of this stage of the process, it is difficult to examine because the APA of 1946 does not require agencies to document or record these exchanges. A researcher can ask an agency about these exchanges, which they are often willing to provide, but the groups participating during stage 1 do not necessarily want to go on record. Scholars are still investigating the reasons why.

Inevitably, those who are going to be impacted by a rule created by an agency are the individuals who are going to participate in the process. Research suggests business groups often dominate the submission of public comments (stage 2); thus, they can impact the language of a final rule (Golden 1998; West 2009). Furthermore, a growing body of research suggests that the pre-rule stage is the current access point to make an impact (Cook and Rinfret 2013; Hoefer and Ferguson 2007; Rinfret 2011a, b). But the question becomes, What happens after a rule is finalized—what can groups do to make an impact? Recall that during stage 3 of the rulemaking process groups can use litigation to achieve their desired outcome after a final rule is published in the *Federal Register*. Moreover, a rule cannot become law until pending courts cases are resolved (Kerwin and Furlong 2011). To examine how litigation can impact the outcome of a final rule, we examine the Alaskan polar bear.

In 2007, the United States Fish and Wildlife Service (FWS) proposed an NPRM in the *Federal Register*, asking for public comment about whether the agency should list the polar bear as a threatened species and, if so, how much habitat should be set aside for the polar bears' survival. The U.S. FWS used the Endangered Species Act (ESA) of 1973 as its statutory authority to propose this rulemaking. More specifically, under the ESA a species can be classified or listed as endangered or threatened. "Endangered" means this species is on the brink of extinction, whereas "threatened" is used to explain that there is concern the species could become extinct. In this rulemaking, the FWS received over one million public comments and determined approximately 187,000 acres of designated critical habitat were necessary for the survival of the polar bear.

PHOTO 4.4
Skating on thin ice: polar bears and the climate change rule
iStock / Coldimages

Although this rulemaking was finalized in 2008, the storyline continues. In particular, environmental groups such as the Center for Biological Diversity were upset that the species was not listed as endangered because, as a threatened species, reduced protections or exemptions can occur (Rodriguez 2011). In turn, other groups and the state of Alaska argued the rule was unnecessary altogether because the polar bear was already protected by state law and did not need federal intervention (Rodriguez 2011). After the finalization of this rule, lawsuits ensued and the industry perspective was that the science and data were not enough to set aside critical habitat for the polar bear. Federal judge Emmett Sullivan ruled in 2011 that the FWS rationales to list the polar bear were "well supported and that opponents failed to demonstrate that the listing was irrational" (Rodriguez 2011).

In 2015, the question was whether or not the extraction of petroleum resources or coal-burning power plants in the region near the habitat of polar bears were aiding in the decrease of the species' habitat. This question is still under investigation, and we encourage you to consider what is at stake that drives the complexities of this issue—climate change, the U.S. economy, and the future of the polar bear. Regardless, this story about the polar bear demonstrates that even though the rulemaking process is in place, groups that are not satisfied can try to influence the outcome of a final rule through the courts. The courts are the final decider (unless Congress decides to pass new legislation in lieu of a rule), and polar bears are still a threatened species.

AFTER A RULE BECOMES A LAW

Once a federal or state rule becomes a law, we move on to the implementation phase. The implementation and ongoing compliance with regulations involve two crucial populations:

regulators and members of the regulated community (businesses and other regulated entities). These are the individuals on the front lines (sometimes also referred to as street-level bureaucrats or front-line workers) of policy implementation who are largely responsible for the success or failure of that policy (Lipsky 1980; Maynard-Moody and Musheno 2003; Riccucci 2005). As with rulemaking, regulators use a process to examine the day-to-day practices of a regulated entity and to make sure the organization is in compliance with the law. Moreover, on average, a regulator can often be responsible for overseeing five to three hundred companies per year (Pautz and Rinfret 2013). This average depends upon the policy area and government agency. But before we turn to an investigation of how a regulator would review the practices of a regulated entity, it is first important to describe state and federal regulators.

Within an environmental context, state regulators are often responsible for implementing a large majority of policy (Pautz and Rinfret 2013). For instance, many states across the United States have drinking water regulators. The goal is to ensure compliance with the Safe Drinking Water Act (see Chapter 10). Typically, these individuals work for a state's environmental protection agency. Let's say a local mobile home park uses a well for drinking water, but this water becomes contaminated. Due to the contamination, a drinking water regulator and the operator of the mobile home park could work closely together to address the issue and to prevent health risks for the community. Together, the regulator and the mobile home park operator could ban the use of drinking water until it was properly tested and safe for consumption.

An example of the type of work a federal regulator oversees is the mining of coal. The mining of underground coal has been categorized as one of the most hazardous occupations in the world (U.S. Department of Labor 2015). One of the most important safety precautions for underground mining is proper ventilation for workers. If ventilation is not provided, deadly results can and have occurred. As a result, the federal Mine Safety and Health Administration (MSHA) regulators have the statutory authority under the Federal Coal Mine Health and Safety Act of 1969 to monitor underground mining practices. An MSHA regulator would examine underground mines to make sure proper equipment and ventilation are provided for miners in order to help prevent respiratory diseases from coal dust.

State and federal regulators run the gamut across policy areas. But, in order to make sure public policy is carried out as intended by the law, a regulator will conduct a site visit of a local mobile home park that reported drinking water contamination or to make sure a mine has safe working conditions for employees. The process to ensure compliance with the law is often described as an inspection process or site visit. In order to better understand the inner workings of these practices, we examine how a regulator would inspect a dry-cleaning facility. We use this particular example, then, to describe why understanding the interactions between a regulator and businesses are also essential to understanding U.S. policy implementation.

Regulating Your Local Dry Cleaner

To demonstrate the processes a regulator might take when visiting a company, we use a local dry cleaner as an example—we use the pseudonyms Sam, the regulator, and Sunny, the owner and operator of Sunny's Cleaners, to unpack the process.

Sam, the regulator, arrives unexpectedly at Sunny's Cleaners at 8 a.m. on a cold winter day. Upon arrival, Sam announces to the dry-cleaning attendant that he would like to meet with Sunny's manager to conduct a site visit. Sunny, the owner of Sunny's Cleaners, makes his way to the customer pickup counter and greets Sam. Sam asks Sunny if they could meet in his office to discuss any issues or concerns before he begins his site visit of Sunny's Cleaners. Sunny lets Sam know that he believes his company is in compliance with the law, and notifies staff that Sam will be walking around the floor to examine their dry-cleaning practices. Sunny and Sam, however, discuss some issues that occurred during the last site visit—Sunny's Cleaners had a malfunctioning machine that was spewing chemicals into the air. Sunny told Sam this issue had been corrected.

Next, Sam conducts a physical inspection of Sunny's Cleaners, walking around the operations floor and watching the dry-cleaning process. Sam knows this is often the stage in the inspection process in which something could arise. And, unfortunately, Sam did find a dry-cleaning machine that appeared to be leaking a blue substance onto the floor. More specifically, dry-cleaning machines are required to have a spin pan underneath each machine; this was missing. Sam, uncertain of the substance, scratched his forehead and knew he could just point out the problem to Sunny, which could lead to a quick fix. However, if the substance were a health violation, he might have to formally write up or document the violation, which is never easy to do. The other issue was that Sunny's Cleaners had a violation a couple of years ago, which would mean Sam would have to write a notice of violation, which the company would have to address immediately. Sam decided to ask Sunny what the substance was. Sunny replied it was just detergent; the company had just purchased a new machine and forgotten to install the spill pan. Luckily, this was a quick fix, and one of Sunny's employees placed the spill pan under the machine.

After several hours, Sam's site inspection of Sunny's Cleaners was complete. Sam asked Sunny if they could debrief from the day and discuss the substance on the floor. Sunny knew Sam had to document the incident to follow his agency's procedures. The two men said their goodbyes and Sam drove back to his office to write up his report. Upon completion, Sam took his report to his supervisor and they discussed the inspection from the day. Although the aforementioned example appears to be seemingly straightforward, and without conflict or controversy, it does not always unfold this way. In our example, it appears that Sam and Sunny have a working relationship, but this is not always the case. We now turn to research about how the approach a regulator uses or the response a business practices can impact the outcome of policy implementation.

THE GOOD, THE BAD, AND THE UGLY

Although we provided a snapshot into the details of a site visit, we have only begun to scratch the surface of the inner workings of this process. More specifically, regulatory relationships are essential to understanding U.S. regulations more broadly. In our dry-cleaning example, what if Sam and Sunny did not have a cordial relationship? Instead, what if Sam just wrote a notice of violation without first discussing the issue with Sunny? Or what if when Sam asked Sunny about the substance, Sunny just brushed off the situation? These are all plausible responses that are driven by different regulatory approaches to a problem.

As a result, the approach a regulator employs to achieve compliance can vary dramatically and has been studied extensively by scholars.

The focus by many scholars has been to understand how the relationships between the regulator and the regulated organization during a site visit impact the implementation of policy (Bardach and Kagan 2002; Hawkins 1984; Hutter 1998). We borrow from Pautz and Rinfret (2013) to unpack what might explain the variation in approach among regulators. As Figure 4.6 suggests, the enforcement style a regulator uses can be classified into three different categories: (1) **precision-based style**, (2) **intention-based style**, or (3) **mix of enforcement styles**.

Precision-Based Some scholars would classify this regulatory approach as by the book, or strict in terms of ensuring the regulated community is compliant (Bardach and Kagan 2002). Key attributes of this style, based on past study, include (1) rules orientation, (2) consistency, (3) tough enforcement, (4) deterrence through enforcement actions, and (5) some degree of adversarialism. Regulators who embrace this approach think regulations have to be enforced as they are written in order to be effective—in other words, they have to "go by the book" (Bardach and Kagan 2002). This approach ensures all regulations are applied uniformly and with little room for deviation in terms of compliance assessment. Regulators who express this style believe they are compelled to enforce the rules as written, without deviation. For example, if Sam the regulator used a "by the book" approach, Sunny's Cleaners would have been given a notice of violation, which could create a bad relationship between the company and the regulator. However, Pautz and Rinfret (2013) suggest we say "precision-based" instead of "by the book," "strict," or "rules-oriented" to more accurately describe this type of regulatory style. "Precision" is a positive term used to describe accuracy and care, which are traits in a regulator who represents this approach.

FIGURE 4.6

Enforcement Style

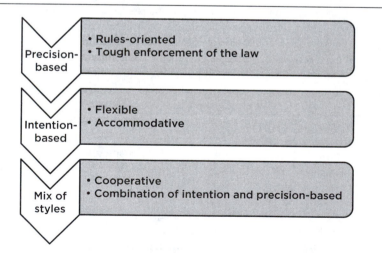

Intention-Based This type of regulatory style has also been categorized as flexible, results-oriented, or flexible/accommodative. The regulatory approach used by Sam in our dry-cleaning example is representative of this approach. In particular, Sam the regulator used cooperative or conciliatory means to secure compliance with regulations. He worked with Sunny's Cleaners to convey that it needed to install a spill pan and they worked together to address the situation. It is presumed this approach would lend itself to a more positive relationship with the company.

Yet it could be argued that this regulatory style may be perceived as soft, easily manipulated, and ripe for regulatory capture (i.e., regulator acts on behalf of the interests of the company instead of the public). Put simply, this label indicates regulators with this style are easily taken advantage of and succumb to the regulated community. Instead, Pautz and Rinfret (2013) illustrate the "intention-based" enforcement style better conveys that regulators who embrace this style examine the intentions of the regulated facility. This is because they consider the intent of the regulation.

Mix of Enforcement Styles Historically, scholars suggested regulatory enforcement styles occur in a binary fashion—intention or precision-based. However, subsequent research has demonstrated that the regulator might employ each approach in varying combinations depending on the circumstances, settings, or policy area (Hutter 1988, 1989; May and Winter 2000). One might question why a regulator would personify both approaches during a site inspection. We suggest this is because different circumstances warrant different behaviors. For instance, if Sunny's Cleaners was a chronic violator and routinely problematic, wouldn't Sam react differently? Thus, regulators who embrace a mixed enforcement style prefer a combination of various tactics and tools as they seek compliance from the regulated community.

To articulate the use of a mixed approach, Pautz and Rinfret (2012), in a nationwide study of over 1,200 state environmental regulators, found regulators are shifting toward cooperative relationships, and inevitably use a combination of approaches when working with regulated businesses to achieve environmental compliance. The assumption is that collaborative relationships will move beyond an "us versus them" mentality that pits a regulator against a business. Nonetheless, if regulators and a company work together, compliance is more easily achieved.

At this juncture, you have a big picture of the processes and day-to-day approaches used by regulators. But inspection processes can also be fraught with controversy, just like rule-writing. In order to understand how to navigate some of these complexities, we examine why the Animas River in Colorado turned orange in the summer of 2015 (see Photo 4.5).

Regulators are also confronted with issues that can be difficult to manage. For instance, what happened to cause the Animas River in Colorado to turn orange during the summer of 2015? More specifically, in August 2015 the EPA took the blame for the leakage of wastewater into the Animas River (Marcus, Benjamin, and Shinn 2015). But before we can understand why the EPA took the blame, we need to understand the details of the story.

The Gold King Mine, which closed in the 1920s, sits above the Animas River near Durango, Colorado. Some local residents have argued the abandoned Gold King Mine should be classified as a Superfund site (classified by the EPA's Comprehensive Environmental Response, Compensation and Liability Act of 1980 as a contaminated

PHOTO 4.5
The Animas
turns orange.

Helen H. Richardson/
The Denver Post via
Getty Images

site with hazardous substances) due to the toxic levels of mining waste that could spew into the Animas. And, according to Parker (2015), this mine is part of the ever-growing 50,000 in the western United States that are vacant, potentially wreaking havoc; but the cleanup of all of these vacant mines would cost almost $24–54 billion in taxpayer dollars.

Moreover, there were concerns presented by Colorado game and fish authorities about the vacant Gold King Mine—the trout population, plentiful for twenty years, was on the decline in 2014. Nevertheless, it could not be determined the wastewater from the Gold King Mine was the culprit (Parker 2015). Therefore, due to lack of resources and budget cuts, the EPA used a government contractor to examine the Gold King Mine, and the goal was to install a pipe to drain the water so the EPA could eventually plug the mine, keeping the contaminated water away from the river (Thompson 2015). Unfortunately, this did not work, and on August 5, 2015, the mine's water turned the Animas River water a blood-red orange. Individuals living near the river could choose whether or not to drink the water, and in September 2015 the pH levels of the water were similar to that of vinegar (Parker 2015).

Although the outcome of this case is unfortunate, it is also the case of what happens when a regulator is trying to regulate a company that is no longer in business. The approach the EPA was taking was to plug the mine to prevent catastrophe. These steps did not work in this case, but for some local communities, such as Durango or Silverton, Colorado, "If public reaction is any indication, the disaster has woken up Durangoans to not only how important the river is, but also what is going on upstream. And they're likely to exert whatever pressure they can on their neighbors up in Silverton to accept, even embrace, Superfund and a comprehensive cleanup effort" (Thompson 2015).

THE FUTURE OF REGULATORY POLICY

As this chapter demonstrates, understanding the complexities and details of the U.S. regulatory arena is an important, yet overlooked, area of public policy. We have documented in this chapter the role that rule-writers and regulators play in implementing public policy. These individuals make sure the peanuts we eat on a plane or the new e-cigarettes' smoke are safe for us, the consumer. In the final few pages of this chapter, we offer some innovative approaches to foster citizen engagement for the future.

We previously noted participation in rulemaking is often dominated by those who are impacted by a rule. For example, the BLM's rule for the disclosure of chemicals used in hydraulic fracturing contained public commenters from the natural gas industry, those impacted by the rule. Nevertheless, it is also important for *everyone* to understand the rulemaking process, especially since information is easily accessible with the submission of public comments via the Internet. The electronic submission of public comments is a relatively new phenomenon, however, something that federal agencies have worked on in order to increase the level of awareness for the general public about the process. This approach has increased the level of accessibility from the days by which you would have to submit written comments to agencies via snail mail.

Moreover, with the Obama administration's commitment to an open and transparent government, the goal is to ensure federal agencies are indeed providing timely, accurate, and accessible information to the general public. As described above, Regulations.gov has aided agencies in providing information videos about the rulemaking process and how to submit a comment for an agency's proposed rule.

In addition to the transparency or availability of Regulations.gov, the *Federal Register* recently received a facelift. Recall that Regulations.gov is the portal where a person or group would submit or review public comments, and the *Federal Register* is the daily publication of agency rules. In July 2010, the *Federal Register* celebrated its seventy-fifth birthday. In order to honor this milestone, Federal Register 2.0 was created. According to David S. Ferriero, a U.S. archivist, the objective was to make the *Federal Register* website more user-friendly so that information would be accessible and readable (Federal News Staff Radio 2010). Therefore, WestEd Interactive, a web development team from San Francisco, studied the *Federal Register* by examining over ten years of data to make the website more interactive. This research helped to create GovPulse.US, an application (app) that allows individuals from across the United States to track regulations by region. And, according to GovPulse.US, "GovPulse was built to open the doors of government to the people they work for. By making such documents as the *Federal Register* searchable, more accessible and easier to digest, GovPulse seeks to encourage every citizen to become more involved in the workings of their government and make their voice heard on the things that matter to them, from the smallest to the largest issues" (GovPulse 2015).

A facelift for the *Federal Register* or a new app may not be enough to entice the average American to consider rulemaking or participate in its processes. Because of this, Cornell University recently launched the Regulation Room (http://regulationroom.org/). This project, organized by Cornell's CeRi (Cornell eRulemaking Initiative), is a collaborative research group of faculty and students across disciplines—law, computer science, and conflict resolution—to overcome barriers regarding effective online civic engagement. The goal of this pilot program is to engage individuals in how to participate in rulemaking and to provide meaningful public comments. As part of the program, CeRi has been working with the DOT to provide an online venue or the Regulation Room for individuals to discuss proposed rules (Regulation Room n.d.).

Interestingly, one of the first proposed rules discussed in the Regulation Room was the Department of Transportation's peanut rule. This particular rulemaking discussion received over 24,000 visits to the Regulation Room website and provided a means for the agency to reach stakeholders to understand how to participate and ways to read the proposed rule. The Regulation Room, according to Lipowicz (2011), has moderators to help explain information, and key points for each rule instead of having someone try to read through a lengthy government document. Nonetheless, these examples demonstrate ways agencies such as the DOT are trying to enable us to participate in a process we might not have heard about before reading this chapter. Before we conclude the chapter, we offer our everyday citizen connection section. This segment uncovers how you can help to encourage regulatory innovation.

Everyday Citizen Connection

You already know from reading this chapter that regulations impact your everyday life, from eating peanuts on a plane, to smoking e-cigarettes, to the practices of Sunny's dry cleaners. But how can you make a difference beyond submitting a public comment on the *Federal Register* or attending a public hearing? The vast majority of college students are extremely technologically savvy. Because of this, you can make regulations better. Students just like you are enhancing regulatory compliance. If you have a friend who attends Sonoma Tech or Clemson University, you might want to reach out to them. Why? Sonoma Technology developed air-beam sensors that can be placed in the palm of your hand to track air pollution when you are walking down the street. These data from your palm device could then be reported back to a central computer system. Clemson University developed Intelligent River, which monitors pollution in rivers using geospatial sensors (Giles 2014). So why not use this information to team up with your computer science classmate to create an app for the *Federal Register* or Regulations.gov?

Not everyone has the background to develop a new sensor, so what can you do if you are a policy wonk? We suggest taking notes from students at the University of Pennsylvania (UPenn). UPenn has a forum called RegX. The goal of this forum is to bring all the regulatory players together—businesses, students, faculty, regulators, and the public to create the "regulatory excellence molecule" (Coglianese 2015). Through information sharing across entities, RegX wants to demonstrate how far-reaching and impactful regulations are—from environmental protection, to financial risks, to preventing disease. RegX might sound expensive or a difficult endeavor to pull off. If you love policy, why not start your own campus forum? Use one of your own student organizations to invite a panel of guests to discuss a regulatory topic. Or have your local state regulatory affairs experts come to campus to explain the rule-writing process, why it is important, and internship opportunities. This could inform others across campus about the far-reaching aspects of regulation and how they might get a job after graduation.

Discovery Question:

Visit your campus homepage. What types of regulations do you think impact your own campus on a daily basis? Why? Are these regulations beneficial or a hindrance?

CONCLUDING THOUGHTS

In this chapter we provided public policy students a roadmap to understanding regulatory policy from process (rulemaking) to implementation (compliance). The rulemaking process occurs over several stages: from pre-rule, to notice of proposed rulemaking, to final rule; but most important, it allows for public input into agency decision making. Technological advances, such as Federal Register 2.0, Regulations.gov, or Cornell University's Regulation Room, are recent attempts to engage us to become involved in agency policymaking. Moreover, the work of a regulator should not go unnoticed, since these individuals ensure that those who are regulated are in compliance with the law.

We encourage students to continue to think about and research this part of public policy due to the ever-increasing federal congressional gridlock. Because of congressional gridlock, it does not mean that policymaking has come to a halt; instead, we should focus our attention on the role of federal and state agencies in U.S. public policymaking. Increasing our knowledge about how and why policies are made within administrative agencies is important for the future of public policy more broadly.

GLOSSARY TERMS

Administrative Procedure Act (APA) of 1946   77
delegation of authority   76
intention-based style   88

mix of enforcement styles   88
precision-based style   88
regulation   74
rule   77

shift of responsibility   76
statutory law   74

DISCUSSION QUESTIONS

1. Go to the *Federal Register* and find a final rule of your choice. Upon selection, how would you trace this rule through the stages of the federal rulemaking process? Did you include all of the stages? Why or why not?

2. U.S. regulations are not created in a vacuum. In what ways are other branches of government involved or influence agency decision making? Which branch of government do you think is most influential and why?

3. Often, citizens are concerned that the U.S. bureaucracy yields too much power in decision making. What are the ways the other branches of government can hold state and federal level agencies accountable?

4. What is the U.S. *Federal Register*, and how can someone submit a public comment for agency consideration? Why is it important for citizens to access and influence the rulemaking process?

5. Out of the future alternatives for regulatory policy, which approach will engender the most participation from U.S. citizens?

6. Take two class periods and design an agency public hearing simulation based upon a state or federal rule. Divide the class into groups—agency experts (conduct the hearing), citizen group (provides public comment), and pro/con groups pertaining to the rule. Discuss the differences between substantive comments versus value-laden comments and how an agency reconciles to inform the language of a rule.

SUGGESTED RESOURCES

Suggested Websites

Federal Register, https://www.federalregister.gov/
Regulations.gov, https://www.regulations.gov/

Suggested Books or Articles

Goodsell, Charles T. 2004. *A Case for Bureaucracy: A Public Administration Polemic.* Washington, DC: CQ Press.

Kerwin, Cornelius, and Scott Furlong. 2011. *Rulemaking: How Government Agencies Write Law and Make Policy.* Washington, DC: CQ Press.

Pautz, Michelle C., and Sara R. Rinfret. 2013. *The Lilliputians of Environmental Regulation: The Perspective of State Regulators.* New York: Routledge.

Suggested Films

The Cove, DVD, directed by Louie Psihoyos (2009: United States), http://www.imdb.com/title/tt1313104/

Fed Up, DVD, directed by Stephanie Soechtig (2014: United States), http://www.imdb.com/title/tt2381335/?ref_=nv_sr_1

Food, Inc., DVD, directed by Robert Kenner (2009: United States), http://www.imdb.com/title/tt1286537/?ref_=fn_al_tt_1

NOTES

1. U.S. presidents can also use executive orders to drive regulatory processes, but these are based upon congressional law or statute.

2. See Montana's official state website: http://liv.mt.gov/public/goals.mcpx.

for CQ Press

Sharpen your skills with SAGE edge at **http://edge.sagepub.com/rinfret.** **SAGE edge for students** provides a personalized approach to help you accomplish your coursework goals in an easy-to-use learning environment.

Economic Policy and Public Budgeting

with Emily Kaylor

5

GREEN EGGS AND HAM AND THE FEDERAL GOVERNMENT SHUTDOWN IN 2013

In 2013, congressional Republicans and the Obama White House could not agree on the federal budget, and it was during this time that Sen. Ted Cruz (R-Texas) read the classic Dr. Seuss tale *Green Eggs and Ham* on the Senate floor. After all, during a filibuster, the politician holding the floor of the chamber can talk about whatever he likes, so long as he keeps talking and remain standing. It is also worth mentioning that bathroom breaks are not permitted. Recitation of the widely known children's story was just a part of Senator Cruz's efforts to filibuster the federal budget days before funding of the federal government was set to run out.

The federal government—like any other organization—has a budget, and to operate, Congress must pass a budget each fiscal year, which runs October 1 through September 30. The then-freshman senator from Texas launched a filibuster, lasting over twenty-one hours, in an effort to stop Congress from passing the budget and forcing the federal government to shut down (O'Keefe and Kane 2013). Although Senator Cruz's filibuster focused on efforts to undo the Affordable Care Act (ACA), also known as "Obamacare," he and his like-minded congressional colleagues were able to bring the daily operations of the federal government to a halt, since a federal budget was not passed into law for the start of the federal fiscal year on October 1, 2013—which was also the date the ACA took effect. The shutdown lasted from October 1–16, 2013.

Federal government shutdowns are not uncommon in U.S. history, but it had been nearly twenty years since such an event had happened. We examine the causes of the shutdown and the implications for government and citizens alike as we study economic policy and public budgeting. The federal

LEARNING OBJECTIVES

Readers of this chapter will be able to:

1. Articulate foundational concepts associated with economic policy and the involvement of the federal government

2. Explain key indicators of the economic condition of an economy

3. Differentiate between monetary and fiscal policy

4. Discuss the intricacies of the federal budget process at a macro level

5. Identify key statutes and government agencies involved in economic policy

government has to operate with a budget, but unlike individuals or businesses, that budget has to be passed by Congress. In the fall of 2013, President Barack Obama faced opposition from the Republicans, who retained control of the House of Representatives, while the Democrats controlled the Senate. Both parties were deeply divided over a host of issues, including the levels of spending by the federal government and spending that pertained to the looming implementation of the Affordable Care Act, the president's signature health care law passed in 2010. As both parties dug their heels into their opposition of each other's priorities, they were unable to come together to pass a budget for the 2014 federal fiscal year, which would start on October 1, 2013. Without a budget, the federal government stopped working and the shutdown lasted sixteen days before both sides came together to get the government back up and running.

The federal government shutdown—what does that really mean? More than one million federal government employees had to report to work anyway, even though the government shutdown meant their time cards and paychecks were not being processed. Federal employees who were deemed essential—mostly individuals whose jobs dealt with national security, including the members of the Capitol police force—still had to go to work. Everyone else had to stay home. And before you think this would be great, remember that the millions of federal employees had bills to pay, including rent and mortgage payments, and were told they could not do their jobs for the foreseeable future. For instance, environmental inspectors at the U.S. Environmental Protection Agency (EPA) were told, Do not come to work, there is no need to inspect facilities that might be polluting the nation's environment, and there is no need to process permit applications for companies that want to build new facilities to manufacture goods. The national parks and Smithsonian museums were also shut down because park rangers and museum guides were deemed nonessential. Accordingly, all those tourists on vacation hoping to enjoy the nation's parks and museums found closed signs. Americans who depended on assistance from the government, including Women-Infant-Children programs and some low-income housing assistance, did not get their aid, either. The American public became irate with Congress, and after more than two weeks the shutdown ended and the federal government resumed normal operations. Interestingly enough, the government shutdown ended up costing taxpayers more than if the government had remained open (Carroll 2014).

This story reminds us that although topics such as economic policy and the federal government budget may seem unappealing and with little direct effect on our lives, that simply could not be further from the truth. Finally, it bears repeating that the federal government is the nation's single largest employer and major driver of the nation's economy, so anything other than "business as usual" can have major effects on the nation's economic well-being and impact the world economy.

OVERVIEW OF ECONOMIC POLICY AND PUBLIC BUDGETING

The health of a nation is tied in large measure to the health and stability of its economy. Simply put, the **economy** refers to the wealth and resources of a particular region or country; also included are the goods and services produced and consumed and the value ascribed to them and their management. In other words, the economy of the United States is comprised of all the resources, from people and natural resources, including coal, and the utilization of those resources to produce goods and services—including cars and schools—and how those goods and services are managed and consumed. Within the United States, there are smaller economies, including state economies (indeed, California on its own has an economy far bigger than many countries), and regional economies. The management of those economies varies, depending upon the types of economic structures in place.

Types of Economies and Economic Policy Definition

The type of economy a region or a nation has sets the contours of the policies that govern that economy. While there are many ways to classify economies, we start with the most basic types. On one side of the spectrum is a **free-market or laissez-faire economy**, in which goods and services are produced in the market as determined by the demand of consumers and the supply of producers without any interference by government. The market refers to the venue or institution in which the exchange of goods and services occurs. At the other end of the spectrum is a **command or centrally planned economy**, in which the government controls all aspects of the economy and owns everything. In this type, the government determines what goods and services will be produced and owns and operates the producers. The former Soviet Union is an example of this economic form.

Economies around the world and in the United States operate at various points along this spectrum in some combination or mix of these two extremes. Many countries, including the United States, have a **capitalist economy**, in which the market largely determines the production and consumption of goods and services, but there is a role—albeit limited—for the government. In the case of the United States, for example, the federal government sets workplace safety standards for employees who make consumer electronics and ensures that products sold in the market meet minimum safety standards. However, the government does not control or dictate the types of electronic devices that are available to consumers; nor does it tell consumers what to buy.

The involvement of government in the economy brings us to a formal definition of economic policy. **Economic policy** is the umbrella term used to encapsulate any number of public policies related to the economy, including decisions about taxation, government spending, and subsidies for various industry sectors. Views on economic policy are often rooted in various approaches to the economy or preferences about the role of the economy and government. These different views are rooted in several theoretical perspectives on the economy.

Economic Theories

If you have ever taken an introductory economics course or read an article about the economy, you probably read words such as *laissez-faire, Keynes,* or *trickle-down.* Here we take a quick dive into three of the most common economic theories: classical, Keynesian, and supply-side. Keep in mind there are numerous other economic theories to study, but these will get you started with a basic understanding of some different approaches.

Classical economic theory draws on laissez-faire ideas whereby individuals act according to their own self-interests to make economic decisions. Additionally, classical theorists teach that consumer spending drives a country's overall economic growth. This school of economic thought believes that markets function best with little or no government intervention: a free market. The great classical economic theorists include John Stuart Mill and Adam Smith. Mill based much of his economic and philosophical thought on utilitarianism, accepting government intervention in the market only to provide the greatest happiness for the greatest number of people. Smith, best known for *The Wealth of Nations*, argued that rational self-interest and competition lead to national economic prosperity. If sellers are left to compete freely without government intervention, supply and demand will reach equilibrium as sellers are forced to match prices or offer the consumer something better.

In contrast, John Maynard Keynes, father of **Keynesian economic theory**, believed that government intervention was necessary for a successful market. Aggregate demand, or total spending, drives economic output and is influenced by public and private economic decisions. Rather than affecting prices in the marketplace, this theory contends that changes in aggregate demand affect employment. Unlike classical economic theory, Keynesian economics teaches that government spending spurs growth. These economists support government intervention, though limited, to recover from periods of recession. A good example of Keynesian economics in action was Franklin Delano Roosevelt's New Deal program in the wake of the Great Depression.

Finally, **supply-side economic theory** reasons that capital investment and lowering barriers, such as tax rates and government regulations, lead to economic growth. Supply-side economics believes in some government intervention to implement policies that reduce regulatory burdens on producers. These policies could include reducing the frequency with which businesses must report sales taxes or allowing for an online registration process to save time and money for a start-up company that must be licensed. None of these economic theories eliminates government intervention, but it aims to provide the least restrictive government regulation. This limited government approach is associated with the "trickle-down" economic policies most attributed to President Ronald Reagan. Trickle-down theorists contend that tax cuts and other incentives for investors and businesses at the top will lead to economic benefits for those at the bottom.

SIZE AND SCOPE OF THE U.S. ECONOMY

Before we get too caught up in the various aspects of government involved in the U.S. economy, we need to start by grasping the current size and scope of the economy, which also enables us more fully to comprehend the magnitude of shutting down the federal government and its effects on the economy. Measuring the economy of any nation (and even state economies) is generally done by assessing its **gross domestic product (GDP)**. The GDP is the nation's total production of goods and services for a single year. GDP for the United States is over $19 trillion, representing about a quarter of the entire world's GDP. In 2016, the U.S. GDP grew by 1.5 percent, which was over 1 percent slower than in 2015 (U.S. Bureau of Economic Analysis 2017). Later in the chapter we will look at the history and growth of U.S. GDP.

GDP is just one of several measures that are used to assess the size and scale of an economy. Other important measures, including unemployment rates and inflation rates, help to understand the overall health of an economy. The **unemployment rate** is the percentage of people in an economy who are looking for work but do not have a job. It is important to remember that the unemployment rate does not account for the people who do not have a job and may not want one, for the people who cannot work due to illness or disability, or for the people who may have given up looking for a job. In the United States, the Bureau of Labor Statistics (BLS) tracks these figures and reports them monthly. In 2016, the U.S. unemployment rate averaged 4.9 percent (U.S. Bureau of Labor Statistics 2017). Table 5.1 provides historical unemployment figures in the United States (U.S. Bureau of Labor Statistics 2017).

For a healthy and robust economy, a nation would want its unemployment rate to be as low as possible. Most economists will agree that since there will always be fluctuation as people leave jobs and search for others, there will always be some percentage of unemployment—often referred to as the natural unemployment rate. As a point of historical comparison, during the Great Depression, unemployment rates in the United States peaked at around 25 percent.

Another measure of an economy's health is its inflation rate. **Inflation** is the rise in the cost of the same basket of goods over time; it is a measure of the purchasing power of the dollar. Put differently, inflation is essentially the rise in the price for a gallon of milk year to year (and any other goods and services, for that matter). If the price of a gallon of milk increases each year, you need more money to buy the same gallon of milk over time, which means the purchasing power of your dollar is going down because you can buy less with it. This can be problematic for the health of an economy, and periods of massive rises in inflation rates are known as **hyperinflation**. However, some level of inflation is a good sign for an economy. By contrast, **deflation** is the drop in the price of the same goods over time; deflation may seem like a positive, since purchasing power rises, but it is not. When goods and services are cheaper over time, the decline in prices indicates an economy in which the supply for products exceeds demand for them. And then prices have to be discounted and firms take losses for the excess inventory, which means profits go down, adversely impacting the stock market. In an economy, the pursuit is equilibrium between demand and supply for goods and services.

Inflation is typically assessed via the Consumer Price Index (CPI). The U.S. Bureau of Labor Statistics computes the CPI by pricing a basket of goods that includes items ranging from breakfast cereal and milk, to televisions, to airline tickets, to postage stamps, to haircuts (U.S. Bureau of Labor Statistics 2016). Table 5.2 displays CPI and the percentage change (U.S. Census Bureau 2012).

The measures of the economy discussed thus far inform overall assessments of the state of an economy and help observers make conclusions about whether the economy is growing or contracting. Typically, a healthy economy is one that is growing—meaning it is increasing in the goods and services that are produced and consumed. Accordingly, Americans and elected officials are particularly focused on economic growth. Economists will often describe that economies follow cycles of growth and contraction, brought on by various forces. Figure 5.1 depicts the growth and contraction of the U.S. economy in terms of percentage change in U.S. GDP.

Periods of prolonged contraction in GDP are referred to as economic recessions, and if that contraction continues, then it is termed

TABLE 5.1

U.S. Annual Unemployment Rates, 1995–2016

Year	Unemployment Rate
1995	5.6
1996	5.4
1997	4.9
1998	4.5
1999	4.2
2000	4.0
2001	4.7
2002	5.8
2003	6.0
2004	5.5
2005	5.1
2006	4.6
2007	4.6
2008	5.8
2009	9.3
2010	9.6
2011	8.9
2012	8.1
2013	7.4
2014	6.2
2015	5.3
2016	4.9

Source: U.S. Bureau of Labor Statistics.

TABLE 5.2

U.S. Consumer Price Index, 1990–2010

Year	Consumer Price Index	Percent Change
1990	130.7	5.4
1995	152.4	2.8
1998	163.0	1.6
1999	166.6	2.2
2000	172.2	3.4
2001	177.1	2.8
2002	179.9	1.6
2003	184.0	2.3
2004	188.9	2.7
2005	195.3	3.4
2006	201.6	3.2
2007	207.3	2.8
2008	215.3	3.8
2009	214.5	–0.4
2010	218.1	1.6

Source: U.S. Bureau of Labor Statistics, CPI Detailed Report-January 2017, page 90.

an economic depression. A **recession** is defined by economists as two or more quarters of negative economic growth—or declines in GDP. Recessions may also be marked by rises in unemployment rates and declines in consumer spending. The United States experienced an economic recession in 2008. However, politicians may refer to any slowdown in economic growth—even if there is slow growth—as a recession for political purposes. Sustained, long-term negative growth of the economy is referred to as a **depression**. The United States experienced a period of economic contraction, better known as the Great Depression, beginning with the stock market crash of 1929 and continuing into the 1930s. During this time, GDP fell by more than 30 percent.

Public Opinion and the Economy

So far we have covered a lot of terms and ways of measuring the robustness of the economy; here, we focus on what Americans think about the economy and their consumption of that information. Americans routinely indicate that the state of the economy is a driving factor in their opinions about politics and which politicians they support. In presidential elections, the health of the economy is often a predictor of whether an incumbent president will be reelected. And with some other areas of public policy, such as environmental policy, public support for various policy initiatives is typically only feasible when the economy is robust. In periods of economic downturn, Americans are unlikely to support policy efforts in "quality of life" areas, as they are more focused on the economy improving. In the lead-up to the presidential election in 2016, Americans were mixed in their opinions about the economy under President Obama. According to an ABC News/*Washington Post* poll, 49 percent of respondents said they were about the same in terms of their financial situation from when Obama became president, while the remaining 50 percent were evenly split between reporting they were better or worse off (ABC News/*Washington Post* Poll 2015). Heading into the 2016 presidential election, 53 percent of Americans thought the economic conditions of the nation were good in September 2016, up more than eight points since the spring of that year (Kopan and Agiesta 2016). Six months into the Trump administration, views of the new president's handling of the economy were mixed, with 43 percent approving and 41 percent disapproving of his performance (Struyk and Hauk 2017).

In addition to assessments about one's own financial situations, Americans share with pollsters their opinions about the broader economy and tax structure. In a CNN/ORC poll in February 2016, 71 percent of respondents said the economic system in the United States generally favors the wealthy, whereas only 27 percent said the system is fair to all. Regarding taxes, polls over time indicate Americans do not think the wealthy and corporations pay their fair share. The same ABC News/*Washington Post* poll mentioned above found that 65 percent of respondents thought corporations paid too little in taxes, while 19 percent said they paid their fair share, and only 9 percent thought corporations paid too much in taxes. A Gallup poll asked similar questions about individual taxes and found that 61 percent of its respondents thought the wealthy in America paid too little in taxes.

FIGURE 5.1

Growth and Contraction of the U.S. Economy, 1930–2016

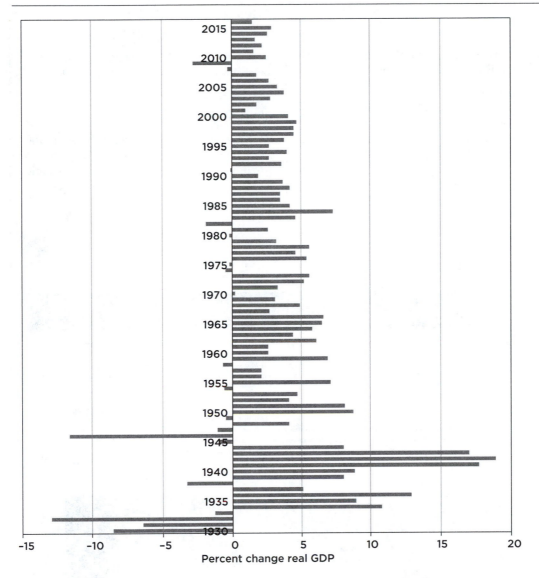

Source: Chart made from Bureau of Economic Analysis data: http://www.bea.gov/national/index.htm#gdp.

In this chapter's Telling Stories with Data section, you can unpack some of these opinions by exploring the data in your local area. These opinions are likely informed by the complexities of economic policy. In the subsequent sections, we consider the primary types of economic policy—monetary and fiscal—and then explore the public budgeting process, along with government expenditures and revenues.

Box 5.1: Telling Stories with Data

Using the Bureau of Labor Statistics to Explore Regional Economic Data

The discussion of economic policy to date has focused on national-level data. While the health of the economy is important nationally, it is also essential to explore data on a state and even regional level. After all, for many voters, everything is local, especially the economy. On the Bureau of Labor Statistics website (https:// www.bls.gov/), you can scroll down a bit and find economic information by region and state. Go there and explore data for your home state.

What do you think?

How does your state or region compare to the condition of the national economy? How might differences in state versus national economic condition affect your neighbors when they vote for political candidates?

FIGURE 5.2

Bureau of Labor Statistics

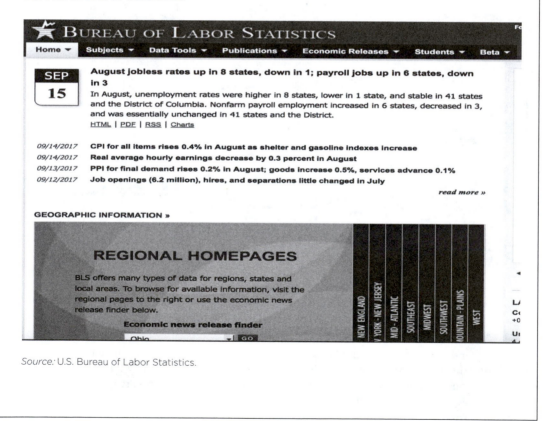

Source: U.S. Bureau of Labor Statistics.

Monetary and Fiscal Policy

The health of the economy is a function of both monetary and fiscal policy. **Monetary policy** deals with decisions concerning the supply of a nation's money, while **fiscal policy** is the term for government decisions surrounding the revenues it takes in and how it spends that money. Taken together, monetary and fiscal policy comprise the economic policies of a nation.

Monetary policy has a significant impact on a nation's economy, since it is the way that the money supply is controlled. In other words, the volume of currency out for people to have in their wallets and for banks to loan is a function of the government's efforts to control that supply. At first glance, this may make little sense, but remember: U.S. currency (just like many other currencies around the world) is little more than the fancy paper, replete with counterfeiting prevention technologies, it is printed on. The American dollar has value because we think it does, not because it is backed up by anything of value. Initially, U.S. currency was backed by gold and silver. This meant that anyone holding U.S. dollars could go to a bank and get the equivalent amount of precious metals; this was a means of ensuring faith in the paper money that was used in transactions. In the twentieth century, most nations abandoned this standard. Now, paper money in the United States has value because we can exchange it for goods and services. Accordingly, the federal government via the Federal Reserve System controls how much paper currency (and coins, for that matter) is available in the economy as a means of ensuring its value. This is monetary policy in a nutshell. If the federal government wanted to pay off its debts, for example, it could simply order the U.S. Mint to print more dollar bills, and then that money could be used to retire our debts. But if the Mint printed truckloads of dollars, would those dollars be worth the same amount to the nation's creditors? Simply put: no, they would not. Maintaining a delicate balance of money in the economy is tremendously important.

The Federal Reserve System, or the Fed for short, is essentially the central banking system for the United States. Many other nations have national banks, and the United States did have formal central banks—remember the Bank of the United States?—but Congress allowed those bank charters to expire, and the current system has been in place since 1913. The Fed is largely outside the control of politicians, even though the president appoints the members of the Board of Governors, but those terms are fixed and staggered. To control the nation's money supply and endeavor to maintain the health of the economy, the Fed lends money to member banks at "discount rates" determined by the Fed; buys and sells Treasury bonds; and ensures that banks are in compliance with regulations, including the reserve requirements.

Let us work through an example to help us understand basic operations of the banking system to explore how the Fed controls the money supply. When consumers go to the bank and deposit money, banks in turn use this money to lend to other individuals (e.g., student loans, mortgages, car loans) or to firms. When you borrow money from the bank, you get a sum of money—let us say, enough to buy a house for $150,000. But because the bank is loaning you money, the bank has to generate a profit, so you are charged an interest rate. In 2017, mortgage rates were about 4 percent for a thirty-year, fixed-rate mortgage. So you have thirty years to pay the bank back the $150,000 you borrowed, at the rate of 4 percent a year. This means you will end up paying the bank back about $257,800.

To loan you the money, the bank uses deposits from its various account holders to come up with that sum of money. As a result, the bank does not actually have on hand the money all of its depositors have in their accounts at that bank. Under normal circumstances, this is not a big deal, since the likelihood that all the depositors are going to show up at the bank tomorrow and ask for all their money is highly unlikely.

The Federal Reserve, or Fed for short, requires banks to keep a certain percentage of all the money depositors have in that bank on hand at all times—this is known as the reserve requirement (or cash reserve ratio). During the day-to-day operations of a bank, its cash reserves fluctuate and the bank may need to borrow money to make sure it complies with the reserve requirement. The Fed sets the interest rate at which banks borrow cash from one another. If the Fed wants more money in the economy, it will lower the interest rate so it becomes cheaper to borrow money. If the Fed wants less money in the economy, it will increase the interest rate so it becomes more expensive to borrow money. Since the financial crisis of 2008, the Fed has held these interest rates at historic lows, which ultimately results in an increase in the money supply and very low interest rates.

As mentioned in the example of the home loan, mortgage rates today are around 3 or 4 percent, which is extremely low. In the early 1990s, mortgage rates were about 10 percent, down from highs of 17 and 18 percent in the early 1980s. Compare these figures to the example mentioned earlier, and now the total amount due to the bank with a 10 percent rate is $473,890, or $769,865 with a 17 percent rate. By making it cheaper to get loans today, the Fed is encouraging people to borrow money and invest in homes, college educations, cars, new business ventures, and so forth to stimulate the economy. Keep in mind, though, that too much spending will ultimately drive up prices and increase CPI—and therefore inflation—since demand goes up. The Fed engages in a delicate balancing act of keeping the money supply in line with promoting economic growth—but not too much, because then inflation can be a major problem. Controlling the supply of money and how cheap it is for individuals and firms to borrow money is a bit more complicated than presented here, but this is the general gist of the efforts.

Fiscal policy, by contrast, is a bit more straightforward. Simply put, fiscal policy comprises the decisions the government makes about its revenues and its expenditures. It was fiscal policy that shut down the federal government in the fall of 2013. It is fiscal policy that rankles many Americans as April 15 looms every year and taxes are due to the Internal Revenue Service (IRS). And it is fiscal policy that determines government spending on public health programs, Social Security, new warplanes, environmental protection, and everything else. Unlike monetary policy, which is largely removed from politicians and politics, fiscal policy is under the control of Congress and the White House. To delve into the particulars of government spending and revenues, we begin by exploring the basics of the federal budget and its process.

THE FEDERAL BUDGET

We delved deeply into economic theory and policies to establish a foundation that enables us to understand budgets, which are essential for implementing any public policy. Individuals, families, businesses, and governments all rely on budgets to properly manage their revenues and expenses. Budgets are not just numbers on spreadsheets. According to the Government Finance Officers Association, budgets are policy documents, financial plans, operations guides, and communications devices.

You might be wondering how a budget can express policy or communicate executive initiatives. Looking at a budget and its history shows trends in priorities and ideas.

For example, if the president proposes a new grant program to encourage housing development in urban areas, it must be funded in the budget. A new line item will be included to demonstrate the administration's commitment to this initiative, and the amount of the money it allocates to the new program can convey to the public how important it is to fund. Additionally, if the president thinks an agency has not been allocating its resources properly, the president may reduce the funding to that agency. There may never be a quote or an article written about the inefficiencies of the agency, but if its funding goes down in the president's budget proposal, then it can communicate that POTUS does not think the agency is doing its job.

Budget Process

The budget process is probably much more complicated than it should be. Below is a broad overview of the process (see Figure 5.3). However, what is supposed to happen and what actually happens are two very different realities. Let us start with a discussion of what should happen.

Agencies are supposed to submit budget requests to the Office of Management and Budget (OMB) in the fall, generally requested by October 1, since that is when the fiscal year starts and OMB believes agencies should have all the data they need to provide projections for the next fiscal year. OMB officials review the agency requests that may require more information or modifications from the agency and they compile the recommended budget, which is sent to the president in January and must be submitted to Congress by the first Monday in February. By mid-February the Congressional Budget Office (CBO) should provide budget and economic outlook reports to the Senate and House Budget Committees, which must report a concurrent resolution by April 1. A concurrent resolution must be passed by both chambers of Congress but does not require a presidential signature because it does not have the full force and effect of a law. This concurrent budget resolution is formulated through committee hearings with the consideration of the president's requests and the CBO reports. Since the House and Senate usually pass different versions of the resolution, members of Congress work out the differences in conference committee (as discussed in Chapter 1) before finalizing the concurrent budget resolution by April 15.

As stated above, this budget resolution does not go to the president for signature or veto and is not law. Therefore, appropriations bills must be passed to accumulate into a budget bill that requires presidential approval. House and Senate appropriations subcommittees formulate the twenty-four appropriations bills, one per committee. However, tradition says that appropriations, like tax and revenue-raising bills, originate in the House and are sent to the Senate for approval or amendments. As with the budget resolution, if the appropriations bills from each chamber look different, then they must be reconciled in conference committee by the end of June. The final versions are sent to the president for their signature of approval or veto decision.

Now, here is an overview of how the budget is created in recent fiscal years. Generally speaking, the internal processes of the agencies and OMB happen close to their suggested timelines. Additionally, the president usually gets the budget request to Congress by early February. Congress is where the process seems to fall prey to politics and the slow nature of the legislature. If the appropriations bills are not passed and signed by October 1, the start of the fiscal year, Congress must pass a continuing resolution to ensure that agencies continue to receive funding (and this is what did not happen during the 2013 government shutdown).

FIGURE 5.3

Overview of the Federal Budget Process

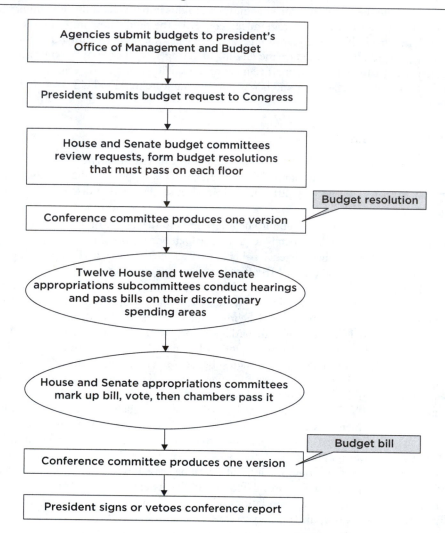

This allows the government to function and people not to experience a gap in benefits while Congress works out its differences and hopefully agrees upon a proper budget. All twelve necessary appropriations bills have been promptly enacted only four times since fiscal year 1977, while in all the other fiscal years at least one continuing resolution was needed (Tollestrup 2014). In the absence of a continuing resolution or appropriations bills, a government shutdown occurs, as was the case in 1995 and 2013, among the eighteen other funding gaps in U.S. history.

There are many forces that drive the budget process and create obstacles. The threat of a government shutdown is one that most politicians do not want to have to explain to their constituents. Election cycles play into this fear, but sometimes legislators' constituencies are pressuring them to let the shutdown happen to prove a point to Washington and its wasteful spending habits. Adding to the complications of the budget process is revenue forecasting. The budget is based on revenue projections that are imperfect. There are five common revenue forecasting methods, each of which will provide a different number on which to base a budget, which makes the process even more unpredictable.

Government Revenues and Expenditures

In order to fully understand the budget, you must realize where the government gets its money and how it distributes it to various programs.

Revenues

In fiscal year 2016, the U.S. government raised approximately $3.2 trillion (Congressional Budget Office 2017). This massive amount of revenue is made up of a variety of taxes and fees that the government levies on its citizens. As can be seen in Figure 5.4, individual income taxes make up the majority—almost half—of all revenue for the federal government. The second-highest revenue source is payroll taxes, which include disability insurance, hospital insurance, and other social insurance taxes. In general, the main source of revenue for the federal government is the personal income tax, while states rely on sales taxes and localities rely on property taxes. Many of the other

FIGURE 5.4

Federal Government Revenues, 2016 (in billions of U.S. dollars)

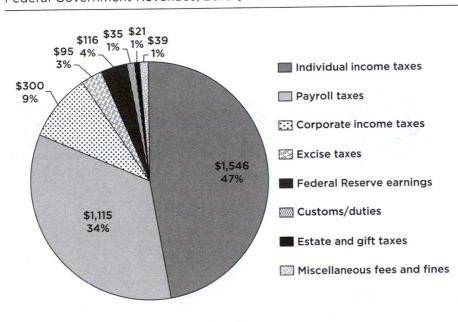

Source: Congressional Budget Office, January 2016.

taxes are self-explanatory, but you may be wondering about excise taxes. Excise taxes are those paid when one purchases a certain good. For the federal government, its major source of excise tax revenue is gasoline. While gas only makes up approximately 3 percent of the annual revenues for the government, you may feel the burden of the gas tax when you go to fill up your car next time.

The main source of revenue is individual income taxes. Table 5.3 shows the seven tax brackets for 2016 and how an individual's rate changes depending on the method of filing: single, married filing jointly, married filing separately, or head of household. The income tax is administered by the Internal Revenue Service, a bureau of the U.S. Treasury Department. In order to change the tax code, Congress has to pass legislation. The president can make recommendations for tax changes, but Article I, Section 7, of the U.S. Constitution requires that all bills raising revenue must originate in the House of Representatives and then receive Senate approval and presidential signature. The tax code is complicated by a series of credits and deductions that individuals can take advantage of to reduce their tax burden. Credits are items that can be subtracted from the tax dollar number that you owe while deductions are subtracted from your income before calculating your tax. As of January 2017 there were twenty-one credits and twenty-nine deductions in the federal tax code, such as the earned income tax credit, education credits, charitable contributions deduction, mortgage interest credit, and student loan interest deduction. These credits and deductions provide individuals with ways to save money but also reduce the tax base, which reduces government revenue.

Expenditures

The U.S. government spent about $3.8 trillion in fiscal year 2016. Figure 5.5 shows how the spending is split up among mandatory programs, discretionary funds, and interest on the debt. While reading or talking about the federal government's budget problems, you may have heard the terms *mandatory* and *discretionary spending*, but not fully understood

TABLE 5.3

Federal Income Tax Brackets, 2016

2016 Tax Rate	Single Filers Income	Married Filing Jointly Income	Married Filing Separately Income	Head of Household Income
10%	Up to $9,275	Up to $18,550	Up to $9,275	Up to $13,250
15%	$9,276 to $37,650	$18,551 to $75,300	$9,276 to $37,650	$13,251 to $50,400
25%	$37,651 to $91,150	$75,301 to $151,900	$37,651 to $75,950	$50,401 to $130,150
28%	$91,151 to $190,150	$151,901 to $231,450	$75,951 to $115,275	$130,151 to $210,800
33%	$190,151 to $413,350	$231,451 to $413,350	$115,726 to $206,675	$210,801 to $413,350
35%	$413,351 to $415,050	$413,351 to $466,950	$206,676 to $233,475	$413,351 to $441,000
39.6%	$415,051 or more	$466,951 or more	$233,476 or more	$441,001 or more

Source: Courtesy of Department of the Treasury, *Your Federal Income Tax, 2017*.

FIGURE 5.5
Federal Government Spending, 2016 (in billions of dollars)

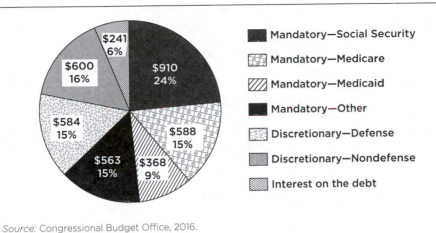

Mandatory—Social Security
Mandatory—Medicare
Mandatory—Medicaid
Mandatory—Other
Discretionary—Defense
Discretionary—Nondefense
Interest on the debt

Source: Congressional Budget Office, 2016.

what they mean. Mandatory spending is required by existing law and generally consists of social programs like Medicare, Social Security, and veterans' benefits. This is money that Congress cannot touch when drawing up the budget and generally comprises about 60 percent of the spending budget. Out of the $3.8 trillion spent in fiscal year 2016, $2.4 trillion was mandatory (Congressional Budget Office 2017). That means Congress only had $1.4 trillion to "play with" when trying to balance the budget. However, the interest on the debt can also be considered **mandatory spending** and out of congressional reach. So that leaves us with discretionary spending. **Discretionary spending** consists of defense and nondefense spending. Fiscal year 2016 defense spending totaled $584 billion, approximately $139 billion of which was spent on personnel. The remaining defense money goes to operation and maintenance, procurement, research and development, and military construction that includes family housing. Nondefense spending, totaling $600 billion in fiscal year 2016, is really what Congress looks at when it talks about making cuts. This spending includes things like transportation, health, international affairs, justice, natural resources, community development, commerce, administration costs, and many other general categories (Congressional Budget Office 2017). It is important to know the difference between mandatory and discretionary spending so that you can have a better understanding of the impact that they have on the deficit and debt, and why these problems cannot change overnight.

Debt and Deficit

When the government spends more than it receives in a given year, it experiences a **deficit**. The **debt** is the accumulation of each year's deficit, or how much the U.S. government owes. As explained above, in fiscal year 2016, the U.S. government spent $587 billion more dollars than it raised, so that would be its 2016 deficit. This $587 billion deficit adds to the already accumulated multitrillion debt held by the public.

The United States has always had publicly held debt. It started after the Revolutionary War, when the Compromise of 1790 was reached and the national government assumed the states' debts. Since then, we have pretty much always been in debt as a country—and, of course, some times have been worse than others. War generally results in a lot of borrowing, and World War II was the largest debt as a ratio of GDP we have probably ever seen. Debt during the world wars was generally financed through the sale of U.S. Treasury bonds. Since the days of Harry S. Truman, the largest debt to GDP increase occurred during the Reagan administration, while the best decreases occurred during the Truman, Clinton, and Eisenhower administrations (Clemons 2012). The federal debt to GDP ratio drastically climbed during George W. Bush's presidency, due in large part to the Iraq invasion and in response to the Great Recession, but it has been on the decline and is generally projected to continue its downward trend. However, with the debt currently exceeding $20 trillion, a debt-free United States seems a distant dream.

As with almost anything in public policy, there are pros and cons to the debt. Borrowing in the short term can be good to spur economic growth. As was the case in the Great Recession, President Bush's administration tried to anticipate the pending recession by providing tax credits and business investment incentives that reduced government revenues. The revenue reduction meant the government had to borrow more, and when the recession really hit, only the passage of the American Recovery and Reinvestment Act could provide the necessary spark for struggling businesses and workers. Debt allows a government to function and perform public services like building infrastructure in its most desperate times. However, as is seen now, with about 6 percent of government spending going to it, interest on the debt is a huge problem and a large expense. With any loan, there is interest, and interest compounds. You may be paying the interest on your student loans for years before actually making payments on your principal. It is the same with the government debt. The debt sits there and accumulates interest at varying rates. This is a negative on debts and why borrowing money is not a sustainable method of running a public or private entity. When a government is forced to allocate funds to pay off large debts, then it is less prepared for any crisis that may arise and require millions of dollars for aid, such as a hurricane like Katrina or another terrorist attack like 9/11. If one of these kinds of crises were to happen tomorrow, with our current $20 trillion debt, the United States would be ill prepared to help and would probably have to take on even more debt. This debt burden means we must redistribute funds in the budget in order to pay back the debt instead of investing more money in new opportunities that could make us a world leader in the newest technology.

HISTORY AND DEVELOPMENT OF ECONOMIC POLICY

The development of the United States and its meteoric rise from rebellious colony to world superpower, both militarily and economically, in just a few hundred years was due in large part to the sound economic footing of our founders, notably Alexander Hamilton (c.f. McCraw 2012). In this section, instead of discussing the transition of the country from an agrarian to an industrial economy and how that affected the market, we look at a few turning points in history that give the big picture of U.S. economic policy.

Founding Period

The Revolutionary War and the beginning of our country left the states with great debt. In order to prevent these debts from hindering the progress of the new country, the first secretary of the Treasury, Alexander Hamilton, recommended the national government assume the states' debts and allow for a clean slate. Unfortunately for him, this had to pass Congress, and Congress was just as politically divided back then as it is now. The Assumptions Bill failed to pass multiple times, so rumor has it that Secretary of State Thomas Jefferson hosted an infamous dinner party between Hamilton and James Madison to sort out the issues of the new country: where to locate the capital and the assumption of the approximately $25 million of state debt (Public Broadcasting Service 2007). There were sixteen potential locations suggested for the capital city, and Madison argued for a location on the Potomac River. The debts were held by wealthy businessmen who some wanted to bind to the national government's success or failure while others feared the influence these businessmen would have on the new Congress. Additionally, some states had paid off most of their debts and thought other states should have to do the same, while others thought that assuming the debts would allow the nation to move forward as one economic body in the international market. Since Congressman Madison was a powerful Virginian, he promised to deliver votes in favor of assumption in return for Hamilton publicly supporting the location on the Potomac as the new capital city, now Washington, D.C. The Compromise of 1790 can be considered the start of economic policy and debt in the United States.

Treasury Secretary Hamilton may best be known not only for being the face on the $10 bill—and now the subject of the hit Broadway musical—but also for proposing the First Bank of the United States. Congress chartered the nation's first central bank in 1791 for twenty years at the great objection of Thomas Jefferson. The First Bank of the United States functioned much like a hybrid of what we know today as the Federal Reserve Bank and the Treasury Department. It issued the national currency that needed to be created as each state previously had its own currency, helped fund the debt assumed from the states, and regulated private banks. Even though it saw success as the first central bank, the Bank of the United States' charter was not renewed by Congress in 1811 due to the public perception that it was unconstitutional because it imposed restraints on private, state-chartered banks that were not considered under its jurisdiction. In 1816, however, a Second Bank of the United States was established partly to help the nation after the War of 1812 brought up concerns of instability and British rule. The charter expired in 1836, and like the first bank, it was not renewed.

Growth of Government Spending

On October 29, 1929, also known as Black Tuesday, the U.S. stock market crashed and the Great Depression officially began. You might be wondering what a stock market crash really means. Investors dumped shares at an unprecedented rate because stock prices were increasing as production was decreasing. People were deciding to get out of the market because they could not justify the cost compared to the projected future earnings of businesses. Millions of worthless shares were sold and traded on Black Tuesday and the days leading up to it. With the failure of the market, consumers stopped spending, which led to businesses cutting wages and laying off workers. The more than ten million unemployed had to borrow exponentially in order to keep themselves and their families afloat.

Banks began to fail as investors backed out in the unstable economy, and President Herbert Hoover could do nothing to stop the worst economic disaster in U.S. history.

Enter President Franklin Delano Roosevelt. He convinced Congress to pass the Emergency Banking Act that saved the banks by allowing the Federal Reserve Bank to issue currency so banks could help their citizens, which may be considered the first government bailout. The most famous work of Roosevelt, however, is a series of social programs known as the New Deal. These programs, like the Public Works Administration, Tennessee Valley Authority, and Works Progress Administration, all put people back to work at the expense of the federal government. This investment paid off because it not only created jobs but also built infrastructure necessary for the long-term success of the country like roads, dams, bridges, and schools. It was the government investing in the economy and hoping to spur growth in a time of unprecedented depression. And many government entities, such as the Federal Deposit Insurance Corporation (FDIC), were created during this period.

Although the New Deal seemed like a great stimulus package for a suffering economy, the United States did not truly recover from the Great Depression until after its entrance into World War II. During wartime, a nation must drastically increase its manufacturing capabilities, which requires a lot of human capital. The war effort put millions of Americans back to work, some in the military and others in the factories. The New Deal undoubtedly did much to keep the economy growing during the Great Depression, but the war efforts were what really got the country out of its hole.

The problem with wartime economic growth, however, is the aftermath. Wars end and people come home needing jobs. The economic boom provided by the war sustained America's growth and provided job opportunities for all who needed them. It was a period of great postwar economic prosperity. But economic prosperity fades, and social challenges added to the struggle of America in the 1960s. President John F. Kennedy was assassinated in 1963 and Vice President Lyndon Johnson now found himself as commander in chief fighting what he called the "war on poverty." He was able to pass some tax cuts that provided temporary relief to a struggling country, both economically and socially. With unrest in the civil rights movement and struggling Americans, Johnson was able to make the food stamp program permanently funded in addition to passing the Economic Opportunity Act of 1964. The aim of this legislation was to create opportunities for youths without having to obtain a college education. It also provided funding for Volunteers in Service to America (VISTA) and Head Start, both of which are frequently discussed today. VISTA participants generally go into urban areas to provide social services to individuals in return for some kind of student loan forgiveness and small stipend. Head Start's goal is to help children from low-income families ensure they are at the same developmental stage as their higher-income counterparts when they reach school age. Johnson's legislation in addition to the expansions of Medicare and Medicaid contributed to the growth of government spending that was seen in the 1940s to recover from the Great Depression.

As seen in Figure 5.6, there are noticeable bumps in government expenditures around World War I and World War II. World War II set off a pattern of increased government spending that would not dip below prewar levels ever again. The Johnson administration expenditures of the 1960s set off an even greater pattern of increases in government spending. The New Deal of Roosevelt and the Great Society of Johnson are two eras that explain the immense government spending we see today in addition to setting the precedent that in times of trouble the government will, and probably should, spend to invest in the economy.

FIGURE 5.6
U.S. Government Outlays, 1914–1978 (in millions of dollars)

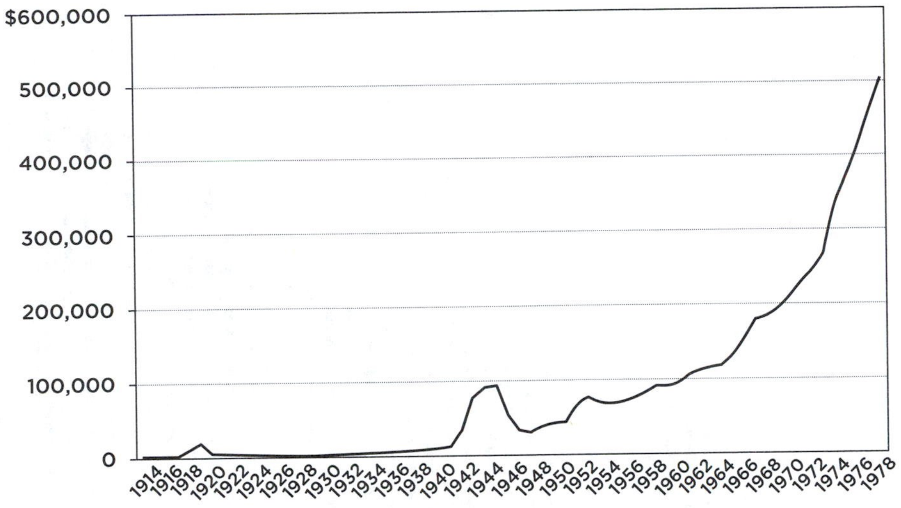

Source: The White House, Office of Management and Budget, Historical Tables.

Great Recession and Government Response

President Johnson began a period of unprecedented government spending, even more so than Roosevelt's New Deal programs. This increased spending lasted through the Nixon, Ford, Carter, Reagan, Bush I, Clinton, Bush II, and Obama eras, as seen in Figure 5.7. The United States has not only experienced ever-increasing government expenditures since 1948, but also has seen a large, steady jump since 2008. Here we explore the Great Recession and what has put us into a pattern of spending meant to stabilize our economy.

Throughout the 1990s and early 2000s, the United States experienced a positive financial market where mortgages and other sources of debt were readily approved, whether applicants were fully vetted for their ability to pay or not. Because of this, lots of mortgages were approved. These institutions sought to profit by trading mortgage bundles and assuming the risk, but because many mortgages were issued with adjustable rates, payments were reduced and more borrowers defaulted. Housing prices fell and demand for homes increased rapidly, so it became a buyers' market where homes sold for well below market value. An unprecedented number of homeowners were foreclosing and filing for bankruptcy while the stock market plummeted and investment banks struggled. Because of these poor economic situations, the government decided a bailout was necessary. In 2008, the Bush administration decided to step in by having the Treasury Department take over Fannie Mae and Freddie Mac while the Federal Reserve Bank bailed out American International Group.

Nothing could stop the bubble from bursting. America saw its biggest stock market crisis since the Great Depression. In 2008, Congress passed the Troubled Asset Relief Program (TARP) to bail out major financial institutions and ensure the continuation of

FIGURE 5.7

U.S. Government Outlays, 1980–2016 (in millions of dollars)

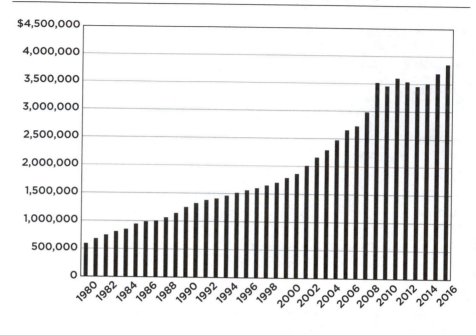

Source: The White House, Office of Management and Budget, Historical Tables.

investment activities and citizens' borrowing. Some of the institutions saved by TARP were well-known names like Citigroup, JPMorgan Chase, Wells Fargo, Goldman Sachs, Morgan Stanley, and PNC Financial Services. Additionally, the Bush II administration agreed to spend approximately $17.4 billion to bail out the auto industry. General Motors and Chrysler, two of the largest auto manufacturers in the United States, were aided by government intervention and major financial support. The Federal Reserve Bank injected over $1.25 trillion into the economy by lowering its discount rate to less than 1 percent and then to 0 percent. This increased the money supply and encouraged banks to give loans that would allow citizens to spend more and infuse the economy with capital.

President Obama signed two pieces of legislation aimed at recovering from and preventing another Great Recession. First, the American Recovery and Reinvestment Act was passed in 2009 to act as a stimulus package and aid the recovery from the Great Recession, but the details of that bill are described later in this chapter. In 2010, the Dodd-Frank Act became law to provide stricter regulations on the financial industry. Dodd-Frank's main goal is to prevent another bailout by stipulating that if Wall Street fails, then it must pay rather than have the government and taxpayer dollars save a failing entity. It also created a few new bureaucratic entities including the Federal Stability Oversight Council, Bureau of Consumer and Financial Protection, and Office of Credit Ratings. These new governmental organizations should monitor national and international economic stability threats, oversee consumer accounts to investigate any unfair or deceptive practices, and oversee credit rating companies like Moody's, respectively.

MAJOR ECONOMIC POLICY AND BUDGETING STATUTES

With the brief review of the history of economic policy in the United States, we highlight in this section some essential statutes for this area of policy.

Federal Reserve Act (1913) The Federal Reserve Act of 1913 created the Federal Reserve System. This system encompasses twelve regional Federal Reserve banks and requires a Board of Governors to oversee it. With this law, Congress established priorities of maximizing employment, stabilizing prices, and moderating interest rates. Since financial stability is the goal, the Federal Reserve Act empowers the Federal Reserve System to regulate and supervise the banking industry and to formulate monetary policy.

Budget and Accounting Act (1921) Before the Budget and Accounting Act of 1921, the federal budget process did not exist. Money was spent through appropriations passed through various committees, and if an executive agency wanted money, it submitted requests to the committees that had spending jurisdiction. As you can imagine, this was a disorganized process that led to redundant requests and the misallocation of funds. To create a more accountable, organized system, Congress passed the Budget and Accounting Act, which mandates that a president submits his budget to Congress. The Government Accounting Office (now called the Government Accountability Office) was created by this law. The GAO watches over executive agencies so that they are doing the work assigned them by Congress. It acts as an external audit agent to improve government efficiency (Mikesell 2014). The Bureau of the Budget, now the Office of Management and Budget, was also established to help manage the new executive budget process.

Glass-Steagall, or the Banking Act (1933) The Glass-Steagall Act separates commercial and investment banking activities. Many of the problems that arose in the commercial banking industry were believed to have been ripple effects from Wall Street, so Congress decided to pass the Banking Act of 1933 to create separation. It is commonly named for the bill sponsors Senator Carter Glass and Representative Henry Steagall (Irwin 2015). Glass-Steagall was repealed and replaced in 1999 by the Gramm-Leach-Bliley Act to allow American banks to offer a wider array of banking services. This has led to the rise of some of the largest banks, like Citigroup, JPMorgan Chase, and Bank of America, which have combined assets of about $6.5 trillion (Irwin 2015).

Congressional Budget and Impoundment Act (1974) The Budget and Accounting Act of 1921 formalized the role of the executive branch in the federal budget process; yet Congress did not have strict guidelines until the Congressional Budget and Impoundment Act of 1974. This legislation created the Congressional Budget Office. The act stipulated numerous budgetary provisions, including the congressional budget process that has been described in this chapter, changing the start of the federal fiscal year to its current date of October 1, requiring the president to submit a tax expenditure analysis, and eliminating presidential impoundment power (Mikesell 2014).

Economic Growth and Tax Relief Reconciliation Act (2001) Known as one part of the Bush tax cuts, the Economic Growth and Tax Relief Reconciliation Act of 2001 included individual income tax rate reductions, doubled the per child tax credit, reduced the estate and gift tax rate from 55 to 45 percent by 2007, increased retirement savings contribution ceilings, and expanded education credits and deductions (Tax Policy Center 2016). This legislation had a sunset provision so that its tax policy changes would revert to their previous versions in 2010. However, it was extended by the Tax Relief, Unemployment Insurance Reauthorization, and Job Creation Act of 2010, and the American Taxpayer Relief Act of 2012 made the rates for taxpayers with annual incomes of $400,000 or less permanent.

Troubled Asset Relief Program (2008) The Troubled Asset Relief Program (TARP) was passed in October 2008 to address issues of financial instability. In response to the economic turmoil, Congress passed TARP and authorized $700 billion to provide capital to banks and an influx of cash to credit markets and employers, particularly the auto industry. The Treasury Department, however, reports that only $37.2 billion of the authorized funding will be used. In the end, people were able to keep their homes, jobs were slowly restored, and the biggest financial crisis since the Great Depression was nearly avoided.

American Recovery and Reinvestment Act (2009) Passed in response to the Great Recession, the American Recovery and Reinvestment Act of 2009 was a $787 billion economic stimulus package. The bill saved or created 1.6 million jobs per year through 2012 and led to $689 billion of tax cuts (Superville 2014). It increased the earned income tax credit rate to 45 percent for families with three or more children and allocated $25 billion for recovery zone bonds issued in 2009 and 2010 (Tax Policy Center 2016). Not only was it a job creator and tax cut measure, it also improved roads and bridges, invested in better infrastructure for water and public utilities, increased health care and food stamp programs for the unemployed, augmented state Medicaid assistance, and increased funding for Pell Grants and research.

MAJOR ACTORS IN ECONOMIC POLICY

With our focus on the implementation of policy and its relevance in the everyday lives of citizens, it is important to explore the major actors in each policy area; and while undoubtedly there will be some repetition in the discussion of actors over the coming pages, it is worth remembering how influential certain actors can be. Indeed, these are the major actors discussed in news stories about economic policy.

Congress

It should already be evident how involved the nation's primary lawmaking body is in all areas of policy, and economic policy is no different. As you have seen in this chapter, Congress is responsible for crafting budgets and passing them into law (constituting fiscal policy). Additionally, Congress creates laws regarding taxes, economic benefit programs, government subsidies—quite honestly, nearly all the legislation Congress passes has on some level to do with money. More specifically, a host of congressional committees involve themselves in economic policy; in the House of Representatives, those committees include: Appropriations, Budget, Energy and Commerce, Financial Services, Small Business, and Ways and Means. In the Senate, relevant committees include: Banking, Housing, and Urban Affairs; Budget; Commerce, Science, and

Technology; Finance; and Small Business and Entrepreneurship. Finally, Congress has a Joint Committee on Taxation. In addition to passing laws that have to do with various aspects of economic policy, Congress is often the body that creates the rest of the government agencies that are tasked with carrying out policy. Recall that it was Congress that chartered the Banks of the United States and then chose not to renew their charters. Additionally, Congress created the Federal Reserve Bank and the Congressional Budget Office, among others.

President

The president, as a constitutional officer, is highly involved in all areas of policymaking, and economic policy is no exception. Recall that the president reviews legislation that Congress passes and can sign or veto that legislation. Regarding economic policy, as we discussed earlier, the president is central to the federal budget process in that the president—along with the White House Office of Management and Budget—puts together the very first draft of a federal budget and submits it to Congress early in the calendar year. It is often the president's policy agenda that drives congressional legislation, and nearly all policy initiatives require funding. Finally, as the chief executive of the United States, the president oversees all of the federal agencies tasked with implementing policy, from the Internal Revenue Service (IRS) to the Securities and Exchange Commission (SEC).

Government Agencies

A plethora of federal government agencies are involved in economic policy, and a number of them merit mention here as we continue our look at actors involved in this area. Here we examine the agencies that play a significant role in this policy arena.

Congressional Budget Office The CBO was created as part of the 1974 Budget Control and Impoundment Act to provide Congress nonpartisan and timely analysis on fiscal policy. The CBO scores various policy proposals and assesses the budget implications of those policy endeavors. Supporters and opponents of various policy initiatives often wait anxiously for CBO scoring, as it is a highly respected entity in assessing the financial costs of a proposed policy and can make or break efforts of lawmakers. The CBO only assesses the financial impacts of a proposal and does not render any sort of recommendation about the merit of a proposal.

U.S. Department of the Treasury The U.S. Department of the Treasury has a range of responsibilities, including printing money in its Bureau of Engraving and Printing. While printing money and producing coins are probably the most public functions of the department, the Treasury also advises the president on economic and financial issues in order to ensure America's financial security. The department has been in the news recently for announcing that Harriet Tubman would replace President Andrew Jackson on the $20 bill.

Internal Revenue Service The IRS is a bureau within the U.S. Department of the Treasury. The agency dates back to the Civil War, when a Commissioner of Internal Revenue was created by Congress to raise funds for the war effort. The IRS of today came about in 1913 with the ratification of the Sixteenth Amendment, which empowers the federal government to collect income taxes. Its mission is to "provide America's taxpayers top quality service by helping them understand and meet their tax responsibilities and enforce the law with integrity and fairness to all." Americans know the IRS as the agency that collects taxes for the federal government. The agency collected $3.1 trillion in 2014 and processed about 240 million tax returns (Internal Revenue Service 2016).

Federal Reserve System The Fed was created in 1913 by Congress as the central banking system for the United States. In addition to being the nation's central bank, the Fed manages the money supply and aims to provide stability for the financial and banking sectors. There are four major components to the Fed: (1) the Board of Governors, (2) the Federal Open Market Committee (FOMC), (3) the twelve regional Fed banks, and (4) member banks. These regional banks oversee banking operations in their region and carry out the policy of the system. Finally, there are private banks that are members of the Federal Reserve System.

Office of Management and Budget The OMB is responsible for the implementation of the president's budget strategy for the executive branch. There are a variety of offices within OMB that carry out the five critical processes of the White House office: budget development and execution, management and oversight, coordination of executive agencies, legislative clearance and coordination, and implementation of executive orders and presidential memoranda (Office of Management and Budget 2016b). Originally known as the Bureau of the Budget under the Treasury Department, OMB is part of the Executive Office and reports directly to the president to help manage every executive department and agency in the federal government. The budget process begins with OMB gathering budget requests from each agency and compiling them into the president's budget, which is submitted to Congress for consideration.

Council of Economic Advisers The Employment Act of 1946 established the CEA within the Executive Office of the President. The members of the CEA and their staff of approximately thirty-three prepare the Economic Report of the President, research economic development trends, and provide the president with their suggestions for national policies that spur economic growth.

Securities and Exchange Commission The SEC was created in 1934 to protect investors; maintain fair, orderly, and efficient markets; and facilitate capital formation (U.S. Securities and Exchange Commission 2016). Five commissioners—no more than three of the same political party—work to ensure that laws and rules governing the securities industry protect individuals and businesses choosing to participate in the securities market. Securities include stocks, bonds, and options that allow business entities to raise new capital and secure investment from individuals and other entities. The SEC aims to reduce fraud and promote fair investment practices where everyone has access to the same information.

Federal Trade Commission The FTC, created in 1914, is an independent agency comprised of five commissioners who aim to protect consumers, maintain competition, and advance performance (Federal Trade Commission 2016). They do so by being associated with busting trusts and preventing market collusion that manipulates and harms consumers. Businesses and individuals can be investigated by the FTC on suspicions of identity theft, monopolistic behaviors, and deceptive practices.

Federal Deposit Insurance Corporation The FDIC is a government-run corporation that guarantees depositors their money if a bank should fail. You may have noticed the FDIC stickers in your bank's windows. Created in 1933 by Congress in the Banking Act, the FDIC was a response to the bank failures that contributed to the Great Depression. The agency "maintain[s] stability and public confidence in the nation's financial system by insuring deposits; examining and supervising financial institutions for safety and soundness and consumer protection; making large and complex financial institutions resolvable; and managing receiverships" (Federal Deposit and Insurance Corporation 2016).

ISSUES AND CHALLENGES

The complexities of economic policy present enough issues themselves, but there are some current challenges that further exacerbate work in this policy area. These include (1) political polarization, (2) debts and deficits, and (3) global markets and free trade.

Political Polarization

One of the most commonly heard phrases today is, "We are more polarized than ever before." For Americans, this phrase generally refers to the political polarization and the divide that exist between Republicans and Democrats. Budgets, taxes, trade policies, and other economic issues are not immune to this polarization. On the contrary, they are extremely controversial and usually central issues of the polarization. Democrats want to tax in order to spend, while Republicans want to cut taxes and spending. The issues are not black and white; there is no right or wrong side. These are two different philosophies about how to manage money and make decisions. Republicans view the government as an entity that should be more fiscally responsible, where it focuses on providing services at the cheapest cost and allowing people to keep their incomes. They also consider states to be the best providers and would delegate much economic and social authority from the nation to the states. Democrats view government as more of a service-delivery entity that should be efficient in its operations but to which citizens must pay a fee in order to get quality opportunities. They believe the national government should bear the responsibility for providing economic opportunities for all. Unfortunately, in our current two-party system, political polarization will continue to be a challenge for our domestic and international economic decisions for years to come.

Debts and Deficits

As explained earlier, when the government spends more than it receives in a given year, it experiences a deficit, and the debt is the accumulation of each year's deficit, or how much the U.S. government owes. Political polarization may best be seen in the issue of the debt ceiling: the limit set on the amount of money the U.S. government can borrow to pay its obligations. If the government exceeds the debt ceiling, then the Treasury Department may not pay for expenditures that have already been approved through the budget or appropriated in bills. Not only does reaching the debt ceiling prevent the Treasury Department from paying current obligations, but it can also affect the U.S. credit rating and cause economic instability. It affects the ability of citizens to collect their benefits and government employees to get paid. Democrats argue that raising the debt ceiling was necessary to make payments and continue as a functional government; Republicans demand that the debt ceiling should only be raised if spending is cut on an equivalent basis. Without cutting spending, the government will just continue to raise the debt ceiling to meet obligations and will never have an incentive to balance its budget. Both sides have valid arguments, as one wants to ensure that people do not see interruptions in their benefits and the other wants the country not to spend more than it raises. The challenge of the debt ceiling is nothing new, as the United States has modified the debt limit fourteen times since 2001, and it even contributed to the 2013 government shutdown.

Global Markets and Free Trade

Technology drives the economy, and information is the new currency. Not only must our workforce keep up in the rapidly changing market, but we must also be aware of changes in trade. Another phrase you've probably heard: "we live in a global world." What does that mean, and how does it affect the average citizen? With advances in technology and the ease of travel, employers have a diverse pool of workers from which to choose and Americans have to learn to keep up. The challenge here is ensuring that Americans are trained properly to contribute to the rapidly changing market. Globalization and the exchange of information demand that the United States take a serious look at trade deals like the Trans-Pacific Partnership (TPP) and the Transatlantic Trade and Investment Partnership (TTIP). TPP aims to open trade by reducing tariffs—taxes on imports—so there is a reduced financial burden on business. TTIP loosens regulations on environmental standards, data privacy, and financial institutions hopefully to encourage growth. Both of these deals have to do with reducing regulatory barriers to trade and generally are considered to benefit large multinational corporations. The fear that accompanies these trade deals is that jobs may be lost in the United States. However, they also offer potential economic growth, as trade can open the market and provide new opportunities. Next, we bring our discussion back to the connections ordinary citizens have with economic policy today and in the future.

Everyday Citizen Connection

The old adage "money doesn't buy you happiness" is worth recalling here, and while money does not buy happiness, it is necessary for everything the government does. Let us start with something probably near and dear to you: the cost of college. Many of us pay for college tuition by taking student loans. The biggest provider of student loans is the federal government (FAFSA forms, anyone?). If your loans are not from the government, the private borrower from which you got student loans is regulated by the federal government.

In addition to student loans, many other forms of assistance are available from federal and state governments to offset the tuition at colleges. Additionally, the cost of public colleges is generally influenced significantly by state governments and state politics. State legislatures, like in Ohio, have recently been setting caps on tuition. This may sound great for students: it forces colleges whose costs are not observing the same moratorium to look to make up that money in other ways, including student fees.

Besides the cost of working hard and earning a college degree, many of us have credit cards and bank accounts. The federal government oversees the operations of banks and has plenty to say about what banks and financial institutions can and cannot do to consumers. The actions of the Fed impact the interest rate our credit card companies charge us. The same is true for car loans and home loans, among others. All of this is just the tip of the proverbial iceberg when it comes to economic policy in our daily lives.

Presumably you are enrolled in college, maybe taking on student loans, all in the hopes of getting a good job that will give you a paycheck for doing something you love. In case you have forgotten, part of that paycheck goes to the federal government, the state government, and in some cases, even the local government in the form of taxes. This tax revenue, along with other streams of income, is what funds the government to create and maintain the roads you drive on to get to and from campus, ensure the safety of the buildings in which you take your classes, and protect the safety of the food you eat on the run between classes. As Americans, we ask the government to do a lot—after all, did you have to worry that the banana you ate this morning as you dashed to class was going to make you sick? Probably not. And your hope is that the taxes you pay today will provide you health care and even some supplemental income when you retire. The point is it is virtually impossible to escape the impact of economic policy in your life. But it would seem that you probably would not want to, either. After all, are you going to pave the road in front of your house when the government has no revenue?

Beyond the ways that this policy area touches most aspects of your everyday life, there are lots of professional opportunities to consider. Budget analysts in local, state, and federal government agencies are vital in understanding, forecasting, and planning the work of government. Economists are employed extensively by government entities to facilitate these aspects as well. The entire banking and financial sector is governed by an extensive array of laws and regulations that require individuals to implement and oversee. As we discussed earlier in this chapter, organizations like the FDIC, SEC, FTC, along with many others, need committed and passionate civil servants to ensure the health and integrity of the nation's economy. Related: tax professionals both inside and outside of government are important. While much could be said about how quickly things change, one certainty is the need for hardworking individuals to ensure the well-being of the nation's economy.

Discovery Question:

Take a look at the website of one of the agencies discussed here, such as the FDIC or SEC. Explore some of the current topics or efforts. What are these agencies up to, and how does their work affect economic policy?

CONCLUDING THOUGHTS

Underlying the implementation of government policy is money. Furthermore, the government's income and spending also constitute its own area of policy, especially given the size and scale of the U.S. government. This chapter has discussed underpinnings of economic policy and provided a window into the government's budgeting process. A comprehension of these topics is necessary as we move into discussions of other substantive policy areas, since all policies require money and have an impact on our economy. The complexities of the process and policy decisions are only touched on in this chapter, but it is already clear that the government's revenues and expenditures are far more complicated than a household budget.

These complexities are particularly important as we consider economic policy in the future. In particular, the political polarization facing elected officials as well as citizens is unlikely to change in the near future, thereby complicating economic policy decisions. The demands of the citizens and their representatives for government action are going to cost money, and lately those costs exceed the government's income. As a result, we are going to continue having conversations about debts and deficits. As the nation is part of a world economy, the influence and behavior of other markets are likely to exude influence as well. It remains to be seen how the vote by the United Kingdom to leave the European Union—better known as "Brexit"—in the summer of 2016 will affect the U.S. and world economies. Suffice it to say that economic policy and public budgeting are more involved than simply numbers on a spreadsheet. How we spend money and the priorities for that money tell us a lot about the nature of the country and its values. The revenues the government spends come from taxes, and there is much debate over how the government collects taxes from its citizens. We close the chapter with our Policy Choices section to examine some of the options concerning the federal tax system.

POLICY CHOICES: THE FEDERAL TAX SYSTEM

Due to seven tax brackets, multiple types of taxes, and numerous credits and deductions, the federal tax system can be described as complicated, confusing, and complex. As we've discussed, taxes are necessary for the government to raise revenue and fund its mandated operations. However, there is discretion in what types of taxes the government demands and how it administers them. Here we present a few ideas that have been presented as adaptations to our current tax structure to reduce the number of headaches around tax season.

Policy Choices: Federal Tax Policy

Choice #1: Increase Taxes on the Rich	Choice #2: Consumption Taxes	Choice #3: Flat Tax	Choice #4: Eliminate Credits and Deductions
Our current tax system is progressive. It taxes higher-income individuals at increased rates. The thought process behind increasing the rate on the richest Americans is that the top 1 percent of wage earners do not pay proportionally what they owe because of exemptions or loopholes that they utilize. The Treasury Department reports that the top 1 percent of wage earners in the United States pay approximately one-third of their salaries to the U.S. government in taxes. Raising taxes on this group of Americans could bring in much-needed revenue, but the unknown is if an increased tax rate would discourage top wage earners from investing in the economy.	Consumption taxes are taxes on choices made by the consumer like sales taxes. However, income and consumption taxes are not equal. Taxes on income are generally stable and predictable, based on labor statistics. Consumption taxes, however, are almost entirely dependent on the current status of the economy and completely unpredictable because we cannot assume what people are going to purchase or how they will behave. Income taxes are such a large source of revenue for the federal government that consumption taxes would have to be accompanied by increases in other revenue sources that include controversial topics like severance taxes, user fees for public services, taxes on trade, or something else.	A flat tax rate simplifies the tax code by establishing a consistent tax rate across all income brackets. This would streamline the system, but it would shift the tax burden from the rich to the middle class because the flat rate would probably be greater than what most Americans pay now to make up for the reduced rate that the wealthiest would experience. As discussed earlier, there are currently seven federal tax brackets. These cause confusion, and when filling out your tax forms, if you do not understand into which bracket you fall, then you may be in for some tax penalties rather than that nice refund check you were looking forward to.	Reducing credits and deductions available for taxpayers undoubtedly simplifies the tax code without changing tax rates and our progressive structure. It would close loopholes that are used predominantly by richer individuals who can hire professionals who understand the code to file their taxes. This option would broaden the tax base, as everyone would have to pay the rate assigned to their income bracket and not allow for exceptions, which is a policy generally advocated by financial and economic professionals. Broadening the base can also allow for a reduction in rates while still seeing the government take in equivalent revenue amounts.

GLOSSARY TERMS

capitalist economy   97
classical economic
   theory   97
command or centrally
   planned economy   97
debt   109
deficit   109
deflation   99
depression 100
discretionary
   spending   109

economic policy   97
economy   96
fiscal policy   103
free market or laissez-faire
   economy   97
gross domestic product
   (GDP)   98
hyperinflation   99
inflation   99
Keynesian economic
   theory   98

mandatory spending   109
monetary policy   103
recession   100
supply-side economic
   theory   98
unemployment rate   98

DISCUSSION QUESTIONS

1. There are many types of economies; which do you find the most compelling, and why?

2. Economic policy and public budgeting are essential topics in considering government action, yet few citizens grasp the complexities associated with them. What would it take for citizens to better understand these processes? How would a better understanding of the processes enhance civic discourse?

3. What should the role of government in the economy be? What can that role be in practice, considering the existing interconnectedness of government and the economy today?

4. You have probably been taught some basic concepts behind money management and not spending more than you earn. Is it appropriate for the government to adapt these basic principles to spend more than it takes in? Should there be some kind of check and balance on government borrowing?

5. What do you think is the biggest issue facing our national economy: spending decisions, politics, tax policy, balanced budgeting, states' rights, international trade, or something else? Why do you think it is the biggest issue? What should be done about it?

SUGGESTED RESOURCES

Suggested Websites

Center on Budget and Policy Priorities, http://www.cbpp.org/

Economic Report of the President, https://www.whitehouse.gov/administration/eop/cea/economic-report-of-the-President

Government Accountability Office Tax Reform, http://www.gao.gov/key_issues/tax_reform/issue_summary

Internal Revenue Service Tax Statistics, https://www.irs.gov/uac/tax-stats

U.S. Bureau of Labor Statistics, http://www.bls.gov

Suggested Books or Articles

Ahamed, Liaquat. 2009. *Lords of Finance: The Bankers Who Broke the World*. New York: Penguin.

Geithner, Timothy F. 2015. *Stress-Test: Reflections on Financial Crisis*. New York: Broadway Books.

Levitt, Steven D., and Stephen J. Dubner. 2009. *Freakonomics*. New York: HarperCollins.

McCraw, Thomas K. 2012. *The Founders and Finance: How Hamilton, Gallatin, and Other Immigrants Forged a New Economy*. New York: Belknap Press.

Rubin, Irene. 2013. *The Politics of Public Budgeting: Getting and Spending, Borrowing and Balancing*. Washington, DC: CQ Press.

Sorkin, Andrew Ross. 2010. *Too Big to Fail: The Inside Story of How Wall Street and Washington Fought to Save the Financial System—and Themselves*. New York: Penguin.

Wildavsky, Aaron, and Naomi Caiden. 2003. *The New Politics of the Budgetary Process*. 5th ed. New York: Longman.

Suggested Films and Other Media

The Big Short, DVD, directed by Adam McKay (2015: United States), http://www.imdb.com/title/tt1596363/videoplayer/vi1593618969?ref_=tt_ov_vi

Hamilton: An American Musical, by Lin-Manuel Miranda (2015: United States), https://www.youtube.com/channel/UCKhSqWRvBtjlivrs_xeT5aQ

Too Big to Fail, DVD, directed by Curtis Hanson (2011: United States), http://www.imdb.com/title/tt1742683/

Wall Street, DVD, directed by Oliver Stone (1987: United States), http://www.imdb.com/title/tt0094291/

Wall Street: Money Never Sleeps, DVD, directed by Oliver Stone (2010: United States), http://www.imdb.com/title/tt1027718/?ref_=nv_sr_1

Sharpen your skills with SAGE edge at **http://edge.sagepub.com/rinfret. SAGE edge for students** provides a personalized approach to help you accomplish your coursework goals in an easy-to-use learning environment.

LEARNING OBJECTIVES

Readers of this chapter will be able to:

1. Understand what is meant by the crime rate and how it is determined

2. Explore issues of mass incarceration, deterrence, recidivism, and gun control

3. Assess the role of history, politics, and the courts in crime and public policy

GUNS ON CAMPUS: SAFETY OR RISK?

April 16, 2007, should have been a beautiful spring day on college campuses, with students thinking about finals and the end of the school year. Instead, it was ugly, devastating, and surreal. At 7:15 a.m., Seung Hui Cho, a twenty-three-year-old student at Virginia Polytechnic Institute and State University (Virginia Tech), shot and killed two people in the dorm. That would have been horrific enough, but he was not done. Just over two hours later, he entered a classroom building, chaining and locking the doors behind him. Armed with a 9-millimeter handgun, a 22-caliber handgun, and with hundreds of rounds of ammunition, Cho went from room to room shooting people. In all, twenty-seven students and five faculty were killed and seventeen more students injured before Cho turned the gun on himself as police closed in on his position. Cho earned a dubious spot in history by killing the most people ever on a college campus.

PHOTO 6.1
Thousands gather in a candlelight vigil to mourn the thirty-two people killed during the mass shooting at Virginia Tech in 2007.

Robert Gauthier/*Los Angeles Times* via Getty Images

In the aftermath of this tragedy came calls for new policies. The U.S. Department of Education fined Virginia Tech for failing to give prompt, campus-wide warnings that a gunman was still at large after the first shooting in the dorm. Following the shooting, early-warning systems were examined on campuses throughout the country. Universities and colleges increased campus security and instituted new policies about how and when to warn students of potential dangers on campus. Campus lockdown procedures were reviewed and strengthened, and many campuses practiced those procedures, in a similar manner to tornado or fire drills.

Changes in these policies drew little criticism, as students, their parents, faculty, and college administrators wanted safe places to learn. However, one policy became very controversial: allowing guns on campus. In some states, including Colorado, Idaho, Kansas, Mississippi, Oregon, Texas, Utah, and Wisconsin, state legislators argued that mass-shooting events demonstrated a need to ease existing firearm regulations and allow concealed-carry weapons on campuses. Other states, such as California, Florida, Georgia, Illinois, Louisiana, Massachusetts, Michigan, Missouri, New Jersey, New York, and North Carolina, enacted state laws banning guns on public university grounds. They believed tightening restrictions on the presence of weapons on college campuses would help prevent events like the one at Virginia Tech. Other states left it for individual public universities and colleges to determine whether or not to allow concealed weapons.

Which position is correct, and who should decide what policy to adopt? Recent studies suggest two findings. First, college campuses are increasingly prone to gun violence. The Citizens Crime Commission of New York City reviewed 190 incidents at 142 colleges from the 2001–2016 school years. The study revealed that shooting incidents increased 153 percent and casualties increased 241 percent, calling the last five years an "epidemic" in gun violence on college campuses, as over 437 people—most of them students—were shot (Cannon 2016). So, too, elementary and high schools are not immune from gun violence. A horrific mass shooting occurred in 2012 at Sandy Hook Elementary School, claiming the lives of twenty children and six adults. In the first two months of 2018 two high school shootings, one in Benton, Kentucky, and one in Parkland, Florida, killed nineteen people and injured twenty-eight. Despite precautions, gun violence in schools continues.

Second, studies indicate that controlling gun violence is not as simple as allowing guns on campus or on school grounds. Allowing people to carry weapons may actually increase violent crime, according to researchers at the Brennan Center for Justice. They found a 10 percent average increase in violent crime in states that adopted right-to-carry laws. The Citizens Crime Commission also found that states with ready access to guns were more likely to have gun violence on campuses. Twelve states accounted for 64 percent of the gun violence on college campuses, and these states had more gun dealers, no requirement for universal background checks, easy access to purchasing assault weapons, or no limits on the number of guns purchased (Cannon 2016, 3).

A 2016 study by Johns Hopkins University also found that having concealed-carry laws did not deter mass-shooting events. From 1966 to 2015, less than 10 percent of high-fatality mass shootings in America, whether on college campuses or elsewhere, took place in "gun-free zones," or where carrying guns is prohibited (Webster et al. 2016). A similar analysis, by the National Bureau of Economic Research, found that only 13 percent of mass shootings from 2009 to 2015 occurred in gun-free or gun-restricted zones (Michaels 2016). This runs contrary to the argument of concealed-carry advocates that "gun-free zones" provide ready targets for shooters, since they know that no one will fire back at them.

Arguments about the right to have guns on college campuses or bans on semi-automatic weapons, such as the AR-15 rifle used in the Parkland High School shooting, are reflected in larger debates about gun control and crime. Mass shootings, especially in schools, are important public policy issues that must be addressed. However, this chapter takes a broader look at crime and criminal justice policies. The chapter explores the history of crime and punishment and various approaches to deterring crime. We look at relationships between drug use and crime; the roles of national, state, and local government in fighting crime; and the role of race in arrests and incarceration.

We look at **criminology**, or the study of crime, to inform our understanding of how, why, when, and where crime occurs, and explore our **criminal justice** system of enforcing laws, investigating crimes, prosecuting and punishing criminals, and rehabilitating persons convicted of a crime (Roufa 2016). Both of these fields (criminology and criminal justice) shape policies that deal with crime. The chapter ends with U.S. incarceration rates, the problem of escalating prison costs, and the special challenge of capital punishment. Finally, we return to the topic of gun control, considering possible policy choices to prevent future massacres at the hands of someone with a gun.

....

OVERVIEW OF CRIME IN AMERICA

People have different views on the extent of crime in the United States, the causes of crime, the kind of punishment that should occur, what to do about mass shootings, and whether or not the death penalty is good public policy. Let's begin by looking at the types of crime and the crime rate in recent U.S. history.

Types of Crime

Crimes are actions that are prohibited by federal and state governments because they are deemed to be harmful to society. Crimes are defined by criminal law, which determines whether a person should be punished by imprisonment, fines, or both. Crimes that are punishable by more than one year in prison are felonies, such as murder, kidnapping, or robbery. Less serious crimes, such as shoplifting, with sentences of less than one year, are called misdemeanors.

Crimes may be classified into four broad categories. The first is personal crime, where the crime results in injury or harm to a person or persons. Examples of violent crime include assault and battery, kidnapping, rape, and homicide. When an individual acts with premeditation and intent to kill, prosecutors will charge that person with first-degree murder. A second category is property crime, which involves the taking or interference with the property of another. Examples include auto theft, burglary, robbery, and larceny. A third type of crime is inchoate. Inchoate crimes include crimes that were in progress but never completed, or assisting another person with a criminal act. Examples include conspiracy and aiding and abetting. The final category is statutory crime. This includes crimes that are specifically proscribed by state or federal laws, in addition to the ones set out in the previous categories. Many alcohol- and drug-related crimes are statutory crimes, as are traffic offenses.

The state or national government prosecutes criminal cases on behalf of the people. In contrast, civil cases typically involve private disputes between individuals or organizations. Both criminal and civil cases are heard in federal or state court, depending on **jurisdiction**. Jurisdiction is an important concept that refers to the ability of a court to hear a case. Contrary to popular belief, the most serious cases are not necessarily prosecuted in federal courts. Most criminal cases are heard by state courts, which have broad jurisdiction. For example, robbery is a crime that is most often tried in state courts as violating state law.

Criminal cases where the United States is a party, such as crimes that occurred on federal property, involved a federal employee, or violated federal laws or the U.S. Constitution, are heard in federal courts. For example, the crime of robbery would be tried in federal courts if the individual robbed a bank insured by the Federal Insurance Deposit Insurance Corporation (FDIC), an agency of the U.S. government. If the individual robbed a local convenience store, gas station, or residence, however, that person would be prosecuted in state court.

It is also possible for an individual to be prosecuted for violating both state and federal laws. An historic example is the case against four police officers charged with beating Rodney King, an African American man, after a high-speed chase in 1991. The officers were tried in California state court in 1992, and acquitted of assault charges. The acquittal verdict prompted riots that took more than fifty lives and caused over $1 billion in property damages in Los Angeles (Mydans 1993). The officers were subsequently charged with violating King's civil rights and tried in a federal court; two of the four were convicted.

The interplay between federal and state criminal courts is discussed in greater detail later in the chapter. The bottom line, however, is that state courts are the workhorses of the criminal justice system, prosecuting more than 90 percent of criminal cases in the country, hearing over eighty-six million cases in 2015, as shown in Figure 6.1. Note that 21 percent, or about one in five cases, heard in state courts is a criminal case; the majority of cases, 54 percent, involve traffic violations. The next section traces the incidence of crime over time in the United States.

FIGURE 6.1

Types of Cases Heard in State Courts, 2015

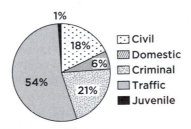

Total: 86.2 million cases.

Source: Adapted from R. Schauffler, R. LaFountain, S. Strickland, K. Holt, & K. Genthon. *Examining the Work of State Courts: An Overview of 2015 State Court Caseloads*, p. 3. National Center for State Courts, 2016.

One essential element measuring the status and scope of crime in America is the **crime rate**, which refers to the incidence of crime that is then standardized by the population. Crime rates are often expressed by the type of crime, or total crime, per 100,000 people. Crime rates of communities, cities, states, or the nation help us better understand the extent of crime in any given location. The **incarceration rate**, another important indicator of crime, is defined as the number of persons in local jails, state prisons, and federal prisons per 100,000 residents (Bureau of Justice Statistics 2015). Let's look first at the crime rate.

The U.S. Crime Rate

A favorite talking point of some politicians is the increase in crime and the need for more police and security measures. Local media frequently report crimes that happen in certain communities, making it seem like crime is rampant everywhere. However, deciphering the U.S. crime rate is a bit more challenging, and depends on if one refers to the overall crime rate or a particular type of crime or location, or if one looks at data over a short time frame.

The Federal Bureau of Investigation (FBI) within the U.S. Department of Justice compiles annual statistics on crimes reported by law enforcement agencies across the country. The **Uniform Crime Reporting Program** (UCR) is a nationwide, voluntary effort among local police departments and sheriffs that started in 1930. Four publications, including *Crime in the United States*, the *National Incident-Based Reporting System, Law Enforcement Officers Killed and Assaulted*, and *Hate Crime Statistics*, are prepared each year to guide the understanding of policymakers, criminologists, criminal justice scholars, and others about crime and its incidence. Over time, UCR has become a key source of information about the rate of criminal activity in America.

Looking at the trend shown in Figures 6.2 and 6.3 based on UCR data, we see that the long-term trend for violent crimes, such as murder, rape, or aggravated assault, has been in decline. Figure 6.2 shows that the rate of violent crime peaked in 1991, with 758 offenses per 100,000 people; by 2014, the rate had dropped by more than half, to 365 per 100,000 people (Robertson 2016; U.S. Department of Justice 2016). Also shown in Figure 6.3, the murder rate declined from a high of about 10 murders per 100,000 people in 1979 to less than 5 murders per 100,000 people in 2014. (The September 11, 2001, terrorist attacks are not included in these calculations.)

Another database used to report the crime rate is the Bureau of Justice Statistics' National Crime Victimization Survey (NCVS), which is the nation's primary source of information about who has been a victim of crime. The NCVS surveys 90,000 households each year, asking about violent crimes as well as property crimes that may have occurred. Ongoing since 1973, this database includes crimes that may not have been reported to the police. Looking at Figure 6.4, we see a similar trend to the UCR data. The trend reveals a crime rate (indexed to the year 1976) that has declined broadly with respect to all types of crimes.

Explaining Decreases in the U.S. Crime Rate

The fact that crime rates nationwide stand at lows not seen since the 1960s is heartening news. Crime, which once was thought to be unstoppable and unmanageable, seems to have plateaued, at least for now. This phenomenon leads policy analysts and criminologists to

FIGURE 6.2

U.S. Violent Crime Rate, 1960–2014

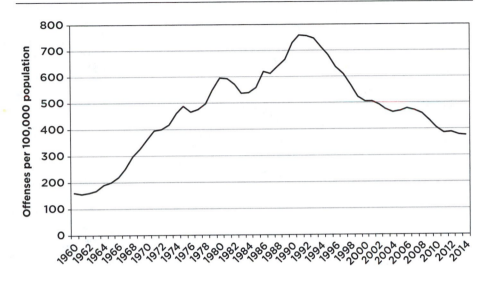

Source: FBI Uniform Crime Reports.

FIGURE 6.3

U.S. Murder Rate, 1960–2014

Source: FBI Uniform Crime Reports.

FIGURE 6.4

National Crime Victimization Survey Crime Rates, 1976–2012

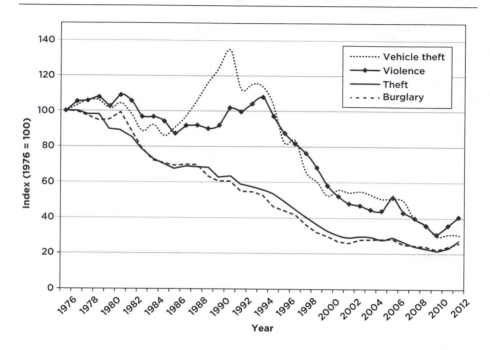

Source: Graham Farrell, Nick Tilley, and Andromachi Tseloni, "Why the Crime Drop?," *Crime and Justice* 43 (2014): 421-490.

a central question: Why has crime fallen? Undoubtedly, there is no single explanation for the drop in crime, but scholars have sought to identify major causes.

Scholars who study trends in the crime rate have attempted to explain reasons for the decrease in crime. Farrell, Tilley, and Tseloni (2014) hypothesize that improvements in the quality and quantity of security devices, such as electronic immobilizers on new vehicles or home security systems, is one factor explaining reductions in the crime rate. They also argue that crimes are linked, so that a decrease in vehicle theft may subsequently decrease violent crimes, as shown in Figure 6.5.

In turn, while violent crime and motor vehicle theft have declined, opportunities for crime over the Internet and cell phones have increased. Thus, it may be that a different type of crime (e-crime) will increase, while other types of crime (car theft) decrease (Farrell, Tilley, and Tseloni 2014). The Bureau of Justice Statistics reported that 17.6 million Americans, or about 7 percent of U.S. residents age sixteen or older, were victims of identity theft in 2014, but that number will likely increase. In 2017, Equifax, one of three credit-reporting companies in the United States, reported that cybercriminals accessed the personal information of as many as 143 million Americans, making it one of the worst cybersecurity breaches to date. However, as people become more aware of cybercrime, they are also taking actions to help prevent it. About 85 percent of U.S. residents took some kind

FIGURE 6.5

UCR Violent Crime, Including Homicide, and Motor Vehicle Theft Rates per 100,000 Population, 1960–2012

Source: Graham Farrell, Nick Tilley, and Andromachi Tseloni, "Why the Crime Drop?," *Crime and Justice* 43 (2014): 421-490.

of action to prevent identity theft, including checking credit reports, shredding documents with personal information, or changing passwords on financial accounts (Bureau of Justice Statistics 2015).

A study by the Brennan Center for Justice (Roeder, Eisen, and Bowling 2015) found that increased numbers of police and decreased use of crack cocaine were among the factors that helped start a downward trend in the crime rate in the 1990s. So, too, were demographic factors such as an aging population, increases in income, and consumer confidence. Law enforcement's use of a new database to manage crime called CompStat also contributed to crime rate declines from 2000–2013. Both the number of police on the street, and how police fight crime, are important.

The Brennan Center study further found that the things we commonly think of as decreasing the crime rate had no or little influence. For example, the use of the death penalty does not deter crime; nor do right-to-carry gun laws. Perhaps the most interesting observation from the study is that there is a limited effect of incarceration on the crime rate. In other words, putting more people behind bars does very little to reduce the crime rate.

This seems counterintuitive, but if you are familiar with the economic concept of diminished returns, it makes sense. We get a lot of public benefit by putting very violent criminals in prison. But swelling the prison population to include nonviolent drug offenders provides negligible crime control benefit. The study noted that California, Michigan, New Jersey, New York, and Texas have reduced their prison populations and crime in those states has not gone up. In fact, it has continued to fall (Roeder et al. 2015).

Public Perceptions about Crime

Given the downward trend of crime in the country over the last few decades, one wonders why perceptions are that crime is on the rise. One reason may be as noted above: different types of criminal acts, such as those using the Internet, are replacing more traditional types of crime, such as home burglary.

Public perception is also influenced by high-profile crimes, such as mass shootings in schools, including those described in the opening to the chapter. Mass shootings prompt national media attention, which in turn influences our understanding about crime. After the 2018 shooting at Marjory Stoneman Douglas High School in Parkland, Florida, students marched for gun control, taking their pleas to the state capital, Tallahassee, and to Washington, D.C. This kept the media spotlight on gun control.

Another reason why the public perceives an increase in crime is that politicians often like to talk about crime as a way to get voters' attention. Sometimes, this is in response to a tragedy, such as a mass shooting. Other times, however, politicians describe year-to-year trends, which can lead to erroneous conclusions. For example, in 2016, presidential candidate Donald Trump campaigned on ridding major cities of crime, especially in the inner cities of places like Chicago. He noted in a July 11, 2016, speech, "Our inner cities are rife with crime. According to the *Chicago Tribune*, there has [*sic*] been more than 2,000 shooting victims in Chicago alone this year" (Robertson 2016). He referenced the city's newspaper story, which noted an increase over the same period in 2015. Chicago would end 2016 with what was described by the *Chicago Tribune* as a "soaring pace of violence," with 4,368 shooting victims and 762 homicides—the most since 1996, when there were 796 (*Chicago Tribune* 2017; Rosenberg-Douglas and Briscoe 2017). Chicago had more murders that year than Los Angeles or New York (Martin 2016).

However, two items are worth emphasizing. The first is that, as a matter of public policy, it is better to look at long-term trends rather than do a comparison from year to year. Trends over decades, as shown in Figures 6.2 to 6.5, provide a more accurate accounting of the crime rate. One should not put too much stock in year-to-year differences. A second point is that a few U.S. cities have increases in crime while the trend for the nation is in decline, or holding steady. Analysis by the Grawert and Cullen (2016) of the thirty largest cities in the United States showed that half of the increase was attributable to just three cities: Baltimore, Maryland; Chicago, Illinois; and Washington, D.C. Other big cities, such as New York, have not experienced increases in the crime rate.

Staying with the Chicago example, we see another point worth noting regarding the crime rate. Just as some cities have spikes in crime while others do not, some communities within Chicago have greater incidences of crime than other communities. The city of Chicago aggregates reported crime from the Chicago Police Department's Citizen Law Enforcement Analysis and Reporting System, or CLEAR. This database, accessible through the Chicago Data Portal, provides a map of the incidence of crime, as well as the type of crime reported. Astute real estate agents use this dataset in selling properties in areas with lower incidences of crime. However, more important for public policy is that the dataset, and ones like it in other cities, should provide guidance as to where to direct more public safety personnel, install better lighting, advance neighborhood protection programs, or focus economic stimulus programs, rather than make blanket statements about an entire city.

A final item of note regarding the crime rate and public perception takes us back to our opening story about the horrific shooting at Virginia Tech and subsequent arguments for and against guns on campus or in public schools, and the reasons for gun violence. In Chicago, Police Superintendent Eddie Johnson lamented that gun violence was endemic to the city's West and South sides, and cast blame on a "national climate against law enforcement" and lax sentencing guidelines for repeat gun offenders. By his reasoning, more public support for police and stronger punishments for persons engaged in gun violence would help keep crime in check. Others, however, would argue for more gun ownership among citizens, adopting the oft-quoted argument of National Rifle Association (NRA) CEO Wayne LaPierre that "the only thing that stops a bad guy with a gun is a good guy with a gun" (Arter 2012). Reflecting that sentiment after the school shooting in Parkland, President Trump suggested that teachers with gun expertise should bring their weapons to school to protect children in their classrooms.

Still other policymakers point to a decrease in street stops by police and a decline in arrests, as well as abysmal and dangerous conditions in some neighborhoods prone to drive-by shootings (Rosenberg-Douglas and Briscoe 2017). They observe, too, the economic disparity among Chicago communities. In an interview, the Reverend Jesse Jackson suggested, "You can't police poverty. You must eliminate poverty. You must educate children, employ parents, and provide transportation. Chicago's inner city has been treated unlike the rest of the city, and the results are predictable.... We need an even playing field for opportunities, for education, health care and job training" (Martin 2016).

It seems clear that criminologists, policy analysts, politicians, and policymakers have very different views on the crime rate, the reasons for crime, and possible solutions. It's no wonder that public perceptions may inaccurately perceive escalating crime. Still, despite some year-to-year upticks, especially in a few cities such as Chicago, and continued mass shootings, the *overall trend* for crime has been in decline for the last few decades. Next, let's look at the incarceration rate and the phenomenon of mass incarceration.

The U.S. Incarceration Rate

Americans put a lot of people in jail. The most recent incarceration rate reported by the Bureau of Justice Statistics is 670 adults per 100,000 U.S. residents (Carson 2014). (The incarceration rate for males is 1,242 per 100,000; females have a much lower rate of 82 per 100,000.) Over 2.2 million people are behind bars in the United States, representing a staggering increase of 500 percent over the last forty years (The Sentencing Project 2017). In 2015, 1 in every 115 adults in the United States was in jail or prison. The number of people in prison is so high that America has the dubious distinction of being the world's leader in putting people behind bars, as shown in Figure 6.6. Our incarceration rate is more than the rate of Russia and China combined, and far greater than European countries, leading the nonprofit organization The Sentencing Project to wryly note, "Our criminal

FIGURE 6.6

International Rates of Incarceration per 100,000

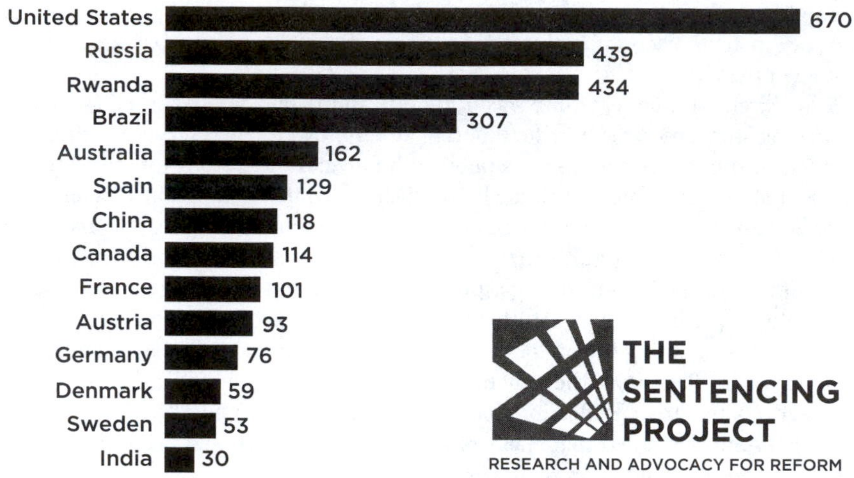

United States	670
Russia	439
Rwanda	434
Brazil	307
Australia	162
Spain	129
China	118
Canada	114
France	101
Austria	93
Germany	76
Denmark	59
Sweden	53
India	30

THE SENTENCING PROJECT

RESEARCH AND ADVOCACY FOR REFORM

Source: Walmsley, R. (2016). *World Prison Brief.* London: Institute for Criminal Policy Research. Available online: http://www.prisonstudies.org/world-prison-brief.

justice system today is like a bicycle stuck in one gear: the prison gear" (The Sentencing Project 2017).

A major contributor to higher rates of incarceration was a shift in policy orientation among state legislatures and the U.S. Congress. Beginning in the 1990s, states and the federal government enacted stricter laws in an effort to "get tough on crime." These included the three strikes and truth in sentencing laws described later in the chapter. By taking away the discretion of prosecutors and judges to impose lighter sentences, prison numbers grew dramatically.

America's policy called the "War on Drugs" aimed at eradicating drug use through strict laws, strong enforcement, and harsher sentences. By 2015, nearly half of people in state prisons were convicted of nonviolent drug, property, or public order crimes; people convicted of drug offenses represented half of federal prison inmates (The Sentencing Project 2017). Most inmates currently in federal prison for drug offenses were convicted of crimes related to marijuana. The Obama administration saw tough drug policies for low-level, nonviolent drug offenses as unjust and pledged to seek early release or lighter initial sentences for these offenders. President Obama granted clemency to more than 1,300 federal prisoners convicted of nonviolent drug crimes, and called for compassionate release of elderly prisoners. The Trump administration, notably Attorney General Jeff Sessions, reversed these policies and sought to impose tough sentences for persons convicted of federal crimes.

Mass incarceration has created another public policy crisis—overcrowded prisons. The courts have taken a dim view on prisons that do not provide enough beds for inmates, finding that to be a violation of the Eighth Amendment protection against cruel and unusual punishment. As a result, state and federal prisons have to accommodate a growing prison population either through early release programs, building more prisons, sending prisoners to local jails rather than state correctional facilities, or putting prisoners in privately run prisons. All of these solutions have potential downfalls, and all of them put a strain on public budgets.

Our incarceration rate, in addition to the human toll on the families of prisoners and the prisoners themselves, is costly. A study done for the Prison Policy Initiative found that the system of mass incarceration costs around $180 billion every year (Wagner and Rabuy 2017). Of that amount, $81 billion is the cost of running corrections systems (prisons, jails, parole, and probation). These costs fall largely on the states, since the states account for the vast majority of people put in prison. Rising costs affect the ability of states to spend in other policy areas. For example, many states spend almost as much on corrections as they do on higher education, and eighteen states, including California, Colorado, Florida, Michigan, Oregon, Pennsylvania, and Vermont, spend more on corrections than on state colleges and universities (Ingraham 2016; National Association of State Budget Officers 2016).

Without efforts to reduce prison populations, another factor is likely to escalate costs, and that is health care for prisoners. The prison population is getting older, and the Bureau of Justice Statistics reports that people over the age of fifty-five are the fastest-growing age group in the U.S. prison population. This trend is unlikely to change in the near future as a result of stricter, mandatory minimum sentences that put people in prison for a long time, sometimes for life. As the population in prison ages, elderly prisoners have increased needs for medical care, including prescription drugs, surgeries for heart and cancer disease, and end-of-life care. In addition to geriatric-related medical needs, elderly prisoners will need added protection from younger, predatory inmates in the general prison population. As states enact policies for an aging prison population, costs will increase (Abner 2006).

Next, let's look at the history of federalizing crime, evolving attitudes about crime, and the role of the media in shaping our perceptions of criminals and criminal activity.

HISTORY AND DEVELOPMENT

Federalizing Crime

At the founding of the country, few crimes were prosecuted in national courts. Crime was viewed as a state and local concern, and law enforcement activities rested almost exclusively with the states. States still prosecute the vast majority of crimes, but Congress has passed laws asserting federal jurisdiction into what had been the long-standing domain of state governments, including laws that dealt with interstate commerce and the misuse of the U.S. mail, such as mail fraud (American Bar Association 1998). This trend continued into the twentieth century, as congressional power to regulate interstate commerce prompted many new laws.

Take, for example, the Prohibition era—those thirteen years when the manufacture, sale, and transportation of alcohol were prohibited by the national government. The Eighteenth Amendment, which banned for the first time alcoholic beverages throughout the United States, and the National Prohibition Act, commonly referred to as the Volstead Act, designed to implement the amendment and define powers of enforcement, greatly increased activity in federal criminal law enforcement. The Volstead Act set the starting date for nationwide prohibition as January 17, 1920, and created a new federal law enforcement agency: the Bureau of Prohibition. This soon gave rise to organized crime and gangsters, the most famous of which was Al Capone, who ran a crime syndicate in Chicago built on illegal alcohol sales. Gangsters ran the operation, and crime increased dramatically. Federal law enforcement officers were soon assisting local and state agents. Eliot Ness and his team of Untouchables became famous for taking down Capone and saw the growth of federal agents in the FBI and the agency known today as the Bureau of Alcohol, Tobacco, Firearms, and Explosives (ATF).

This is perhaps the most famous example of federalizing crime, but the trend includes other crimes, such as crimes that violate civil rights, hate crimes, environmental crimes, and immigration crimes. This creates overlapping jurisdictions (such as we saw in the Rodney King example), and also causes growth in the federal criminal justice system, increasing costs, expanding the power of federal agencies such as the FBI or the ATF, and creating burdens on the federal courts and prisons.

So why would Congress choose to criminalize conduct under federal law, when state laws are on the books? To answer that question, we return to politicians. Federal crime legislation is politically popular, as people perceive that the federal government will act more effectively than state governments. However, the American Bar Association concluded that "increased federalization is rarely, if ever, likely to have any appreciable effect on the categories of violent crime that most concern Americans, because in practice federal law enforcement can only reach a small percent of such activity" (American Bar Association 1998, 18).

In short, while federalization of crime has increased, primarily due to efforts to get tough on drug-related crime, the bulk of the criminal justice system is in the hands of state governments. States were given police powers under the Constitution, and will likely remain the major players in addressing crime and shaping criminal justice policy.

Public Attitudes about the Incidence of Crime

Polling done by Gallup and other organizations suggests that people are concerned about crime in the United States, though not necessarily in their neighborhoods. In 2010, crime and punishment did not rise to the top of most voters' lists of local or state concerns, according to research by the Pew Center on the States (Public Opinion Strategies 2010). In this study, only 2 percent of voters rated crime as the most important problem facing their state. This is true even though most of the voters in the study incorrectly believed the national crime rate was on the rise. Most important, people overwhelmingly supported programs that reduced prison time for nonviolent, low-risk offenders (87 percent; Public Opinion Strategies 2010). Most voters understood the costs of incarceration and wanted to minimize costs while still keeping their communities safe.

The public perception that crime is a problem at the national level, but not in most communities, was confirmed by Gallup polling. When asked by Gallup in 2016 if they worry about crime a great deal, a fair amount, only a little, or not at all, 53 percent of U.S. adults replied they worried a great deal about crime and violence (Davis 2016). In 2017, just after the Las Vegas shooting that killed fifty-eight people, 59 percent of respondents described the problem of crime in the United States as extremely or very serious. However, only 12 percent of respondents believed that crime in the area where they live was extremely or very serious, and 22 percent did not believe crime was a problem at all in their neighborhood (Gallup 2017).

When demographic characteristics of the survey respondents in 2016 are included, several observations are possible. First, people with no college education are twice more likely to worry about crime than are college graduates (70 percent and 32 percent, respectively). Second, nonwhite respondents, and those making less than $30,000 per year, are also more likely to worry about crime.

The same study found increased worry about drug use as well—a valid concern, given that drug overdose deaths in this country continue to increase. The Centers for Disease Control and Prevention estimate that ninety-one Americans die every day from an opioid overdose, noting that the majority of those deaths are related to legally prescribed opioids (Centers for Disease Control and Prevention 2017). Here, again, people with a high school education or less were much more likely to see drug use as a great concern (66 percent) compared with college graduates (22 percent). While one factor for this variation may be that less educated, lower-income respondents live in more dangerous neighborhoods, Gallup pollsters suggest that increased concern about crime might also be due to the extent and type of media coverage of violent crime. Let's look at the role of the media in shaping our opinions about crime.

Media and Crime

Most people come to understand criminal behavior and the U.S. justice system through their consumption of media—what they watch on television or in movies, including both news programs and fictional crime shows. Given this, criminologists have explored the effect that media have on public attitudes about crime. When we view stories of real crime, often sensationalized by the news media, or watch television shows and movies containing fictional violent criminal acts, does it create fear among the general public and influence criminal justice policy attitudes? The answer is mixed. Many studies have found that regular viewers of crime shows are more likely to fear crime (Dowler 2003; Gerbner et al. 1980). Gerbner et al. (1980) observed that extended viewing of television violence resulted in people perceiving a greater threat from crime. The researchers believe that viewers internalize violent images and see the world as a dangerous and dark place. Dowler argued that, in part, this is due to the way criminals are portrayed in the media as greedy, revengeful, brutal, or mentally ill—having characteristics that make them amoral and different.

Take, for example, serial killers. Perhaps the fictitious Hannibal Lecter or Freddy Krueger come to mind. Or maybe you are thinking about the infamous, real-life killer Ted Bundy, whose murderous rampage before he was caught involved at least thirty homicides in seven states, or Jack the Ripper, who mutilated and killed at least five women in the East End of London in 1888. Movies are made about these gruesome criminals, books are written about them, and television crime shows focus on them. But the reality is that serial killers are criminal anomalies—far fewer exist than what we may imagine by watching crime shows, reading thrillers, or going to the movies. Based on FBI crime statistics, serial killings account for no more than 1 percent of all murders in the United States (Bonn 2014). Serial homicide captures our imaginations largely due to the larger-than-life images of serial killers presented by the media.

The effect of sensationalized coverage of crime is that the viewers of crime shows and violent movies see offenders as monsters to be feared. Media not only tend to stereotype persons who commit criminal acts as arch-villains, but many crime shows focus on violence and sex crimes where the perpetrator is unknown to the victim. In reality, most criminal acts involve persons known to the victim. The media overplaying of sensational criminal behavior also masks the reality of property crimes and tends to exaggerate the success of law enforcement to solve cases.

In short, the media distort the reality of who commits a crime and who is a victim. It is not too surprising, then, that people who regularly watch crime drama are more likely to fear crime. The relationship between watching crime shows and increased fear, however, is not absolute. Criminologists have found that the effect of media on increasing fear of impending violent crime is limited because other factors, such as the way we are raised, our exposure to a range of different cultures and communities, and education help temper our understanding about the incidence of crime.

If watching crime drama on television makes us slightly more fearful that we will become victims, can media actually prompt people to become criminals themselves? Scholars have suggested that media may actually cause crime. People may imitate what they see on television or in the movies. They also may learn criminal techniques or become desensitized to criminal acts.

ACTORS IN CRIMINAL JUSTICE POLICY

Many actors are involved in identifying and preventing crime, as others are involved in prosecuting, incarcerating, and rehabilitating criminals. Victims of crimes have rights under our criminal justice system, as they and their families may be traumatized, incapacitated, or worse. This section explores the role of law enforcement personnel, the courts, and the victims of crime.

Federal Law Enforcement Agencies

Law enforcement agencies range from small-town police departments to large federal agencies. At the federal level, sixty-five agencies have some law enforcement duties, many of them housed in the Department of Justice, including the Bureau of Prisons; the Federal Bureau of Investigation; the Drug Enforcement Administration; the U.S. Marshals Service; and the Bureau of Alcohol, Tobacco, Firearms, and Explosives. The Department of Justice is headed by the attorney general, who oversees federal law enforcement operations. Another important federal law enforcement agency is U.S. Customs and Border Protection, one of the largest law enforcement agencies in the world. It employs more than 60,000 people in safeguarding the country's borders, screening cargo, enforcing U.S. trade laws, and preventing terrorists from entering the country.

State and Local Law Enforcement Agencies

State law enforcement agencies are established by the state government, and they vary among the states. All states have an Office of the Attorney General, which serves to enforce state laws, typically housed in a state-level Department of Justice. Many of these state-level departments also house state bureaus of investigation with crime labs and specialized personnel to assist local police. Unlike the U.S. attorney general, who is appointed by the president and confirmed by the Senate, most state attorneys general are elected by the people.

Every state operates a state highway patrol agency to enforce traffic laws and promote traffic safety by inspecting commercial vehicles, ambulances, school buses, and other large vehicles. While state highway patrol personnel have a primary mission to enforce traffic laws, they also possess full law enforcement authority and can enforce any state law.

Most familiar to many people are law enforcement agencies at the local level. These include police departments in towns and cities. Most counties have sheriffs and sheriff's offices created by state governments. Local police departments are tasked with upholding local laws, patrolling neighborhoods, and investigating local crimes. While we tend to think of federal enforcement agencies as the most sophisticated, many large cities have impressive and significant roles in criminal law enforcement. Additionally, many municipalities have community policing programs, where police officers and members of the community partner to solve public safety issues.

Federal and State Courts

Both federal and state courts hear criminal and civil cases. The criminal court process varies slightly among states, but the following is a brief overview of the beginning of the process. The process starts when a prosecutor files charges against an individual accused of committing a crime. This results in an initial appearance, or arraignment, where the charges are read and penalties and constitutional guarantees of a right to legal representation are explained. For felony cases, the next step after the initial hearing is a preliminary hearing. The government must demonstrate that sufficient evidence exists, or probable cause, that the accused individual has committed the crime. If the court finds probable cause, then the case is transferred to a trial court, called a district court. This step ends with the defendant entering a plea (guilty, not guilty, or nolo contendere, or no contest). If a plea of not guilty is entered, bail is set.

If the process is important to ensure the rights of anyone accused of a crime, so, too, are the judges who oversee the trial. Judges must guard against impropriety on the part of the lawyers, or the audience in the court room. They must work closely with the court reporter, who is taking down every word spoken by witnesses and the attorneys. A criminal court clerk must keep all records and files in order. Court coordinators provide further assistance to the jury and to keeping the caseload of the court running smoothly. Given the workload, judges have a demanding role to play. Their ability to exercise discretion, ensuring justice and finding compassion in the sentence, has been influenced by evolving policies explored later, such as "three strikes" laws. Their core duty is to enforce the law, even ones they may find objectionable. A case may be appealed to an intermediate, or appellate, court on the basis of an error in the process, and eventually may reach the state supreme court.

A federal crime is prosecuted in the federal court system, which has a similar process, where cases are heard in federal district courts and may be appealed to a U.S. court of appeals. There are ninety-four federal judicial districts and twelve regionally based courts of appeals.

Crime Victims

Being a victim of a crime can be a life-changing experience. Victims must deal with the trauma of a violent act, or face unparalleled grief. States and the federal government have passed laws to establish victim's rights. These laws require that victims are informed about the criminal justice process, from the arraignment of the offender until that person is released from prison. In most states, victims have the right to be heard during sentencing or parole decisions. Victims also have the right to be protected from threats, intimidation, or retaliation during criminal proceedings. These protections may include police escorts, restraining orders, or even relocation (National Center for Victims of Crime 2012). Federal and state agencies further support and protect crime victims by offering sexual or domestic abuse assistance and partnering with counselors and mental illness specialists. Many states have compensation funds that may cover medical, counseling, or funeral expenses, as well as lost wages that are not covered by insurance or other programs. Victims of crime have a right to seek restitution by offenders, which means that the offender should pay to repair some of the damage that resulted from the crime.

Probation Officers and Parole Officers

These officers perform a vital role in the criminal justice process. Probation officers work with individuals who are given probation instead of jail time. During the time of probation these officers monitor the probationer with the goal of keeping the public safe and also rehabilitating the probationer. They develop treatment plans and report to the court on the progress (or lack thereof) made by the individual on probation.

Parole officers work with individuals who have been released from prison and are serving parole. Parole is an early release of a prisoner that is conditioned upon that person's continued good behavior. Parole officers monitor a parolee, with the goal of helping the parolee reenter society and not commit another crime. Both parole and probation officers schedule regular meetings with their supervisees, and may provide job training or substance abuse counseling to aid in rehabilitation. This works as an important back-stop in the system.

MAJOR U.S. CRIMINAL JUSTICE AND CRIME POLICY STATUTES

As discussed at the beginning of the chapter, there are many types of crimes at the federal and state level, and it is not possible to list them all here. However, policies on sentencing have fluctuated over the last few decades, resulting in two types of laws worth mentioning. One approach that gained popularity in the 1990s is truth in sentencing. **Truth in sentencing,** as the name implies, is designed to reduce any uncertainty about the amount of time an offender must serve in prison. By 1999, forty-one states and the District of Columbia had passed laws implementing some form of the truth-in-sentencing requirement (Sabol et al. 2002). Most states required offenders to serve 85 percent of their imposed sentence; some states eliminated parole release and imposed determinate sentences. The aim was directed to the severity of punishment approach, as policymakers reasoned that individuals may choose not to commit a crime if they knew there was little or no chance of an early release.

Another law that gained prominence in the 1990s is referred to as "**three strikes.**" Directed at repeat offenders, this policy imposes stiff sentences, ranging from twenty-five years to life imprisonment, on persons convicted of a third felony. Twenty-six states and the federal government have "three strikes" laws in place. The federal law provides a good example. In 1994, Congress passed the Violent Crime Control and Law Enforcement Act, creating a powerful "three strikes" provision to deal with violent repeat offenders

(Harris 1995). Under the federal "three strikes" provision, a defendant receives mandatory life imprisonment if he or she is convicted in federal court of a serious violent felony and has two or more prior convictions in federal or state courts, at least one of which is a serious violent felony. The other prior offense may be a serious drug offense (Harris 1995). Policymakers believe that criminals facing life imprisonment would be deterred from committing additional crimes, and that keeping career criminals behind bars would decrease crime. Prosecutors also can use three strikes as leverage over first- and second-time offenders.

However, three strikes laws have been sharply criticized. One critique is that "three strikes" can violate an individual's guarantee under the Eighth Amendment to be protected from cruel and unusual punishment. Take, for example, the case of *Lockyer v. Andrade*. The defendant in the case, Leandro Andrade, stole $150 worth of children's videotapes from two separate stores in 1995. Andrade had committed unarmed burglary in 1983. As bad luck would have it, California had passed its three strikes law the year before Andrade took nine videotapes from two discount stores. Worse for Andrade, the prosecutors were able to elevate these petty thefts from misdemeanors to felonies. Thus, Andrade was tried under the newly fashioned three strikes provision and sentenced to fifty years in prison. Had the "three strikes" law not been in place, Andrade might have served a year for petty theft, or even three years as a repeat offender (Chemerinsky 2003). Though the conviction was overturned in the Ninth Circuit U.S. Court of Appeals as a cruel and unusual punishment, the U.S. Supreme Court reversed. Without intervening clemency by the governor of California, Andrade will be eighty-seven years old before he is released from prison (he was thirty-seven at the time of his conviction).

A third criticism is that the severity of punishment has been shown to be less effective than the certainty of punishment. To put it simply, "three strikes" laws and other tough-on-crime measures are not powerful deterrents. For one thing, deterrence theory assumes that human beings act rationally (Wright 2010). Drug and alcohol use may impair the ability to think clearly about the consequences of any actions. Also, someone acting passionately in the moment may not stop to consider what will happen if he or she breaks the law. Other criticisms of three strikes laws are that they are disproportionately applied to persons of color—a topic of the next section—and that prison overcrowding often results.

Capital Punishment

Sentencing someone to death is the ultimate punishment, and has been part of America's criminal justice policy since before the founding of the country. The first recorded execution occurred in 1608, in the Jamestown Colony of Virginia, and colonies soon adopted laws imposing the death penalty, sometimes for minor offenses such as stealing grapes or chickens (Death Penalty Information Center 2017). By the mid-1800s, public opinion in some states began to shift away from capital punishment. Michigan was the first state to abolish the death penalty for all cases except treason; Rhode Island and Wisconsin abolished the death penalty for all crimes. However, in the 1930s, criminologists persuasively argued that the death penalty was a necessary social measure to curb crime, and once again, the death penalty found public support. By 1950, public sentiment turned away from imposing the death penalty, and fewer death sentences were imposed (Death Penalty Information Center 2017).

Beginning in the 1960s, cases were brought to the courts arguing that the death penalty was a violation of the cruel and unusual punishment guarantees of the Eighth Amendment. Advocates of abolishing the death penalty argued that the imposition of capital punishment was too arbitrary. They had some facts on their side: repeated studies revealed a pattern of either race-of-victim or race-of-defendant discrimination. For example, in Louisiana, the odds of receiving a death sentence were 97 percent higher for offenders who murdered a white person than for those whose victim was black (Death Penalty Information Center 2018). The U.S. Supreme Court effectively voided death penalty laws across the country in 1972, in *Furman v. Georgia*. In a 5–4 split decision, the Court ruled that states' laws governing the death penalty were not imposed uniformly. After this case, states worked to improve the process of capital punishment. Four years later, in *Gregg v Georgia*, the Supreme Court upheld the new state policies regarding the death penalty, and that the death penalty, properly applied, did not violate the Eighth Amendment. However, capital punishment remains controversial. Box 6.1 explores public support for capital punishment over time.

ISSUES AND CHALLENGES

Deterrence and Recidivism

A key question any student of public policy interested in crime and punishment should ask is simply: Does punishment prevent crime? More broadly, how can policymakers lower the incidence of crime? **Deterrence** is the inhibition of criminal behavior, or discouraging a crime because the potential perpetrator fears the consequences of his or her behavior. Criminals may be deterred in two ways. The first is by increasing the *certainty* or likelihood of being caught. Calculating the risk of apprehension is familiar to any driver going over the speed limit who has slowed down on a public highway when in view of state troopers or police officers. We reduce our speed because we perceive that the likelihood of getting a ticket is much greater in the presence of law enforcement. Another way that criminal behavior may be deterred is by the *severity* of punishment. In this case, potential offenders weigh the consequences of their actions and conclude that the risk of punishment is too severe. Capital punishment, or the death penalty, provides a stark example of how severe a punishment may be.

Another core challenge in criminal justice policy is keeping someone who has committed a crime from doing it again. If correctional policies work, then a person should not relapse into criminal behavior. **Recidivism** is measured by criminal acts committed by an individual that results in a subsequent arrest, reconviction, or return to prison with or without a new sentence within three years after the individual is released (National Institute of Justice). Studies of recidivism rates are not encouraging. The Bureau of Justice Statistics studies find that most prisoners commit additional crimes. One study tracked over 400,000 prisoners over a five-year period, with sobering results: nearly 77 percent of released prisoners were rearrested within five years, and over half were arrested within the first year of release from prison. Over 82 percent of property offenders committed another crime and were arrested (Durose et al. 2014). Policies to lessen recidivism include job training and education, drug or alcohol rehabilitation programs, as well as providing ongoing support in the community. Staying away from gangs can

Box 6.1: Telling Stories with Data

The Death Penalty

As of 2018, thirty-one states and the federal government permit the death penalty to be imposed in murder and treason cases. Between 1976 and 2018, 1,469 executions have taken place (Death Penalty Information Center 2018). As shown in Figure 6.7, the majority of Americans still favor imposing the death penalty on persons convicted of murder. However, public support was less in 2016 (49 percent) than in the previous forty years. Opposition to capital punishment has correspondingly increased, as people acknowledge the risk of putting an innocent person to death, the disparate imposition of the death penalty for persons of color, and the growing belief that it is not an effective crime deterrent (Masci 2017). Execution methods have also become suspect after media reports of botched executions using lethal injection or the electric chair.

What do you think?

Looking at the graph, it appears as though the two lines (showing support and opposition) are coming together. Comparing the two trends, do you think the number of people opposed to the death penalty will soon exceed the number of people expressing support for it, as happened in 1966? Why or why not?

FIGURE 6.7

Public Support for Capital Punishment, 1936–2016

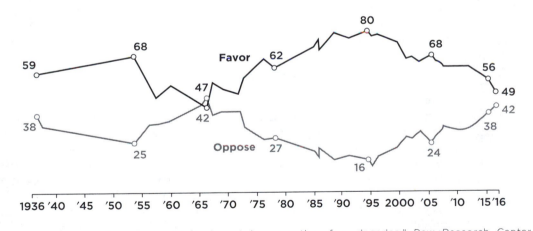

Source: "Support for death penalty lowest in more than four decades," Pew Research Center, Washington, DC (September 29, 2016), http://www.pewresearch.org/fact-tank/2016/09/29/support-for-death-penalty-lowest-in-more-than-four-decades/.

be effective. Hooley (2010) notes that the most important determinant of whether an individual released from prison will reoffend is the peer group of the offender once he or she is released from prison.

Crime and Race

A reality of crime and U.S. public policy is the existence of a racial divide in the conviction and punishment of persons of color when compared to white Americans. In the early decades of the twentieth century, remnants of the overt discrimination after the Civil War resulted in many black men receiving poor representation, unfair trials, and long prison sentences—or worse. The infamous case of Ed Johnson illustrates this point. In 1906, Johnson, a black man, was charged with raping a white woman. He was convicted in a Tennessee court and sentenced to death, even though more than a dozen witnesses testified that he was working at the time and there was no direct evidence linking him to the crime. After the U.S. Supreme Court issued a stay on the execution in order for the case to be appealed, a lynch mob grabbed Johnson from the county jail and hanged him from a bridge outside of town. No one from the lynch mob was indicted (Spohn 2015).

Today, much of this kind of flagrant racism has been addressed. Black defendants are no longer tried by all-white juries, with scant evidence, denied bail or attorneys. The days of vigilante lynch mobs are over. However, inequities persist. Persons of color are more likely to be prosecuted, given longer sentences, and receive the death penalty. The proportion of blacks in state and federal prison has increased dramatically since 1918, when blacks represented 22 percent of the prison population. That percentage continued to increase until blacks comprised over half of the prison population by 1990 (Spohn 2015). The U.S. Bureau of Justice Statistics reported in 2014 that 35 percent of state prisoners were white, 38 percent were black, and 21 percent were Hispanic—a troubling statistic, since whites comprised 62 percent, Hispanics 17 percent, and blacks just 13 percent of the general U.S. population in 2015 (U.S. Census Bureau 2015). A study by The Sentencing Project revealed that African Americans are incarcerated at five times the rate of whites, and in five states (Iowa, Minnesota, New Jersey, Vermont, and Wisconsin) it is close to ten times the rate (Nellis 2016). The Pew Center on the States study noted similar overrepresentation of persons of color in prison, and that among black men aged twenty to thirty-four, one of every nine was incarcerated (Pew Center 2008).

Criminologists offer varying explanations for the overrepresentation of persons of color in U.S. prisons. Some scholars observe that the racial disparity is due to the fact that persons of color have higher arrest rates and, therefore, higher incarceration rates (Blumstein 1982). However, more recent research suggests that higher arrest rates may be poor surrogates for higher rates of crime, as the act of arresting an individual may itself be biased. They suggest that racial biases, including racial profiling and targeting of inner cities, also explain different arrest and incarceration rates. Racial profiling by law enforcement is the practice of targeting people for suspicion of crime based on race, ethnicity, religion, or national origin (National Institute of Justice 2013). The American Civil Liberties Union, and other organizations, fights racial profiling, noting that it violates the U.S. Constitution's equal protection guarantee, is ineffective, and alienates communities from law enforcement.

Yet another factor that helps explain higher incarceration rates between persons of color and white Americans is the shift of policy toward stricter sentences for drug offenses. Harsher drug laws that started in the 1980s accelerated the arrest of African Americans.

In part, this was due to a law enforcement focus on street crimes, which prompted more arrests of young black males. A 2009 Sentencing Project study found much higher arrest and incarceration rates for drug offenses for African Americans between 1995 and 2005. African Americans comprised approximately 13 percent of the drug users but accounted for 36 percent of drug arrests and 46 percent of drug convictions during this time (Mauer 2009).

While the factors explaining the relationship between race and crime are complex, these disparities suggest the need for continued scrutiny by policymakers. As one scholar observed, "The fact that more than half of the young black men in any large American city are currently under the control of the criminal justice system (or saddled with criminal records) is not—as many argue—just a symptom of poverty or poor choices, but rather evidence of a new racial caste system at work" (Alexander quoted in Spohn 2015, 58).

Juvenile Crime

Yet another issue in criminal justice policy is under what conditions juveniles should be treated as adults. Juveniles who commit crimes face an escalating set of punishments, based on the type of crime, location, state law, and inclination of the prosecutors and juvenile court judge. These authorities decide whether to handle the situation informally, file a petition to request an adjudicatory hearing, or move to a waiver hearing. A waiver hearing transfers juveniles to criminal court so they may be tried as adults. The Juvenile Justice and Delinquency Prevention Act of 1974 required states to keep youth under the jurisdiction of the juvenile court and out of adult jail. Therefore, as long as juveniles are tried as juvenile delinquents, they enjoy protection under the law. The law also provided funds for states to address state and local juvenile justice programs. However, once states permitted youth to be tried as adults, the law did not apply.

Like the three strikes and truth in sentencing policies that began in the 1990s, state legislatures also moved to lower the minimum age at which a juvenile may be waived into the adult system. Getting tough on juveniles produced the intended effect. The number of cases sent to criminal courts more than doubled between 1988 and 1994 (Furdella and Puzzanchera 2015). Similar to the decline in the crime rate, juvenile court cases have also dropped after peaking in the mid-1990s. The net effect was that juveniles were less likely to be arrested for violent crime and serve time in prison in 2017 than they were twenty years earlier. The juvenile violent crime rate fell 46 percent, and the rate at which youths were sent to prison dropped 53 percent between 2001 and 2014 (Horowitz 2017).

Even though fewer juveniles are prosecuted as adults today than in the 1990s, states still put sixteen- and seventeen-year-olds, and sometimes even younger, in prison after trying them as adults. On any given day, an average of 7,500 youth are incarcerated in adult prisons (Campaign for Youth Justice 2007), and over 2,225 prisoners serving life sentences without the possibility of parole had committed crimes as children (Coalition for Juvenile Justice n.d.).

Children as young as thirteen had been sentenced to effectively spend their lives behind bars until the Equal Justice Initiative brought a lawsuit challenging the mandatory life without parole sentences for children. The organization was successful in making its case, which involved two separate incidents in which fourteen-year-old boys committed homicide. In 2012, the U.S. Supreme Court ruled in *Miller v. Alabama* and *Jackson v. Hobbs* that mandatory life sentences without parole violated the constitutional rights of persons seventeen years old and younger (Equal Justice Initiative 2016). In a 5–4 decision, the Court held that children must be given an opportunity for parole, as life imprisonment represented a disproportionate punishment for children (*Miller v. Alabama*).

While tough-on-crime advocates continue to feel that trying children as adults reduces crime, studies have reached opposite conclusions. One study by the MacArthur Foundation (2015) showed that children under the age of eighteen in adult corrections facilities face harsher settings, experience more developmental problems, and reoffend at higher rates that juveniles in juvenile correctional facilities. Moreover, they typically lack access to educational resources or rehabilitation programs.

Another issue is that youth in adult prisons are especially vulnerable to victimization because of their age and size. Less than half of the states offer additional protections for incarcerated youth in adult prisons (for example, requirements that juveniles be kept separate from adults). Children in adult prisons are twice as likely to be assaulted by staff, and 50 percent are more likely to be attacked with a weapon than are children housed in juvenile facilities (Coalition for Juvenile Justice n.d.). Not surprising, children in adult prison are thirty-six times more likely to commit suicide than are children in juvenile facilities (Campaign for Youth Justice 2007).

Other studies suggest that incarcerating children in adult facilities also increases the likelihood that young offenders will commit additional crimes, and that those crimes will be more serious and violent in nature (Kolivoski and Shook 2016). Kolivoski and Shook (2016) also found that the younger the age of the juvenile, the higher number of prison misconducts that person is likely to have. Misconduct is perhaps understandable, as juveniles are also more likely to be victimized in prison.

Mass Shootings

The chapter opened with the horrifying mass shooting at Virginia Tech in 2007, when thirty-two people were killed, prompting debates about gun control and the right to carry guns on college campuses. It would be nice to say that mass shootings are part of the past, but sadly, that is anything but the case. Over 1,620 mass shootings occurred between December 2012, when a gunman walked into Sandy Hook Elementary School and killed twenty children and six adults (including his mother) before shooting himself, and February 2018, when a former student shot and killed seventeen people at Stoneman Douglas High School (*The Guardian* 2018; Lopez 2017). Bookmarked between these tragedies are memorable mass shootings. A gunman opened fire on an outdoor concert on the Las Vegas Strip, killing fifty-eight people and wounding over five hundred others in 2017, to date the largest mass shooting in U.S. history. He used a device called a bump fire stock on his weapon, effectively turning it into a machine gun. A little over a month later, another gunman entered a small church in Sutherland Springs, Texas, and opened fire, killing twenty-six people in the largest mass shooting in Texas history. While these mass shootings are remarkable for the number of people murdered, they have become commonplace, as this country averages more than one mass shooting every other day. (A mass shooting is defined as involving four or more victims.)

Studies consistently show that the mass shootings in the United States are unique in the world. America has nearly sixteen times the number of gun-related homicides than other developed countries. The United States also has more guns—lots more guns—than other countries. Americans own over 40 percent of the civilian-owned guns in the world, but represent about 5 percent of the world's population. Gun control advocates point to data that show countries with greater control over the access to weapons have far fewer mass shootings. As discussed in the opening vignette, states with more guns have more gun deaths. Gun ownership advocates, embracing the position of the NRA point to the Second Amendment, which guarantees the right to bear arms. The NRA has long been an influential group in the national gun debate, and has effectively blocked efforts to limit gun ownership.

However, increasingly vocal citizen groups, spearheaded by the Parkland students in 2018, are advocating for the ban of semiautomatic weapons and accessories like bump fire stocks, universal background checks, raising the age at which a person can purchase a semiautomatic weapon from eighteen to twenty-one years old, and other methods of gun control. Controlling the incidence of mass shooting requires new public policy approaches, as well as a careful conversation about gun control.

In sum, issues and challenges in addressing deterrence and recidivism, rethinking tough-on-crime laws, racial disparities, the extent to which juveniles should be treated as adults when they commit crimes, and the uniquely American problem of mass shootings present opportunities to create new policies. Capital punishment presents ongoing challenges in its proper application and in decreasing levels of public support. We offer an everyday citizen connection for you to consider crime more broadly.

Everyday Citizen Connection

If you've never experienced a crime or viewed a prison, you may be thinking, "So what does this have to do with me?" The answer is that crime and public policy involve all of us. How we maintain public safety, while at the same time being a just society, has implications for our democracy. Keeping us safe is a primary obligation of government—but so is protecting our freedoms and our constitutional guarantee to equality. If we are to maintain both a fair and humane country, how we treat persons who commit crimes is important. We need to think carefully about when, and for how long, to incarcerate someone who commits a crime. After all, every person in prison is someone who cannot contribute to the social fabric of society. We need to consider the importance of the criminal justice system and the need for fair trials and due process—something the founding fathers saw as critical to our democracy.

Moreover, we should look broadly at the policy implications of mass incarceration, not only as a matter of humanity, but as one that takes a vast fiscal and social toll. As Joseph Stiglitz observes, "When 1 in 28 children has a parent in prison, the cycle of poverty and unequal opportunity continues a tragic waste of human potential for generations" (Stiglitz in Roeder et al. 2015, 1). As noted in this chapter, the estimated costs of incarceration exceed $80 billion per year; add the cost of policing, prosecuting, and providing criminal courts and the annual cost reaches nearly $200 billion. To put this in perspective, the budget of the EPA in 2016 was approximately $10 billion. The cost of incarceration exceeds the state budgets of Alabama, Nebraska, North Dakota, and Tennessee combined. Money spent on incarceration is money that can't be spent other ways, such as to fund education, make college affordable, provide for environmental protection, or add to our social safety net for people in need.

Discovery Question:

Take a moment and consider another country. Use this country to do a basic research search on how its prison system is designed. Are the data similar to those of the United States? Why or why not?

Policy Choices: Gun Control

Choice #1: States' Choice in Gun Control/Status Quo	Choice #2: Universal Background Check	Choice #3: Ban on Assault Rifle
In recent years, there have been a number of mass shootings in the United States. Despite this growing number nationwide, many state governments and interest groups believe that states should retain the right to pass laws relating to gun control rather than creating federal laws on gun control. While some states have chosen to pass additional background checks as a response to mass shootings, other states have responded by passing laws to allow concealed handguns without concealed-carry permits in the United States. Thus, some states have responded to the increase in mass shootings by adding additional restrictions, while others have responded by passing laws with increased access to concealed- or open-carry laws. For instance, Texas recently allowed for open-carry in most public places as of January 1, 2016. In regards to proposed sweeping federal regulations, twenty-four states have proposed to fight any federal legislation on gun control and insist gun control policy should be left to the states. Many opponents of increased federal restrictions to gun control laws focus on unreliable data on gun violence, ownership, and sales.	About 40 percent of guns purchased in the United States are done without a background check. A recent poll after the Orlando nightclub shooting in 2016, which killed 50 people and wounded 53, found that 92 percent of Americans favored a universal background check when purchasing a firearm. While a federal universal background check might be a challenge to pass in Congress, many states are closing the loophole by requiring background checks at the state level. Federal law prohibits firearm possession by a number of classifications including felons, fugitives, certain domestic-violence offenders, and those found to be a danger to themselves or others due to mental illness or involuntarily committed to a psychiatric institution. These restrictions, however, are only limited when purchasing through a federally licensed gun dealer and do not apply to gun shows or to private or online sales of firearms. Therefore, many people restricted from federally licensed firearm sales can still purchase firearms through other dealers. The proposal to expand background checks seeks to close such loopholes in current legislation.	Those who carried out the mass shootings in Parkland, Florida; Orlando, Florida; Sutherland Springs, Texas; Las Vegas, Nevada; Newtown, Connecticut; and Aurora, Colorado, to name a few, used assault-style rifles to inflict a large amount of causalities. Proponents of a national assault rifle ban believe that such a ban would restrict an assailant's ability to carry out mass shootings. Assault rifles were banned under Title XI of the Federal Violent Crime Control and Law Enforcement Act of 1994. Subtitle A: Public Safety and Recreational Firearms Use Protection Act banned the possession, transfer, and manufacturing of certain semiautomatic and large-capacity firearms. This ban expired in 2004. Neither the Bush II administration nor Congress sought to renew the ban. Those who oppose the ban on assault rifles argue that only a small percentage of gun crimes are committed with assault-style weapons. However, those who support the ban report the percentage of crimes that used assault rifles decreased by one-third while the ban was in place. Proposed bans on assault-style weapons seek to expand the number of types of weapons included in the ban,

Policy Choices: Gun Control

Choice #1: States' Choice in Gun Control/Status Quo	Choice #2: Universal Background Check	Choice #3: Ban on Assault Rifle
However, such lack of reliable data could be a result of gun lobbyists' desire to restrict federally funded research on gun control. For example, in 1996, the NRA succeeded in removing funding from the Centers for Disease Control and Prevention (CDC), the primary federal agency studying gun violence. Since then, there have been few conclusive studies on gun control in the United States, creating a challenge for evidence-based decision making.	Opponents of this legislation do not believe that those banned from federally licensed dealers intend to purchase firearms legally. Therefore, the expansion of background checks would be highly ineffective at reducing access to firearms. However, proponents of the ban believe it would make it more challenging for those restricted from purchasing firearms to do so under a universal background check.	impose background checks on current owners of guns under the ban, and prohibit the trade of assault-style weapons. The focus on the ban would be weapons with large-capacity machines or guns that are able to fire multiple rounds in a short amount of time. After the shooting in Parkland, stores such as Dick's Sporting Goods indicated that semi-assault weapons would not be sold. A March to Save Our Lives in March 2018 hoped to draw political attention on a nationwide ban.

Sources: Tamara Lytle, "Gun Control: Will Recent Shootings Spur New Laws?" *CQ Researcher*, July 25, 2016, http://library.cqpress.com/cqresearcher/cqr_ht_gun_control_2016, accessed March 5, 2018; Barbara Mantel, "Gun Control: Should Lawmakers Tighten Firearm Restrictions?" *CQ Researcher* 23, no. 10 (March 8, 2013): 233–56, http://library.cqpress.com/.

CONCLUDING THOUGHTS

This chapter looked at crime and policy in America. We learned that public attitudes and policy positions regarding crime change over time, and that our crime rate is lower today than during the peak of the 1990s. Media can shape our perceptions about the incidence of crime, as we see many violent crimes reported on the news, on television shows, and at the movies. Mass incarceration, a phenomenon of the tough-on-crime laws, makes the United States the number one country in the world for putting people in prison. As we enter a new era, policymakers will need to consider how to address racial discrimination, prison overcrowding, how to prevent recidivism, and whether or under what conditions capital punishment should be imposed. All of these policy issues touch in some way the use of guns in our country. We pay a heavy price for gun violence, which leads us to policy choices about the extent to which our Second Amendment constitutional guarantee to bear arms should be limited by public policy. One hopes that the mass shootings will never happen again, but the way we remain safe on college campuses, schools, and other public or private venues will require informed decisions about guns and gun control.

GLOSSARY TERMS

crime rate   130

criminal justice   128

criminology   128

deterrence   144

incarceration rate   130

jurisdiction   129

recidivism   144

"three strikes"   142

truth in sentencing   142

Uniform Crime Reporting
Program   130

DISCUSSION QUESTIONS

1. How would you describe the crime rate and public perceptions about crime?

2. What accounts for the rise of mass incarceration, and what problems does mass incarceration present?

3. What evidence do you see of racial discrimination in sentencing policies?

4. Do you support capital punishment? Why or why not?

5. Which of the issues described in this chapter seem most important to you?

SUGGESTED RESOURCES

Suggested Websites

Coalition for Juvenile Justice, http://www.juvjustice.org/

Crime and Justice Research Alliance, http://crimeand justiceresearchalliance.org/

Death Penalty Information Center, https://death penaltyinfo.org/

National Institute of Justice, https://www.nij.gov/Pages/welcome.aspx

Prison Policy Initiative, https://www.prisonpolicy.org/

The Sentencing Project, http://www.sentencingproject.org/

Suggested Books or Articles

Alexander, Michelle. 2012. *The New Jim Crow: Mass Incarceration in the Age of Colorblindness.* New York: The New Press.

Campaign for Youth Justice, 2007. *Jailing Juveniles: The Dangers of Incarcerating Youth in Adult Jails in America.* Report from the Campaign for Youth Justice. November 2007. http://www.campaignforyouthjustice.org/Downloads/NationalReportsArticles/CFYJ-Jailing_Juveniles_Report_2007-11-15.pdf. Accessed March 5, 2018.

Scheingold, Stuart A., and Malcolm M. Feeley. 2011. *The Politics of Law and Order: Street Crime and Public Policy.* New Orleans: Quid Pro Quo Books.

Wilson, James Q., and Joan Petersilia. 2011. *Crime and Public Policy.* 2nd ed. New York: Oxford University Press.

Suggested Films

Dead Man Walking, DVD, directed by Tim Robbins (1995: United States), http://www.imdb.com/title/tt0112818/

The House I Live In, DVD, directed by Eugene Jarecki (2012: United States), http://www.pbs.org/independentlens/films/house-i-live-in/#

In the Land of the Free, DVD, directed by Vadim Jean (2010: United States), http://mobfilm.com/projects/in-the-land-of-the-free/

12 Angry Men, DVD, directed by Sidney Lumet (1957: United States), http://www.imdb.com/title/tt0050083/?ref_=nv_sr_1

The Untouchables, DVD, directed by Brian De Palma (1987: United States), http://www.imdb.com/title/tt0094226/?ref_=nv_sr_1

for CQ Press

Sharpen your skills with SAGE edge at **http://edge.sagepub.com/rinfret.** **SAGE edge for students** provides a personalized approach to help you accomplish your coursework goals in an easy-to-use learning environment.

Education Policy

LEARNING OBJECTIVES

Readers of this chapter will be able to:

1. Explain and describe the way in which education is structured in the United States

2. Understand how U.S. public schools have transformed from one-room schoolhouses to online learning

3. Assess the roles of various stakeholders in education policy and evaluate solutions for the future

BEHIND THE CURTAIN OF A PUBLIC EDUCATION

Are you thinking about becoming a teacher? Your answer is probably no, and you are not alone. Over the last decade, there has been a steady decline in enrollment in teacher education programs across U.S. colleges (Westervelt 2015). To understand why, we turn to a story from one of the author's mothers—a recent retiree from a public middle school in rural Ohio.

My mother graduated from high school and pursued a two-year associate's degree in paralegal studies. She worked in a law firm for several years, got married, and started a family. The demands of being a legal secretary for a large firm were not conducive for a mother of three, so she decided to go back to school to become a teacher. She fed her kids dinner each night and then drove an hour (one way) to the University of Akron to take coursework to become certified in K–12 education. She wanted to become a teacher not only to work in the same building as her own children, but to give back to her community. She eventually got a job teaching fifth grade at a nearby middle school where many of the children came to school hungry because their parents either forgot to feed them or did not have the money to buy food. But she was committed to ensuring that every student receive access to a high-quality public education regardless of their socioeconomic standing.

After a twenty-five-year career, she opted for early retirement. When asked if she would suggest that college seniors pursue a career in teaching, she paused and eventually stated:

> The flexibility or benefits of being a teacher are no longer glamorous. Teachers are demonized by the media and even politicians as lazy and incompetent. I was not lazy, nor were my colleagues. You work from 6 a.m. to 6 p.m. and in the summer you get ready for the next

year. The job is so important, but the current climate is hard and the constant focus today is teaching to a test. If your students do poorly on a standardized test, you don't get funding. Most of my students didn't have parents to help them go over homework, let alone food to eat. It is a hard, yet rewarding job.

She noted that being critiqued is part of any job, but that parents, the general public, and elected officials forget what a public education is supposed to be about. Her teaching career was enjoyable, yet she retired early because of the constant pressures to "teach for the test" or the politics of school funding. She encouraged us to discuss with our own students the inner workings of our U.S. educational system by looking behind the curtain and exploring the relationships—or the lack thereof—between our K–12 and higher education experiences.

To honor the experiences of this former teacher, this chapter attempts to pull back the curtain to understand the complexities of U.S. education policy. The U.S. education system is complex, and as a result, this chapter only begins to remove some of the layers. We start with an overview of education policy in the United States, detailing key aspects of primary and secondary education while also discussing the role of higher education. We pay particular attention to the roles that state and federal actors play in influencing our educational system. Our understanding is guided by a web of actors, including but not limited to the president, Congress, federal agencies, governors, teachers, parents, and students. Although this chapter is not exhaustive, the primary objective is for you to understand some of the challenges we face and how to devise plausible solutions if you decide on a future career in education at the local, state, or federal level.

···

OVERVIEW OF U.S. EDUCATION POLICY

Education is defined as knowledge or development, and **education policy** is the collection of laws that guide education. In the United States, education is often defined as a distributive policy—it provides benefits for an entire community, but can also be defined morally and politically. Education is defined morally because it helps individuals within a country to increase their knowledge or social mobility. It is political because it informs individuals about issues and how to become involved (Kraft and Furlong 2017).

Understanding the Structure of a U.S. Education

The U.S. education system structure is complex and a classic example of federalism, as described in Chapter 3. Regardless, unlike any other country, a U.S. education is primarily the responsibility of state and local governments instead of the national government, as there is no provision for education in the U.S. Constitution.

Remember that under the Tenth Amendment, "The powers not delegated to the United States by the Constitution, nor prohibited by it to the States, are reserved to the States respectively, or to the people." Accordingly, state and local governments control primary and secondary education. Primary education is for students ages five to eleven (typically kindergarten through fifth grade). **Secondary education** contains students ages twelve to eighteen (typically sixth through twelfth grade). For students ages five to eighteen, the term K–12 is often used. The federal government focuses more on higher education (e.g., community colleges and colleges) for individuals ages eighteen or older due to its historical role in U.S. education policy, to which we turn later in this chapter.

Table 7.1 expands upon some of the key differences between federal, state, and local authority. We begin with an examination of some of the overarching responsibilities of the federal government in U.S. education policy more broadly. The federal government's role in U.S. education surrounds three broad areas: policies related to education funding, collection of data and research, and enforcement of discrimination laws (Chen 2016). Congress passed the Elementary and Secondary Education Act in 1965 to provide federal grants to improve the public education system in the United States. The U.S. Department of Education (DOEd) ensures the implementation of national policy and conducts research to evaluate national educational trends and patterns. Additionally, the DOEd's Office of Civil Rights enforces U.S. civil rights laws to prevent discrimination for programs or activities that receive federal funding (Office of Civil Rights 2017). In 2016, for example, the DOEd stated that all students, including transgender students, can attend school in an environment free from discrimination based upon sex.

Moreover, and something that might interest you as a college student, is the College Scorecard (see Photo 7.1). This is also administered by the DOEd, which collects national data about colleges across the United States, such as how much it will cost to attend a particular college or the probability of obtaining employment upon graduation. Let's say you wanted to pursue a four-year degree in public administration and the location did not matter—the College Scorecard generates a list of schools that have this degree program available, the cost to attend, graduation rate, and earnings potential after graduation.

By way of comparison, state and local governments work together to oversee public education for their respective state. As Table 7.1 indicates, their involvement with education includes: allocation of funds for public schools; setting standards for curriculum; licensure for schools, teachers, and staff; and the election or appointment of members for school boards. We use the analogy of a pie to examine the allocation of education funds per state. The ingredients of the education funds pie are generated by us, the taxpayers. However, state actors (e.g., governors, state legislatures, local school boards) determine the size of the slice of pie that is received. Although the federal government does provide each state, on average, 9–10 percent of the financial support for state education (Center for Public Education 2018), each state determines how much of its *entire annual state budget* it will contribute to K–12 education and public colleges.

The allocation varies from state to state. For example, in Alabama 55 percent of the state budget is allocated toward education, Florida 40 percent, and Vermont 87 percent

TABLE 7.1

Local, State, and Federal Roles

Set Standards for Curriculum	Federal Government
• Licensure for schools, teachers, and staff • Elect or appoint members of school boards	• Makes policies related to education funding • Collects data and research • Enforces discrimination laws

(Center for Public Education 2018). Within these state education allocations, state legislatures and governors designate the amount that each school district and public college or university receives within these state allocations. However, these allocations often do not cover the amount needed to fund your local high school or current college. The remaining amount of money needed to run K–12 public education is primarily raised from a local **property tax,** or in some cases, gasoline or tobacco taxes can be earmarked to support education. Higher education is funded through additional revenue streams such as tuition and research grants.

PHOTO 7.1 College Scorecard

U.S. Department of Education.

Once education funds are allotted, we need to consider what mechanisms are put into place to ensure implementation. Put simply, standards are implemented by state and local actors. Let's turn back to our opening vignette of our recently retired public school teacher to describe how this works. The state of Ohio's Department of Education works with county or city school boards to set the standards for curriculum and licensure requirements for teachers. In most states, public education is divided into local school districts. The school district is managed by a school board, which can set educational requirements and planning education needs of a community (Center for Public Education 2018). For example, Ohio's Department of Education has a checklist for all school districts to use across the state that determines what type of classes and how many credits a graduating high school senior must complete in order to graduate. Teachers and staff are hired based upon educational and state licensure requirements and annually rated on their performance (e.g., accomplished, skilled, developing, or ineffective).

With our broad definitions regarding both systems—K–12 and higher education—it is also important for us to understand the status and scope of education policy and how they relate to the history and development of education in the United States.

Status and Scope

Longitudinal research allows us to explore the twenty-first-century status and scope of education in the United States. Measures of educational success range from graduation rates, diversity, and where the nation ranks internationally. Let's consider some data to observe where the United States currently stands:

- From 2000–2013, the high school dropout rate declined by 5 percent (Kent 2015).
- Since 2002, school-aged children have become more diverse—one out of five children is Latino (Kent 2015).
- Since 1997, the percentage of minority enrollment in public elementary and secondary schools has increased by almost 20 percent (Kent 2015).
- On average, the United States spends $115,000 per pupil, but ranks thirty-fifth in math and twenty-seventh in science internationally (Kent 2015).

- As of 2014, 51 percent of five- to eight-year-olds knows how to use a computer (Clemmitt 2013).
- Millennials (eighteen to thirty-three years of age) are on track to become the most educated generation to date (Kent 2015).

On the surface it appears the United States has improved in terms of decreasing the high school dropout rate, increasing the diversification of public schools, and providing access to technology in the classroom. And, although the millennial generation is on track to having the highest percentage to receive a high school education, the question remains: How do we define the term *education*? Does our conceptualization of being educated mean students successfully completing their graduation requirements and taking standardized tests, or are students well versed in how to conduct research, critically think about a problem, or—most important—are they effective public speakers? As our previously stated overview noted, it depends on state and local requirements.

Nonetheless, do these statistics uncover what is going on behind the curtain of our U.S. education system? For many Americans, the largest challenge is how we pay for our public education—property taxes. Cory Turner (2016) from National Public Radio explains that "America's schools have a money problem" and demonstrates this through an interactive map for us to explore in Box 7.1: Telling Stories with Data.

More specifically, the web link provided in Box 7.1 demonstrates that the resources your state spends on your K–12 education can impact the decision you make whether or not to attend college or what college you select. For example, does your high school have a guidance counselor? This person can serve as the gatekeeper to providing high school students with assistance in deciding whether or not to attend college. Nevertheless, if your public high school generates less property tax than the state next door or a nearby city, does

---

Box 7.1: Telling Stories with Data

Using Maps to Explore Education Funding

When you open National Public Radio's map (https://www.npr.org/2016/04/18/474256366/why-americas-schools-have-a-money-problem), you can explore two schools in Illinois to demonstrate that where you live impacts the education you receive. We explore our own states to visualize the money spent on K–12 education (per pupil): Colorado spent $8,985, Montana $11,017, and Ohio $11,354.

What do you think?

Does it matter that Ohio spends more on per pupil education than Montana and Colorado? Put differently, what's the connection between what someone spends on college and what a state spends per pupil for K–12 education? Some argue the amount of money spent on K–12 education does impact the education you receive.

this create inequities? The straightforward answer—property taxes vary from neighborhood to neighborhood, and in turn, so do the resources school districts have to provide for a public education—the books or courses that are available for selection.

This just scratches the surface on K–12 public education. What about the costs of a college education? The average debt for a U.S. college graduate is $30,000 (National Center for Education Statistics 2017). But maybe we ignore this because we are used to our "free" public education (K–12). Regardless, in 1984, the cost of a four-year college education, on average, was $10,210. In 2015, the average cost was $21,728 (National Center for Education Statistics 2017). Our Canadian neighbors pay approximately $5,000 per year for college, on average. Our current successes and concerns provide a snapshot into the educational landscape. However, in order to best understand how our educational system has evolved, we first explore the history of our U.S. educational system. This allows us to recognize where we came from and how we can move forward.

HISTORY AND DEVELOPMENT OF THE U.S. EDUCATION SYSTEM

Much of our education policy history is guided by statute, but before we turn to this, we highlight some of the major historical milestones. This overview provides an important baseline to understand our education policy past, which informs our present.

Colonialism and Mann

The idea of a free K–12 education did not always exist; in fact, it is a relatively new idea (*Education News* 2013). Originally, children learned to read and write in church, but many colonists realized this was not sufficient. By the early 1600s, colonies began partially to fund grammar schools, which were limited to young men. Unless they were from wealthy families that could afford a private education, young women were limited to picking up reading and writing skills at home (*Education News* 2013).

By the 1800s we began to see a change in our public education due to the work of Horace Mann. The Common School Movement, led by Mann, wanted every child to receive an education funded by local taxes. Moreover, Mann preferred a high-quality education, with standardized grading and common standards. He desired an educational system that did not vary from district to district, but instead a homogenized public school system (*Education News* 2013). The motivations behind Mann's efforts were due in part to his notion that an educated citizenry engendered civic participation, and therefore political stability. And, as a result, his efforts led to more than 100,000 one-room schoolhouses across the United States.

By way of comparison, higher education did not receive a great deal of attention until the U.S. economy slowly shifted from agriculture to industry in the nineteenth century. Accordingly, in 1862, Congress passed the Morrill Act to create land-grant colleges to create a highly skilled labor force to meet the needs of a growing, industrialized society. The goal for land-grant colleges was—and is to this day—to train students in engineering and technical agriculture in states such as Iowa, Kansas, Michigan, Ohio, Pennsylvania, and Texas. From here, the U.S. educational system becomes a bit more complex, with concerns surrounding the diversification or fairness of an education.

Challenges and Change

The description of Mann's Common School Movement appears simplistic in comparison to the 1950s and 1960s—among the most significant periods in U.S. education policy history. In 1954, the landmark Supreme Court case *Brown v. Board of Education* challenged *Plessy v. Ferguson* (1896), which held that schools could be separate based upon color as long as equal accommodations were provided. Many black students in schools across the southern United States did not receive equal accommodations, and the Court intervened, noting that the schools should be desegregated. For almost ten years, the desegregation of southern schools was met with resistance until the passage of the 1964 Civil Right Act, which attempted to end segregation in schools and banned employment discrimination based upon a person's race, religion, sex, or national origin. Yet we still see how this exists today, which we discuss more in Chapter 8.

To continue the efforts of the civil rights legislation and maintain national educational standards, the Elementary and Secondary Education Act (ESEA) of 1965 was enacted under President Lyndon Johnson. The ESEA serves as a foundation for our education system today. As mentioned above, state and local governments control U.S. education; however, the federal government provides some funding for state and local governments. The ESEA offered "new grants to districts serving low-income students, federal grants for textbooks and library books, funding for special education centers, and scholarships for low-income college students. Additionally, the law provided federal grants to state educational agencies to improve the quality of elementary and secondary education" (U.S. Department of Education 2017). The 1970s brought additional protections for gender discrimination with the passage of Title IX. In particular, any school—K–12 or higher education—that receives federal funding cannot discriminate based upon an individual's sex. When we consider the implications of Title IX, we often think about the role it plays in sports. Because of this legislation, women cannot be discriminated against when wanting to play a sport, and it ensures that the same numbers of sports teams are available for men and women in schools across the United States.

More recent ESEA reauthorizations include—but are not limited to—President George W. Bush's No Child Left Behind Act (NCLB) of 2002 or President Barack Obama's Every Student Succeeds Act (ESS) of 2015. Although standardization and a quality education have been at the foundation of U.S. education since the 1800s, President Bush wanted to increase standards by requiring annual testing in reading and math for Grades 3–8. Each state needed to identify standards for students to meet: receive free and reduced lunches, provide adequate special education services, and support English language learners. Schools with majority low-income children were labeled Title I schools and were required to meet adequate yearly progress. If the standards were not met, the school could select a new leadership team and students could attend another school. Although "NCLB was intended to increase standards in public schools nationally [it] has actually declined since implementation" (Reckhow 2013, 19).

NCLB came to an end with President Obama's Every Student Succeeds (ESS) in 2015, though ESS still honors some of the basic tenets of NCLB, such as how best to address underperforming schools. The law created a new national center for literacy for students with disabilities and dyslexia to enhance reading and writing. Students are still tested each year, but the state determines the test and accountability measures—parents, however, can now opt out of state standardized states contingent upon state law. New York has one of the largest opt-out movements, with about 20 percent of students not taking standardized tests per year (Strauss 2016). With these examples, we begin to see how schools have transformed since Mann's framework of the 1800s. This transformation continues with **school choice** and the digital revolution.

Choice and a Digital Revolution

Today's schools are marked by change due to choice and technology. School choice began to gain traction in 2002 with the passage of NCLB. Recall that if a student attended an underperforming school she could choose to attend a different school. Within this framework, a small pilot program was established to provide students with a voucher to attend another school. This other school could be a private or religious school. The concern was that federally funded dollars would then be used for students to attend a religiously based private school, which could be in possible conflict with the Constitution's establishment clause; yet the Supreme Court deemed these practices acceptable in 2002. As a result, in 2004, Congress appropriated over $14 million for a voucher program in Washington, D.C., where students in underperforming schools could choose to attend a school of their choice.

School choice ranges from vouchers to magnet/charter schools. So what is the difference? A **voucher** provides public money for students to attend the school of their choice. Students can choose to attend another public school or magnet or charter school. A magnet school is publicly funded but focuses on a particular topic area, such as the sciences or the arts, and typically, students have to apply to attend the school. Dallas's School for the Talented and Gifted is an example of a magnet school that places an emphasis on advanced placement curriculum for high school students (*U.S. News & World Report* 2017). Charter schools are privately funded and not religious, but free for students to attend. For example, the rapper Pitbull opened his own charter school in Miami, Florida—the Sports Leadership and Management Academy for sixth through twelfth grades (Sanchez 2013).

In addition to school choice, the educational landscape has changed due to technology. After all, "The Information Age is only decades old. But many scholars argue, that, eventually, digital technology will change everything, including concepts of learning, as surely the greatest upheavals in history have done" (Clemmitt 2013, 213). In 2010, Wyoming was the first state to appoint a director of distance learning, and San Francisco's Flex School was the first public school to offer blended learning (a combination of in-person and online learning). Connecticut granted authority for students to complete their high school degree via online coursework. And Idaho requires all students to take two or more online courses to graduate from high school.

As technology advances, we are brought back to our introductory story—tight school budgets are not available across all school districts to keep pace. For example, many rural schools across the nation do not have the bandwidth for Internet connection, or old buildings need to be rewired to become twenty-first-century schools. Moreover, many college students in student teaching training programs do not have college curriculum to train the next generation of students (Clemmitt 2013).

Summarizing U.S. education policy history, we see how our system has evolved from one-room schoolhouses to students taking courses online to graduate. Yet the system seems complex, more so than those in some of the substantive policy chapters in this textbook. To evaluate if Americans are happy with the free education they receive, we turn to related

Gallup polling data. Since 1999, Gallup has asked Americans, "How satisfied are you with the quality of education students receive from K–12?" In 1999, 47 percent of respondents were satisfied, and in 2015, 43 percent were (Gallup 2015). Gallup has consistently asked Americans to rate their confidence in public education since 1973. In 1973, 58 percent of Americans had a great deal of confidence in the public school system. By way of comparison, the level of confidence dropped significantly in 2012 to 29 percent (Gallup 2015).

MAJOR EDUCATION POLICY STATUTES

The aforementioned historical context for U.S. education policy is essential to understand present concerns and the major actors involved. Before we move on to additional contemporary issues and concerns, we highlight some of the major statutes that define U.S. education policy by briefly discussing their major provisions in chronological order.

Major U.S. Education Laws

Morrill Act of 1862 The Morrill Act created land-grant colleges, which were federally controlled pieces of land granted to states to create and endow higher education institutions. The focus was to educate people in practical sciences (e.g., agriculture, military science, engineering).

Elementary and Secondary Education Act (ESEA) of 1965 This act worked to ensure all people, specifically those with disabilities, mobility problems, learning difficulties, or who live in poverty, access to education. It also promoted higher standards and accountability in state-run school systems. The ESEA has been reauthorized every five years (e.g., NCLB).

Family Educational Rights and Privacy Act (FERPA) of 1974 FERPA applies to all schools that receive funding from the Department of Education. The law allows parents the right to inspect and review the student's education records. If it is believed they are incorrect, it allows them to request that a school correct the records. The law also dictates what the schools can release to other entities.

Education of Handicapped Children Act of 1975 (Individuals with Disabilities Education Act [IDEA] of 1990) Originally the "Education of Handicapped Children Act" of 1975, it was amended and changed to IDEA in 1990. This law ensures that special education and individually required services are made available to all children with an "identified disability." It also works to make sure the disabled are provided with employment preparation and independent living skills, while also protecting the families of the disabled. Last, it offers assistance to educational service agencies in providing for the education of children with disabilities.

Improving America's Schools Act of 1994 This is a reauthorization of the ESEA. It created the Title I program, which gives additional assistance to disadvantaged students, and provided reforms for charter schools, safety in schools, Eisenhower Professional Development, Native American education, and technology and infrastructure improvements.

Goals 2000: Educate America Act of 1994 This act focused on increasing high school graduation rates, knowledge in STEM topics, and the social and emotional aspects of a child's growth. It set the foundation for NCLB and provided a framework to quantify every aspect of student progress.

No Child Left Behind Act (NCLB) of 2002 NCLB focused heavily on "standards-based education reform." The goal was to establish standard metrics upon which students could be evaluated, enabling individual students to then improve and succeed. It was replaced in 2015 with the ESSA.

Every Student Succeeds Act (ESSA) of 2015 The latest reauthorization of the ESEA, ESSA limits the federal government's role in elementary and secondary education, moving more accountability and responsibility to the states—a shift from the previous ESEA reauthorizations. The standardized testing that was so widely criticized in NCLB is retained in ESSA, albeit slightly less frequent.

This review of education policy statutes is not exhaustive but provides an overview of key pieces of legislation from past to present. As the chapter suggests to this point, education policy is complex and interconnected by a multitude of actors. The next section explores what role institutional and noninstitutional actors play in the creation and implementation of education policy.

MAJOR ACTORS IN U.S. EDUCATION POLICY

As we noted at the beginning of this chapter, much of the heavy lifting in U.S. education policy originates at the state and local level—teachers, governors, or school boards, to name a few. However, our core federal institutions also play an important role in setting the national landscape. Therefore, we discuss how the president, Congress, the courts, and the bureaucracy affect education policy more broadly.

President

Many of us might not realize this, but thirty-four out of our forty-five presidents to date have only had a bachelor's degree. Despite this fact, most presidents have taken an interest in promoting their own educational initiatives. For example, President Benjamin Harrison supported financial aid to teach literacy for southern blacks. President Gerald Ford signed into law the Education for All Handicapped Children's Act of 1975, which provided funding and guidelines for special needs children. And President Bill Clinton touted Goals 2000 so that Americans would be the first in the world in math and science. Moreover, presidents appoint (with Senate confirmation) who oversees the DOEd. This person can shape the direction of federal educational initiatives. For example, President Donald Trump's education secretary, Betsy DeVos, has demonstrated that a larger allocation of federal funding should be used for school choice (e.g., voucher schools). This policy perspective is in contrast with that of President Barack Obama's education secretary, Arne Duncan, whose priority was to focus on using data to make informed education policy decisions, standardization in educational curriculum, and holding colleges and universities accountable through the College Scorecard.

Although most U.S. presidents have focused on K–12 educational initiatives, presidents such as Johnson and Obama emphasized higher education. President Johnson is credited with the creation of the financial student aid system by which students can borrow money from the federal government to attend college and universities across the United States based upon financial need. President Obama has been hailed by many as the higher education president. In our aforementioned example of the College Scorecard, the Obama administration wanted to ensure students knew about the affordability of attending college and the predicted student earning upon graduation for colleges and universities across the nation (Ledermen and Fain 2017). Regardless, education policy is part of each president's platform, but one actor that serves an overlooked role in education policy is the first spouse.

For instance, Lucy Hayes was the first, first lady to receive a college education and promoted education for all, regardless of race. Nancy Reagan was a strong advocate for her Just Say No to Drugs program to inform children about the concerns surrounding drug abuse. And First Lady Michelle Obama aided in efforts to address childhood obesity by partnering with schools across the nation in her Let's Move campaign. This endeavor attempted to address the food offered during school lunches, providing healthier options and exercise for school children. Together, the president and first spouse can impact the direction of education policy in the United States.

Congress

Congress, with its constitutional lawmaking authority, sets national education policy for the United States to be implemented by the states. As our overview of major federal statutes noted, Congress's role has been to provide equal educational opportunities through civil rights legislation and setting national standards to ensure norms across states. The lead committee that oversees education policy is the U.S. House of Representatives' Committee on Education and the Workforce.

Since the 2000s, much of the discourse within the halls of Congress has been on the viability and future of school choice. Congress has appropriated funds for states to provide students the ability to choose which school to attend if their public school was categorized as underperforming. In 2015, Congress began to consider creating tax credits for K–12 students to select private schools if they were opposed to attending a public school in their neighborhood. This approach remains pending as we write this chapter due to the lack of bipartisan support for school choice.

Courts

Throughout history, Supreme Court rulings have had significant implications for U.S. education policy, primarily surrounding the provision of equal protection for students. *Brown v. Board of Education* led to the desegregation of schools in the 1960s, and *Lau v. Nichols* ruled that school boards could not discriminate against non-English-speaking students in 1974.

After the *Brown* ruling, President Dwight Eisenhower had to use the National Guard to enforce the desegregation of schools in the South. And a recent study conducted by the U.S. Accountability Office (GAO) reports that isolated schools, where 75 percent or more of the student population is dominated by one race, have grown since 2000. Many of these schools represent minorities in poverty who have higher dropout rates and offer less college preparatory classes for their students (Toppo 2016). Nonetheless, Supreme Court rulings have attempted to address social issues surrounding segregating schools, but concerns still exist to date. We delve more deeply into these concerns in Chapter 8.

Bureaucracy

The preceding discussion of the main branches of government briefly highlighted some of the major federal actors, yet as Chapter 4 reminds us, we cannot forget about the role that federal agencies play in the implementation and execution of policy. Here is a sample of two specific agencies:

- The **U.S. Department of Education (DOEd)** was formed in 1980. The DOEd is responsible for creating policy for federal financial aid for education and distributing and monitoring those funds. It also collects and disseminates research on schools, guides discourse on key educational issues, prohibits discrimination, and ensures equal access to education (ed.gov).
- The **Federal Trade Commission (FTC)** is designed to help protect consumers and, for education policy, helps in the regulation of for-profit educational institutions.

With these examples, we cannot forget that these agencies impact education policy. Federal agencies serve as education policy experts, collecting and disseminating data and report information so we stay informed about national trends in education. In addition, these agencies continue to protect the American people. In 2015, the DOEd promulgated a rule to safeguard students and taxpayers from predatory institutions that provide financial loans to attend college. This particular rule provides additional precautions for students before they borrow money to pay for school (U.S. Department of Education 2016).

The DOEd and the FTC can also work together to combat educational concerns. For example, in 2016, they filed a lawsuit against a for-profit college, DeVry University, for misleading advertisements to college students. Together, the agencies stated DeVry University made erroneous claims that within six months, 90 percent of college graduates receive employment. As a result, the two agencies have also helped to create the College Navigator (see Photo 7.2) to inform parents and students about potential scams about their selection processes (Smith 2016).

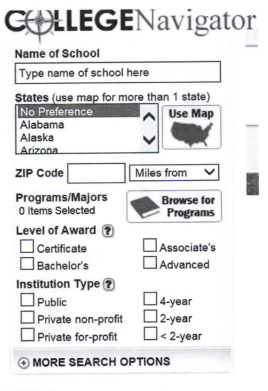

PHOTO 7.2

College Navigator

Federal Trade Commission, https://www.consumer.ftc.gov/articles/0395-choosing-college-questions-ask

STATE ACTORS AND VESTED INTERESTS

Although federal actors can shape or set the direction of U.S. education policy, state, local, and interest groups in education policy are far-reaching. Much like the president and Congress, governors and state legislatures determine how to implement education standards. Recall that the U.S. Constitution does not provide federal control over education policy; therefore, the states get to decide. Although there are national norms to follow, states, in conjunction with local governments, can set curriculum for students, funding allocations for school districts, and teacher certification requirements. In this section, we briefly describe how governors, state legislatures, state agencies, mayors, superintendents, and teachers drive education policy in their respective jurisdictions.

Governors and State Legislatures

Each year governors inform their state legislatures about their goals for specific policy areas and budget allocations. The gubernatorial educational initiatives vary from state to state. For example, Montana is one of the few states that do not allocate state funds to publicly support prekindergarten for children. Therefore, Montana's governor, Steve Bullock, created his own initiative, Early Edge Montana, to garner public support for educational opportunities for his state (Early Edge Montana 2017). In addition, gubernatorial decision making is influenced by their education policy advisers (GEPAs) or the so-called "education policy wonks" who work side by side with their governor to inform state actors, with research and data on how best to move forward with state education policy (Rippner 2015). This cadre of individuals are the experts in educational standards, and inform state legislatures and governors on education policy avenues. For example, in Washington State, these individuals work closely with state legislatures, constituents, and stakeholders to advise and develop education policy initiatives to support a governor's agenda (Washington Governor: Jay Inslee 2017).

We cannot forget the powerful part that state legislatures play in education policy. Since there is a variance across the states, two of the best resources to track state legislation are the National Conference of State Legislatures and the Education Commission of the States. Together or independently, governors and state legislatures can determine the curriculum for public schools. For example, a Republican lawmaker in Arkansas's legislature proposed a bill to ban Howard Zinn's *A People's History of the United States* from their public school libraries and classrooms (WBUR 2017). The concern was that this particular book was too liberal for students. By way of comparison, governors and state legislatures have worked together to design how sex education should be taught for their respective states. California governor Jerry Brown, for instance, advanced mandatory high school curriculum to prevent sexual assault (McGreevey and Megerian 2015). The education policies that state legislatures enact are then carried out by the state-level department of education and a variety of local actors.

State Expertise

Much like the federal level, each state has its own department of education. The implementation of statewide education policy would not be successful without the expertise

State Contacts

Contact the department of education, the higher education agency, special education agency and adult education agency in your state.

Commonwealths and Territories

- American Samoa
- Federated States of Micronesia
- Guam
- Northern Mariana Islands
- Puerto Rico
- Republic of Palau
- Republic of the Marshall Islands
- Virgin Islands

PHOTO 7.3

State Education Departments

U.S. Department of Education, https://ed.gov/about/contacts/state/index.html

of state-level departments of education. Experts within a state education department are responsible for crafting standards to meet national standards set by legislation such as NCLB or President Obama's Race to the Top program. The oversight of each state department of education varies; we suggest visiting the website listed in Photo 7.3 to examine what your own state's department of education oversees.

Nonetheless, individuals within state education agencies serve as the architects and implementers of education policy. The education policy experts help to maintain and analyze data inputs and outputs on a range of topics, from graduation rates to teacher certification programs.

Mayors, Superintendents, and Teachers

Shifting to the local level, mayors across the nation do not necessarily yield an official authority in education, but they can shape school budgets, boards, and direction for educational improvements. Mayors can serve as a loud voice in large metropolitan areas such as New York City. Bill de Blasio, the mayor of New York City, can promote his own initiatives to create public support to pressure governors and state legislatures to act. For example, in 2015, Mayor de Blasio stated he wanted additional funding to meet his goal to have all

New York City children read by the third grade (Lemire 2015). Rural mayors can work within their local communities by partnering with businesses or community organizations to ensure education stays on the public agenda because an educated workforce can help the economic development of a community.

At the local level, superintendents serve as the powerbroker for their school district by working with governors, state legislators, mayors, and the public. Superintendents can be elected by their city or county or appointed by a governor. A superintendent is essentially the manager or top executive of schools and works with their respective school board to hire staff, implement educational standards, and make decisions about funding. Recall that K–12 public schools are supported by local property taxes and the amount of money a superintendent has to allocate to schools across her district varies from county by county and state.

Nonetheless, there are a multitude of actors at the state and local levels. Yet one of the most important players in education policy are on the front lines—our teachers. Teachers are the unsung heroes of education and ensure our children can read and write. In 2015, 3.6 million individuals were employed as teachers for K–12 education. Despite their important role, only 39 percent of teachers are satisfied with their job, which is a 23 percentage decrease from 2008. Reasons for the decline in satisfaction range from stress levels to lack of funding to ensure a quality of education for their students (Richmond 2013).

Interest Groups

As we describe in each of our substantive policy chapters, interest groups within specific policy areas vie for access to influence outcomes. As Table 7.2 illustrates, education policy has a wide range of interest groups that attempt to enhance the understanding of particular issues for institutional actors, but also influence policies that are created. Some of the more notable, mainstream education interest groups for K–12 education include the National Education Association (NEA) and the National School Boards Association (NSBA). Some additional interest groups that focus on higher education range from the American Association of State Colleges and Universities or the Council for Higher Education Accreditation. To support teachers, the American Federation of Teachers (AFT) is a powerful union organization to protect the rights of teachers.

One interest group with which you might be most familiar is the National Parent Teacher Association (PTA), which serves to meet the needs of communities and parents. The PTA can serve as an influential force across U.S. school districts and has historically served a significant role in a wide range of policy areas, from child labor laws to juvenile justice reform. However, the twenty-first-century PTA has evolved into other individualized organizations such as MomsRising, which focuses on grassroots mobilization for issues surrounding women and mothers.

So far in this chapter, we have examined the history and development of education policy and considered the actors involved. Inevitably, there is interconnectedness among institutional and noninstitutional actors. But what about you, the student—where do you fit in the education policy web? To illuminate how well we all intersect, we use what is served at lunch for K–12 children.

TABLE 7.2

Examples of Federal Education Agencies

Interest Group	Overview	Find More Information
American Association of State Colleges and Universities (AASCU)	Organization that advocates for 420 member colleges, universities, and university systems	http://aascu.org/Default.aspx
American Federation of Teachers (AFT)	Has 3,000 local affiliates that represent 1.6 million members. Heavily involved in education policy and the political process	http://www.aft.org/
Association of Private Sector Colleges and Universities (APSCU)	Membership organization of career-specific educational programs (for-profit colleges and universities)	http://www.apscu.org/
Council for Higher Education Accreditation (CHEA)	Largest higher education membership organization in United States, with roughly 3,000 degree-granting colleges and universities	http://www.chea.org/
National Association of State Boards of Education (NASBE)	Centralized board to represent the different state boards of education across the country in nationwide policy discussions	http://www.nasbe.org/
National Education Association (NEA)	Advocates for all education levels from K–12 to higher education regarding federal policy	http://www.nea.org/
National Parent Teacher Association (PTA)	National organization that helps parents within communities organize to advocate for children	http://www.pta.org/
National School Boards Association (NSBA)	A federation of state associations consisting of over 90,000 local school board members. Gives local actors the opportunity to affect policy on the national scale	http://www.nsba.org/

What's for Lunch?

Figure 7.1 illustrates a laundry list of actors involved in deciding what students get to eat for lunch in K–12 schools. Congress established the U.S. Department of Education (DOEd) and the U.S. Department of Agriculture's (USDA) Child Nutrition Services Division to determine the standards for what should be served for K–12 school breakfasts or lunches. But consider a hypothetical scenario: a state legislature passes legislation to ban all junk food from K–12 vending machines, but it is pending the governor's approval. The state legislature justifies this decision based upon data collected from the DOEd and USDA.

Before making his decision, the governor is approached by the statewide PTA, teacher's union, students, state school boards, and the junk food vendor association. PTA members express mixed support for the new legislation because, on the one hand, they want to ensure their children have healthy options, but they also want them to have the freedom to make decisions about what to eat on their own. The junk food vendor association is outraged by this legislation and has held a weeklong protest outside of the governor's office in opposition to the bill.

To cast a wider net to make an informed decision, the governor meets with the teacher's union, students, cafeteria employees, and school boards. In his discussions, he finds that the teacher's union was ambivalent and cafeteria employees demonstrated concern that the junk food in the vending machine was often much cheaper for lower-income students to purchase food than fruit in the cafeteria for lunch. The school boards, much like the governor, heard voices in strong support and opposition. In the end, the governor decides to sign the legislation, based upon data provided by the USDA, DOEd, and research conducted by his own staff.

Although the junk food legislation is a hypothetical example, it demonstrates the myriad actors involved and the intersection of local, state, and federal actors. We close the chapter by addressing current issues and challenges.

FIGURE 7.1

A Tangled Web of Actors

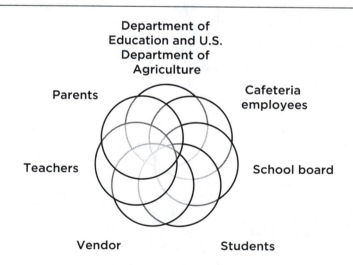

ISSUES AND CHALLENGES

Due to the web of actors involved in unveiling what is behind the curtain of education policy, it is no surprise that there are numerous challenges we face as a nation related to education policy. We explore four challenges: (1) defining a twenty-first-century education, (2) standardized curriculum for technological innovation, (3) connection for K–12 and higher education, and (4) a positive narrative to engender an education workforce for the future.

Paradigm Shift

In the United States, the goal has long been to provide a free public education to everyone regardless of race, class, gender, or socioeconomic status. Furthermore, national policies have sought to address inequities within this system to ensure that students from all backgrounds receive a quality education. Yet how do we define quality education when the implementation of education policy is a piecemeal approach that varies from state to state?

Also, the twenty-first century has seen a shift in our schools. The contemporary public school classroom across the nation is now dominantly defined as majority-minority. Put simply, the classroom is no longer homogeneously defined by race. However, what this shift has illustrated is an increase in student bodies who live in poverty, have a disability, and speak English as their second language. Therefore, as national coordinator for the Broader Bolder Approach to Education, Elaine Weiss suggests:

> Kids who are living in poverty need more, not less, of the supports that help upper-class children thrive. These include small classes, challenging, rich curriculum, individualized instruction, and supportive responses to emotional and behavioral challenges. It also means ensuring a meaningful "floor"—in terms of school readiness, physical and mental health, and nutrition—on which they can stand in order to viably learn. (Strauss 2013)

These disparities can often be linked back to by the funding used per pupil. Therefore, in order to remedy these challenges, a paradigm shift is necessary to provide a funding model that levels the playing field for all children to receive the same education. One thought is to follow the Finnish model, where their national government provides funding based upon the amount of students—if you have more students, you receive more funding. Moreover, if a particular school has nonnative speakers or students with disabilities, they also receive more funding. This is in stark contrast from the U.S. educational model, but a different model for examination.

Curriculum and Technology

We noted at the beginning of the chapter that most students know how to use a computer, and even some states such as Idaho require high school graduates to take online coursework. Yet what standards exist for the incorporation of technology in the classroom when many rural communities in the United States do not have access to high-speed Internet?

The concern is that our nineteenth-century idea of an education has not kept pace with technological advancements of the twenty-first century. Therefore, disparities exist between rural and urban communities in terms of accessibility to technology and training for educators on how best to use technology in the classroom. Moreover, the students who do experience technology in the classroom often enter college classrooms at public universities where professors do not utilize technology and often still use the tell-sell approach. This creates a disconnect between K–12 education and higher education, which in turn affects our economy when training and skills are not available in K–12 and higher education across the United States.

Connecting the Dots

The lack of connection between K–12 and higher education is apparent throughout this chapter. Much of the focus for state and local governments is funding a K–12 education, while the federal government sets standards for states to implement. However, we saw a shift with the Obama administration to focus its attention on higher education.

Yet these endeavors do not unpack the fact that the K–12 education we receive affects the college we decide to attend. Most European countries have programs in **elementary education** that serve as pathways for skills-based training or higher education. This is not to say the U.S. education system will evolve into a European model, but understanding that there is a disconnect and providing opportunities to collaborate in the future are necessary. Minnesota, for example, is working on a major proposal to better connect K–12 and higher education for its citizens. The goal is to close the gap between curriculums in high schools to ensure students are better prepared for a two- or four-year college education (Adams 2012).

New Narrative

Our opening story describes a retired public school teacher who was unsure whether or not she would recommend college graduates to enter a teacher education program. This is due in part to the current rhetoric used by elected officials that label teachers as lazy or overpaid. Such discourse has led to a rapid decline of students enrolled in teacher education programs in U.S. colleges and universities.

The fewer numbers of college students we have graduating from education programs is creating a hiring shortage for K–12 schools. Teachers serve an essential role in providing a free public education for our children across the nation. Recall that Mann wanted a readily accessible public education system in the United States because it creates civic engagement and a stable democracy. Yet the question becomes if the lack of interest in teaching is a detriment not only to our public education system but to society in general. To change the narrative would mean for more teachers to become involved and possibly run for office. Or for parents in local communities to discuss the impact that teachers have at any level on the future of their children.

The challenges described here are ripe for teachers and policy experts to craft plausible solutions to advance a twenty-first-century education. More specifically, such challenges are a call for action for you to become involved in crafting these solutions. Before we conclude, we offer our everyday citizen connection to stimulate additional thoughts more broadly about U.S. education policy.

Everyday Citizen Connection

This chapter delves into the multifaceted layers of U.S. education policy. But let's take a pause for a moment and consider a variety of questions and scenarios to determine if your everyday life ultimately affected your educational pathways.

Let's begin by considering some questions about your high school. Did your high school have a guidance counselor? Did this guidance counselor provide assistance for filling out and explaining college applications or the FAFSA? Or did your parents hire a consulting firm to fill out your forms for you and try to match your interests with the college of your dreams?

Now, let's examine where you grew up. Did you grow up in a rural community? As a result, did your school have the resources to provide AP or college preparatory courses or reliable Internet access? By way of comparison, did you grow up in a large metropolitan area where you could spend your entire senior year of high school at the nearby college taking courses to complete your high school degree? What about art or theater classes? Did your school provide options to explore the arts?

Additionally, how large were your classes in elementary and high school? Were they small, and therefore did you feel you had direct access to your teachers for assistance in your math class that you struggled to conceptualize? Or were you in large classes with over fifty students where you shared a teacher who looked exhausted?

Now, let's consider your family. Did both of your parents work, and did they help you with your homework and take you on college visits? Or are you from a single-parent household, where you rarely saw your parent because they were working? How often did you not have time to do homework because you were taking care of your younger siblings?

These questions matter and expose the variance across states and local school districts on what is available for students and how your life affects your educational pathway.

Discovery Question:

Use the link earlier in this chapter provided by NPR that tracks spending per pupil. Compare how much your county and your roommate's county spent per pupil. Are there differences, and if so, why?

CONCLUDING THOUGHTS

This chapter has only skimmed the surface on the multifaceted and far-reaching implications of U.S. education policy. In our examination of our education history we have shifted from one-room schools to a digital revolution with which many schools cannot keep up due to lack of state or local financial support. And the layers of U.S. education policy are complex due to the varied nature and roles that local, state, and federal actors play.

We can conclude the U.S. educational system has evolved, but collaborative efforts across the government are needed to ensure that students are provided an accessible public education for K–12 that can prepare them for a collegiate career if they so choose. With a sense of urgency for cooperation, we close this chapter with options to consider on how local, state, and federal actors can work together on how best to evaluate our students.

Policy Choices: Student Evaluation

Choice #1: Standardized Testing/Status Quo

With the initiation of NCLB in 2002, standardized testing of students in K–12 became a regular occurrence. Throughout their K–12 educational careers, students commonly have taken well over a hundred standardized tests in reading, math, and other subjects. These tests were intended to guide teachers with what to teach and when to teach it; to accurately track student improvement; and to allow for students, schools, and teachers to be compared to one another. Standardized tests also provide a valuable metric that can be used to evaluate preparedness for the workforce or higher education, which in turn can be used to allocate resources where they are deemed to be the most needed. NCLB also represented a shift toward heavy federal involvement in K–12 education that had historically been left up to the states. This involvement by the federal government and the emphasis on standardized testing, however, has been the target of substantial criticism. Many argue that the sheer number of tests is too stressful for the students

Choice #2: Improved Data Acquisition Methods/Stealth Assessments

ESSA was essentially touted as the antithesis of NCLB, specifically in the realm of standardized testing. It allowed states to cap the number of standardized tests, and removed standardized assessment scores from federal teacher evaluations and also the sanctions received by schools if students did not achieve "adequate yearly progress." However, it still requires annual assessments in the core academic subjects for 95 percent of students. While ESSA still requires standardized testing, it allows some flexibility in the manner in which the tests are conducted and data are gathered. While ESSA has yet to be in place long enough to see its impacts, there are interesting methods of student evaluation that could be included in the implementation of the law. One method would be to administer the same tests, but on a sample of students rather than the entire student population, minimizing the resources and instructional time required as well as limiting undue stress on students and teachers. If the data that are gathered through standardized tests are

Choice #3: Alternative Evaluation Methods

As the world has changed outside of the educational realm, with society requiring different skills and abilities in its workforce, many argue that the education system should adjust to reflect these changes as well. Instead of any form of standardized testing, schools could pursue other evaluation methods that many believe are more representative of an individual's ability to succeed without the stresses and time commitments of standardized testing. These include social and emotional skill surveys, group presentations, video-game-based assessments, and other evaluations that measure creativity and technological abilities, for example, alongside the more traditional academic subjects. These evaluation methods, combined with increased teacher support and a higher level of flexibility in curricula, have proven to be effective internationally and in pilot programs around the United States. This more dynamic and individualistic approach also requires an increased

Policy Choices: Student Evaluation

Choice #1: Standardized Testing/Status Quo	Choice #2: Improved Data Acquisition Methods/Stealth Assessments	Choice #3: Alternative Evaluation Methods
and instructors, and a waste of valuable instructional time. Furthermore, critics assert that these mandated tests result in teachers "teaching to the test"—restricting the learning process so students will achieve certain scores. Some states have gone a step further and tied teacher pay, partly, to their students' scores and progress on the tests, raising questions of the morality of that practice and whether or not students are truly being put first.	unavoidably necessary, there may be other ways for that data to be collected. For example, some computer resources have been released that track every answer a student submits during regular instructional time (via computer learning game, online assignment, etc.). These answers can then be aggregated and ultimately track student progress at the same level that consistent standardized testing can. These practices could alleviate some of the criticisms of standardized testing, while still providing a metric for school and teacher evaluation.	level of state and local government autonomy in education policy, as compared to the days of NCLB.

Source: NPR, "What Schools Could Use Instead of Standardized Tests," January 6, 2015, http://www.npr.org/sections/ed/2015/01/06/371659141/what-schools-could-use-instead-of-standardized-tests.

GLOSSARY TERMS

education policy   155
elementary education   172

property tax   157
school choice   161

secondary education   156
voucher   161

DISCUSSION QUESTIONS

1. Go to the websites of the U.S. Department of Education and the National Council of State Legislatures (NCSL) and find an educational topic of your choice. Upon selection, what data trends did you find? Any areas of concern or promise? Any differences between state and federal examples? Why or why not?

2. College students are no longer enrolling in teacher training programs, and some classify this as an education crisis. To encourage yourself or others to become a teacher, what would you say and why?

3. The lack of coordination between levels of government surrounding education policy is apparent. You have been selected to convene an education summit. Who do you invite and what will you discuss?

4. Research options surrounding school choice. Should the U.S. Congress or your state allocate funding for school choice or spend this money to support or revamp public schools? Why or why not?

SUGGESTED RESOURCES

Suggested Websites

Education Week, http://www.edweek.org/ew/index.html

Education World, http://www.educationworld.com/

State Education Departments, https://ed.gov/about/contacts/state/index.html

U.S. Department of Education, https://www.ed.gov/

Suggested Books or Articles

Rippner, Jennifer A. 2015. *American Education Policy Landscape*. Abingdon, UK: Routledge.

Swail, Watson Scott. 2012. *Finding Superman: Debating the Future of Public Education in America*. New York: Teachers College Press.

Tienken, Christopher, and Carol A. Mullen. 2015. *Education Policy Perils: Tackling the Tough Issues*. Abingdon, UK: Routledge.

Suggested Films

Dangerous Minds, DVD, directed by John N. Smith (1989: United States), www.imdb.com/title/tt0112792

Freedom Writers, DVD, directed by Erin Gruwell (2007: United States), www.imdb.com/title/tt0463998

Waiting for Superman, DVD, directed by Davis Guggenheim (2010: United States), www.takepart.com/waiting-for-superman/index.html

Sharpen your skills with SAGE edge at **http://edge.sagepub.com/rinfret**. **SAGE edge for students** provides a personalized approach to help you accomplish your coursework goals in an easy-to-use learning environment.

Civil Rights and Immigration Policy

8

THE DESERT AND AN ELUSIVE CAT

My uncle, the son of French-Canadian immigrants, was born and raised in New York City, and a former U.S. Air Force pilot turned advertising executive. In the late 1980s, my uncle's advertising agency opened a satellite office in Phoenix, Arizona, and he soon relocated to escape the fast-paced city life to enjoy advertising in the desert. When my sister and I would visit him, we were enamored with the beauty of the Sonoran Desert landscape—something so different from the farming community where we grew up.

During one of our spring break visits, my uncle took us on long car rides to expose us to the grandeur of the American Southwest (e.g., Grand Canyon, Lake Mead). On one particular occasion, we drove to the U.S.–Mexico border, where we could easily put one foot in the United States and the other in Mexico. My uncle lamented that this particular area was also home to an endangered species—the U.S. jaguar. He told a story about how it was rumored that only two male jaguars remained in this part of the United States and he wanted us to experience the same landscape as an endangered species. I truly did not grasp what the jaguar personified until I moved to Flagstaff, Arizona, in 2004 to pursue my doctoral degree in political science.

During my first year as a graduate student at Northern Arizona University I took the class Science Policy. The focus of this course was to expose policy and science students to each other about how best to make public policy in the United States. One of the discussion topics for the course was the proposed legislation from then–U.S. Congressman Duncan Hunter, a Republican from California. Representative Duncan proposed legislation to build a fence along the U.S.–Mexico border to prevent illegal immigration. Instead of discussing this from a political science

LEARNING OBJECTIVES

Readers of this chapter will be able to:

1. Understand the connections between civil rights and immigration policies

2. Explain and describe how U.S. immigration policy has evolved over time

3. Evaluate how official and unofficial actors can shape immigration policy

4. Present different policy approaches for immigration reform

perspective, my professor had us read research reports about the U.S. jaguar—the same jaguar from my uncle's story from the late 1990s.

We learned that, historically, the jaguar populated parts of the southern United States, Mexico, and Central America, but due to population density and hunting, the jaguar's existence came into question. As a result, in the United States, the jaguar was listed as an endangered species—protected by the Endangered Species Act of 1973—because it is on the brink of extinction. To date, two male jaguars had been spotted in southern parts of Arizona. However, the closest female jaguars resided across the border in Mexico. With the creation of a border fence (legislation eventually passed in 2006), the migration patterns were disrupted, lessening their likelihood to migrate and mate (Emrick 2017).

After I completed my graduate course in Science Policy, I drove two hours from Flagstaff to Phoenix to have dinner with my uncle. We reminisced about his jaguar story and I expressed the fact that I had no idea a border fence could inhibit the jaguar's ability to recover as a species. My uncle simply replied, "As a son of French-Canadian immigrants, you think immigration is about people, but it is much more complex than this."

My own experiences in Arizona illustrate that immigration policy is complex and can unexpectedly cross policy areas (e.g., environment). In order to capture the complexities of immigration policy in the United States, this chapter begins by briefly defining civil rights in the United States. This definition serves as a framework for addressing one of the most pressing and controversial policy issues of the twenty-first century: immigration policy. Following is a discussion of how U.S. immigration policy has evolved and the actors involved in its progression. The chapter concludes with a discussion about security and crime, the role of small town USA, and sanctuary cities and refugees, before turning to our choices for immigration reform. By no means does this chapter explore every aspect of immigration policy to date; rather, it provides a concrete overview for students to make their own informed policy choices.

....

OVERVIEW OF CIVIL RIGHTS

Civil rights are the "protections of citizen equality provided by the government" (Ginsberg et al. 2011, 92). This is not to be confused with **civil liberties**, which are protections from the government guaranteed in our Bill of Rights (e.g., freedom of speech, right to privacy). The origins of the civil rights movement can be traced to the U.S. Declaration of Independence, which denied indentured slaves the right to "life, liberty, and the pursuit of happiness." Furthermore, at the inception of the United States, voting rights were only granted to white, male property owners. These examples led to individuals pressing for equality throughout the late 1880s to the early 1900s (e.g., the abolitionist or suffragist movements). Despite the abolition of slavery or the right to vote for women, civil rights issues continue. To understand the far-reaching impacts of civil rights, we explore just a few examples here to demonstrate how civil rights transcend different groups such as American Indians, African Americans, women, the disabled, the aged, and LGBTQ (lesbian, gay, bisexual, transgender, queer).

American Indians are the original inhabitants of the United States. However, American Indians were not considered citizens of the United States until the Indian

Citizen Act of 1924. In addition, American Indians were not allowed to be taught in their own language until the *Lau v. Nichols* (1974) Supreme Court decision (Ginsberg et al. 2011). Nonetheless, one constant concern for American Indians is **territorial dispossession**—historically, tribal people have had their land taken away from them due to their proximity to natural resources (e.g., uranium, tar sands). To demonstrate this point, *Slate* created a time-lapse map to illustrate the loss of land for American Indians over time: http://www.slate.com/blogs/the_vault/2014/06/17/interactive_map_loss_of_indian_land.html. The San Carlos Apache Nation in Arizona, for example, is trying to prevent the sale of its land to mining operations near Oak Flat (Indianz.com 2015). The issue is that some tribal communities want to protect the land in its natural form for sacred practices instead of resource extraction for economic gains.

By way of comparison, we explore how African Americans pressed for equality throughout the 1950s–1960s. One area of concern was that segregated schools did not provide equal education for black and white students. As noted in Chapter 7, the landmark Supreme Court decision *Brown v. Board of Education* (1954) ruled segregated schools were unequal. President Dwight Eisenhower used the U.S. National Guard to enforce the integration of schools in places such as Arkansas's Central High School. Moreover, Figure 8.1 is an example of a literacy test that was required for African Americans living in Louisiana to take in order to register to vote. However, white citizens did not have to take the same test to vote; therefore, the argument can be made that this was a discriminatory practice to disenfranchise African Americans from voting. Because of examples like this, African Americans and other groups pressed for policy action, which led to the Civil Rights Acts of 1964 and 1965, which made desegregation a legal requirement, outlawed discrimination in employment, and barred literacy tests as a requirement to vote, to name a few.

The workplace is also a place where groups organize to curb discriminatory practices. Women, for instance, continue to try to achieve equal pay in the workplace. Women, on average, make 80 percent of what men are paid each year. According to the American Association for University Women (AAUW), women will not achieve pay equity until the year 2152.[1] Some reasons why women will not receive equal pay for over one hundred years include: discrimination, lack of policies for women with children, women are less likely to negotiate for a higher wage, and outdated legislation (e.g., the Paycheck Fairness Act of 1963). Because of such issues women organized a massive nationwide march in 2017 to advocate for policy positions for the advancement of women and other groups. This was the largest organized protest in U.S. history.

Individuals with disabilities in the United States were provided support in 1990 with the passage of the Americans with Disabilities Act. This act ensures that a person's workplace is accessible with ramps, elevators, or other devices necessary for individuals with disabilities. This extends for public and private spaces—for example, movie theaters, public pools, or restaurants. More broadly, consider how an individual in a wheelchair could move from class to class on a college campus. For instance, what if the campus you attend is located on the side of a hill and a student needs to move between classes within fifteen minutes. Without accommodations, this student would find it difficult to attend college classes on a daily basis.

An additional concern is age discrimination and unlawful termination of employment. Let's say an individual is seventy-four years old and still working, when many presume the retirement age is sixty-five. You cannot remove someone from their position based upon their age; the employer must demonstrate valid reasons for removal. However, some states have laws of mandatory retirement ages for specific positions. Ohio judges, for

FIGURE 8.1

Sample Literacy Test

DO NOT WRITE ON THIS CARD

Form No. 3

Applicant must correctly answer any four of the following six questions so as to evidence an elemental knowledge of the Constitution and Government, an attachment thereto, and a simple understanding of the obligations of citizenship under a republican form of government.

1. Limits are placed on the right to vote by the—
   a. National Government.
   b. States.
   c. courts.

2. The Articles of Confederation are—
   a. the Constitution we now have.
   b. a plan for State governm ent.
   c. an early plan of government for the original 13 States.

3. The mail carrier is paid by the—
   a. city.
   b. State.
   c. United States Government.

4. The President is elected—
   a. for four years.
   b. for six years.
   c. for life.

5. The name of our first President was—
   a. John Adams.
   b. George Washington.
   c. Alexander Hamilton.

6. The Congress cannot establish—
   a. churches.
   b. courts.
   c. banks.

Applicant's answers must be provided on Form No. 11 furnished by the Registrar for permanent records.

This card must be returned to the Registrar

Source: Louisiana Voter Literacy Test, circa 1964. Via the Civil Right Movement Veterans website: http://www.crmvet.org/info/la-littest2.pdf.

example, have a mandatory retirement age of seventy, or airline pilots must retire by the age of sixty-five.

You might be most familiar with a twenty-first-century civil rights case that surrounds same-sex couples and their ability to marry. *Obergefell v Hodges*, in 2015, ruled that gays and lesbians have the fundamental right to marry. However, Rowan County (Kentucky) clerk Kim Davis refused to issue a marriage license to a gay couple and served jail time for doing so. Davis argued she could not issue the license due to her religious beliefs and her literal interpretation of the Bible (Dwyer 2017). In turn, the Kentucky governor issued an **executive order** stating that county clerks no longer had to sign marriage certificates for processing. Instead, a marriage certificate could move forward without the signature of the county clerk. The rights and protections for gay, lesbian, bisexual, or transgender individuals continue, though. Even though marriage equality was adopted, many states still do not have policies to protect individuals from firing based upon their sexual orientation.

Civil Rights and Immigration

Civil rights issues are extensive, and we will briefly introduce you to some major concepts here; yet what are the connections to immigration policy? **Immigration** is defined as a person coming to live permanently in a country. **Immigration policy** refers to the guidelines used by a country for allowing individuals entry. Each of the aforementioned civil rights examples identified some, but not all, groups who fight for their equal protection under the law. Additional examples help us to bridge the gap between civil rights and immigration policy.

Mexican Americans initially believed the border between the United States and Mexico was an artificial one. After the Mexican–American War, the 1848 Treaty of Guadalupe Hidalgo "gave all Mexicans living in the ceded territory the option of remaining there or becoming U.S. citizens or of relocating within the new Mexican borders" (Hing 2011, 117). Such sentiments, however, began to change after the Great Depression. Due to the scarcity of U.S. jobs, Mexicans were viewed as migrant workers who were no longer needed and should return to their own country so Americans could get back to work (Hing 2011). As the U.S. economy began to improve, cheap labor was needed in the southern United States and American private employers wanted temporary workers from Mexico. But concerns grew about the level of **undocumented workers** or illegal immigrants—individuals working in the United States without legal documentation and the unfair treatment of these individuals.

The 1964 Civil Rights Act prohibits against national origin discrimination—treating someone differently due to their ethnicity in hiring practices. Congress also passed the 1986 Immigration Reform and Control Act (IRCA), which requires employers to verify foreign workers and provide a pathway for individuals to apply for lawful citizenship. These efforts were short-lived, as enforcement of employer verification was not followed at a high level, and as a result, discriminatory treatment of undocumented workers in the United States continues today. For instance, some states, such as Arizona, created "papers please" legislation requiring police officers to ask individuals for proper documentation if they suspect they are in the country illegally (Duara 2016). Although this practice was voided due to a court settlement, it presents a picture into the ways in which Mexican Americans or undocumented employees can be treated in the United States.

Another type of civil rights discrimination surrounds religion. Religious discrimination is not unfamiliar in the United States—the 1800s experienced strong anti-Catholic and anti-Mormon movements. In order to industrialize the United States before the Civil

War, efforts were made to encourage European immigration to help with the economic development of the United States. Many of these immigrants were Irish Catholics, and as a result, incited fear among Protestants. The concern was that Irish Catholics were an alien menace, or a threat to the religious freedoms of native-born Americans. As a result, the Know-Nothing Political Party formed in the late 1850s. The platform for this political party was to hire only native-born citizens for government employment and require a twenty-one-year residency before a person could apply for U.S. citizenship (Hing 2011).

In 1832, Joseph Smith, the founder of the Mormon religion, was tarred and feathered because he was not "Christian" (Davis 2010). Discriminatory practices toward individuals from Muslim nations significantly increased post-9/11. As Hing (2011) documents, individuals of Middle Eastern descent were told to "go back to their country" despite being born in the United States. Moreover, Figure 8.2 illustrates Gallup polling data from 2011 that asked, "Have you personally experienced racial or religious discrimination in the past year?" Forty-eight percent of Muslim Americans reported in this specific poll that they had experienced discrimination in 2011. Discriminatory acts ranged from death threats to a New York man trying to drive over a Middle Eastern woman (Hing 2011). Figure 8.2 additionally encourages us all to consider further conclusions about discriminatory practices we do not recognize, which is an important foundation for this chapter.

FIGURE 8.2

Experiences of Religious Discrimination, 2011

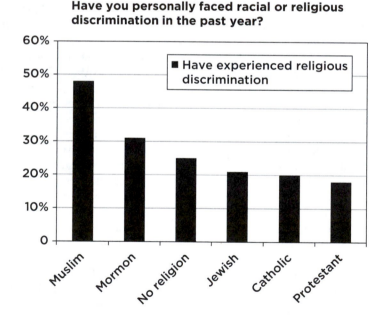

Have you personally faced racial or religious discrimination in the past year?

■ Have experienced religious discrimination

Source: Data from Gallup World, Islamophobia: Understanding Anti-Muslim Sentiment in the West. http://news.gallup.com/poll/157082/islamophobia-understanding-anti-muslim-sentiment-west.aspx.

This section of Chapter 8 briefly defined civil rights in the United States—and, more important, their connection to immigration policy. With our broad definitions, we turn to the status and scope of immigration policy and how they relate to its history and development.

Status and Scope

Presumably most of us know someone (e.g., family, friends, next-door neighbor) who immigrated to the United States. Our opening story illustrated an uncle whose parents migrated from Quebec, Canada, to New York City for work after the Great Depression. Yet what are migration patterns to the United States over time? How do these migration patterns link to U.S. perceptions about immigration more broadly, which could persuade elected officials to pass legislation to represent these viewpoints? In order to address these questions and to provide a broader lens into U.S. immigration policy, we examine the status and scope through three primary lenses: (1) longitudinal trends, (2) public opinion research, and (3) acts of de-Americanization post-9/11.

Longitudinal Trends

Since the 1960s, the Pew Research Center and Gallup have tracked migration trends into the United States. The following is a snapshot into some of these longitudinal data:

- From 1960–2015, the number of immigrants living in the United States increased by approximately 33 million (e.g., in 2015, 43 million immigrants lived in the United States; in 1960, there were 9.7 million).

- In 1960, 84 percent of immigrants migrated to the United States from either Canada or Europe (e.g., Germany, Italy, Poland, Russia); in 2015, this number fell to approximately 14 percent.

- In 2015, 30 percent of foreign-born immigrants were Hispanic and 67 percent were Asian.

- Between 2000–2015, the average percentage of foreign-born individuals living in the United States included:

  - Northeast = 28 percent

  - Midwest = 37 percent

  - South = 65 percent

  - West = 27 percent. (Gallup 2017)

Although the raw data illustrate historical migration patterns, what are Americans' perceptions about immigration? And how do these perceptions affect policies passed by policymakers?

Public Opinion Research

Since 2001, Gallup has tracked responses to this nationwide question: *On the whole, do you think immigration is a good or bad thing for our country today?* In 2001, 62 percent said it was a good thing, 31 percent a bad thing, and 5 percent were mixed. In 2016, 72 percent of respondents said it was a good thing, 25 percent said it was a bad thing, and 2 percent were mixed. From this data collection, it appears Americans' perspectives have changed—immigration is a good thing for the United States. However, do these findings indicate pro–immigration policy perspectives?

After the 2016 election, Gallup asked participants if they were strongly in favor or strongly against the following: *Should we build a wall along the entire U.S.–Mexico border?* The breakdown of responses included:

- 15 percent strongly in favor

- 18 percent in favor

- 25 percent oppose

- 41 percent strongly oppose

- 1 percent no opinion

In examining these responses more closely, 33 percent favor building a wall along the U.S.–Mexico border and 66 percent oppose the construction, with 1 percent having no opinion. The longitudinal data on immigration are rich, and in Figure 8.3 we suggest you research additional results reported by Gallup. Based upon your findings, if you were elected to serve in your state or federal legislature, which policy would you suggest? Would you take an approach similar to President Donald Trump's and encourage the creation of a wall along the U.S.–Mexico border? Or would you, like in states such as Alabama, Arizona, Georgia, Indiana, South Carolina, and Utah, support statewide legislation that requires police officers to ask suspicious individuals to show their papers?[2] Regardless, the public opinion data and elected officials' responses begin to unpack the complexities of the immigration policy conundrum.

Immigration Sentiments

Longitudinal and public opinion data can quantify U.S. sentiments regarding immigration more broadly, but with the advent of social media in the post-9/11 era, we need to consider the process of de-Americanization. The definition of de-Americanization is "a twisted brand of xenophobia that is not simply hatred of foreigners, but also hatred of those who in fact may not be foreigners but whom vigilantes would prefer being moved from the country anyway" (Hing 2011, 260). More specifically, de-Americanization is a process in which someone treats a specific community (e.g., Asians, Mexicans, Muslims) as not part of America. This term is not uncommon in American society, and has been experienced by Japanese, American Indians, and Filipinos throughout the

Box 8.1: Telling Stories with Data

Using Gallup Polling Data to Detect Trends

When you visit Gallup's website: http://www.gallup.com/poll/1660/immigration.aspx, you can explore historical trends about migration patterns in the United States and Americans' perceptions about immigration more broadly.

What do you think?

Located within the Gallup Organization's immigration polling data are trends, over time, regarding what the best policy should be for undocumented immigrants who currently reside in the United States. Take a look at these data and decide what actions or steps you would take as an elected member of the U.S. Congress regarding immigration policy.

FIGURE 8.3

Levels of Government

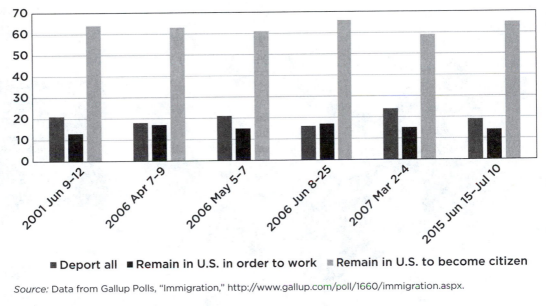

What should be the policy for undocumented immigrants who currently reside in the United States?

■ Deport all ■ Remain in U.S. in order to work ■ Remain in U.S. to become citizen

Source: Data from Gallup Polls, "Immigration," http://www.gallup.com/poll/1660/immigration.aspx.

nineteenth and twentieth centuries. We have seen a resurgence of de-Americanization sentiments post-9/11 with messages of exclusion that someone is not a "true American." You can log onto your favorite social media sites such as Twitter or Facebook and find an array of de-Americanization sentiments about immigrants. Yet when we use terms such as *illegals* or the phrase, "I know an American when I see one," do we pause to consider the impact?

De-Americanization leads to private citizen action and, inevitably, government action. In the 1950s, Mexicans experienced Operation Wetback, in which individuals who came to provide manual labor in the United States were deported back to Mexico. After the bombing of Pearl Harbor at the start of World War II, the U.S. government placed Japanese Americans in internment camps (Hing 2011).

As you examine the results from Figure 8.4 and additional public opinion data findings from Gallup, U.S. immigration policy is not only defined through the lens of civil rights but is a multifaceted and complex substantive public policy area. And to truly understand the evolution of immigration policy we must turn to our history to grasp how the United States, a nation built by immigrants, has viewed immigration "as the source of diversity and criticized as agents of disunity" (Jost 2012, 340).

FIGURE 8.4
E-Verify States

State E-Verify requirements

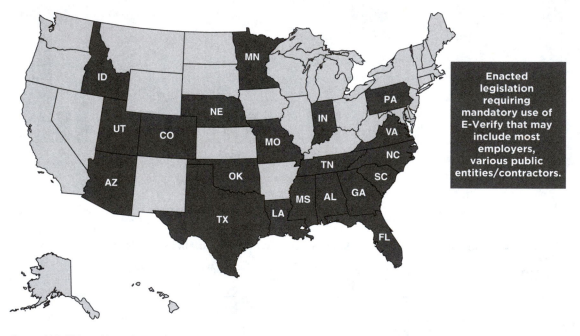

Enacted legislation requiring mandatory use of E-Verify that may include most employers, various public entities/contractors.

Source: U.S. Citizenship and Immigration Services..

HISTORY AND DEVELOPMENT OF
U.S. IMMIGRATION POLICY

Our substantive policy chapters throughout this text have noted that policies are guided by congressional statute. Before turning to the laws that guide our immigration policy decisions, we provide an overview of some of the major historical points.

National Origin Quotas

From the 1790s through the 1950s, the United States pursued a variety of policy approaches that serve as a guidepost to understanding the evolution of immigration policy. Although we do not provide an exhaustive historical overview here, we explore a range of examples, from the Asian exclusive laws, to Ellis Island, to national quotas, to provide a foundation.

In the late 1790s, there was a growing fear of war with France; therefore, President John Adams signed into law the **Alien and Sedition Acts**. These acts allowed the federal government to deport immigrants; they also stated that immigrants could not vote until they lived in the United States for fourteen years. These policies ended with President Thomas Jefferson in 1800, but they demonstrate one of the first immigration policies created by the United States.

In the late 1880s, drawn by the Gold Rush in the western United States, an influx of Chinese immigrants moved to the United States for economic opportunities. Individuals grew concerned that Chinese immigrants would economically displace current residents. Therefore, one of the first significant immigration policies in the United States was the Chinese Exclusion Act of 1882, which barred Chinese immigration for ten years and prevented individuals currently residing within the United States from citizenship (Harvard University Library 2017).

Despite this policy approach for Chinese immigrants, Ellis Island (Photo 8.1) opened in 1892 and served as a federal immigration hub in the mouth of the Hudson River between New York and New Jersey. Individuals from many Western and Eastern European countries traveled to Ellis Island in hopes of finding a new home, often fleeing from disease, famine, or war in their home countries. It is estimated that from 1900 to 1915, up to 5,000 individuals per day arrived at Ellis Island. Upon arrival, medical examinations and legal inspections were made to determine if a person was fit to live in the United States. And, by 1917, under the Immigration Act, all immigrants over the age of sixteen were required to complete a literacy test. If a person was not able to read the test in English, she or he was provided a version in their native language (Ellis Island 2017). Upon reading an excerpt, a person had to interpret the meaning; if not done properly, that person was denied access into the United States (Ellis Island 2017). Hing (2011) provides the example of a Yiddish-speaking woman from Poland who was asked to interpret: "Blessed is the man that walketh not in counsel of the ungodly, nor standeth in the way of sinners, nor sitteth in the seat of the scornful" (51). She could not interpret the meaning of the statement and therefore was denied entry.

Although more than 40 percent of Americans today can trace their family lineage to Ellis Island, because of legislation such as the Immigrant Quota Act of 1921, migration to New York declined (*History* 2017). The Immigrant Quota Act of 1921 required a 3 percent annual entry immigration cap from a country based on the number of those living in the

PHOTO 8.1
Ellis Island
Library of Congress

country of the same nationality. The population of 1890 and its demographics served as the base year for the quota. Anyone applying for immigration status after the fulfillment of the quota would not be allowed entry. This did not apply to certain individuals, including government officials and their families or those visiting as tourists or on temporary business.

The quota approach continued throughout the 1950s, and was also influenced by anti-communist sentiments from the Cold War. Although President Harry Truman strongly opposed these policy perspectives because they created a system by which some individuals were more equal than others, Congress still passed the 1952 McCarran-Walter Act. This act focused on limitations for two key groups—communists and homosexuals. For example, if you indicated on your immigration application that you were part of the Hungarian Communist Party, you could be denied entry. The McCarran-Walter Act additionally contained a provision that excluded individuals "afflicted with psychopathic personality," which was often linked to homosexuals (Hing 2011). As a result, immigration from European countries declined, eventually lessening the need for an allocation system (Jost 2012).

Civil Rights, Amnesty, and Enforcement

The 1960s civil rights movement brought a different framework to immigration policy. As Jost (2012) suggests, "Against the backdrop of the civil rights revolution, national origins system seemed to many also to be antithetical to American values" (340). President John F. Kennedy supported immigration reform that provided a global vision (Hing 2011). As a result, the 1965 Immigration Act abolished the national origin quota system and focused on family reunification. Immigration increased with this new law, and the vast majority migrated from Latin America and Asia. Additionally, the Asian exclusion laws were abolished.

With these new policy methods, growing concerns surrounded undocumented immigrations—individuals migrated to the United States unreported and without documentation. By the 1980s, the Census Bureau estimated that between three to five million undocumented immigrants were living in the United States (Jost 2012). This led to the creation of the Immigration Reform and Control Act of 1986. This particular law attempted to reconcile undocumented immigrants currently living in the United States and the need for labor. Therefore, the goal was to provide a pathway toward citizenship for individuals who had lived in the United States consecutively until 1982 and force employers to verify the status of their employees (Jost 2012).

Concerns continued to mount regarding the Immigration and Naturalization Service's (INS—the federal agency responsible for overseeing immigration entry and reentry) ability to monitor employer and migration activities. As a result, in 1996, the Illegal Immigration Reform and Immigrant Responsibility Act was created to allocate more funding for the E-Verify system for employers to substantiate the status of employees, additional funding for Border Patrol to monitor the U.S.–Mexico border, and the construction of a fourteen-mile fence along the border.

9/11, Dreamers, and Deportation

Right before the September 11, 2001, terrorist attacks, U.S. president George W. Bush, Mexican president Vincente Fox, and members of Congress were working toward immigration policy reform to provide amnesty for Mexicans currently living in the United States (Hing 2011). However, 9/11 changed this direction and instead of a pathway toward citizenship, the Bush administration shifted from legalization to "ways to track, monitor, arrest, prosecute, and deport foreigners who may or may not have been a threat to national security" (Hing 2011, 266). Thus, Congress passed the USA Patriot Act, which authorizes the U.S. attorney general to detain noncitizens without a hearing. Moreover, a newly created agency—the Department of Homeland Security— was the central overseer for immigration policy and monitored migration across the U.S.–Mexico border.

The immigration policy landscape under the Obama administration was concerned with deportation and the "1.5 generation"—children of undocumented immigrants who were born in the United States but often did not realize it until they were old enough to obtain a driver's license. For instance, Jose Antonio Vargas, an accomplished journalist, did not know until he visited his local DMV that he had a fake green card (Jost 2012). Individuals like Vargas support endeavors such as the DREAM Act, which would provide a pathway toward citizenship for children of undocumented immigrants.

In 2016, President Donald Trump declared that in order to prevent illegal immigration, we need to increase our border security through the construction of a wall across the entire U.S.–Mexico border. Opponents of this perspective suggest we need to develop appropriate legal channels for citizenship. Proponents of Trump's policies indicate a wall would decrease crime and prevent acts of terrorism.

In our brief overview of U.S. immigration policy to date, the system has evolved from the utilization of quota systems, to pathways of citizenship, to building a wall. Immigration reform in 2016 and beyond is unclear due to congressional gridlock and Congress's inability to reconcile its differences. Republicans want stricter border patrol, whereas Democrats desire a pathway to citizenship. Nonetheless, scholars such as Nathan Glazer have defined the United States as the "permanently unfinished country," which succinctly defines our evolution of immigration policy to date (Jost 2012).

MAJOR U.S. IMMIGRATION POLICY STATUTES

The historical context for U.S. immigration policy is important to understand contemporary concerns and the major official and unofficial actors involved. We illustrate here, in chronological order, some of the major statutes that define U.S. immigration policy by briefly describing their major provisions before exploring the roles of official and unofficial policy actors.

Select Major U.S. Immigration Laws

Chinese Labor Exclusion Act of 1882 The Chinese Labor Exclusion Act of 1882 specifically targeted Chinese immigration. This act called for a ten-year ban on Chinese laborers in the United States. It both banned those seeking to immigrate to the United States and made it unlawful for those already in the country to remain beyond ninety days after the passage of the act. Chinese immigrants who were already in the United States before the passage of the act were able to remain, but the law made it so Chinese immigrants were unable to naturalize.

Immigration Act of 1882 The Immigration Act of 1882 instated a 50 cent tax for every passenger from a foreign port to any port within the United States. The funds from ports of entry would be collected under the secretary of the Treasury and used to create an immigrant fund for expenses incurred to carry out the act. Some funds were also used to care for immigrants arriving to the United States. The Immigration Act of 1882 excluded ex-convicts and the mentally ill.

1885 Contract Labor Law This act banned the importation of contract labor. Often, contract labor commanded lower wages and undercut domestic wages. Businesses could no longer prepay for passage for any workers or encourage the immigration of workers in any way. Companies could be fined per person for disobeying the law if they were found to have brought in foreign workers. Those caught transporting immigrant workers would also be subject to fines.

1906 Naturalization Act This act moved the Office of Immigration from the Treasury Department to the Commerce and Labor Department. The Office of Immigration was renamed the Bureau of Immigration. The 1906 Naturalization Act required that immigrants must be able to speak English to acquire citizenship.

1917 Immigration Act The 1917 Immigration Act gave the secretary of labor the power to determine the necessity of skilled labor to be imported to the United States. Additionally, this act banned wide-ranging classes of people, including but not limited to: those with mental illness, those convicted of a felony, deported immigrants attempting to return, and unaccompanied children under the age of sixteen. Furthermore, the act banned immigration from most of Asia and the Pacific Islands and required a literacy test. This test was not specific to English literacy, but it required immigrants to read, whether in their native language or the English language.

Immigration Act of 1924 This act required immigrants to obtain visas from their home countries prior to entry in the United States. Preference remained to be given to family members of U.S. citizens and immigrants skilled in agriculture, as well as to their immediate families.

Alien Registration Act of 1940 This act required fingerprinting and registration of new immigrants. Immigrants must possess alien registration card at all times or face fines or possible prison time not to exceed $100 or thirty days. The Alien Registration Act of 1940 allowed immigrants to receive Social Security accounts. The act further allowed for the deportation of criminals.

Migrant Labor Agreement in 1951 The Migrant Labor Agreement in 1951 allowed migrant workers to work temporarily in the United States. This program was started to fill a need for a shortage of labor—particularly in agriculture—as men were drafted into World War II. The program continued after the war, since many migrant workers were paid lower wages than domestic workers. The program, called the Bracero Program, remained in immigration policy until 1964.

Immigration and Nationality Act of 1952 The Immigration and Nationality Act of 1952 maintained the quota system of past immigration policies, including preferences given to skilled labor or those who have family members that are U.S. citizens. It included a provision that excluded those seen as a threat to U.S. democracy or those associated with communism in any way.

Immigration and Nationality Act of 1965 The Immigration and Nationality Act of 1965 abolished national quotas, but it created limited immigration based on the following: unmarried children of U.S. citizens, spouses and unmarried children of permanent resident aliens, people in the professions and exceptional scientists and artists, married children of U.S. citizens, siblings of U.S. citizens, workers with skills needed in the U.S. labor market, and refugees. The limit of immigration from the Eastern hemisphere was set to 170,000 annually and the number of immigrants from the Western hemisphere was limited to 120,000 a year. This new limit would go into effect after July 1968. These limits on immigration resulted in large increases in illegal immigration and policies being drafted to address the increase in illegal immigration.

Immigration Reform and Control Act 1986 This act provided amnesty for illegal immigrants living in the United States continuously after January 1, 1982. Applicants assigned legal status were unable to receive public assistance for five years. This did not include Cuban or Haitian immigrants. Additionally, the act imposed sanctions on businesses that employed undocumented workers.

Immigration Act of 1990 This act serves as the foundation of the current policies on immigration and was built upon the 1965 reforms. The Immigration Act of 1990 stated that immigration would be limited to 675,000 persons per year for all types of immigration. Family reunification remained the primary preference status for immigration. Furthermore, immigrants from countries that were underrepresented by the current U.S. population would be able to apply for entry through a lottery system.

Illegal Immigration Reform and Immigrant Responsibility Act of 1996 This act doubled the size of the U.S. Border Patrol and provided more tools and technology for apprehension and detention. The act also called for increased penalties for those caught smuggling illegal persons across the border or those involved in the production and distribution of fraudulent documents.

Homeland Security Act of 2002 The Department of Homeland Security was created in 2002 and included immigration services. Its mission is to secure America from the variety of threats it faces, including terrorism both domestically and abroad.

Secure Fence Act of 2006 The Secure Fence Act of 2006 was passed to allow the Department of Homeland Security to gain more control over the southern border of the

United States. This act allows the construction of physical barriers and the technology associated with such construction.

This review of immigration policy statutes is not exhaustive but demonstrates a solid overview of significant pieces of legislation. The development of these policies was not made in a vacuum but through the creation of myriad actors—official and unofficial—to which we turn next.

THE ACTORS IN IMMIGRATION POLICY

Notably, throughout this policy area, federal and state governments play a significant role in shaping immigration policy. To delve more deeply into the involvement of institutional actors, we discuss how the president, Congress, the courts, and the bureaucracy affect and shape immigration policy.

President

Presidential perspectives regarding immigration policy have varied over time. As previously noted, President Harry Truman opposed anticommunist sentiments in the 1950s, but his veto was overturned by Congress. During the 1960s, President John F. Kennedy wanted a global approach to immigration policy, demonstrating the United States would be open to immigrants migrating to the United States. President Barack Obama placed an emphasis on children of undocumented immigrants and their pathway toward citizenship, but was strict on deportation through the use of immigration detention centers. These centers are operated by **ICE** (U.S. Immigration and Customs Enforcement), a federal enforcement agency under the direction of the Department of Homeland Security. If someone attempts to cross the border without legal documentation, that person can be placed in a detention center. An immigration judge determines whether that person can stay in the United States or is deported.

In 2016, President Donald Trump's stance toward immigration could be defined as nativist—with policies that protect natural-born citizens. Within his first year in office, President Trump sidestepped Congress through the use of executive orders. A presidential executive order derives from Article II of the Constitution. Presidential executive orders are legally binding and use existing policies to direct the government (e.g., agencies) on how to implement or use resources.

Table 8.1 provides a few examples of President Trump's executive orders in 2017 and their effects on immigration policy. For example, one of the major provisions of Executive Order 13767 is to direct the Department of Homeland Security to use existing statutes to build a wall along the U.S.–Mexico border. Additional executive orders place a ban on people from specific countries from traveling to the United States (Blake 2016). The question becomes whether the use of executive orders is a common practice for presidents. Throughout history, it was not unusual for presidents to issue executive orders. The presidents with the most executive orders are President Franklin D. Roosevelt (over 3,000) and Woodrow Wilson (more than 1,200). President Obama issued 276, and as of March 2018 President Trump issued 60 (*Federal Register* 2018). Furthermore, President Trump is not the first to use executive orders for immigration policy.

TABLE 8.1

President Trump and Executive Orders

Executive Order	Description
Executive Order 13767: Border Security And Immigration Enforcement Improvements	In accordance with the Immigration and Nationality Act (8 U.S.C. 1101 et seq.) (INA), the Secure Fence Act of 2006 (Public Law 109–367) (Secure Fence Act), and the Illegal Immigration Reform and Immigrant Responsibility Act of 1996 (Public Law 104–208 Div. C) (IIRIRA), the executive order cites the critical need for border security due to drug trafficking, human smuggling, and an increase in violent crime as well as acts of terror. The Trump Administration cites the failure of the federal government to enforce current federal immigration laws. The executive order includes the policy of securing the southern border of the US with a border wall and detaining individuals violating federal or state law, including federal immigration law. The executive order aims to end "catch and release" detainment of undocumented immigrants and will return undocumented immigrants to the country from which they came after formal removal proceedings have taken place. This executive order also empowers state and local law enforcement officers to enforce immigration laws in addition to federal immigration officers.
Executive Order 13769: Protecting the Nation from Foreign Terrorist Entry into the United States	The stated goal of the executive order is to protect the American people from terrorist attacks by foreign nationals admitted to the US citing Immigration and Nationality Act (INA), 8 U.S.C. 1101 et seq., and section 301 of title 3, United States Code. This executive order put a 90 day ban on visas issued to "immigrants and non-immigrants." According to the ban, "The United States cannot, and should not, admit those who do not support the Constitution, or those who would place violent ideologies over American law." The executive order does not specify the countries in the ordered ban, but included were Iraq, Iran, Sudan, Libya, Yemen and Somalia. Additionally, a 120 day suspension of the United States Refugee Admissions Program was enacted as part of the executive order as well as a permanent halt of allowed entry of Syrian refugees to the US. The executive order also prioritized claims of refugee status based on religious persecution.
Executive Order 13769: Protecting the Nation from Foreign Terrorist Entry into the United States— Revised	Citing the Immigration and Nationality Act (INA), 8 U.S.C. 1101 et seq., and section 301 of title 3, United States Code, the new travel ban defends the actions of the original executive order with reasons and justifications for the ban by country for five of the six countries included in the original ban. However, this executive order does not include Iraq in the ban as a result of promises of increased cooperation between the Iraqi government and the US and greater confidence in the vetting process between the two countries. This executive order does not include those who are lawful permanent residents of the US, dual citizens traveling on a passport of another country of origin, those who have been already granted asylum before the ban, or any refugee already approved for entry into the US before the executive order was enacted. The constitutionality of this ban is currently being challenging in the court system.

Source: The White House, Presidential Actions, Executive Orders 13767 and 13769, January 2017.

Congress

Congress has the vested lawmaking power to create immigration policy. The numerous immigration laws, which we have already discussed, make up the basis for immigration policy and subsequent enforcement of those laws in the United States. And Republicans and Democrats have had strong policy differences, making immigration reform unsuccessful because of gridlock, or the inability of members of Congress to reach a compromise.

For instance, reform efforts occurred in 2006 and 2007, with discussion about a pathway to citizenship for individuals already living in the United States. Research has shown Republicans are typically against a pathway to legal citizenship because it could: encourage other immigrants to migrate illegally, reward illegal future behaviors, cause a potential drain on the U.S. economy, and become a burden for U.S. services (e.g., medical providers; Doherty 2013). Comparatively, Democrats are concerned about the treatment of undocumented workers by employers and finding mechanisms for citizenship. For example, under President Obama, the Deferred Action for Childhood Arrivals (DACA) program was enacted to allow the children of undocumented immigrants to stay in the United States for at least two years, which can be renewed. The Department of Homeland Security oversees this program. President Trump suggested he would end this program and deport these individuals (Lind 2017).

It remains to be seen what actions members of Congress will take regarding DACA, since the majority of children in the program have been born and raised in the United States (Lind 2017). Consider the broader implications—your college classmate, sitting next to you in class, could be in the DACA program; this person could be deported before the end of the semester. Members of Congress could create policy to prevent the deportation of your classmate. The policy direction for Congress is undetermined at this juncture.

Regardless, Democrats and Republicans are also concerned about what immigration reform would indicate for reelection purposes. The growing Hispanic population in the United States is often referred to as the "sleeping giant" of electoral politics, which could affect the 2018 midterm election outcomes (Ginsberg et al. 2011).

Courts

The courts, past and present, continue to play a pivotal role in shaping immigration policy. The civil rights protections for Americans, or even undocumented immigrants, have been affected by court decisions. The *Lau* decision, as previously discussed, prevented discrimination against non-English-speaking students and allowed Native American students to receive an education in their native language. In another example, *Plyler v. Doe* in 1957 stated that local school districts in Texas could prevent students from attending public schools if a student did not have legal documentation. The Supreme Court ruled this approach unconstitutional (American Immigration Council 2016).

In 2017, President Trump's executive orders listed above were challenged in court. *Washington v. Trump*, a lawsuit filed by Washington State attorney general Bob Ferguson, claims that key provisions in the executive order are unconstitutional, violating the equal protection clause under the Fifth Amendment. Attorney General Ferguson says the ban undermines the sovereignty of the state of Washington. The lawsuit claims that restricting immigration on a national level inhibits Washington's ability to hire immigrants. The lawsuit was upheld and the Trump administration drafted a new executive order on immigration. In *Hawaii v. Trump*, the attorney general of the state of Hawaii, Douglas S. Chin, and plaintiff Ismail Elshikh, the imam of the Muslim Association of Hawaii, including his family and members of his mosque, filed suit. The lawsuit claims the executive order undermines the Constitution by effectively banning individuals from six nations: Iran, Libya, Somalia, Sudan, Syria, and Yemen. The lawsuit claims discrimination under the U.S. Constitution and Immigration and Nationality Act by denying the rights of U.S. citizens to associate with family overseas. Furthermore, the act affects the hiring processes throughout Hawaii, along with international students interested in attending university. The outcomes of these cases are pending in the U.S. Supreme Court.

The Supreme Court will continue to be involved in cases surrounding the rights of individuals, which affects immigration policy to date.

Bureaucracy

The bureaucracy serves as the gatekeepers to immigration policy because federal agencies implement and interpret congressional law. Table 8.2 lists some examples of federal agencies involved with the implementation of immigration policy.

The U.S. Department of Homeland Security (DHS) was created by Congress in 2002 in the aftermath of the 9/11 terrorist attacks. The purpose of DHS is to protect the U.S. homeland, and its responsibilities range from aviation to border security. Within DHS there are specific units, such as ICE or Citizenship and Immigration Services (CIS). Recall that ICE employees are tasked with enforcing federal laws on border patrol, customs, trade,

TABLE 8.2

Agency Actors

Agency	Role	Weblink
U.S. Department of Homeland Security (DHS)	The mission of the DHS is "to secure the nation from the many threats we face. This requires the dedication of more than 240,000 employees in jobs that range from aviation and border security to emergency response, from cybersecurity analyst to chemical facility inspector." The goal of DHS is "keeping America safe."	https://www.dhs.gov/
U.S. Customs and Border Protection (CBP)	CBP is one of the largest law enforcement agencies in the United States. It takes a comprehensive approach to border management and control by combining customs, immigration, border security, and agriculture protection within the same agency.	https://www.cbp.gov/
U.S. Department of State, Bureau of Population, Refugees, and Migration	The bureau provides aid and sustainable solutions for refugees and promotes the United States' population and migration policies.	https://www.state.gov/j/prm/

and immigration in order to promote homeland security and public safety. CIS manages and monitors the E-Verify system. E-Verify is a voluntary program but, as Figure 8.4 illustrates, states determine how to use it. Arizona and Mississippi, for example, require all employers to use E-Verify, whereas California does not use the system. The argument for E-Verify is that it allows employers to check and confirm the legal status of employees, prevents employers from hiring undocumented immigrants, and becomes a "virtual fence" (Meyers 2013). If an individual is hired by a company and that person is undocumented, the employer could face fines. Opponents of E-Verify claim it could lead to discriminatory practices of nonwhite employees (Meyers 2013).

A front-line example of the bureaucracy at work is the U.S. Border Patrol. Within the U.S. Customs and Border Protection Agency is the U.S. Border Patrol. When we think about border patrol, we consider its role in the literal sense—protecting our U.S. borders. However, border patrol employees also work to protect the United States from drug smugglers and to secure coastal waters.

A final example of a federal agency involved in U.S. immigration policy is the U.S. Fish and Wildlife Service. As our introductory story presented, if a president or Congress would issue a law to construct a wall alongside the entire U.S.–Mexico border it could affect endangered species like the jaguar. In order for the wall to be constructed, the USFWS would have to conduct an environmental impact statement to determine the impact a wall would have on an endangered species. Under Section 7 of the Endangered Species Act, any construction of a project using federal dollars is to be reviewed by the USFWS to determine if an endangered species is in the area. The levels of expertise in federal immigration agencies are far-reaching, from technology, to criminal justice, to law. The bureaucracy serves as the gatekeepers to evidence that informs our day-to-day immigration practices.

UNOFFICIAL ACTORS IN IMMIGRATION POLICY

Immigration policy is also affected by outside interests. For instance, if there is fear of economic job loss, members of Congress might find public support for stricter policies for the migration of individuals into the United States. Let's say you live in Texas near the border, and your brother lost his job because his boss hired a recent immigrant with less experience for half the cost. Your brother was upset about the job loss and started supporting immigrant quotas so he would not lose another job in the future. However, your brother began to change his viewpoint when he learned the individual hired to replace him needed the resources to pay for brain cancer surgery for his child. By way of comparison, you live in northern Maine and own a small business where the population is predominantly white males, but you need to diversify your workforce due to new regulations. You become supportive of immigration policies that ban quotas because they could help your company diversify with immigrants encouraged to relocate across the globe.

These hypothetical examples depict the often polarizing, yet personalized, nature of immigration policy. As a result, a variety of interest groups have formed to serve the interests of immigrants migrating to the United States, as well as business owners. Table 8.3 provides a sample list of interest groups that run the gamut from lawyers' associations to global partnerships. But in order to understand the power of vested interests on

TABLE 8.3

Sample of Unofficial Actors

Unofficial Actor	Current Role	Website
American Immigration Lawyers Association (AILA)	Made up of over 14,000 attorneys and law professors. AILA represents U.S. families seeking permanent resident status for close family members. Assists U.S. businesses seeking skilled workers and global talent in their organizations.	http://www.aila.org/
Council for Global Immigration 2016	Provides resources to advance employment-based immigration of highly educated professionals worldwide.	https://www.cfgi.org/
Immigration Equality	Advocates for LGBTQ and HIV-positive immigrations since 1994. Provides services to asylum seekers, LGBTQ immigrant and binational couples and families, detainees and undocumented LGBTQ people living in the United States.	http://www.immigrationequality.org/
U.S. Immigration Reform PAC (USIRPAC)	Represents Americans who want current immigration laws enforced and to support candidates who will support USIRPAC's goals.	http://usimmigrationreformpac.org/

policy decisions, we examine statewide policy directives, minute men, and the American Civil Liberties Union (ACLU).

States

States are at the forefront of immigration policy and serve as key unofficial policy actors. If you are an undocumented immigrant, your residency and state policies affect you daily. The Urban Institute is a nonprofit organization that specializes in social policy and has tracked state immigration policy approaches since the early 2000s. Figures 8.5 and 8.6 illustrate the variance across state immigration policies. We encourage you to use this figure as a baseline to conduct additional research for your own state. In examining your own state, what led to the policies adopted?

As noted in Chapter 7, states set the tone for education policy. Moreover, there are clear connections between educational and immigration policies. States can determine whether or not to provide in-state tuition rates for undocumented immigrants. Supporters of this endeavor believe an educated population helps to boost the state's economy. Opponents suggest it rewards illegal behavior. Twenty-two states have decided, to date, to provide in-state tuition rates for undocumented immigrants.

Health care, another substantive policy area discussed in this text, also has links to immigration policy. Some states provide prenatal care for pregnant undocumented immigrant women. The rationale is that if care is provided, it helps to decrease costs of the uninsured receiving medical attention in the emergency room, which in turn falls on taxpayers to cover.

In-state tuition for unauthorized immigrant students

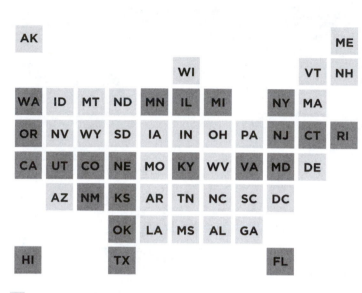

YEAR

2016

POLICY DESCRIPTION
State allows students who meet certain requirements to pay in-state tuition rates at its public colleges and universities, regardless of their immigration status. Eligibility requirements usually include attending a state's high school system for a certain number of years.

State did not have the policy

State had the policy

Medicaid for unauthorized immigrant pregnant women

YEAR

2016

POLICY DESCRIPTION
State provides prenatal care, regardless of a woman's status, through either a state-funded program or through a 2002 CHIP option.

State did not have the policy

State had the policy

Source: © Urban Institute.

The policies states adopt can serve as policy laboratories for the federal government. The federal government created the E-Verify system as a voluntary mechanism for employers to verify the immigration status of their employees. However, some states like Arizona have opted to require the use of E-Verify. Nonetheless, if states and their constituents show strong support or provide evidence of a successful program or policy, the federal government could pursue national legislation as a result.

The Immigration Posse and the ACLU

Although states are crafting their own policies to shape policy direction, vested interests are attempting to present their own perspectives. The Immigration Posse and the ACLU serve as two very different viewpoints.

In 2006, the Immigration Posse formed as a volunteer group under the advice of former sheriff Joe Arpaio of Maricopa County, Arizona. The Immigration Posse is comprised of trained volunteers such as retired sheriff deputies and even Hollywood actors (e.g., Steven Seagal). The goal of the group is to patrol the U.S.–Mexico border for smuggling of undocumented immigrants. The question becomes how a volunteer group can act as law enforcement. Under state law, smuggling is a two-year offense. The argument for the group is that the federal government is not doing enough to protect the U.S.–Mexico border from undocumented immigration; therefore, this organization will help prevent illegal crossings into the state (NBC News 2006).

In stark contrast is the ACLU, with origins that date back to the 1920s. After World War I, concern grew of communism in the United States. As a result, U.S. attorney general Mitchell Palmer used federal law enforcement to raid individual homes without search warrants and deported individuals without a trial. In direct response, a small group of individuals formed a group to protect the civil liberties and rights of individuals (American Civil Liberties Union 2017). Today, the ACLU is one of the country's largest public interest law firms.

Post-9/11, the ACLU is concerned that the United States is risking its civil liberties and rights in the pursuit of security. The ACLU has a network across the United States and continues to prevent unlawful searches and seizures in addition to human rights violations; its fear is that current immigration policies discriminate against particular groups (American Civil Liberties Union 2017).

So far in this chapter, we have examined the history and development of immigration policy, and considered the actors involved. Yet, as a nation built upon immigrants, why do we still discriminate against one another? In our remaining pages, we attempt to address this question through the examination of issues and challenges.

ISSUES AND CHALLENGES

It is unsurprising that we continue to face challenges surrounding immigration. We offer three challenges for consideration: (1) security and crime, (2) small town USA, and (3) sanctuary cities and refugees.

Security and Crime

We have noted in this chapter that two of the largest concerns surrounding undocumented immigration include security and crime. Throughout the 2016 presidential campaign, Republican politicians, such as candidate Trump, lamented that we need stricter immigration reform because without it our crime rates will continue to increase.

According to The Sentencing Project, undocumented immigrants are not the cause for increased crime in the United States. According to its research, undocumented immigrants are incarcerated at much lower rates than U.S.-born citizens (Bernal 2017). Furthermore, U.S. voters often have misperceptions between crime rates and the data. Even though crime rates are not driven by undocumented immigrants, voters in the 2016 presidential election did not believe this because of the constant political rhetoric espoused by politicians. Then–presidential candidate Donald Trump repeatedly claimed that undocumented workers are the cause of crime in the United States. When messages are repeated continuously, voters are more likely to believe them as opposed to data collected by experts. Therefore, elected officials can use public sentiments to engender support for policy approaches. These methods have been repeated throughout time, as the historical overview previously indicated. It is up to us to do our research to determine what is fact and what is fiction.

Sanctuary Cities and Refugees

This chapter only began to scratch the surface of some of the multifaceted layers of immigration policy to date. We discussed the role of policies that have addressed U.S.–Mexico border concerns in addition to national origin quotas. However, a challenge in the twenty-first-century immigration landscape is sanctuary cities. There is no one clear definition of a sanctuary city, but one thing such localities share is they do not ask for a person's immigration status. Cities such as Chicago and Los Angeles have argued they will not participate in discriminatory practices asking someone to show their papers.

In 2016, the Trump administration asked the Office of Management and Budget to come up with a list of sanctuary cities across the United States. In turn, the Trump administration will use this information to decrease federal funds for these cities. The question remains if the president is able to do this; and it is another reason why clearer federal legislation is necessary.

Small Town USA

This chapter has illustrated the divisiveness immigration policy can engender. Yet can small towns serve as examples of how to forge a collective effort toward reform? *High Country News* makes the case through the real-life story of Rosa Sabido from Cortez, Colorado.

Fifty-three-year-old Rosa Sabido has served as her church secretary since 2008. Her legal status for citizenship in the United States remains pending. Until her application is accepted, she has to reapply each year, paying $5,000 to remain in the United States and to avoid deportation. In 2017, her reapplication to stay was denied by ICE. Sabido has no criminal record and pays taxes. Due to fear of deportation, she has relocated to a small apartment inside her church as her community (made up of differing political ideologies) discusses how best to protect her from deportation (Butcher 2017). The question becomes, If others heard stories like Sabido's, could we achieve immigration reform?

Everyday Citizen Connection

This chapter is underscored by a long history of immigration in the United States. Think about the origins of your own family. Is your family part of the many who migrated to the United States by first arriving at Ellis Island? Or did they flee religious persecution in their own country in hopes of a new start in the United States?

If your grandparents are still living, have you taken the time to ask them the origins of your family? If you have not, maybe you should. If your grandparents are no longer living, is there a family member who has a knack for family trees? Maybe you were adopted, and you can use a free source—familysearch.org—to investigate your family. Regardless, when you take the time to understand your own family history, how does this compare to our immigration policy history illustrated in this chapter?

In investigating these questions, compare your answers with your college roommate or friends. What similarities or differences do you share? In connecting the pieces of your immigration puzzle, consider how your family treated others. Does this treatment reflect the policies we have today? Are there new civil rights protections we should consider as a result?

Discovery Question

Based upon your own family history and others, what do you predict the future of U.S. immigration policy will entail? Should we build a wall along the U.S.–Mexico border? What does a wall symbolize? Compare the U.S. wall with the Berlin Wall of the past. What are the similarities and differences?

CONCLUDING THOUGHTS

This chapter is only a glimpse into the vast immigration policies to date. As evidenced in the chapter, our immigration policy is cyclical, from strong pro- and anti-immigration throughout our history. The United States began as a nation of immigrants fleeing from religious persecution. This foundation transcended into policies that have set migration quotas to the voluntary Immigration Posse that patrols the U.S.–Mexico border.

Immigration policy, we conclude, is a constant work in progress, much like the landscape of the U.S. population has changed over time. In 2018, and into the future, immigration is once again at the forefront, and it is up to all actors—official and unofficial—to collectively decide our future. We close the chapter with three options to consider for the future of immigration reform: increase funding for a border wall, prioritize deportations, and provide pathways to citizenship. Ultimately, with any public policy there are a variety of options, and it is up to us to consider them.

Policy Choices: Immigration Reform

Choice #1: Increase Funding for a Southern Border Wall	Choice #2: Prioritize Deportations and Focus on Businesses Hiring Undocumented Workers	Choice #3: Provide Pathways to Citizenship for Current Undocumented Immigrants
Currently, Executive Order 13767: Border Security and Immigration Enforcement Improvements seeks to use the laws already in place including the Immigration and Nationality Act (8 U.S.C. 1101 et seq.), the Secure Fence Act of 2006 (Public Law 109–367), and the Illegal Immigration Reform and Immigrant Responsibility Act of 1996 (Public Law 104–208 Div. C) to tighten border security across the southern United States. U.S. officials citing the need for tightened border security give drug trafficking, human smuggling, violent crime, and terrorism as reasons for increased protection. Executive Order 13767 seeks an end to "catch and release" detainment of undocumented immigrants and will deport those after formal immigration hearings rather than releasing the unauthorized immigrants back into the United States. To increase border security, the U.S. Department of Homeland Security plans to add 5,000 border patrol agents and 10,000 Immigration and Customs Enforcement (ICE) officers, increasing enforcement of current immigration laws throughout the United States.	The estimated eleven million unauthorized immigrants in the United States create enforcement challenges for Customs and Border Patrol, ICE, and the Department of Homeland Security. One solution is to prioritize deportations for unauthorized immigration, focusing on those with criminal records, particularly those with violent or felony convictions. Furthermore, government agencies could prioritize unauthorized immigrants who have recently entered the United States rather than those living in the United States for ten or twenty years. Additionally, the U.S. government could seek to expand enforcement of the 1986 Immigration Reform and Control Act, which made it illegal for businesses to recruit and hire undocumented workers. Businesses employing undocumented workers are circumventing U.S. labor laws by employing undocumented workers at rates lower than domestic workers. Many times, employers hiring unauthorized immigrants pay those workers less than minimum wage and require workers to work more than a forty-hour week without overtime pay.	Offering pathways to citizenship creates an avenue for current unauthorized immigrants residing in the United States to begin to receive the benefits received by permanent legal residents and citizens. A proposal to create Deferred Action for Parents of Americans and Lawful Permanent Residents (DAPA) would allow parents of U.S. citizens or lawful permanent residents to remain in the United States legally provided they have no criminal record and have resided in the U.S. continuously since January 2010. Unauthorized immigrants eligible to apply for legal status would receive Social Security cards after passing a background check. The proposed DAPA program is similar to DACA, or Deferred Action for Childhood Arrivals, which allows those who arrived in the United States before the age of sixteen the ability to remain in the United States for at least two years and receive work authorization.

Policy Choices: Immigration Reform

Choice #1: Increase Funding for a Southern Border Wall	Choice #2: Prioritize Deportations and Focus on Businesses Hiring Undocumented Workers	Choice #3: Provide Pathways to Citizenship for Current Undocumented Immigrants
A proposed wall on the southern border aims to increase border security, particularly of those attempting to cross into the United States without documentation.	Workers are not afforded benefits like Social Security, and businesses do not need to cover such workers under standard U.S. labor law requirements such as worker's compensation. Expanding the U.S. government's ability to penalize businesses hiring unauthorized workers could decrease illegal immigration by making it harder to employ a workforce of unauthorized immigrants.	

Source: Gallup, http://www.gallup.com/poll/1660/immigration.aspx.

GLOSSARY TERMS

Alien and Sedition Acts   187
civil liberties   178
civil rights   178

executive order   181
ICE   192
immigration   181

immigration policy   181
territorial dispossession   179
undocumented workers   181

DISCUSSION QUESTIONS

1. If you wanted to become a U.S. citizen, what steps would you need to take to obtain citizenship? If you are unsure of where to find this information, please watch the following video before answering this question: https://www.youtube.com/watch?v=HllGXBzVkSs

2. You recently learned that you were born in the United States, but you do not have documentation. What steps do you take to obtain citizenship in this country?

3. You have been elected to the U.S. House of Representatives, and based upon your expertise in immigration policy have been asked to sponsor a bill on immigration reform. What three policy options will you pursue and why?

4. What are the economic advantages and disadvantages associated with immigration policy?

5. How can you apply a news event from today (e.g., kneeling during the national anthem) to expand how we define and understand the connections between civil rights and immigration policy?

SUGGESTED RESOURCES

Suggested Websites

American Civil Liberties Union, https://www.aclu.org/

Governing Magazine, http://www.governing.com/

High Country News, https://www.hcn.org/

Immigration/Pew Research, http://www.pewresearch.org/topics/immigration/

National Council on State Legislatures, http://www.ncsl.org/

Pinksourcing Video, https://www.youtube.com/watch?v=k_m5AlsQqcs

U.S. Citizenship and Immigration Services, https://www.uscis.gov/tools/settling-us/welcome-united-states

Suggested Books or Articles

Hing, Bill. 2011. *Defining America: Through Immigration Policy*. Philadelphia, PA: Temple University Press.

Schrag, Peter. 2010. *Not Fit for Our Society: Immmigration and Nativism in America*. Oakland: University of California Press.

Wilkerson, Isabel. 2010. *The Warmth of Other Suns: The Epic Stories of American's Migration*. New York: Knopf Doubleday.

Suggested Films

The Immigrant, DVD, directed by James Gray (2013: United States), www.imdb.com/title/tt1951181/

The Lives of Others, DVD, directed by Florian Henckel (2006: United States), http://www.imdb.com/title/tt0405094/

The Visitor, DVD, directed by Tom McCarthy (2007: United States), www.imdb.com/title/tt0857191/

NOTES

1. American Association for University Women, http://www.aauw.org/

2. The National Immigrant Law Center, which represents immigrant rights, challenged Arizona Senate Bill 1070 because it would encourage police officers to racially profile nonwhite individuals. The National Immigrant Law Center sued Arizona and won a million-dollar settlement that led to the removal of the proof of documentation requirement used by police officers (Metcalfe 2016).

Sharpen your skills with SAGE edge at **http://edge.sagepub.com/rinfret. SAGE edge for students** provides a personalized approach to help you accomplish your coursework goals in an easy-to-use learning environment.

Social Welfare and Health Care Policy

9

LIVING ON $2 A DAY

Imagine being nineteen years old, with a new baby, and living on $2 a day. Such was the situation for Ashley, who was profiled in an article for the *Los Angeles Times* (Edin and Shaefer 2015). Living with her mother, brother, uncle, and cousin in public housing, the cupboards were bare, the refrigerator empty. They had a roof over their heads because of government assistance, but they lacked cash. No one in the household received monetary assistance from the government, and no adult in this extended family could find a job. When the researchers gave Ashley $50 for participating in the interview, it was the most money she had seen in months. She used the money to buy a suitable outfit from the Goodwill secondhand store for a job interview, purchased a bus pass, and headed out to apply for jobs.

The World Bank calls living on $1.90 or less per person per day extreme, or deep, poverty. According to this

PHOTO 9.1
A homeless man begs for money in downtown Los Angeles.
Lucy Nicholson / REUTERS

LEARNING OBJECTIVES

Readers of this chapter will be able to:

1. Understand what is meant by social welfare and poverty

2. Understand how social welfare and health care policy developed

3. Assess the role of history, politics, and public opinion on social welfare and health care policy

4. Identify issues and challenges in addressing social welfare and health care

international organization's estimates, about 11 percent of the world's population lives on less than $1.90 per day (World Bank 2016). But this story is not just from some faraway place in the world; it is also an American story. Researchers at the University of Michigan's National Poverty Center found that the number of U.S. households living on $2 a day or less per person increased from 636 thousand to 1.46 million from 1996 to 2011 (Shaefer and Edin 2012). Many more Americans are poor, though they live on more than $2 a day. The U.S. Census Bureau estimated that nearly 41 million people in the United States lived in poverty in 2016 (Semega, Fontenot, and Kollar 2017). While this is a slight improvement over 2015, when over 43 million people lived in poverty, it still means that nearly 13 percent of Americans are considered poor (Proctor, Semega, and Kollar 2016). Of those, 19.4 million were very poor, with incomes below 50 percent of the poverty threshold.

Safiyyah Cotton is an example of someone living in extreme poverty. She has worked for McDonald's for over a year, making $7.50 an hour to support herself and her two-year-old son. Many companies like McDonald's depend on part-time workers, and Safiyyah works less than forty hours a week, earning less than $8,000 a year—too little to pay for housing, transportation, and food. (Her story is told by CNN Money and available on YouTube.) Or imagine being a veteran who suffers from posttraumatic stress disorder or substance abuse and cannot keep a job. Shunned by family and lacking a social safety net, the veteran may be on the street and homeless. The U.S. Department of Housing and Urban Development estimates that over 39,000 veterans were homeless in 2016 (U.S. Department of Housing and Urban Development 2016). You may have seen a homeless person like the man in the photo above when walking an urban area, or know someone working for minimum wage trying to support a family. You may also be living frugally, while attending college and working a part-time job, perhaps struggling to pay for tuition, rent, food, and books. If so, you are not alone. Estimates are that nearly one in three college students living off-campus is poor (Fang 2013).

These are just a few of the faces of people who are poor. The economic downturn in the aftermath of the 2008 recession brought renewed focus on social welfare policy, as millions of Americans lost their jobs and their homes. Health care also captured public attention during the recession, as increasing numbers of Americans found themselves without health insurance.

This chapter focuses on the role and importance of social welfare policy and health care policy in the United States: two policy areas that address the well-being of Americans. The first half of the chapter provides an overview of social welfare policy, including the history of the laws that shape government's response to poverty. The second half of the chapter presents the evolving nature of health care policy, highlighting current debates as well as long-standing policies that provide health care insurance to Americans. You will see that these two policies are connected, and share a common background. After overviewing the laws and actors in both policies, the chapter presents issues and challenges of social welfare and health care policy into the foreseeable future. The chapter's concluding "policy choices" spotlight the Family and Medical Leave Act, and illustrate the ways in which values influence policy solutions.

OVERVIEW OF SOCIAL WELFARE POLICY

Social welfare policy addresses the well-being of all members of a society—for purposes of this chapter, American society. Social welfare policy represents governmental responses to social problems that arise, responding to well-being issues such as having enough food to eat, having a home, having a secure future in retirement. If you are working, you can see evidence of social welfare policies by looking at your paycheck and seeing deductions for FICA, or the Federal Insurance Contribution Act. That deduction, described in more detail later in the chapter, makes you a part of the Social Security Program, the largest social welfare program in the country. Segal (2016) makes the point that all Americans are part of social welfare programs, as the foundation of a social welfare system is that society (that's all of us) provides for the care for others as well as for themselves. Fundamental to any civil society is a bottom-line expectation of a safety net for people who are in need. However, what should comprise that safety net, and how far it should extend, has been widely debated over U.S. history. Let's begin with a key focus in any social welfare program: addressing poverty. After describing definitions of poverty developed by the federal government, we'll look at conflicting values about welfare within society.

Defining Poverty

Defining who is poor provides an indicator of well-being in America, and also affects the development of public policy and the delivery of social programs. Mollie Orshansky, a federal government worker, developed an official measure of poverty in the 1960s that is still used today. She took the costs of feeding a family a minimally sustainable diet, sometimes referred to as a Thrifty Food Budget, and multiplied that by a factor of three. At the time, the U.S. Agriculture Department estimated that families of three or more persons spent about one-third of their cash income on food. Next, the government, through the U.S. Census Bureau, set **poverty thresholds** based upon the size of a household, such as a family comprised of two adults and two children, and established a minimum income amount necessary to meet basic needs. These thresholds, sometimes referred to as the poverty line, are adjusted annually based upon the Consumer Price Index and serve as an indicator of the number of people with inadequate income to buy food and other goods and services. For example, a family of two with an annual income of $15,569 was below the poverty threshold in 2016; for a family of four, it was $24,563.

Over the decades, the limitations of this way of measuring poverty became apparent as U.S. social and economic conditions changed. For one thing, the measure did not distinguish between the working and nonworking poor. Working poor families faced added child care and transportation costs not accounted for in the thresholds. Also, the measure did not reflect the effects of various other social programs, such as food or housing assistance, that raise disposable income, or increases in Social Security (or FICA) or Medicare payroll taxes that reduce income into the calculation of who is poor. Finally, the official poverty threshold was the same throughout the United States, and did not take into account geographic differences in the costs of living.

To address these limitations, a second measure of poverty, called the **Supplemental Poverty Measure (SPM)**, was developed. The SPM calculates what people spend for basic needs beyond just food. The new measure, first reported by the U.S. Census Bureau in 2010, allows for local variations in rental costs. It also adds noncash benefits such as housing subsidies or low-income energy assistance into the calculation of the poverty thresholds. At the same time, the SPM accounts for additional costs such as child care, taxes, medical expenses paid out of pocket, and transportation costs related to work. In many years, the SPM measure shows a higher poverty rate than that calculated using the traditional method. For example, in 2012, 46.5 million people, or about 15 percent of the population, lived in poverty based on the official measure of poverty; the SPM measure indicated that 16 percent of Americans fell below the poverty line (U.S. Census Bureau 2014).

However, another federal poverty measure, called **poverty guidelines**, identifies who is poor in America. Issued by the U.S. Department of Health and Human Services, these guidelines are a simplified version of the poverty thresholds issued by the Census Bureau. Poverty guidelines are used to determine financial eligibility for many social welfare programs, such as the Children's Health Insurance Program, the Supplemental Nutrition Assistance Program, and the National School Lunch Program. Like the SPM, these guidelines are adjusted for geographic variations, but condense these into just three different regions: one for the forty-eight contiguous states and the District of Columbia; one for Alaska; and one for Hawaii. For example, in 2017, a family of four making less than $24,600 in the forty-eight contiguous states fell beneath the poverty guidelines; that same family making less than $30,750 in Alaska would be considered poor (Institute for Research on Poverty 2017). Whether referring to the official poverty thresholds, the supplemental measures, or the poverty guidelines, few economic indicators are more closely watched or more important for public policy.

Who Is Poor?

The incidence of poverty varies over time, and also by age and racial/ethnic group. As shown in Figure 9.1, African Americans experience poverty at over twice the rate when compared to white Americans (24.1 percent compared to 11.6 percent in 2015). The same is true for Hispanic Americans (21.4 percent compared to 11.6 percent). Figure 9.1 also shows the persistently high numbers of children who are poor (ranging between 15.4 and 19.7 percent from 1968–2015). To put that another way, nearly one out of every five children in this country lives in poverty or near-poverty. Another noteworthy item in Figure 9.1 is that poverty among the elderly has decreased (from 25 percent in 1968 to 8.8 percent in 2015). The decrease of elderly poverty is explained, in part, by increases in Social Security expenditures—explained later in the chapter.

Not shown in Figure 9.1 is that poverty rates also vary by gender. Women between the ages of eighteen and twenty-four are more likely to be poor (21.9 percent) than men of the same age (17.6 percent). The disparity widens between women and men ages twenty-five and thirty-four (18.2 percent and 11.3 percent, respectively; Institute for Women's Policy Research 2014). Several factors contribute to this difference, including the prevalence of women in lower-paid jobs, the gender-wage gap, and being a single mom. More than half of American families who are poor are headed by single women (U.S. Census Bureau 2016).

Poverty rates vary among states and localities. For example, in 2016, less than one in ten people living in New Hampshire were poor. However, nearly one in five residents of Louisiana, Mississippi, New Mexico, and West Virginia lived in poverty. The availability of higher-paying jobs and a more educated workforce contributes to lower poverty rates in states like Colorado, Connecticut, Maryland, Minnesota, or New Hampshire—all of which have rates below 10 percent. The disparity by race is also a factor in poor states.

Box 9.1: Telling Stories with Data

Using Census Data

When you visit the Institute for Research on Poverty website at the University of Wisconsin http://www.irp.wisc.edu/faqs/faq2.htm, you can explore historical trends about poverty, poverty levels by state, and demographic characteristics of people who are poor that has been collected through the U.S. Census. You may want to look at Table 1 at the website, which compares the income-to-poverty ratio by states, and Table 2, which looks at characteristics.

What do you think?

After looking at Figure 9.1, what can you say about who is poor? Which demographic category has changed the least over time? Which demographic category consistently has higher levels of poverty? When you visit the website, looking at Tables 1 and 2, what factors would you consider most important in making policy decisions?

FIGURE 9.1

Official U.S. Poverty Rates in 1968, 1990, and 2015, by Age and Racial Group

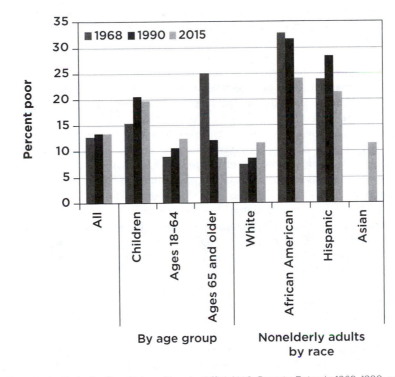

Source: Data from the Institute for Research on Poverty, Official U.S. Poverty Rates in 1968, 1990, and 2015 by Age and Racial Group.

In Louisiana, for example, 14 percent of whites were poor, while 30 percent of blacks and 24 percent of Hispanics were poor (Kaiser Family Foundation 2017). Addressing the causes for these differences in the incidence of poverty is a vexing policy issue.

Public Values and Types of Social Welfare Programs

Social welfare policy reflects the tension between two widely held values in this country. First, Americans value individualism and self-sufficiency. The American Dream reflects this value by embracing the notion that if people work hard they will enjoy prosperity according to their talents and skills—not based on their family's wealth or status. Thus, Americans believe that hard work and individual effort will be rewarded. By extension, many Americans feel individuals should take responsibility for their own well-being by working harder, making good decisions about the money they earn, and committing to improving themselves.

This value conflicts with a second value of social, or collective, responsibility. Most Americans see an obligation to assist people who lack the basic needs of life such as food and shelter. Society should take responsibility to provide necessary resources, jobs, and opportunities to address poverty and to help those who cannot help themselves. Many Americans also feel that government should provide other services that will help societal well-being, such as public education, clean water and air, basic health care, and care for the elderly and disabled.

The tensions between individual responsibility and collective, or social, responsibility are seen in approaches to social welfare programs. **Social insurance** reflects the value of individual responsibility by requiring input into the system by those receiving benefits. Contributions made by employees and/or employers fund the program. Three major social insurance programs exist in this country: Social Security, unemployment insurance, and worker's compensation. Workers pay into Social Security through their FICA taxes in order to receive cash benefits when they retire. To receive benefits, a person must work for a minimum of ten years and be at least sixty-two years of age (full retirement age is calculated based upon the beneficiary's date of birth). The Social Security Administration determines Social Security retirement benefits based upon the amount of money earned each year and the number of years worked. In addition to the retirement benefit, the Social Security Program pays cash benefits to surviving spouses and dependent family members. It also provides support for disabled people through Social Security Disability Insurance, provided that the recipient has worked long enough and paid Social Security taxes.

A second approach to providing social welfare reflects the value of collective responsibility. Here, people are given assistance through programs that are **means-tested**, where eligibility to receive support through a government social welfare program depends on an individual's financial situation. These **public welfare programs** typically will use the poverty threshold or poverty guidelines to determine whether an individual qualifies for assistance. The Temporary Assistance to Needy Families (TANF) Program is a prominent example of a welfare program that provides cash and other kinds of assistance to poor American families. The federal government provides a block grant to state governments, allowing states to determine how to help families in need. However, TANF grants are conditioned on two requirements: (1) that parents seek employment while receiving cash benefits, and (2) that states limit benefits to families to no more than five years. States also must spend state funds on programs for needy families in order to receive the federal grant.

Other public welfare programs include Supplemental Security Income, which pays benefits to disabled adults and children, and the Supplemental Nutrition Assistance

Program (SNAP), formerly known as food stamps, operated by the U.S. Department of Agriculture. To receive SNAP benefits, a person must meet an income test determined by poverty thresholds, and have less than $2,250 in countable resources, such as savings in a bank account (U.S. Department of Agriculture 2017). Other public welfare programs support poor children through food assistance (such as the National School Lunch Program and the School Breakfast Program), or provide nutritional support for low-income pregnant women and their children (up to the age of five), called Women, Infants, and Children (WIC).

Public Support for Social Welfare Programs

If the values of individual responsibility and social, or collective, responsibility are reflected in the types of social welfare programs (social insurance and public welfare), these values are also evident in public opinion polls. These polls consistently show that the predominant value for most Americans is individual responsibility. A *Los Angeles Times*/American Enterprise Institute poll found that public support for these two values persisted with little change for thirty years, between 1985 and 2015 (Lauder and Lauter 2016). As shown in Table 9.1, while poor and nonpoor respondents alike believe that government is responsible for the well-being of its citizens (29 percent in 2015), most Americans do not believe the government bears the main burden of taking care of the poor. Americans both below and above the poverty line feel individuals bear the greatest responsibility for their own well-being (66 percent in 2015; 69 percent in 1985).

That does not mean, however, that Americans want to end social welfare programs. As shown in Figure 9.2, the majority of Americans polled in a Pew Research Center

TABLE 9.1

Opinions about Welfare Responsibility

Which statement comes closest to your position: "The government is responsible for the well-being of all its citizens and it has an obligation to take care of them" or "People are responsible for their own well-being and they have an obligation to take care of themselves"?

Government	2015	1985
Below poverty level	38%	24%
Above poverty level	26%	24%
All respondents	29%	24%
People	2015	1985
Below poverty level	57%	69%
Above poverty level	70%	67%
All respondents	66%	69%

Source: Adapted from Thomas Suh Lauder and David Lauter. 2016. View on Poverty: 1985 and Today. *Los Angeles Times* and American Enterprise Institute Poll. http://www.latimes.com/projects/la-na-pol-poverty-poll-interactive/.

FIGURE 9.2

Public Support for Budget Cuts, 2017

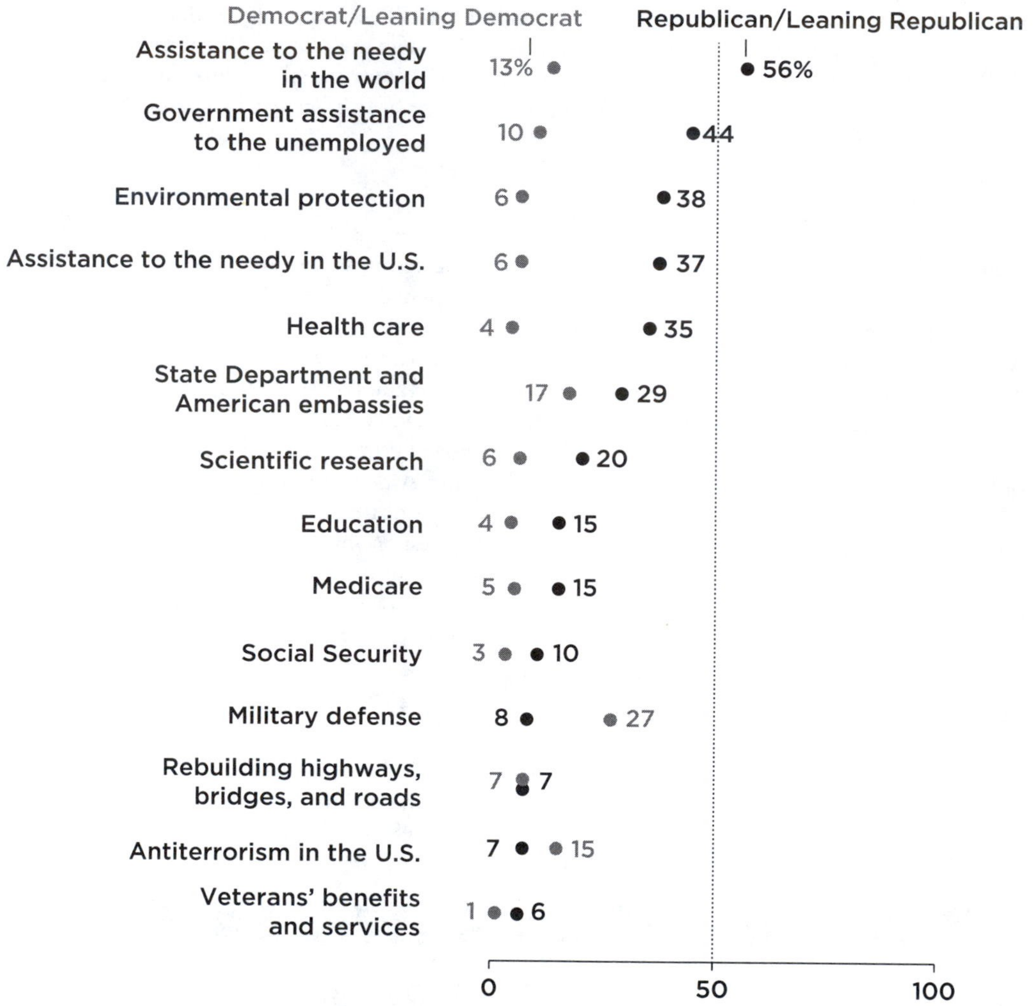

	Democrat/Leaning Democrat	Republican/Leaning Republican
Assistance to the needy in the world	13% ●	● 56%
Government assistance to the unemployed	10 ●	●44
Environmental protection	6 ●	● 38
Assistance to the needy in the U.S.	6 ●	● 37
Health care	4 ●	● 35
State Department and American embassies	17 ●	● 29
Scientific research	6 ●	● 20
Education	4 ●	● 15
Medicare	5 ●	● 15
Social Security	3 ●	● 10
Military defense	8 ●	● 27
Rebuilding highways, bridges, and roads	7 ●● 7	
Antiterrorism in the U.S.	7 ●	● 15
Veterans' benefits and services	1 ●● 6	

0   50   100

Source: "Few Americans support cuts to most government programs, including Medicaid" Pew Research Center, Washington, DC (May 26, 2017), http://www.pewresearch.org/fact-tank/2017/05/26/few-americans-support-cuts-to-most-government-programs-including-medicaid/.

survey conducted in 2017 favored continued federal government support for assistance to the needy; only 6 percent of Democrats and 37 percent of Republicans felt government spending on social welfare should be cut (Gramlich 2017). Virtually no one polled supports cutting assistance to veterans (only 1 percent of Democrats and 6 percent of Republicans favor such cuts); few Americans support cuts to education, Social Security, and Medicare.

Some major differences are apparent by political party affiliation. For example, while only 10 percent of Democrats support cuts to government assistance for the unemployed, 44 percent of Republicans support cuts. Republicans are also more likely than Democrats to support cuts to health care (35 percent and 4 percent, respectively). The largest difference by political party is found in cuts to international aid for needy people throughout the world. Here, 56 percent of Republicans, or people leaning toward being Republicans, would support budget cuts, while 13 percent of Democrats would support cuts to international aid.

In sum, most Americans support social welfare programs, though differences exist between Democrats and Republicans in how much funding should be devoted to means-tested programs. Most Americans favor programs that reflect the value of individual responsibility. The next section explores the history of social welfare programs.

HISTORY AND DEVELOPMENT OF U.S. SOCIAL WELFARE POLICY

Understanding long-held American values helps set the context for the history and development of social welfare policy in this country. These values, as is true for many policy areas, influence the eventual policies adopted to address social needs. Different approaches in social welfare policies are driven in large measure by predominant values, and by changes in the economic condition of the country. This section briefly describes the major policy shifts in social welfare programs.

Poor Houses and "Outdoor Relief"

In the early 1800s, the U.S. government did not provide much in the way of social welfare for its citizens. Poor people were left largely to fend for themselves, or to seek assistance from charitable organizations. Government antipoverty efforts were largely in the realm of local and state governments, and focused on housing the poor. These poorhouses, also known as almshouses or workhouses, were never widespread, in part because housing came with expectations for its temporary residents. For example, New York's Society for the Prevention of Pauperism forced residents of its poorhouses to work—something that was formalized when the New York legislature passed the County Poorhouse Act of 1824, requiring county governments to build a poorhouse and also to teach the occupants to engage in constant industry, remain sober, and learn the value of being thrifty. Most poorhouses were also miserable places to be, offering a last refuge for the frail, disabled, and elderly, and also for orphaned children.

The Civil War brought more people into poverty, especially in the South. African Americans struggled to survive the postwar devastation, unfavorable laws, and political circumstances, often having little alternative but to engage in share-cropping for landowners. African American families often moved from farm to farm in order to make a meager living. Also poor were the people who lived in the mountain hollers of Kentucky, Tennessee, West Virginia, and other Appalachian states. Beginning in the late 1800s, many Appalachians eked out a living in coal mines or subsistence farming. (Appalachia still has some of the highest poverty rates in the country.)

PHOTO 9.2

"Migrant Mother," by Dorothea Lange. Destitute pea pickers in California in 1936. This mother, age thirty-two, became the face of people in poverty during the Great Depression.

Dorothea Lange / Library of Congress

Policies toward the poor began to change, allowing people in need to live with family or friends instead of in poorhouses. In exchange, the government would supply a small amount of financial support to the family. This program was called "outdoor relief" and set the stage for addressing poverty through some form of cash assistance. In arguing that both poorhouses, or "indoor relief," and family aid, or "outdoor relief," were necessary policies addressing the plight of the poor, a report from the annual session of the National Conference of Charities and Corrections in 1890 observed, "The public, generally, prefer, for reasons of sentiment, and oftentimes of good sense, the use of family aid rather than the separation of households and the sequestration of persons in great establishments, where individuality is lost in the mass, and persons are known by a numeral rather than a proper name" (quoted in Virginia Commonwealth University's Social Welfare History Project, 2017). The first Board of Public Welfare, established in Kansas City, Missouri, in 1910, paid men in script to work in a rock quarry in exchange for room and board, and groceries for their families (Hansan 2011a). This sentiment persists today, as policymakers and the public prefer to keep families intact.

The New Deal and Social Security

The most significant period for changes in U.S. social welfare policy came during the Great Depression, which began with the stock market crash of 1929 and continued for over a decade. Misery for many people followed as countries around the world sank into a deep depression. Economic conditions were dire; local, state, and charitable organizations were overwhelmed. A value shift toward community responsibility was needed. Franklin D. Roosevelt, elected president in 1932, campaigned on a promise to create government solutions that would end the Great Depression. By 1933, unemployment reached 25 percent, and those who had jobs saw wages cut nearly in half. Roosevelt pushed for a range of programs and new federal agencies as part of what was referred to as the New Deal. One agency was the Works Progress Administration, which provided jobs for unemployed people while improving parks, bridges, post offices, and other public places. The Civilian Conservation Corps was established to help younger workers find useful work. The Federal Emergency Relief Administration was created to make grants to states, which in turn could help its citizens with relief payments. In this way, government itself put people to work as businesses were reluctant or unable to hire workers.

In his message to Congress in 1934, Roosevelt observed that in complex and industrialized societies people needed "security against the hazards and vicissitudes of life. Fear and worry based on unknown danger contribute to social unrest and economic demoralization. If, as our Constitution tells us, our Federal Government was established among other things 'to promote the general welfare', it is our plain duty to provide for that security upon which welfare depends." His Executive Order No. 6757 established a committee, headed by Frances Perkins, the first woman to serve as U.S. secretary of labor, to provide recommendations for a program that would provide security in old age, and assist persons who were sick or disabled.

The result was the most important policy that emerged from the Great Depression: the Social Security Act of 1935. Title II of the law established the Old Age, Survivors Insurance Program, referred to today simply as **Social Security**, based on providing a form of social insurance for workers. Workers would pay into the Social Security Trust Fund, and in turn, receive monthly checks when they retire. The amount of Social Security would vary based upon the amount paid in payroll taxes, age at retirement, and other factors. Social Security was therefore distinct from welfare, where cash assistance is based on financial needs of an individual. Thus, benefits derived from Social Security were not means-tested, in that people who reach retirement age will receive Social Security regardless of their financial situation. Another feature of the Social Security Program is that it is work related and, with few exceptions, compulsory for workers. Employees typically cannot opt out of paying Social Security, or FICA, taxes. Social Security worked as envisioned, becoming the primary source of income for America's elderly, with seven out of ten beneficiaries deriving more than half of their income from Social Security benefits (Hansan 2011b).

Unemployment Insurance and AFDC

The law established another kind of social insurance program: unemployment insurance. Unemployment insurance protects individuals when they lose their job. The program levies a payroll tax on employers that, in turn, may be drawn on when workers become unemployed through no fault of their own. This unemployment insurance compensation is limited to two years, as a temporary support for people while they seek other employment.

In his signing statement, Roosevelt noted:

> We can never insure one hundred percent of the population against one hundred percent of the hazards and vicissitudes of life, but we have tried to frame a law which will give some measure of protection to the average citizen and to his family against the loss of a job and against poverty-ridden old age.... It will act as a protection to future Administrations against the necessity of going deeply into debt to furnish relief to the needy. The law will flatten out the peaks and valleys of deflation and of inflation. It is, in short, a law that will take care of human needs and at the same time provide the United States an economic structure of vastly greater soundness. (Roosevelt 1935)

Though most of us think of Social Security benefits when we think of the Social Security Act, other provisions are important. Title I provided for federal/state cash assistance for the needy elderly, Title X for the blind, and Title IV provided aid to dependent children living in poor families. Prior to Title IV, poor families relied on mothers' pension programs offered by state governments. These programs provided cash support for families where no father was present. This aid enabled mothers to remain at home to care for dependent children. By 1935, all but two states had mothers' pension laws (Dear 1989). That did not mean, however, that these laws provided adequate support to widows. In 1930, only 3 percent of the 3.8 million female-headed households received assistance from mothers' pension programs (Dear 1989). Moreover, virtually no assistance was given to minority families, and implementation across the country was uneven, with some states simply not implementing the law.

Aid to Dependent Children under Title IV shifted the locus of control to the federal government. For the first time, the federal government accepted responsibility for helping support needy children by giving cash assistance to their mothers. By underwriting state programs, and overseeing that support was given to all eligible families, the federal government broadened the reach and fairness of cash-assistance welfare programs (Page and Larner 1997). The federal government would pay one-third of the state's expenditures; state and local governments paid two-thirds of the cost. Initially, Congress approved a maximum federal payment of $6 per month for the first child and $4 per additional child, but with no limit to the number of families supported (U.S. Department of Health and Human Services n.d.). Interestingly, cash support was given only for the children, not the adults in a family. A 1950 change to the law provided federal funds for an adult caring for children; in 1962, the program added a second adult to the aid formula. Correspondingly, the name was changed to Aid to *Families* with Dependent Children, or AFDC.

However, the amount given to families through AFDC varied greatly by state, as states were free to establish benefit levels. These differences persisted over the decades. In 1994, the median state grant was $366. However, a poor family of three in Alaska, the state with the most generous benefits, received $923 per month under AFDC; the same family of three living in Mississippi received just $120 (Page and Larner 1997, 22). Despite state-by-state differences, no state was particularly lavish in cash assistance to needy families. No state's benefit level kept pace with inflation, and the value of the benefit dropped nearly in half between 1970 and 1994 (Page and Larner 1997). Nonetheless, families who met poverty threshold eligibility requirements were entitled to receive support. AFDC was in place as the nation's most visible cash assistance program for the poor from 1935–1996. Roosevelt would later observe that if Congress did nothing else but pass this bill, the session would have been "regarded as historic for all time" (Roosevelt 1935).

The Great Society and Connecting Health Care to Social Welfare

After World War II, a robust U.S. economy helped lift many Americans from poverty. From 1940 to 1960, the postwar boom brought new jobs, massive building, and educational opportunities. The American Dream seemed possible for many American families. However, not all Americans were so lucky. Unskilled workers, migrant farmers, minorities, and female-headed households suffered in the midst of a strong economy. Nearly one in five rural Americans and four out of ten nonwhite Americans lived in poverty during the mid-1960s (Marx 2011); what was needed was a major initiative to address poverty and racial discrimination, and that is what happened through a series of programs that comprised the Great Society.

The Great Society was promoted by President Lyndon B. Johnson with the twin goals of eliminating poverty and racial injustice. President Johnson saw these as not only policy priorities, but also moral issues. In 1963, just five days after taking the oath of office after the assassination of President John F. Kennedy, he urged Congress to enact civil rights legislation to honor President Kennedy's memory. The Civil Rights Act became law in 1964, banning discrimination in public accommodations and in the workplace, as described in Chapter 8.

In 1964, President Johnson declared he would fight an unconditional war on poverty to "not only relieve the symptoms of poverty, but to cure it, and above all, prevent it" (Johnson 1964). It was a big statement, and one that would result in what came to be called the "War on Poverty," a major part of the vision of a Great Society. Johnson launched his Poverty Tour, visiting Appalachian families and other rural areas, calling attention to the plight of the poor. By May, Congress passed the Poverty Bill, also known as the Economic Opportunity Act. This law established the Office of Economic Opportunity to implement new federal programs that were part of federal efforts to address poverty, including the Jobs Corps, the VISTA program, the federal work-study program, and the Head Start program.

PHOTO 9.3
President Johnson shakes the hand of an Appalachian resident during his Poverty Tour of Appalachia in 1964.
Cecil Stoughton / LBJ Library

Other laws formed the basis of Johnson's efforts to combat poverty. Perhaps the most important passed in 1965, and amended the Social Security Act. These 1965 amendments connected social welfare and health care policy by creating Medicare and **Medicaid**—important components of U.S. health care policy today. President Johnson saw that the lack of adequate health care for the elderly left them vulnerable to poverty, and that health care and social welfare policies were connected. Prior to Medicare, nearly half of all Americans over the age of sixty-five did not have insurance, either because they could not afford it or because private insurance companies terminated their policies (Social Security Administration n.d.). A second health care program, Medicaid, was also part of the 1965 amendments to the Social Security Act. Medicaid was designed to provide health coverage for low-income people, who were also unable to find health insurance. The amendments also expanded Social Security benefits for retirees, widows, and the disabled.

The Food Stamp Act passed in 1964, with a goal of preventing hunger by providing food stamps that the poor could exchange for food in grocery stores. The Elementary and Secondary Education Act of 1965, described in Chapter 7, established the Title I program to distribute funding to schools and school districts with a high percentage of students living in poverty. This law made a policy connection between the importance of a quality education and the ability for individuals to rise out of poverty.

President Johnson said he wanted to be the president who helped the poor find their way, and he was successful. Through the Great Society programs, the poverty rate went from 22 to 13 percent—the greatest one-time reduction in the history of this country. However, the Great Society and War on Poverty social programs had critics. Conservatives argued that these programs were expensive, and many of the programs received reduced funding, or were eliminated over the years. Other critics felt that these programs went to the "undeserving poor" who took government assistance but did not work. Johnson's successor, President Richard Nixon, was a conservative who felt the Great Society programs excessive; nonetheless, he worked to expand food stamps and implemented the Earned Income Credit—a cash supplement from the federal government for the working poor.

Welfare Reform through TANF

Another important event in social welfare policy occurred in 1996, after several decades of criticism of the welfare program, AFDC, established as part of the Social Security Act of 1935. As described earlier, AFDC provided cash assistance to families with children who lived below the poverty threshold. Conservatives believed that AFDC fostered dependency on government social welfare programs and that recipients were ill-inclined to look for jobs. Welfare dependency would pass from one generation to another, critics argued, keeping poor families perpetually in poverty. Starting in the 1970s, the derogatory term *welfare queen* was used to stigmatize women, especially African American women, on cash assistance, suggesting that women engaged in fraud or otherwise manipulated their eligibility for welfare. President Ronald Reagan referred to "welfare queens" in arguing for welfare reform, and the term persisted through the 1990s, despite little evidence of welfare fraud. Also misunderstood by critics were the costs of providing welfare to families under AFDC, which for thirty years never exceeded 1.2 percent of the federal budget (Dear 1989).

Reforming welfare became a major campaign issue in 1992 and in the midterm elections of 1994. Republicans in the House introduced bills to cut welfare; President Bill Clinton also promised changes to AFDC. The country was coming out of a recession that had put 33 percent more families on AFDC assistance, and 81 percent of Americans wanted welfare reform (Rothman 2016). The result was the Personal Responsibility and Work Opportunity Reconciliation Act of 1996, which replaced AFDC with a program called Temporary Assistance to Needy Families, or TANF. TANF limited lifetime welfare benefits for recipients to five years; mandated the head of every family to find work within two years or lose benefits; and required unmarried teenage mothers to live at home and stay in school to receive benefits. Anyone convicted of a felony drug charge would get neither food stamps nor cash assistance.

TANF is delivered as a block grant to states, giving states latitude in determining the mix of cash assistance, work-support (such as child care assistance), and other services (such as funding pregnancy prevention and family support initiatives). In addition to work requirements for recipients, TANF changed the obligations of the federal government to fund this program. AFDC was directly tied to how much states spent for cash assistance to low-income families; if states spent more, the federal funding went up as well. Under the new law, the amount the federal government spent on welfare was effectively capped by the amount allotted to the TANF block grant. Adjusted for inflation, the value of federal funding for TANF has declined by about 25 percent (Congressional Budget Office 2015, 5). Many policy analysts suggest that TANF is successful, in large part, because of the work requirement and the added flexibility provided to states. They point to decreases in welfare caseloads and more women in the workforce. Other analysts find mixed success, noting that TANF's "work first" policies are fine as long as the economy is strong and there are no serious barriers to employment. In the absence of sustainable employment opportunities with jobs that allow family incomes to increase, TANF is unlikely to be a sufficient safety net (Brookings Institution 2006). We now turn to health care policy.

OVERVIEW OF HEALTH CARE POLICY

Health care policy covers everything from the type, coverage, and design of health insurance plans to the array of laws and regulations that cover insurance policies, hospital care, the cost of medical care, government health insurance programs, public health activities, and regulations that oversee the operation of hospitals and clinics—just to name a few. Most Americans who have health insurance coverage get their policies from their employers, or if they are under the age of twenty-six, through their parents' insurance. Contrary to the rest of the developed world, America's health care programs are primarily provided by private insurance companies, rather than by the government. Americans over the age of sixty-five, the disabled, the poor, and children whose parents cannot afford private insurance are the exception: they are covered under government health care programs, notably Medicare and Medicaid.

For much of the history of U.S. health care policy, this meant that private companies decided whether or not to cover an individual, and could reject persons based upon pre-existing conditions or if the person was otherwise deemed to be a high risk for needing health care, such as the elderly. Insurers could also decide how much to charge, and when to increase premiums. In turn, employers decided whether to offer insurance programs to employees, and if they did, how much of the insurance cost to cover. In effect, providing health care was like providing a business service for many Americans—a service that increasingly higher numbers of Americans could not afford.

Government-Run Insurance Programs: Medicare, Medicaid, and CHIP

As mentioned in the previous section, health care and social welfare policies connect to provide a safety net for low-income and elderly Americans. You'll recall that this connection was most evident in the Great Society programs of the Johnson administration, and particularly through the 1965 amendments to the Social Security Act. President Johnson understood that the only way to keep the elderly from slipping into poverty was to provide them with health insurance. Today, **Medicare** provides insurance for people over the age of sixty-five, people under sixty-five with certain disabilities, and people with end-stage renal disease. It's a social insurance program, like Social Security, and designed to be paid for through payroll taxes. If you're working, you'll see a deduction for Medicare on your paystub. Medicare Part A provides for hospital insurance. Most people receiving Medicare will not pay a premium for Part A because they or their spouse paid payroll taxes. Medicare Part B provides medical insurance that covers doctor's services, outpatient care, physical therapy, and some home health care services. Prescription drugs are also covered, but this part of Medicare is provided by private companies. People who opt to enroll in Part B and the prescription plan will pay premiums. In 2015, over 55 million people were beneficiaries of Medicare.

Medicaid provides medical insurance for low-income families, people with disabilities, and people who need long-term care. Medicaid programs exist in all states, but states administer their programs differently. In 2017, over 69 million people were covered by Medicaid. People enrolled in Medicaid do not pay premiums, as the costs are funded jointly by state and federal governments. The Children's Health Insurance Program (CHIP), established in 1997, provides health insurance and preventative care for uninsured American children. This program primarily covers children from uninsured working families whose income makes them ineligible for Medicaid. States received federal grants to run the CHIP program. In 2016, 8.9 million children were enrolled in the CHIP program.

These are critical programs in providing health care to low-income households and the elderly. When all government health insurance programs are considered, 130 million people receive health care at reduced costs, or at no cost at all (in the case of Medicaid and CHIP). Roughly 22 percent of people in the United States are covered by Medicaid or CHIP alone. Public insurance covers virtually everyone over the age of sixty-five, but also 43 percent of children under the age of eighteen, and 20 percent of people between the ages of eighteen and sixty-four (Centers for Disease Control and Prevention 2017). Still, over 28 million people under the age of sixty-five were uninsured in 2016—but that represents a drop from 47 million in 2010, the year the Affordable Care Act was passed, which is described next.

The Affordable Care Act and Beyond

Prior to 2010, unless you were part of a government program (Medicare, Medicaid, or CHIP) you hoped to receive health insurance coverage through your employer. Most employers paid for most of the costs of insurance premiums, and you paid any remaining amount. If you were not so lucky, you either were uninsured or paid the full cost for health insurance through other venues. Given this system, it was not surprising that over 47 million Americans, or roughly 18 percent of the population, were uninsured in 2010. More troubling was that nearly half of uninsured Americans had not been covered by health insurance for five years or more (Garfield, Licata, and Young 2014).

People opted to go without health insurance either because they could not afford it or because they could not get coverage due to preexisting conditions. As shown in Figure 9.3, health expenditures per capita had increased dramatically from 1960 to 2010. In 1970, the United States spent an average of $356 per person, or about $75 billion. Just forty years later, per person costs ballooned to $8,402 per person, or about $2.6 trillion (Kaiser Family Foundation 2012). Policymakers understood that these escalating health care costs, coupled with high numbers of uninsured Americans, were significant challenges threatening the fabric of a just society—the issue was figuring out how to solve this vexing and expensive public policy problem.

President Barack Obama made addressing the health care crisis a primary policy-making goal, as did Democrats in Congress. In July 2009, then–Speaker of the House Nancy Pelosi introduced a bill to overhaul the health care system, while Democrats in the Senate introduced another bill. For the next eight months, these bills were hotly debated. In March 2010, Senate Democrats used the budget reconciliation process to get the votes necessary to pass the bill, which was signed by President Obama on March 23, 2010. Significantly, the bill passed largely along political party lines, with all Republicans voting against it.

Key Provisions of the ACA

The legislative result was the Patient Protection and Affordable Care Act, or simply the Affordable Care Act or Obamacare (ACA). The ACA focused on expanding coverage, controlling health care costs, and improving the delivery of health care services. Some key provisions of the ACA are shown in Table 9.2. After the ACA passed, health insurers could no longer deny coverage based upon preexisting conditions; nor could they drop the benefits provided to patients.

FIGURE 9.3

National Health Expenditures per Capita, 1960–2010

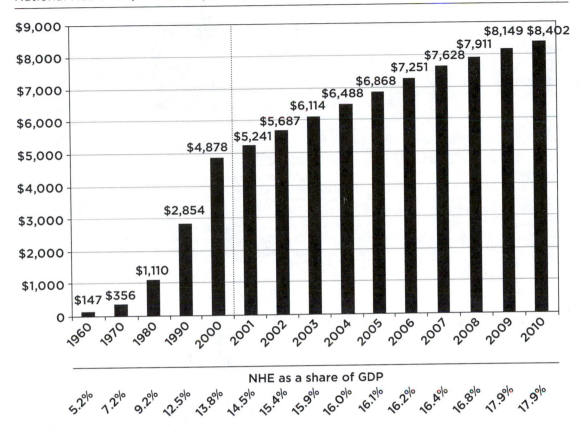

Source: The Kaiser Family Foundation's State Health Facts, https://www.kff.org/report-section/health-care-costs-a-primer-2012-report/. *Data source:* Centers for Medicare and Medicaid Services, Office of the Actuary, National Health Statistics Group at http://www.cms.hhs.gov/NationalHealthExpendData/ (see Historical; NHE summary including share of GDP, CY 1960-2010; file nhegdp10.zip).

It's hard to imagine a more contentious rollout of a new law. The federal website failed to work properly, and some states were not prepared for public interest in the new health exchanges. Republicans in Congress vowed to replace ACA, finding it expensive and intrusive, especially the requirement that all people have health insurance. Some states did not expand Medicaid, but thirty-one states did. Repealing and replacing the ACA was a major campaign promise of President Donald Trump, but efforts in 2017 proved unsuccessful, in part because of strong public opposition. Sen. Bernie Sanders (D-VT) and others argued in 2016 that all Americans should be covered by a national insurance system, perhaps by making Medicare available to everyone, but was unable to translate that idea into public policy. Why is it that we have been unable to formulate a health care policy, and why is

TABLE 9.2

Key Provisions of the Affordable Care Act

Guaranteed Coverage: Health insurers cannot deny coverage based on current or prior health.

Essential Health Benefits: Each policy contains minimum coverage standards, including annual health exams. Children can remain on their parents' health coverage until age twenty-six.

Individual Mandate: With few exceptions, all adults must purchase health insurance or pay a noncompliance penalty to the IRS.

Health Insurance Exchanges: Individuals may purchase coverage through a state or federal exchange.

Low-Income Subsidies: Individuals and families with incomes less than 400 percent of the poverty level are eligible for a cost-sharing subsidy from the government.

Employer Mandate: Companies with over fifty employees are required to provide health insurance to employees who work more than thirty hours per week.

Medicaid Expansion: Medicaid eligibility expanded to 133 percent of the federal poverty level. The U.S. Supreme Court subsequently upheld a constitutional challenge to this expansion, as long as this was a voluntary decision made by state governments. The federal government financed 100 percent of the costs of expansion until 2016, incrementally lowered to 90 percent in 2020 and subsequent years.

PHOTO 9.4

In early 2017, people gather outside Rep. Pat Meehan's (R-PA) Springfield office, protesting against GOP plans to dismantle Obamacare and revamp Medicaid.

NICHOLAS KAMM/AFP/Getty Images

our system of health care so complicated? To answer that question, one needs to explore the history of health care policy.

HISTORY AND DEVELOPMENT OF U.S. HEALTH CARE POLICY

Like social welfare policy, people have different opinions about health care policy. To some, providing health care is a government obligation and fundamental human right; to others, health care is a benefit provided to working Americans through private insurance companies. These two positions emerged as health care evolved over the decades.

Early Efforts to Establish Health Care

The push for a government-funded health care system has its roots in the progressive reforms of the 1880s through the early 1900s. Reformers looked to European countries that had health care as part of social insurance programs. Germany provided compulsory sickness insurance as early as 1883; by 1912, Austria, Britain, Hungary, the Netherlands, Norway, and Russia had similar programs. Denmark, France, Sweden, and Switzerland offered health care subsidies for workers (Palmer 1999). These programs were adopted throughout Europe with the primary goal of protecting the economy from lost wages due to sickness and stabilizing incomes; they evolved to include payment for medical expenses.

Progressives wanted a similar program in the United States. However, the federal government took no action to provide health insurance, leaving policymaking to state governments. In turn, states left health care to local governments, or to charitable organizations. One reason why Congress did not move to enact health care laws was the lack of organized political pressure. Unlike many European countries, America did not have a strong labor party or a politically forceful working class.

In 1906, the American Association of Labor Legislation (AALL) campaigned nationally for health insurance. In 1912, Theodore Roosevelt was the first presidential candidate to campaign for national health insurance. Supported by the American Medical Association, the AALL introduced a model bill in 1915. Under the bill, the working class—including the working poor and their children—would receive health care, sick pay, maternity benefits, and a small death benefit (Palmer 1999). Employers, employees, and the government would share in costs for the program.

However, other political forces soon allied against the bill. Surprisingly, the American Federation of Labor was one of them. This large labor union saw compulsory health insurance as limiting individual rights and also weakening unions by usurping social welfare benefits they provided to union members. Private insurance companies also opposed the bill. These companies provided life insurance policies, and saw the death benefit as an encroachment into their business. Finally, the U.S. entrance into World War I doomed the bill. Values played a role this time: Americans opposed anything that Germany provided—including what they saw as German socialist insurance.

Health Reform Efforts after the Great Depression

From 1917 to 1935, medical costs increased, the Great Depression put many people out of work, many families had little or no food, and the economy was on the ropes. President Franklin Roosevelt and his administration considered including health coverage in the Social Security Act (described in the previous section), but ultimately decided against it. Roosevelt felt that providing unemployment insurance and benefits for old age were more important. A separate bill was introduced in 1939, called the National Health Act, but did not find sufficient congressional support to pass.

Four years later, the bill was refashioned as the Wagner-Murray-Dingell Bill. Senators pushed for national health insurance funded in part by a payroll tax. This bill was introduced every session for fourteen years, but never passed. Organized interest groups, including those from the medical field, saw national health insurance as a threat to private health providers. In its editorial against the bill, the American Medical Association (AMA) warned that a "dominant bureaucracy would be created which would end free enterprise in the United States and alter the whole way of American life" (*Journal of the American Medical Association* 1943).

President Harry Truman continued to call for national health insurance. He argued against opponents who said that universal health insurance was tantamount to socialized medicine. Again, the AMA came out against Truman's proposal, saying that doctors would be slaves to the government. Once reelected, Truman pushed hard for the bill, having campaigned on a national health care. However, opponents lobbied just as hard, raising the specter of a socialist America. During this time of anticommunist sentiment, framing the issue of national health care as a socialist policy proved successful. Truman's proposal died in a congressional committee.

At the same time, private insurance plans offered through businesses and unions provided health care to some of the population—enough to mute any further effort at health care reform. Additionally, Blue Cross organizations, which acted like nonprofits, helped address health care concerns by charging everyone the same premium regardless of age or preexisting conditions (Noah 2007). This would soon change, as both Blue Cross and private insurers began adjusting premiums on the basis of relative risk—unhealthy people would pay more, or simply not be insured.

The 1960s through 2017: Government Steps In

President Johnson's efforts to build a Great Society included health care (discussed in the social welfare section). Johnson, echoing Roosevelt and Truman, believed that health care was a right, and that the lack of coverage kept people in poverty. This time, however, the focus of health care reform was not to provide universal health care, but rather to provide it to senior citizens and the poor. Social Security had been in place for thirty years, and worked well in allowing older Americans to retire. However, the elderly were increasingly joining the ranks of the uninsured. The policy result was Medicare and Medicaid, part of the Social Security Amendments of 1965. These government-run programs are at the heart of U.S. health care policy today, covering persons over age sixty-five, the disabled, and poor families.

From the 1970s through the 1990s, health maintenance organizations, or HMOs, proliferated as the costs of providing health care rose for the majority of Americans who did not qualify for the means-tested Medicaid program or were not old enough to receive Medicare. HMOs lower costs by contracting with doctors and medical facilities for services. People with HMO insurance plans had to get treatment from "in network" providers—providers under contract in order to be covered by their insurance. HMOs were not enough, however, to stem the growing expense of insurance coverage. Employers were increasingly reluctant to provide health care—or opted to increase the share of premium costs that employees would pay as a way of sharing the pain of rising costs from insurance companies.

In part due to high costs and decreasing insurance coverage by employers, in part due to the recession of 2008, by 2010, nearly one out of every five people in the country were uninsured. President Obama made health care his signature issue, and the ACA was passed.

ACA Repeal Attempts under President Trump

In 2017, Republicans in Congress saw their chance to repeal and replace Obamacare, or the ACA. They drafted legislation, called the American Health Care Act, which would have repealed subsidies for poor and middle-class families, replacing the subsidies with refundable tax credits based on age as well as income. This drew sharp criticism from AARP (American Association of Retired Persons), an organization that had its roots in fighting for health care for senior citizens. The proposed bill also repealed the individual mandates, and eliminated the requirement that employers with over fifty employees provide health insurance. Finally, it altered the Medicaid expansion program. After analysis by the Congressional Budget Office suggested that 24 million more Americans would be uninsured by 2026, including 14 million by 2018, public sentiment turned against the bill.

Republicans tried to repeal the ACA and replace it with their version of health care policy twice during the summer of 2017. Both attempts were defeated. Public pressure to keep Obamacare, meanwhile, was high. It seemed that many Americans realized the benefits of the ACA, and now supported keeping it in place. For the first time, the ACA was supported by over half of Americans, who now understood that they would potentially pay more for health insurance, and might lose it altogether, if restrictions were lifted on preexisting conditions. As of 2018, health care policy is at a crossroads: keep ACA as is, change the law, or start with something new. Time will tell the direction of America's health care policy.

MAJOR U.S. SOCIAL WELFARE AND HEALTH CARE STATUTES

The historical context for U.S. social welfare and health care policy helps illuminate major components of the federal social welfare and health care systems. Listed here, in chronological order, are some of the major statutes that define these policy areas, along with brief descriptions of key provisions.

Select Major U.S. Social Welfare and Health Care Laws

Emergency Relief and Construction Act of 1932 This law was the first significant attempt by the national government to offer financial assistance to states overwhelmed by providing public relief programs to address large-scale unemployment as a consequence of the Great Depression. This was followed by the Federal Emergency Relief Act of 1933, which authorized the federal government to distribute more than $1 billion in grants to states to help meet the costs of providing public assistance.

Social Security Act of 1935 This act is considered one of the bedrock laws of Franklin D. Roosevelt's New Deal program designed to address the needs of citizens during the Great Depression. At that time, over half of the country's elderly population were poor. The act provided benefits to retirees, financed by payroll taxes, and lump-sum death benefits to surviving spouses or children (added in 1939). Title IV of the act established the Aid to Dependent Children (changed to AFDC). The act also provided for unemployment insurance, public health services, and maternal and child welfare.

Federal Insurance Contributions Act of 1939 Part of the 1939 amendments to the Social Security Act of 1935, this law shifted the taxing provisions to the Internal Revenue Code. The law provided for a federal payroll tax, known as FICA taxes, to be imposed on both employees and employers in order to fund Social Security payments and Medicare.

Social Security Amendments of 1965 This act amended the Social Security Act to provide a federal health insurance program for persons age sixty-five and older called Medicare. Benefits included up to ninety days of hospital services; up to one hundred home health service visits after a hospital stay; and medical benefits including doctor visits, outpatient care, and medical supplies. Medicare established a federal health insurance program as well for certain younger people with disabilities, and people with end-stage renal disease. The amendments also established Medicaid, designed to provide health coverage for low-income people.

Family and Medical Leave Act of 1993 This act entitles eligible employees of covered employers to take *unpaid*, job-protected leave for medical or family reasons for up to twelve weeks. Such reasons include the birth or adoption of a child; to care for a spouse, child, or parent; or to address a serious health condition of the employee. Covered employers include private-sector employers with fifty or more employees, public organizations of any size, and public or private elementary or secondary schools. Eligible employees are those who have worked for a covered employer for at least twelve months, with at least 1,250 hours of service.

Personal Responsibility and Work Opportunity Reconciliation Act of 1996 This act replaced AFDC with Temporary Assistance for Needy Family Programs (TANF), a block grant program for states to provide cash assistance to needy families. Cash assistance was time limited and came with work requirements for most recipients. States were given more flexibility, but federal funding under TANF was capped.

Patient Protection and Affordable Care Act of 2010 Also known as the Affordable Care Act or Obamacare, the law was created to make health care more affordable and accessible to Americans. It requires insurers to offer plans to people with preexisting conditions, and to cover basic treatments that may not have been offered under existing plans. The law required everyone to obtain insurance, or face a fine imposed by the IRS. The law created a health insurance exchange, or marketplace, where individuals could shop for health insurance plans, and provided a subsidy for low-income people who had to pay for insurance.

MAJOR ACTORS IN SOCIAL WELFARE AND HEALTH CARE POLICY

The president, Congress, the courts, and the bureaucracy affect and shape social welfare and health care policy.

The President

Whether it is President Roosevelt advancing New Deal social welfare programs or President Obama fighting for health care reform, presidents command the bully pulpit and set the agenda for policymaking. They rely on Congress to pass legislation that reflects their policy priorities. This was true for Roosevelt and Obama, who enjoyed the support of their political parties, as well as President Johnson, who advanced his Great Society policies with the help of Congress. This is not always the case, however. President Trump campaigned on repealing Obamacare, and his party (Republicans) controlled both the House of Representatives and the Senate. Despite holding the majority, he was unable during his first year to force the repeal of Obamacare.

Congress

Congress formalizes most public policies, health care and social welfare among them. Both policy areas captured the attention of Congress at certain periods of time. As suggested by Punctuated Equilibrium Theory (described in Chapter 2), the power of media attention and events can alter long-standing policies. Therefore, Congress passed the Social Security Act in the wake of the Great Depression; Congress amended that law in 1965 as part of Johnson's War on Poverty (described in Chapter 8).

Courts

Courts ultimately decide the constitutionality of policies. In the case of health care, the U.S. Supreme Court was asked to determine whether the ACA violated the federalism principle of the Constitution, as described in Chapter 3. In a case arguing that the law was unconstitutional because it violated states' rights (the Medicaid expansion provision) the Court ruled that as long as a state could opt out of expanding Medicaid, there was no constitutional infringement. Other provisions of the ACA were deemed constitutional. Thus, the courts played a pivotal role in allowing the new law (ACA) to be implemented.

Federal Bureaucracies

New laws need bureaucracies to implement them, and social welfare and health care policies are no exception. Several federal agencies play important roles in these policies. Perhaps the most prominent is the Social Security Administration, which administers the Social Security Program including the traditional retirement program as well as disability and survivors benefits. The U.S. Census Bureau determines the poverty threshold, while the U.S. Department of Health and Human Services determines the poverty guidelines and implements the TANF program. An agency inside the Department of Health and Human Services, the Centers for Medicare and Medicaid Services, administers both of these health care programs, as well as the CHIP program and the federal Health Insurance Marketplace. The U.S. Department of Agriculture implements various food assistance programs, including the Supplemental Nutrition Assistance Program (SNAP).

State Governments

Departments in state governments help to implement national social welfare and health care programs, most notably TANF and ACA. States participate in funding social welfare and health care assistance, and determine the level of benefits recipients receive. Medicare and Social Security, on the other hand, are administered by the federal government. You'll recall that in Chapter 3, states were described as policy innovators, and many social welfare and health care reforms are modeled on state programs. For example, the ACA was modeled after a health care program in Massachusetts.

Unofficial Actors

In addition to institutional actors, one should not forget the many interest groups that weigh in on existing policies, helping to bring new policy solutions to the formal agenda. In social welfare policy, a number of organizations exist to advance the needs of the poor. Poor people are not active politically, nor are interest groups for the poor powerful in Washington, but their needs are represented by groups such as the Center for Budget and Policy Priorities. AARP powerfully advocates for persons over age fifty, which brings the organization into discussions about health care and social welfare policies. Pharmaceutical and insurance industries spend millions of dollars to advance their interests in health care policy. Think tanks, like the Kaiser Foundation, provide data on the extent and characteristics of poverty but also have been great sources of information regarding health care reform.

ISSUES AND CHALLENGES

By exploring the history and development of social welfare and health care policies, we see the persistence of many issues—we haven't solved poverty; people are still uninsured and lack basic health care. This section explores three of the thorniest issues: income inequality, the cost of being poor, and universal health care.

Income Inequality

A vexing issue for social welfare policy is the predominance of income inequality. The United States has the highest-level inequality among industrial nations. More troubling, the pace of income inequality is unrivaled in the world. To put it another way, the wealthiest people in this country are prospering at far higher rates than poor and middle-class Americans—staggeringly so. According to data compiled by the Economic Policy Institute, from 1979 to 2007, income in the United States grew by 36.9 percent. However, the wealthiest 1 percent more than doubled their income (a 200 percent increase), while the remaining 99 percent saw incomes increase less than 19 percent. In 2016, the average annual income of the top 1 percent of Americans was $1,153,293, while the average income of everyone else was $45,567 (Sommeiller et al. 2016). Coming out of the recession (2009–2012) showed that disparities were even worse—the bottom 99 percent actually lost income during the recovery, while the top 1 percent of the population saw incomes rise by nearly 37 percent.

This income inequality did not just happen—it was created by government policies. Tax policies and other policies have increasingly benefited the wealthy, with tax cuts going disproportionately to the richest Americans. Also, much more could be done to improve economic mobility, or that ability to get better jobs. Instead of the American Dream, many Americans find that it is hard to break into higher-income categories, particularly if they are not able to afford advanced education. Providing a safety net for the poor in America will be more easily achieved if everyone benefits from growth in the economy.

The High Health Cost of Being Poor

Being poor in America is costly to your health. Studies reveal that poor people tend to be less healthy than more affluent people. They live in areas with fewer health care resources available to them, and hospitals and medical facilities are closing their doors in low-income areas, choosing to relocate in the suburbs and well-to-do neighborhoods. As a result, even if the poor have health insurance through Medicaid, CHIP, or Medicare, they likely live in "primary care shortage areas." Additionally, many poor people live in urban areas with higher rates of pollution and are more susceptible to environmental pollutants such as lead. Thus, they suffer increased incidences of asthma, lead poisoning, and other toxic exposures. One way to measure this high cost of being poor is to look at the death rate. A Centers for Disease Control and Prevention study found that the death rate before the age of seventy-five was 480 per 100,000 people in low-income counties; the rate was 345 in higher-income counties (*Pittsburgh Post-Gazette* 2014). Thus, poverty and poor health are connected issues.

Universal Health Care Coverage and Single-Payer Health Care

Many Americans support a shift to a single-payer or universal health care system. A **single-payer health care system** defines a way of financing health care where one entity, usually the government, is responsible for paying for insurance for all citizens. Governments are the "single payer," typically paying health care expenses through collected taxes. A closely related, but broader, concept is **universal health care**. The World Health Organization defines universal health coverage as individuals receiving the health services they need without suffering financial hardship. Simply put, health care services are available to everyone.

When countries see health care coverage as a fundamental right, they seek to provide universal coverage. It's a goal that all United Nations member states have agreed to try to achieve, and nearly every developed country in the world provides some sort of universal health care. Most of these are public insurance plans that are run by national governments (for example, the UK's National Health Service). The United States stands apart from European countries, Australia, Canada, China, New Zealand, and Russia, as all of these countries provide some form of universal health care. Even developing countries such as Costa Rica, Cuba, and Kyrgyzstan provide citizens access to health services.

Why has a shift to universal health care coverage been unattainable in this country? As illustrated in the political fight to end the Affordable Care Act, health care reform pits the desire for affordable health care insurance coverage against controlling the costs of providing insurance and charges of socialized medicine. Costs of the public insurance programs such as Medicare and Medicaid have risen at an alarming rate, giving ammunition to conservatives who resist shifting to universal coverage. However, the cost of private health care insurance has increased even more. Also troubling is the fact that increasing numbers of Americans will not be able to be covered by their employers. Whatever policy approach is eventually chosen, it is essential to understand that every year people are pushed into poverty or suffer financial hardship because of out-of-pocket expenditures on health services.

Everyday Citizen Connection

This chapter opens with living on $2 a day. Consider how your life would change if you had to live on about $60 a month, with no job prospects. Even for the working poor, financial security is often out of reach. No one can predict the future, and many Americans are just one paycheck or one catastrophic illness away from falling into poverty. As of 2018, the federal government mandated a minimum wage rate of $7.25 per hour. Assuming that you worked full-time (2,080 hours in a year—no vacations; no time off for sickness or bad weather), you would earn $15,080. The 2018 Federal Poverty Guideline for one person is $12,140. So you are living above the level of financial eligibility for certain federal programs. Now, imagine there were three persons in your household—the poverty level is $20,780.

Discovery Questions:

How many more hours would you have to work to be above the poverty line if you were the head of a three-person household? What about if you were sick, needed to take some time off for family reasons, or your employer reduced your hours?

Next, estimate what a family of three might need for basic living every month: food, clothing, rent, utilities, transportation costs to and from work, possible child care, savings, and health care. Compare your estimate with both the minimum wage income for a month and the poverty level income for a month. Are you having trouble making ends meet? This is what life is like for the working poor.

CONCLUDING THOUGHTS

This chapter explored two interconnected policy areas: social welfare and health care. Tracing the history and development of these policies illustrates that Americans have felt quite differently about solutions to the challenge of lifting people out of poverty and meeting health care needs. The values that are brought into these policy arenas (individual or collective responsibility) shape policy solutions. Furthermore, the force of events such as the Great Depression, and the persuasiveness of presidents such as Franklin Roosevelt, Lyndon Johnson, and Barack Obama, have created opportunities for major new shifts in social welfare and health care policies. Time will tell if the country is able to provide a sustainable safety net; to address income inequality and wage discrimination; as well as to answer the call for an affordable, just, and robust health care system.

Policy Choices: Social and Welfare Policy—Family Leave

Choice #1: Family and Medical Leave Act and Employer's Choice/Status Quo	Choice #2: State Funds for Paid Family Leave	Choice #3: Federal Paid Family Leave through a Taxation or a Savings Fund
The Family and Medical Leave Act was enacted in 1993. FMLA states that employers and public agencies with fifty or more employees must provide up to twelve weeks of unpaid leave and a continuation of health benefits for the birth or adoption of a child, to care for a spouse, a parent or a child who has fallen ill or one's own health issues. In order to qualify, employees must have worked for a company for at least a year and logged 1,250 hours within that year to receive benefits under the Family and Medical Leave Act.[1] Because of these stipulations, including the size of the organization or company, only about 60 percent of workers are eligible under the Family and Medical Leave Act.[2] While the Family and Medical Leave Act allows for a variety of family and medical leave, it does so without compensating employees during their time away. Such unpaid time can create a financial burden for employees, especially those in lower-income brackets. Many top businesses choose to offer a competitive benefits package, including paid family leave. For instance, accounting firm Deloitte LLP announced in September 2016 that it will now offer sixteen weeks of paid family leave for its employees.	While the Family and Medical Leave Act offers up to twelve weeks of leave, it is still unpaid. Millions of Americans at or below the poverty level would most likely find it a financial burden to take twelve weeks of unpaid time off. Therefore, the Family and Medical Leave Act does little to alleviate this burden. With the absence of a federal mandate on paid family leave, a handful of states have passed laws regarding paid family leave. In California, 1 percent of workers' payroll is paid to both state disability insurance and paid family leave insurance. This state fund provides employees 55 percent of their salary up to a maximum of $1,000 per week. In New Jersey, the state covers two-thirds of the average worker's wages or up to $584 per week.[5] Washington State covers $250 per week for up to five weeks for a newborn or newly adopted child.[6] Hawaii, New York, and Rhode Island also replace a nominal amount of income for employees seeking leave.	The United States is the only nation out of forty-one industrialized countries that does not offer some type of federal paid parental leave, according to the Organisation for Economic Co-operation and Development (OECD).[8] Of those forty-one industrialized nations, Austria, Bulgaria, Czech Republic, Estonia, Hungary, Japan, Latvia, Lithuania, Norway, Slovakia, and Sweden all offer over a year's worth of paid leave. Even federal workers in the United States do not receive paid family leave. Instead, U.S. federal employees patch together family leave through sick and vacation time. While many Americans view family leave as an individual issue and others do not wish to have the government intervene in their family lives, with increasing numbers of dual working parent households, the issue of family leave is becoming more prevalent in American society today. A federal paid family leave policy could be formed by raising taxes on the entire American population. However, such sweeping tax increases are consistently unpopular. In many other countries, Social Security–type funds are set up with employers and employees paying into the fund. The U.S. federal government could set up a federal Family Medical Leave Fund like those currently in place in California, Hawaii, New Jersey, New York, Rhode Island, and Washington, in which employees and employers can pay into the fund as a percentage of a company's payroll expense.

(Continued)

Choice #1: Family and Medical Leave Act and Employer's Choice/Status Quo	Choice #2: State Funds for Paid Family Leave	Choice #3: Federal Paid Family Leave through a Taxation or a Savings Fund
Law firm Arnold and Porter, LLP offers eighteen weeks of paid maternity leave for the primary caregiver and six weeks for the secondary caregiver.[3] While many Fortune 500 companies compete for top talent with benefits packages including paid family leave, those in lower-skilled jobs are less likely to receive compensation for family leave and are the most likely to need it. In fact, only 13 percent of workers in 2017 received paid family leave through their employers.[4]	With only six states offering some form of paid family leave, this still leaves millions of Americans without a policy on paid family leave. According to a Pew Research poll, 46 percent of households have two parents working full-time compared to 30 percent in 1970.[7] With more American families having both parents working full time, the desire for paid family leave will continue.	Employees across the United States would then receive the benefit of that fund for certain circumstances including caring for a family member with a serious medical condition and for parental leave. Another option could be a federally mandated Family Medical Leave savings account that functions like a Health savings account allowing workers to save for family and medical leave through a pre-tax savings fund. Those who are not working or retired would not be subject to pay into a fund benefiting workers. However, such a savings fund would still create challenges for low-income workers that struggle to establish any type of savings accounts living paycheck to paycheck.

Sources:

[1] T. S. Bernard, "In Paid Family Leave, U.S. Trails Most of the Globe," *New York Times,* February 22, 2013. http://www.nytimes.com/2013/02/23/your-money/us-trails-much-of-the-world-in-providing-paid-family-leave.html. Accessed April 21, 2017.

[2] C. C. Miller, "Americans Agree on Paid Leave, but Not on Who Should Pay," *New York Times*, March 23, 2017. Accessed April 21, 2017, from https://www.nytimes.com/2017/03/23/upshot/americans-agree-on-paid-leave-but-not-on-who-should-pay.html

[3] Bernard, "In Paid Family Leave, U.S. Trails Most of the Globe."

[4] Y. Hara and A. Hegewisch, "Maternity, Paternity, and Adoption Leave in the United States," Institute for Women's Policy Research, issue brief no. A143, updated 2013, pp. 1–15. Washington, DC: Institute for Women's Policy Research.

[5] Bernard, "In Paid Family Leave, U.S. Trails Most of the Globe."

[6] Hara and Hegewisch, "Maternity, Paternity, and Adoption Leave in the United States."

[7] E. Patten, "How American Parents Balance Work and Family Life When Both Work," Pew Research Center, November 4, 2015. Accessed April 21, 2017, from http://www.pewresearch.org/fact-tank/2015/11/04/how-american-parents-balance-work-and-family-life-when-both-work/

[8] G. Livingston, "Among 41 Nations, U.S. Is the Outlier When It Comes to Paid Parental Leave," Pew Research Center, September 26, 2016. Accessed April 21, 2017, from http://www.pewresearch.org/fact-tank/2016/09/26/u-s-lacks-mandated-paid-parental-leave/

GLOSSARY TERMS

means-tested   210
Medicaid   217
Medicare   219
poverty guidelines   208
poverty thresholds   207

public welfare programs   210
single-payer health care
   system   229
social insurance   210
Social Security   215

social welfare policy   207
Supplemental Poverty Measure
   (SPM)   207
universal health care   229

DISCUSSION QUESTIONS

1. Why do you think most Americans believe that poverty is best solved by the individual, rather than by government?

2. What factors account for the inability to address shortcomings in health care policy in the United States? What similarities and differences do you see when considering the development of social welfare and health care policy?

3. Assume you have been elected to the U.S. House of Representatives and have been asked to sponsor a bill on health care reform. What one or two policy options will you pursue and why?

4. What do you think is the most important change made in social welfare policy over the decades? How about health care policy?

SUGGESTED RESOURCES

Suggested Websites

Center on Budget and Policy Priorities, "Policy Basics: An Introduction to TANF," https://www.cbpp.org/research/policy-basics-an-introduction-to-tanf

Economic Policy Institute, "Inequality Is," http://inequality.is/

The Henry J. Kaiser Family Foundation, http://www.kff.org/, especially: http://www.kff.org/state-category/demographics-and-the-economy/people-in-poverty/ and http://www.kff.org/health-reform/

Institute for Women's Policy Research, https://iwpr.org/

The Social Welfare History Project, Virginia Commonwealth University, http://socialwelfare.library.vcu.edu/

U.S. Social Security Administration, www.ssa.gov

Suggested Books or Articles

Brill, Steven. 2015. *America's Bitter Pill: Money, Politics, Backroom Deals, and the Fight to Fix Our Broken Healthcare System.* New York: Random House.

Edin, Kathryn J., and H. Luke Shaefer. 2015. *$2.00 a Day: Living on Almost Nothing in America.* Boston, MA: Houghton Mifflin Harcourt.

Reid, T. R. 2010. *The Healing of America: A Global Quest for Better, Cheaper, and Fairer Health Care.* London: Penguin Books.

Suggested Films and Other Media

1.5 Million Americans Are Living on Less Than $2 a Day, PBS (2015: United States), https://youtu.be/wyieyMwWgoM

The Dust Bowl, DVD, directed by Ken Burns (2012: United States), http://www.pbs.org/kenburns/dustbowl/

Obama's Deal, PBS (2010: United States), https://www.pbs.org/wgbh/frontline/film/obamasdeal/

Poor Kids, PBS (2017: United States), https://www.pbs.org/wgbh/frontline/film/poor-kids/

"This Is Life on $7.50 an Hour." *CNN Money*. September 15, 2015, https://youtu.be/-SCB1t28nDU

for CQ Press

Sharpen your skills with SAGE edge at **http://edge.sagepub.com/rinfret**. **SAGE edge for students** provides a personalized approach to help you accomplish your coursework goals in an easy-to-use learning environment.

Environmental and Energy Policy

10

A WEB OF ACTORS WHEN DISASTER STRIKES

On April 20, 2010, the single most devastating marine environmental disaster began to unfold when the *Deepwater Horizon* drilling rig off the Gulf Coast exploded, releasing 210 million gallons of oil before the well was capped and sank (U.S. Coast Guard 2011). Eleven rig workers lost their lives. The rig, owned by British Petroleum (BP), operated by Transocean, suffered an explosion, and it took eighty-seven days for the well to stop gushing oil from deep below the seabed into the Gulf. These are essential facts, which are not debated. Much of the rest of the story is complicated by the multitude of actors involved. Lawsuits, research, and blame all continue years later while substantive policy has not been implemented, unlike after the 1989 spill from the oil tanker *Exxon Valdez*. Here, we focus on the actors involved in the spill response to illustrate the complexity of environmental and energy policy.

Think for a moment and brainstorm all the actors involved in the response to the explosion of this drilling rig. How many actors have you come up with? Odds are, you might have missed a few. Now, consider this list of actors involved in responding to the disaster:

- U.S. Coast Guard
- U.S. Department of Defense
- state of Alabama
- state of Florida
- state of Louisiana
- state of Mississippi

LEARNING OBJECTIVES

Readers of this chapter will be able to:

1. Describe the origins of environmental and energy policy in the United States and understand the effects of those histories on present-day policy

2. Explain the scope and scale of environmental and energy issues today

3. Assess the roles of various stakeholders in environmental and energy issues today

- state of Texas

- U.S. Fish and Wildlife Service

- U.S. Department of Homeland Security

- U.S. Department of the Interior

- Minerals Management Service

- National Oceanographic and Atmospheric Administration

- U.S. Department of State

- Centers for Disease Control

- National Park Service

- National Geospatial Intelligence Agency

- National Aeronautics and Space Administration

- U.S. Geological Survey

- U.S. Environmental Protection Agency

- Occupational Safety and Health Administration

- U.S. Department of Agriculture

- British Petroleum

- Transocean

- Haliburton

- media

- environmental groups

- energy industry trade groups

- tourism agencies

- economic development agencies

- citizens

And while we could go on for pages with this list, we are going to stop there. The number of actors involved in the response to this spill and its ensuing cleanup helps demonstrate the complexities of environmental and energy issues. The point of this brainstorm has been to demonstrate that while it might seem like only a handful of individuals and organizations might be involved in environmental and energy issues, in reality that list is much longer. Furthermore, while it may also have seemed a foregone conclusion that major legislation would have followed, just as the Oil Pollution Act of 1990 followed the

Valdez spill, on reconsideration it is not so surprising that it did not after this accident. Imagine if you had that many organizations to coordinate for an event on campus!

······································

You do not have to look far to find debates about environmental issues or energy problems in the United States. From concerns over hydraulic fracturing, or "fracking," for natural gas buried in shale formations underground, to the latest battery technology for electric vehicles, including the sleekly designed Teslas, to Pope Francis's 2015 encyclical on climate change, environmental and energy issues are ubiquitous. However, these frequent debates often make these issues seem far more simplistic than they really are, or just political fodder for politicians who prefer hearing themselves speak. In this chapter, we will explore environmental policy and energy policy and provide everyday citizens a context for understanding the latest news story or a politician's speech about one of these topics.

Environmental policy and energy policy are interrelated, but they each have their own unique attributes, so we will consider the history and development of them independently before discussing their current statuses and challenges for the future. We will discover—as is the case with other areas of public policy—that environmental and energy issues are much more complex than politicians, in their campaign rhetoric, might have us believe, but we will also realize that policy choices leave ample room for opportunity to address the challenges as citizens see fit, and there are countless ways everyday citizens can get involved in these issues.

OVERVIEW OF ENVIRONMENTAL AND ENERGY POLICY

As our introductory story of this chapter indicates, environmental and energy policy areas are heavily intertwined, but we suggest that examining each area separately is necessary in order to understand broad definitions, the scope and significance of these policy areas, as well as their history and development. Then we will bring the two policy areas together toward the end of the chapter to investigate current challenges.

Understanding U.S. Environmental Policy

Environmental policy is a broad, umbrella term that encompasses government action, or inaction, related to the natural environment. The term includes efforts to control pollution and prevent it, as well as the management of natural resources and their use, efforts to protect endangered and threatened species, and efforts to promote sustainable use and development of natural resources. Without a doubt, environmental policy is expansive and covers a range of issues surrounding air, water, land, plants and animals, and pollution.

Since the use of resources (e.g., coal) is often an energy source, it is easy to make the argument that energy policy is a part of environmental policy. However, given the complexities associated with our energy use and supply, this area of policy is increasingly referred to as its own area, despite obvious overlaps, and we address it separately later in the chapter.

With this broad definition established, we unpack the topic by examining its current scope and status. Undoubtedly, the United States' natural environment has seen significant improvements in its condition since the mid-twentieth century and the advent of modern environmental policy; however, there is still much to be done, particularly as we understand the new and emerging threats facing the environment. Here, we consider three major areas of environmental concern: air quality, water quality, and waste generation.

Status and Scope

The nation's air quality has seen major improvements since the passage of the modern Clean Air Act in 1970. And these improvements have been realized with a growing economy and increasing energy consumption. Consider the following changes in air quality emissions for "criteria" air pollutants (as defined by the Clean Air Act) from 1980 to 2016 according to the U.S. EPA:

- 85 percent decrease in the national average of carbon monoxide,

- 31 percent decrease in ground level ozone,

- 99 percent decrease in lead,

- 61 percent decrease in nitrogen dioxide,

- 42 percent decrease in particular matter (PM2.5), and

- 87 percent decrease in sulfur dioxide. (U.S. EPA Air Quality Trends 2016)

While most of these pollutant levels are below national standards, these are national assessments and there are many locations around the country that have pollution levels above national standards; for example, consider the many air pollutant alert days, often in the summertime. However, rates of respiratory illness continue to cause concern as millions of people still live in counties with air quality concentrations that exceed federal government standards (U.S. EPA Air Quality Trends 2016). Follow the links presented in Box 10.1 to explore the data where you live and your air quality.

The United States has approximately 3.5 million miles of rivers and streams, and while rivers do not routinely catch fire as the Cuyahoga River did in the 1960s, only a small portion of those waterways are assessed as "good" by the U.S. EPA. More specifically, of the 3.5 million miles, just about half a million miles are assessed as "good," while 564,499 miles are determined to be "impaired," and the evaluation is similar for the lakes, bays, coastline, and wetlands (U.S. EPA Watershed Assessment 2015). An impairment designation is when there is pollution from a host of sources, including agriculture, runoff from fields and pavement, municipal discharge, air deposits, industrial sources, and other nonpoint sources.

The condition of the waterways and overall air quality have much to do with the volume of waste generated in the United States and how that waste is managed. In 2013, Americans generated about 254 million tons of trash, which means that is approximately

0.8 ton for each person for the year, or 4.4 pounds of waste per person, per day (U.S. EPA 2015 Municipal Solid Waste). This represents a steady upward trend in the volume of waste produced annually in the United States since 1960. In addition, about 34 million tons of hazardous waste—waste that cannot be disposed of in municipal landfills, such as oil, medical waste, chemicals, and so forth—are generated annually (U.S. EPA 2011).

With statistics such as these, it is not unexpected that the government has long been involved in environmental policy. Although environmental policy has ebbed and flowed with political inclinations and the disposition of the American public, the government's involvement is unlikely to change dramatically in the future. Much has been done regarding the nation's environment, but much remains as we learn and understand more about our relationship with the natural environment. Exploring the history and development of environmental policy helps provide some perspective on today's current challenges.

HISTORY AND DEVELOPMENT OF ENVIRONMENTAL POLICY

The history and development of environmental policy in the United States is rich and much lengthier than you might expect. Therefore, we illustrate some of the high points in our introduction to this particular policy arena. Although the environmental movement is typically thought of as beginning in the mid-twentieth century, early American colonists were concerned with the use and management of their natural resources, and some of the founders of the nation also paid particular attention to land management and resources. In the late 1800s and early 1900s, the beginnings of the modern environmental movement took root.

As industrialization brought with it urbanization, sanitation and other health concerns mounted. And these trends, along with tales of adventure from the West, fostered a desire

PHOTO 10.2

Cuyahoga River fire

Bettmann / Contributor

for outdoor recreation activities. Two dominant perspectives of the natural environment emerged, setting the foundation for understanding U.S. environmental policy of the past and present. **Conservationists**, such as President Theodore Roosevelt, embraced the idea that natural resources can and should be used in a responsible manner for human flourishing. The environment, with this perspective, is valued because of its value for humans. **Preservationists**, by contrast, including John Muir, founder of the Sierra Club, believed nature had intrinsic value itself and should be protected for future generations. The first national parks were established in the early years of the twentieth century, and the nation's first pollution control laws were passed by local—and then state—governments by the 1920s, typically based in concerns over human health effects of pollution.

Birth of the Modern Environmental Movement (1960s and 1970s)

After the United States survived the Great Depression and achieved victory in World War II, the nation had time to focus on other, perhaps less pressing, "quality of life" issues now that security and economic stability had been reestablished. For many of these quality of life policy areas, like the environment, this context is crucial. With this founding and timing, major focusing events took on special significance and catapulted the environmental movement.

Rachel Carson, a biologist with the U.S. Bureau of Fisheries, wrote a nontechnical best-selling book, *Silent Spring*, in 1962 that warned Americans about the dangers of the pesticide DDT. The book galvanized the public and brought criticism to the chemical industry in the United States. Additionally, during the 1960s, major environmental problems gained national attention with the rise of the modern news media. For example, the Cuyahoga River in Ohio, one of the most polluted waterways in the United States, caught fire multiple times during the 1950s and 1960s, thereby drawing alarm about the state of the nation's waterways (see Photo 10.2). Oil spills, including off the coast of Santa Barbara, California, drew additional concern. And the nation celebrated the first Earth Day on April 22, 1970.

These **focusing events**, along with many others, shaped the political and governing context that gave way to some of the first federal-level environmental laws. The 1960s and 1970s were arguably the most productive time for the passage of environmental laws (see Table 10.1). The first efforts at air quality laws were passed in 1963 and culminated with the 1970 Clean Air Act. Other significant environmental laws—which will be discussed in greater detail in a subsequent section—included the National Environmental Policy Act of 1969, the Clean Water Act of 1972, the Resource Conservation and Recovery Act of 1976, and the Federal Land Policy and Management Act of 1976. Before President Ronald Reagan's election in 1980, the law commonly known as "Superfund" was also passed that established a "superfund" of money to clean up toxic sites and prosecute those responsible. The passage of these laws was made possible by widespread and bipartisan support of

Americans and their elected leaders in Congress. While President Richard Nixon was a Republican, he worked with a Democratic-controlled Congress on environmental issues. He used his authority to create the U.S. Environmental Protection Agency via executive order in 1970 to coordinate the nation's environmental policy.

Changing Course (1980s)

By the 1980s and the election of Ronald Reagan as president, Americans and their governmental institutions had had more than a decade of experience with environmental laws and were beginning to demand changes to the government's approach in this policy arena. For the first time since the modern environmental movement began, environmentalism was now on the defensive as concerns over costs, negative effects on the economy, and burdensome government intervention were increasing worries. Numerous efforts were made by the administration to roll back environmental regulations at the federal level and shift the focus from the national government to state and local governments in this area.

These actions coincided with the governing philosophy of the Reagan administration, which wanted to devolve responsibilities from the federal government to state and local governments in an effort to decrease the level of governmental intrusion in the market and lives of individuals. In keeping with these aims, federal agencies saw significant cuts to budgets and staffing, especially the U.S. EPA (Layzer 2014, 104). And the political appointees to head these agencies, including Gale Norton at the EPA and James Watt at the Department of the Interior, translated Reagan's ideology into agency action. Finally, the White House endeavored to keep government regulations under control with the signing of Executive Order 12291, which required cost-benefit analyses of new regulations and mandated that new regulations be submitted to the White House Office of Information and Regulatory Affairs (OIRA) to ensure tighter control (see Chapter 4 for additional explanation).

Although many of these efforts were initially greeted positively by the public, those sentiments changed by the mid-1980s and in the wake of growing public concern about various environmental issues. With public demand, Congress pushed back on many of the White House's efforts and managed to reauthorize the Superfund legislation that provided funds to clean up toxic sites. Changes in public sentiment came in part from major

TABLE 10.1

Select Major U.S. Environmental Laws

Year	Law
1969	National Environmental Policy Act
1970	Clean Air Act Amendments
1972	Federal Water Pollution Control Amendments (Clean Water Act) Federal Insecticide, Fungicide, and Rodenticide Act Marine Mammal Protection Act Coastal Zone Management Act
1973	Endangered Species Act
1974	Safe Drinking Water Act
1976	Resource Conservation and Recovery Act Toxic Substances Control Act Federal Land Policy and Management Act National Forest Management Act
1977	Clean Air Act Amendments Surface Mining and Reclamation Act
1980	Comprehensive Environmental Response, Compensation, and Liability Act (Superfund)
1986	Emergency Planning and Community Right-to-Know Act Superfund Amendments and Reauthorization Act
1988	Ocean Dumping Act
1990	Clean Air Act Amendments Oil Pollution Act Pollution Prevention Act

events such as the explosion at the Union Carbide chemical plant in Bhopal, India, and the nuclear meltdown at a plant in Chernobyl, Ukraine.

U.S. concerns regarding the environment led the presidential candidates in the 1988 election to profess their environmental aspirations. George H. W. Bush claimed to be the first "environmental president," but this record was put to the test when he confronted a significant environmental disaster when the *Exxon Valdez* tanker ship ran aground in Prince William Sound, Alaska, destroying a pristine habitat for generations by spilling approximately 11 million gallons of oil due to human error. This event precipitated passage of the 1990 Oil Pollution Act, which aimed to prevent these sorts of spills in the future. Also in 1990, major amendments to the Clean Air Act were passed with White House support. The George H. W. Bush administration, like its predecessor, favored market-based approaches to environmental protection but did make more environmentally friendly appointments to federal agencies.

Diffused Attention in the 1990s and Early 2000s

The 1992 election brought Bill Clinton to the White House along with Al Gore as vice president. Environmentalists greeted the new administration with excitement, as Gore had been a prominent environmentalist in the Senate and there was much optimism that environmental gains would be achieved with the Democratic-controlled 103rd Congress. However, that hope dissipated quickly as Republicans took control of Congress for the remainder of the Clinton administration. Legislatively, the Clinton administration focused its efforts on other issues, including failed health care reform and successful welfare reform as Republicans sought to fulfill their campaign promises of reducing regulation and government spending. Federal appointments for environmental agencies were seen to be more environmentally friendly, and President Clinton used executive orders to achieve some environmental goals, particularly in the final years of his eight-year administration. Notably, the Clinton administration supported international efforts to address climate change with the 1997 Kyoto Protocol, but the White House chose not to submit the treaty for formal ratification, as the Republican Senate indicated little chance of endorsing the agreement. Indeed, much of the focus during the Clinton administration was elsewhere, both in terms of legislative priorities and scandal.

Diffused attention to environmental issues continued into the twenty-first century with the election of George W. Bush in 2000 and the aftermath of the terrorist attacks on September 11, 2001. The George W. Bush administration entered office with pledges to undo much of the Clinton-era environmental policy and reduce government regulation. In particular, the newly elected president tried to open government lands to drilling, including the Arctic National Wildlife Refuge (ANWR) in Alaska. However, in the wake of the terrorist attacks, wars in Afghanistan and Iraq, and ensuing economic turmoil, the Bush administration focused much of its attention on national security matters and energy concerns.

Legislatively, the Bush administration oversaw passage of several environmental initiatives, including the 2003 Healthy Forests Restoration Act, which, despite its name, did little to improve the nation's forests (Vaughn and Cortner 2005). While the act ostensibly focused on the health of forests by clearing underbrush, the law allowed logging companies to clear much more than that and harvest large-diameter trees. In terms of federal agencies, Bush's appointees brought a mixed environmental record. His first EPA administrator, former New Jersey governor Christine Todd Whitman, was seen positively, but she quickly resigned over very public fights with the White House. Internationally, the Bush administration removed the United States from all efforts to combat climate change globally and declined to participate in international negotiations.

Executive Action in the 2010s

George W. Bush's successor, Barack Obama, renewed hope that environmental issues would once again feature prominently on the national agenda; however, those hopes did not last long. The Obama administration focused its domestic efforts on passing the Affordable Care and Patient Protection Act—better known as Obamacare—and its international efforts were focused on national security and growing instability in the Middle East. Although the Obama White House had a Democratic-controlled Congress for part of Obama's first term, the Republicans regained control quickly and stymied any efforts at environmental legislation. The Waxman-Markey bill, which would have provided for a carbon "cap and trade" program, passed the House in 2009 but failed to make it to the Senate for a vote. As a result, the environmental efforts taken halfway into this decade are largely the result of executive action.

Key events have defined this decade so far. As noted in our opening story, in 2010 the nation confronted its worst environmental disaster to date with the explosion of a drilling rig, the *Deepwater Horizon,* in the Gulf of Mexico, which spewed oil for nearly ninety days before it could be contained. Eleven individuals perished in the explosion and more than 200 million gallons of oil were spilled into the Gulf. Despite these staggering figures, no legislation followed. Government agencies that oversee drilling, however, were restructured and the Minerals Management Service in the Department of the Interior was gutted and restructured.

Although major environmental legislation has not been passed under the Obama administration, some notable policies were passed that had significant provisions for research and development, including the American Recovery and Reinvestment Act. Concerns about climate change have grown louder in the second decade of the twenty-first century, and the Obama administration worked internationally to reach bilateral agreements with China to curb **greenhouse gas emissions**. Under this administration, the United States also participated in crafting and signed the Paris Climate Agreement in 2016, which endeavors to strengthen the world's response to climate change by keeping global temperatures below two degrees Celsius above preindustrial levels by having participating nations set and achieve their own emissions goals. Environmentalists praised the Obama administration's announcement that it would deny TransCanada's request to build the Keystone XL pipeline extension in November 2015. Additionally, the EPA has promulgated significant regulations that have major implications for the energy sector in the United States and demand measures to reduce emissions, including the Clean Power Plan rule. Many of these regulations, however, are being challenged in the court system.

Donald Trump's presidency is likely to result in significant changes to environmental issues. His campaign rhetoric indicated that he thinks climate change is a hoax, perhaps created by China (Wong 2016). And in the opening months of his administration, he announced the United States would formally withdraw from the Paris Climate Agreement. In practical terms, withdrawal from this agreement means little, since it was never submitted to the Senate for ratification; however, in broader terms, it signals

PHOTO 10.3

Signing of the Paris Climate Agreement

FRANCOIS GUILLOT/ AFP/Getty Images

that a major contributor of greenhouse gas emissions is walking away from efforts to deal with the issue. His appointments to key government agencies bring to leading roles individuals whose commitment to environmental protection is questioned. Scott Pruitt is Trump's EPA administrator, and while Pruitt was attorney general of Oklahoma, he routinely sued the U.S. EPA in an effort to block environmental policy actions, questioning the need for governmental action. Pruitt has stated that the science does not support climate change, and he is taking action to see dramatic cuts to the agency he now heads (Puko 2017). While it is too soon to tell what the long-term impacts of these appointments and regulatory actions will be for environmental issues, it is already obvious that there is a fundamental shift in the new administration's approach to these issues.

Environmental policy has taken center stage in U.S. history—during the 1960s and 1970s—and we have seen periods when it was relegated to the background—notably the 1990s and early 2000s. While the preceding discussion is far from an exhaustive history of U.S. environmental policy, it provides important context for where environmental policy is today and likely where it is going in the near future. An important piece of this history is public opinion regarding environmental issues and its influence.

Citizens galvanized governmental efforts in the 1960s and 1970s, and public opinion supported continued efforts. In April 1970, 53 percent of the public believed reducing pollution was one of the nation's top three problems, and by 1978, 50 percent of the public was willing to accept slower rates of economic growth in order to protect the environment (Layzer 2014, 80–81). By 1980, however, only 24 percent of the public believed pollution reduction was a top problem, and a quarter thought environmental laws had gone too far (Layzer 2014, 81). Yet public support for environmental protection was sufficient to compel Congress to block some of Reagan's most egregious environmental rollback efforts; and, according to a 1990 Gallup poll, three-quarters of respondents considered themselves environmentalists (Vaughn 2007, 24). Additionally, by the early 1990s, Americans thought the government was spending too little and not doing enough to protect the environment (Dunlap 2002, 22).

More recently, public opinion on environmental issues has been mixed. By 2011, 54 percent of Americans said economic growth should take precedence over environmental protection—the first time that economic considerations have trumped environmental ones (Gallup 2013). Recent years have seen this percentage shift to 50 percent favoring environmental protection and 41 percent advocating economic growth (Gallup 2014). Since 2000, the percentage of Americans who think the government is doing too much in terms of environmental protection increased from 10 percent to 16 percent in 2013, while the percentage of Americans who think the government is doing too little has decreased from 58 to 47 percent over the same period (Gallup 2013). Americans remained concerned that the condition of the environment will be worse for the next generation; in April 2017, 57 percent of Americans thought the environment would be worse, only 12 percent thought the environment would be better, and 29 percent said the environment would be about the same (CBS 2017).

The actions of the Trump administration in this policy arena are not widely supported; for example, 55 percent of those polled oppose the withdrawal of the United States from the Paris Climate Agreement (NPR/*PBS NewsHour*/Marist Poll 2017). And 65 percent of respondents do not think the Trump administration should remove government regulations already in place that are intended to combat climate change (Quinnipiac University 2017a, b). Public opinion continues to shift regarding environmental issues, but general support for the government's role in environmental protection remains steadfast despite political rhetoric that indicates the contrary. The role of public sentiment is equally important with energy concerns, and we will see that perhaps the public is even more engaged in energy policy matters as the direct connection to household budgets is apparent.

Our discussion of environmental policy yields several points worth underscoring. First, the approach to this policy area in the United States is largely reactive. Once environmental problems become evident and public pressure mounts, only then the government typically takes action. Second, there has been demonstrable improvement in the health and condition of the natural environment, but as we make progress with one challenge—for instance, chlorofluorocarbons (CFCs)—scientific research and knowledge grow and we uncover new, vexing issues. Third, the complexities of environmental issues themselves are rivaled by the complexities associated with numerous stakeholders involved in the issue, and the same holds true as we explore energy issues in the next section.

UNDERSTANDING U.S. ENERGY POLICY

Although environmental and energy concerns are interrelated, we opt to consider each area independently because of the complexities of each policy area. Much like our definition of environmental policy, **energy policy** refers to government action or inaction that deals with issues related to the production, distribution, transportation, and consumption of energy. In other words, energy policy has to do with how the country uses energy and where that energy comes from. Energy resources are interconnected with environmental and natural resource policies and concerns. However, energy policy is also linked to U.S. economic and national security policy. The visible manifestations of energy policy are often very pronounced because most Americans have a sense of current gas prices and monthly energy bills to power, heat, and cool our homes, whereas many Americans may be less clued into environmental concerns because they are often less tangible.

Status and Scope

With the often daily presence of energy policy—perhaps even more so than environmental concerns—Americans in the modern era are hugely dependent on energy to power our daily lives. Where our energy comes from is significant because it determines our nation's energy policy. Before we can investigate the nation's policy decisions about energy, we first must detail our energy supply and the rates of consumption, as these considerations drive policy decisions.

The United States' energy supply continues to be dominated by fossil fuels, which are fuel sources that come from the decaying plants and animals in the ground that have been converted to energy over millions of years of heat and pressure. Fossil fuels include the energy sources we most often think of—coal, oil, and natural gas—that come out of the ground. These sources are sometimes called nonrenewable sources because once they are consumed, they are not readily replaced. To date, fossil fuels represent the cheapest forms of energy in terms of dollars per unit of energy, but there are significant environmental and geopolitical considerations to their ongoing use.

By contrast, renewable sources of energy, which include geothermal, solar, wind, hydro, and biomass, are easily replaced after their use. Often these sources are touted as the environmentally friendlier option over fossil fuels, but it is important to note that these sources of energy are far from perfect, as there are concerns about the destruction of habitat, water use, and impact on endangered species associated with these sources. For example, advocates of wind power point out the lack of pollution associated with turning wind turbines; however, critics allege that besides the often unsightly wind turbines, these turbines also disrupt the migratory patterns of birds.

With multiple sources of energy, the nation's production of energy is varied, but still dominated by fossil fuels. Figure 10.1 overviews energy production in the United States in 2016.

In 2019, 83 quadrillion British thermal units (Btus) were produced domestically, and of that, only 12 percent were from all renewable sources combined (U.S. Energy Information Administration 2017). Natural gas—which has increased in production in recent years—along with coal and oil, continues to be the source of most of the nation's domestic power. Although the sources of domestic production of energy have been generally consistent in recent years, the nation's consumption of energy continues to grow. In 2014, according to the U.S. Energy Information Agency, Americans consumed 98.460 quadrillion Btus, up from 34.61 quadrillion Btus in 1950. Figure 10.2 explains the growth in consumption from 1950 to 2014.

FIGURE 10.1

U.S. Energy Production, 2016 (in quadrillion Btus)

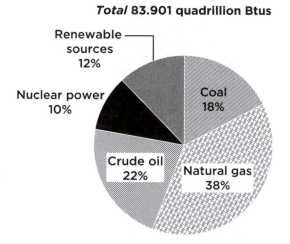

Total 83.901 quadrillion Btus

Source: U.S. Energy Information Administration, Monthly Energy Review, August 2017. Available at www.eia.gov/mer, accessed September 20, 2017.

FIGURE 10.2

U.S. Energy Consumption, 1950–2014

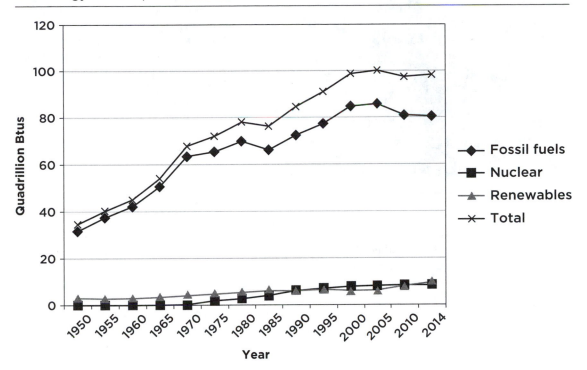

Source: U.S. Energy Information Administration, Monthly Energy Review, August 2017. Available at www.eia.gov/mer, accessed September 20, 2017.

Overall consumption reflects an upward trend, as does the use of fossil fuels—until recently, when that source appears to be reaching a plateau. Despite a lot of conversation regarding renewable sources of energy, they still represent a meager part of the nation's energy sources, in part due to government policy. Nuclear energy continues to represent a steady source of power, but it has seen neither a rapid increase nor decrease as a source. A quick glance of these numbers reveals that Americans use more energy than is produced domestically; therefore, much of our energy has to be imported, resulting in significant economic and geopolitical considerations and ramifications.

The nation's consumption of energy—particularly in the era of technological innovation and increasingly indispensable technological devices in our pockets—is unlikely to change, as its growth has continued since the Industrial Era. Therefore, the nation's energy policy is of paramount significance. Indeed, it is easy to assume that the United States has a coherent policy, but simply put, it does not. Much of our energy policy has been piecemeal and reactive to crises or other significant factors; as a result, the government's efforts are even more disparate than its environmental policy. Since the start of the twenty-first century, we have seen government renew its focus on energy concerns, particularly as energy relates to national security concerns and economic considerations. Unrest in the

Middle East—which is a source, but not the leading source, of the nation's foreign energy supplies—continues to drive concern, and the rapid rise in gas prices in the early 2000s, coupled with a sluggish economy, have focused governmental efforts on devising a comprehensive energy policy. First, we will consider the history and development of energy policy in the United States; then, we will assess at what level of government and among which organizations that energy policy might be implemented, and where it could be going in the future.

PHOTO 10.4
Three Mile Island nuclear plant
Owen/Corbis via Getty Images

HISTORY AND DEVELOPMENT OF ENERGY POLICY

The history and development of energy policy have been less concerned with contamination and pollution hazards and more focused on how and where to access the energy resources the nation needs, along with steps the government should take concerning development of those resources. But, with that said, it would be mistaken to think the United States has a robust, comprehensive energy policy. Prior to the 1970s, the federal government's involvement in energy policy was on the development of nuclear energy for the civilian market and oversaw the creation of the forerunner of the Nuclear Regulatory Commission (NRC), the Atomic Energy Commission.

Crisis in the 1970s

Energy policy of the 1970s is defined by crisis. In 1973, the Organization of the Petroleum Exporting Countries (OPEC) imposed an oil embargo on the nation in response to the United States' support of Israel in the Yom Kippur War. As a result of this embargo, oil prices quadrupled and unleashed significant economic ramifications for the United States. In response to these production cuts, the U.S. government instituted a number of policy actions to decrease energy use, including imposing daylight savings time, instituting a national speed limit of 55 miles per hour, and increasing research and development for energy resources and energy efficiency practices.

As a result, by the mid-1970s, energy policy was a priority for the federal government. For instance, in 1975, the first corporate average fuel economy (CAFE) standards were established for cars. In 1977, the Department of Energy was established, which consolidated several existing government agencies related to energy, and Congress passed the National Energy Act in 1978. This act, which incorporated many of President Jimmy Carter's priorities, included the partial deregulation of natural gas pricing, support for renewable energy sources, and the creation of a market for small energy producers. The dominant source of energy, though, was coal, and little consideration was given to the environmental impacts of mining for and using coal. Because of these efforts, energy conservation improved, but that improvement was due more to a slowing economy and decline in energy-inefficient industries than to behavior changes by consumers. While government policies were plentiful, there was little coordination among them, and many often supported contradictory aims.

Deregulation in the 1980s

As we saw with environmental policy in the 1980s under the Reagan administration, similar efforts unfolded related to energy issues as well. The Reagan administration brought with it a fundamental shift in views on the role of the government—notably the federal government—in society in that governmental power should be kept at the state and local level. Policies of deregulation and greater market control were evident in Reagan's administration. The major emphasis was on ensuring reliable and cheap supplies of energy for the country with the rest being left to market forces. In 1982, President Reagan signed Executive Order 12287 to remove federal control over crude oil and petroleum products. He also tried, albeit unsuccessfully, to abolish the Department of Energy. Additionally, tax breaks for energy-efficient technology and renewable energy programs were cut. Furthermore, support for nuclear energy was increased during the 1980s, even in the wake of the near-meltdown at Three Mile Island in Pennsylvania in 1979 and the nuclear meltdown in 1986 in Chernobyl, Ukraine.

The George H. W. Bush administration endeavored to develop a more coherent energy policy with its National Energy Strategy, which championed a balance between energy conservation and production. But priorities of revising CAFE standards and opening the Arctic National Wildlife Refuge (ANWR) were not achieved. Licensing for nuclear plants was streamlined, and there were additional calls for greater conservation through energy efficiency of appliances and buildings.

Toward a Comprehensive Energy Policy in the 1990s

By the 1990s, the United States was increasingly reliant on imported energy as domestic production declined. President Bill Clinton promised a shift in energy policy with initiatives promoting energy efficiency and the research and development of renewable energy sources. The Clinton administration also proposed an energy tax—often referred to as the BTU tax, based on the heat output of fuel (or BTUs)—with the expectation that billions of dollars would be raised while reducing the United States' use of fossil fuels; but this proposal went nowhere with Congress.

Moreover, throughout the Clinton administration, Congress thwarted efforts for energy policy. For instance, the Republican-controlled Congress blocked the U.S. Department of Transportation's efforts simply to evaluate current fuel economy standards for cars (CAFE standards), much less consider increasing them. CAFE standards for the 2003 model year were 6 percent lower than fifteen years prior (Kraft 2015, 192). Nonetheless, cheap energy and the stagnation with CAFE standards fueled the growth of the sport utility vehicle (SUV) market in the United States. As with environmental policy, the nation's priorities were occupied elsewhere in the 1990s, and political scandal ensured focus elsewhere.

Energy and National Security Concerns in the 2000s

With national security concerns taking a prominent role in the United States after the attacks of September 11, energy concerns were reframed as a national security matter—much like they were in the 1970s. President George W. Bush, who took office in January 2001, charged his vice president, Dick Cheney, with convening an energy task force. The plan created by the task force called for major increases in fossil fuel extraction on U.S. public lands and nuclear energy sources. The goal of the Cheney plan was to reduce the burdensome environmental regulations that stifle energy production in the United States. The task force found itself the subject of much scrutiny as representatives of the energy industry featured prominently while environmental and other public interest groups were kept out of conversations. Ultimately, the task force was focused on increasing energy supply with little regard to decreasing energy demand and consumption. Due to increased public scrutiny, the offer by the task force fared poorly in Congress.

However, in 2005, Congress passed the Energy Policy Act, which was the first major energy legislation since 1992. The act expanded traditional energy sources and nuclear power, provided billions of dollars in tax credits and subsidies for energy producers who generated more energy, offered tax credits for citizens who purchased renewable energy systems or bought hybrid vehicles, and promoted programs to encourage states to conserve energy. Notable in this act were the items that were not included, such as no new CAFE standards or greenhouse gas (GHG) emissions regulation, and no requirements for renewable power. Then, in 2007, the Energy Independence and Security Act of 2007 did change the CAFE standards for the first time since 1975, mandating a new fuel economy standard of 35 miles per gallon by 2020.

The presidential election year of 2008 saw gas prices hit record highs, adjusted for inflation. Many Republicans emphasized the need to increase energy supplies in the United States, while Democrats talked about conservation and decreasing energy demand. Conversations also swirled around endorsing drilling offshore by both political parties. With the rise in gas prices in 2008, the nation experienced the first decrease in demand for gasoline in recent memory, which is notable. By 2008, the nation imported just over half of the oil it consumed (Kraft 2015, 190).

The economic downturn of 2008 and 2009 shaped energy policy history to the present day. The American Recovery and Reinvestment Act of 2009, better known as the "Stimulus," was wide-ranging, and included $39 billion to the Department of Energy alone and another $80 billion in spending, tax incentives, and loan guarantees to promote energy efficiency, renewable energy sources, mass transit, "clean coal," and fuel-efficient vehicles. The early 2010s saw the first steep decline in oil imports, due in large part to the increase in domestic production along with improvements in efficiency. To date, the nation is still grappling with a comprehensive energy policy that addresses supply and demand and balances environmental concerns as well.

The election of Donald Trump to the presidency will likely change the nation's approach to energy policy. During his campaign, Trump promised the return of coal industry jobs; however, this approach might be difficult in the current global landscape, in which the industry has seen jobs decline for years, due in large part to the automation of the industry and shifting energy sources that increasingly favor natural gas and even renewables (Plumer 2017). The Department of Energy's head under the Obama administration was Dr. Ernest Moniz, a nuclear physicist. The Trump administration selected former Texas governor Rick Perry as secretary of energy, who reportedly misunderstood the position and role of the agency, thinking the job would entail being a "global ambassador for the American oil and gas industry" rather than steward of the nation's nuclear arsenal and an overseer of research and development of energy technologies (Shelbourne 2017).

Summarizing U.S. energy policy history, we see times in which concerns were focused on supply and ensuring energy resources from foreign sources, and we see other times in which there were glimmers of focus on addressing energy demand and consumption. As with many areas of public policy, there is a certain ebb and flow to energy policy, and it often has a lot to do with public opinion. When it comes to the public's interest in energy issues, much of it comes from the fluctuations in gas prices. Just about all Americans who drive a car regularly can tell you about what the price of a gallon of gas is because of their routine purchase of it and the ubiquitous presence of gas stations prominently displaying the price of gas. This keeps energy concerns more in the forefront of citizens' minds than other less tangible concerns, such as the health of a nearby river. To understand public opinion on energy more broadly, Gallup has routinely asked whether Americans prioritize the development of energy sources or the protection of the environment. In 2001, 52 percent of respondents said they favored environmental protection, whereas only 36 percent prioritized development of energy supplies (Gallup 2001). In 2010 and 2011, 50 percent of respondents preferred energy development to environmental protection (Gallup 2011). Americans overwhelmingly think it is very important for the nation to be energy independent—92 percent of respondents thought it very or somewhat important in a 2017 poll—and more than two-thirds believe the nation can fight climate change while protecting jobs (Quinnipiac 2017a, b).

A related Gallup poll question asked respondents whether they favor an emphasis on conservation or production for the nation's energy policy; from 2008 until 2013 (when the most recent data are available), a larger percentage and majority of respondents always favored conservation over production (Gallup 2013). And respondents in polls routinely report that they are strongly in favor of the development of alternative energy sources over traditional fossil fuels. In a 2013 Gallup poll, 59 percent of respondents favored an emphasis on alternative energy development, 31 percent favored continued reliance on fossil fuels, and 7 percent favored a combination approach (Gallup 2013). Ansolabehere and Konisky (2014) studied contemporary public opinion on energy issues and made several broad conclusions: (1) what citizens want depends on the alternatives before them; (2) Americans do not think about energy sources, they simply want cheap *and* clean power; and (3) citizens want cleaner energy, and that matters more than economics (Ansolabehere and Konisky 2014).

MAJOR ENVIRONMENTAL AND ENERGY POLICY STATUTES

It is necessary to learn the historical context for environmental and energy policy from the past to understand the present. Before we move on to additional contemporary issues and concerns, we highlight major statutes that define environmental and energy policy and briefly discuss their major provisions. We emphasize these major statutes because they define environmental policy and energy policy, and having a working knowledge of these statutes is imperative in understanding and conversing in these policy areas. The highlights of these statutes are reviewed in chronological order.

National Environmental Policy Act of 1969 The National Environmental Policy Act of 1969 (NEPA, pronounced *NEE-pa*) is arguably the foundation of American environmental policy because it requires the federal government to consider the environmental impacts of proposed projects and mandates that environmental impacts are minimized. NEPA entails environmental assessments (EAs) and/or environmental impact statements (EISs), which often take years to complete, to ensure environmental harms are considered in decision making. This statute also established the White House Council on Environmental Quality (CEQ) to advise the president on environmental policy matters.

Clean Air Act of 1970 While this 1970 statute is typically referred to as the Clean Air Act, it is a major overhaul of clean air acts passed in 1963 and 1967 that had little regulatory power. The 1970 act mandated, for the first time, national air pollution standards and enforcement mechanisms. It requires the EPA to determine national primary and secondary air quality standards for substances it determines to be hazardous to air quality and human health. Additionally, states are required to devise their own state implementation plans (SIPs) to achieve the standards set by the federal EPA. These requirements, while seemingly dated, are highlighted in the chapter's opening case study about regulating greenhouse gas emissions, as it is up to the EPA, according to the Congress that passed this law and via subsequent Supreme Court decisions, to determine what is an air pollutant.

Federal Water Pollution Control Act Amendments of 1972 This statute is better known as the Clean Water Act; as with the CAA, this statute represents major updates and amendments to water pollution laws passed in the 1960s. The Clean Water Act set national water quality goals, established a permitting system for firms that want to discharge wastewater into the nation's waterways, and created programs to help local governments build and maintain their wastewater treatment plants (WWTPs). It is worth noting that President Nixon vetoed this legislation, expressing concern about inflation, but Congress easily overrode the veto.

Endangered Species Act of 1973 This law was passed to give the federal government power to protect species that are in danger of becoming extinct. Under the ESA, the U.S. Fish and Wildlife Service determines whether a species is "threatened" with extinction, or more gravely, "endangered" of extinction. If a species is designated with either label it becomes protected, and development or any other activities that might adversely impact that species are thwarted, including a multimillion-dollar public works project, in one case, because of the snail-darter fish in Tennessee.

Safe Drinking Water Act of 1974 Much like this statute's name implies, the SDWA authorizes the federal government to set standards to safeguard the quality of public drinking water supplies around the country. Furthermore, it calls on the government to regulate state programs to protect underground water sources.

Energy Policy and Conservation Act of 1975 This piece of legislation was a response to the oil embargo and endeavored to increase energy production and supply, notably through establishing corporate average fuel economy (CAFE) standards; created the nation's strategic petroleum reserve (SPR); and gave the federal government power for oil price controls.

Resource Conservation and Recovery Act of 1976 RCRA (pronounced *REC-ra*) requires the EPA to determine regulations for the handling of hazardous waste; more specifically, the EPA has devised standards for the transportation, storage, and disposal of all hazardous waste.

National Energy Act of 1978 The National Energy Act is the umbrella title for a collection of laws that were passed, including the Energy Tax Act, the National Energy Conservation Policy Act, the Power Plant and Industrial Fuel Use Act, the Natural Gas Policy Act, and the Public Utility Regulatory Policies Act, which were all part of the government's ongoing response to the oil crises of the 1970s. These various efforts tried to ensure the nation's supply of cheap and reliable energy, encourage conservation, and develop domestic supplies of energy.

Comprehensive Emergency Response, Compensation, and Liability Act of 1980 More commonly known as "Superfund," this law authorizes the federal government to respond to environmental emergencies, clean up hazardous waste sites, and identify the responsible party after the environmental threat has passed. To orchestrate the cleanup, the law creates a "superfund" of money—initially $1.6 billion—to ensure funds are available to clean up environmental messes. The law also creates legal mechanisms to trace back and hold legally accountable responsible parties for the mess. Superfund quickly exhausted its fund and was reauthorized with additional resources in 1984.

Clean Air Act Amendments of 1990 These amendments to the Clean Air Act passed in 1970 represent major changes for the regulation and protection of air quality. This statute addressed acid rain and ozone depletion, and created a new permitting program for stationary sources, among many other facets. It also included provisions for ordinary citizens to sue over compliance with the law.

Energy Policy Act of 2005 This legislation was the result of the energy task force headed by Vice President Dick Cheney. The act encompasses a range of measures, including increasing domestic sources of energy, such as coal; providing grants for development of various energy technologies and sources; and extending daylight savings time by four or five weeks, among others. The act includes provisions for tax credits for homeowners who make energy improvements and for energy companies to develop domestic sources of energy, both renewable and nonrenewable sources.

Energy Independence and Security Act of 2007 The purpose of the act was to promote the nation's energy independence from foreign sources by focusing on fuel economy, biofuel development, fuel efficiency of vehicles, and improving the energy efficiency of public buildings. Initially the act had provisions to cut subsidies to the petroleum industry to promote energy independence, but those provisions were cut.

Although this review of the major pieces of environmental and energy legislation is by no means exhaustive, it encompasses the significant, much-discussed policies in this arena. Of course, passing legislation is only the first hurdle—and by some accounts, an easier obstacle than implementation. In the next section, we explore the major policy actors in environmental and energy policy.

MAJOR ACTORS IN ENVIRONMENTAL AND ENERGY POLICY

An overarching theme of this text is an emphasis on the practical realities of public policy, and that includes a particular focus on the implementation of policy. To investigate how environmental policy and energy policy are actually realized, we need to explore the major policy actors in this arena. As with the other policy areas discussed in this text, the constitutional actors play a significant role.

Congress

The U.S. Congress is responsible for passing all the previously discussed legislation in these areas, along with numerous other acts, and is the gatekeeper for major efforts. Congress is responsible for devising the strategy of the federal government in any policy arena, and just as action is significant, so is inaction. Linking back to the chapter's opening story, it is noteworthy that Congress has chosen not to address the federal government's role in protecting citizens and the environment from catastrophic oil spills since the *Deepwater Horizon* tragedy, even though it promptly did so after the *Exxon Valdez* disaster. Regardless of your own perspective on the issue and what you think is the responsibility of the government on this topic, Congress's inaction is action. Inaction is a statement of what this institution thinks about a particular issue.

In addition to passing legislation (or not), Congress is also responsible for overseeing a multitude of federal government agencies tasked with implementing the policies Congress passes. After all, Congress works hard to pass legislation; it wants to make sure that its intentions are being carried out as it intended. As a result, Congress spends a good deal of time holding hearings into how implementation is unfolding. And congressional committees convene hearings to explore emerging issues. Indeed, these tasks are important in any policy arena, including environmental and energy concerns. One might expect that there are only a handful of committees with responsibility in these policy arenas, but you would be mistaken. Table 10.2 provides a list of all the congressional committees and subcommittees that are involved in environmental and energy policy concerns in the 115th session of Congress.

A quick perusal of this list easily leaves one wondering if the list of committees that do not have oversight in these areas is shorter! Needless to say, Congress has a lot of involvement in environmental and energy concerns.

President

Another significant actor is the president. As we have explored previously, the president does much to set the nation's agenda. For example, when Barack Obama was elected

TABLE 10.2

Congressional Committees and Subcommittees in the 115th Congress with Jurisdiction over Environmental and Energy Policy Issues

House

- Agriculture

  Commodity Exchanges, Energy, and Credit
  Biotechnology, Horticulture, and Research
  Conservation and Forestry

- Appropriations

  Agriculture, Rural Development, Food and Drug Administration and Related Agencies
  Energy and Water Development, and Related Agencies
  Interior, Environment, and Related Agencies
  Labor, Health and Human Services, Education, and Related Agencies
  Transportation, Housing and Urban Development, and Related Agencies

- Energy and Commerce

  Energy
  Environment
  Oversight and Investigations

- Natural Resources

  Energy and Mineral Resources
  Federal Lands
  Fisheries, Wildlife, Oceans and Insular Affairs
  Indian, Insular, and Alaska Native Affairs
  Oversight and Investigations
  Water, Power, and Oceans

- Science, Space, and Technology

  Energy
  Environment
  Oversight
  Research and Technology

- Transportation and Infrastructure

  Aviation
  Coast Guard and Maritime Transportation
  Highways and Transit
  Railroads, Pipelines and Hazardous Materials
  Water Resources and Environment

Senate

- Agriculture, Nutrition, and Forestry

  Rural Development and Energy
  Conservation, Forestry, and Natural Resources
  Nutrition, Agricultural Research, and Specialty Crops
  Livestock, Dairy, Poultry, Marketing, and Agricultural Security

(Continued)

TABLE 10.2 (Continued)

• Appropriations

Agriculture, Rural Development, Food and Drug Administration, and Related
  Agencies
Energy and Water Development
Department of the Interior, Environment, and Related Agencies
Transportation, Housing and Urban Development, and Related Agencies

• Commerce, Science, and Transportation

Aviation Operations, Safety, and Security
Consumer Protection, Product Safety, Insurance, and Data Security
Oceans, Atmosphere, Fisheries, and Coast Guard
Surface Transportation and Merchant Marine Infrastructure, Safety, and Security

• Energy and Natural Resources

Energy
National Parks
Public Lands, Forests, and Mining
Water and Power

• Environment and Public Works

Clean Air and Nuclear Safety
Fisheries, Water, and Wildlife
Superfund, Waste Management, and Regulatory Oversight
Transportation and Infrastructure
Green Jobs and the New Economy

Sources: GovTrack.us, accessed September 21, 2017; Senate.gov, House.gov.

president, he quickly signaled his major legislative priorities, notably health care. The issues that a president feels passionate about are likely to compel congressional action one way or another, given the president's control of the "bully pulpit." Presidents who express clear commitment to certain issues generally see at least modest legislation on those issues. If a president is not interested in a policy issue, it is unlikely that Congress will take action.

Besides steering the legislative priorities of Congress, the president is the head of the executive branch of government—or, more succinctly, the president is in charge of all the agencies that implement the policies Congress passes. The president appoints the heads of those agencies (with Senate confirmation) and the president plays a role in setting the budgets for those agencies. As Chapter 4 noted, actions of those agencies are also reviewed by the White House via the Office of Management and Budget (OMB) and, if those actions are regulatory, by the Office of Information and Regulatory Affairs (OIRA) as well. These White House offices provide a clear path for presidents to influence executive agency actions.

Federal Courts

The third major actor—albeit one that often escapes notice—is the federal court system and the Supreme Court of the United States. The courts are tasked with reconciling disputes, and there are plenty of disputes about government action in environmental and energy policy. The interpretation of the courts about the constitutionality and actions of federal agencies is significant. It is also worth noting that court challenges can take years—even decades—so quick answers are unlikely. The time it takes to litigate disputes in any policy area can have a significant impact on the implementation of policy.

Executive Agencies

The preceding discussion of each of the three political institutions invariably brings up the work of federal government agencies. Although they feature less prominently in the public spotlight, these agencies are the organizations tasked with taking vague statutes, general policy directions from presidents, and often unspecific mandates from courts, and realizing policy goals in the best interests of the public. By no means is this an easy task in any policy arena, and as with congressional committees, there are a host of agencies that have overlapping responsibilities and interests in implementing environmental policy and energy policy. Here, we review a handful of the most prominent agencies.

- The **U.S. Environmental Protection Agency** is a federal agency created by President Nixon's executive order in 1970. The U.S. EPA's mission is to protect human health and the environment. Though not a cabinet-level agency, the agency's head, an administrator, is typically given cabinet rank. The agency is headquartered in Washington, D.C., and has ten regional offices. It is divided into various offices including Air and Radiation, Chemical Safety and Pollution Prevention, Office of Enforcement and Compliance Assurance, Office of Environmental Information, Office of Land and Emergency Management, and Office of Water, among others. In 2016, there were more than 15,000 employees, but the Trump administration has overseen a diminishing workforce and proposed cutting the agency budget by about a third.

- The **U.S. Department of Energy** is a cabinet-level agency created in 1977 with a mission "to ensure America's security and prosperity by addressing its energy, environmental, and nuclear challenges through transformative science and technology solutions." The agency implements policies involving nuclear power, fossil fuels, and alternative energy sources. This smallest of the fifteen cabinet agencies also oversees the national laboratories that deal with nuclear energy. It is organized around three major offices—nuclear security, science and energy, and management and performance—and it is overseen by a cabinet secretary, currently Rick Perry. In 2015, it had an enacted budget of $27.4 billion, with approximately 14,000 employees (and more than 94,000 contractors; Department of Energy FY 2016 Congressional Budget Request). Within the DOE, there are numerous smaller entities, including the Energy Information Administration (EIA), which is a great source of information about the nation's energy supplies and consumption.

- The **U.S. Department of the Interior** manages most of the nation's public lands and all of the energy resources on those lands. Created by Congress in 1849, the Interior Department's mission is "protecting America's great outdoors and powering our future." It accomplishes this mission through the efforts of many subunits, including the National Park Service, the Fish and Wildlife Service, the Bureau of Land Management, the U.S. Geological Survey, and the Bureau of Ocean Energy Management, among many others. As with other cabinet agencies, the Department of the Interior is headed by a secretary, who is currently Ryan Zinke. More than 69,000 employees comprise this agency, and in 2015 it had a budget of $17.8 million (U.S. Department of the Interior 2015).

- The **Federal Energy Regulatory Commission** (FERC) is an independent agency that oversees energy management authority, including exercising jurisdiction over sales, licensing, pricing, and pipeline rates. Put differently, FERC regulates interstate sale and transmission of energy. The commission's forerunner was created in 1920 by Congress to coordinate the development of hydroelectric power. FERC became the organization it is today during the energy crises of the 1970s. It is a self-funding entity, meaning it pays for its operations from the fees it charges the energy industry, which it regulates. As with other commissions, it is governed by five commissioners who are presidential appointments but serve five-year terms.

- The **Nuclear Regulatory Commission** is responsible for the safe use and environmental security of nuclear energy for nonmilitary purposes. This includes the operation of nuclear reactors, materials, transportation, storage, and disposal of nuclear waste. The NRC is overseen by five commissioners, appointed by the president for fixed terms. This commission was created in 1974; its headquarters are in Rockville, Maryland, with four regional offices throughout the country. The agency employs around 4,000 people, with a budget of about $1 billion (U.S. Nuclear Regulatory Commission 2015).

It should be noted that these are only the major federal government agencies that have jurisdiction in environmental and energy matters. Most of the fifty states have agencies in each of them that deal with these issues as well. In other words, in addition to the U.S. EPA, there are fifty state environmental agencies, along with one for the District of Columbia. There are also agencies at the federal and state levels that deal with natural resources. And, in some cases, there are also local environmental agencies. For example, in Ohio, the state grants authority to oversee air quality to local, regional entities. Even without providing lengthy lists of all of these agencies in all fifty states, it is clear that the complexities of doing environmental and energy policy easily rival those of passing such policies.

Interest Groups and Lobbyists

Just as is the case in other policy areas, environmental and energy concerns have their own collection of interest groups and lobbyists. These entities range from mainstream environmental advocacy groups, including the Sierra Club and the Natural Resources Defense Council, to the more radical groups, such as the Earth Liberation Front. Businesses are also represented in this area by the U.S. Chamber of Commerce and state equivalent organizations and trade associations, including the National Manufacturers Association, and industry groups, such as America's Natural Gas Alliance. These groups work to educate stakeholders about environmental and energy policy matters and influence the work of all governmental actors on these topics.

Thus far in our chapter, we have explored the history to contextualize the development of environmental and energy policy in the United States and considered the actors involved in creating and implementing policy in these areas. The next section helps illustrate how the involvement of these actors intersect; we use an example from 2014, when the Supreme Court determined the EPA's fate in its efforts to regulate greenhouse gas emissions.

Greenhouse Gases Go to Court

In June 2014, U.S. Supreme Court justice Antonin Scalia rebuked the U.S. Environmental Protection Agency (EPA), saying, "We are not willing to stand on the dock and wave goodbye as EPA embarks on this multiyear voyage of discovery" (*Utility Air Regulatory Group v. Environmental Protection Agency* 573 U.S. ____ [2014]). The Court's opinion goes on to chastise the EPA, saying "it should have known better"; nevertheless, by most accounts, this decision represented a "win" for the U.S. EPA in its efforts to regulate greenhouse gas (GHG) emissions and combat climate change. As a result of this case, the EPA can regulate GHG emissions generated by facilities that are already regulated for other, "conventional" pollutants. This decision enables the EPA to continue working to achieve its mission of protecting human health and the environment. However, those efforts will continue to engender controversy without clear guidance from the public and lawmakers. The long-fought court battles surrounding GHG emission regulations are the result of outdated laws, countless stakeholders, and the nation's unwillingness to address climate change—instead, they prefer to push it aside.

Congress mandated the EPA, via the Clean Air Act, is able to define air pollutants and promulgate standards to curb the ill effects of those pollutants. The major challenge facing the EPA with GHG emissions is that we did not know what greenhouse gases were really about in 1970 when the Clean Air Act was passed. Therefore, put differently, we have a law that is more than four decades old that is trying to cope with twenty-first-century environmental issues. Regardless of what you think the government should do about air pollution—or climate change, for that matter—you might concede that a law that is almost half a century old is going to prove challenging today, especially as it concerns science and technological innovation.

In addition to the antiquated laws and accompanying regulatory structure, environmental issues involve pretty much everyone. The government, at all levels, national, state, and local—politicians, the civil servants in government agencies, citizens, companies, consultants, scientists and researchers, the media, and anyone else you can think of—probably has something to say about environmental issues and climate change. Now, put them all together and expect them to agree and get something done. While many policy areas involve a multitude of stakeholders, environmental ones—since we all share the same air—involve everyone. As taxpayers, we care how the government spends money. As consumers of resources, we care about the limits that might be placed on that consumption. As humans, we care about the health of the environment upon which our existence depends. And now we have to figure out together—since we embrace democratic principles—specific thresholds of what is an acceptable level of pollution and what is too much. And, do not forget, it can be very difficult for scientists to figure out what level of pollution is too much and what the ill effects might be in the future, since those determinations involve modeling and educated guesses.

In light of these considerations, it is hardly surprising that the United States has dragged its feet in addressing climate change. Accordingly, much of that inaction has resulted in a fragmented, haphazard approach in which some government agencies endeavoring to serve the public's interest strive to do what it can to curb pollution within its statutory confines that are nearly half a century old. Our elected leaders, who might offer clear guidance in one direction or another regarding climate change, avoid meaningful decisions on the issue as the political campaign is becoming a permanent fixture in American politics.

In the final sections of the chapter we unpack some of the current issues and challenges for these issues and consider how the average citizen is affected by the actions in these policy arenas.

ISSUES AND CHALLENGES

Given the plethora of actors, existing statutes, and long histories with environmental and energy issues in the United States, it is unsurprising that there are numerous challenges for the nation as we contend with energy and environmental concerns. In particular, we focus on five challenges: (1) the lack of a coherent, cohesive policy; (2) politicization; (3) the role of science in policy debates; (4) false trade-offs between the environment and the economy; and (5) the notion of the commons.

Lack of a Coherent, Cohesive Policy

Throughout our discussion of the creation of public policy and exploration of specific areas of policy, the fragmentation of policy is evident. Given the piecemeal approach to policy issues, the reactive and incremental nature of our policymaking processes, and the federal structure of government in the United States, it is hardly surprising that environmental policy and energy policy lack a comprehensive and cohesive structure. During different periods and responding to different facets of these issues, policymakers have cobbled together disparate policy options in an effort to deal with different challenges. The result is an amalgamation of policies that may or may not be coherent, may or may not be cohesive, and may or may not be contradictory. For example, in the 1970s, when major pollution control statutes were being passed, the approach was to deal with types of pollution in isolation from one another. In other words, air quality concerns were wrapped up in the Clean Air Act, and other pollution concerns were not a part of those policy solutions. Fast-forward forty years, and we now understand that making changes to improve air quality and reduce emissions at a firm might result in higher levels of hazardous waste. However, the system of air pollution control laws largely exists in isolation from other considerations. The practical implications are that the same firm deals with a separate air inspector, and separate waste and water inspectors who may or may not (and probably do not) talk to one another. As a result, compliance with and reducing environmental impacts can be even more challenging. Today, we understand the interconnected nature of addressing environmental concerns, but our patchwork system of laws is how it has been for decades. Modifying that regulatory structure is very hard, and even if the political will is in place to overhaul the system, the speed of those changes is best described as glacial. Ultimately, government regulators, firms, and citizens are left with a byzantine system of regulation that is at best disjointed and at worst contradictory.

Politicization

One does not have to look far to see the signs of how polarized our politicians and our electorate have become. The deep political divides are not new, as the nation has been deeply divided before. The entrenchment of both political sides is due to a variety of factors, including the increasingly permanent campaign for political office—or to use Rosenbaum's (2015) language, we have succumbed to the "tyranny of the electoral cycle" (29). With regards to environmental and energy issues, positions on these topics have increasingly become a litmus test for political candidates, much in the way positions on social issues have been in years past. More specifically on the issue of climate change, to be in line with the Republican Party's platform, candidates must profess skepticism in the science substantiating climate change, while Democratic Party candidates must profess belief that the planet's climate is changing because of human activities. It is worth noting that such positions are ultimately questioning facts and scientific information. The science on climate change is settled; the debate should be over what, if anything, the government should do about climate change rather than debating the facts. Nevertheless, in the United States a politician's stance on climate change is increasingly as important as the same candidate's position on abortion or taxes.

Role of Science in Policy Debates

The politicization of issues is emblematic of broader challenges associated with complex scientific and technical issues and how they are distilled for policy debates, often in thirty-second sound bites. As everyone who has ever taken a science class knows, the scientific method drives scientific understanding. That method requires careful, methodical study to observe phenomena and explain them, and that method takes a lot of time. Scientists rarely, if ever, prove that one thing causes another. Just think about the latest nutrition or diet study you heard reported in the news—this week chocolate is good for you, next week it will be bad for you. What is missing in those headlines at the bottom of the screen is understanding the nuances of the studies and the difficulty in proving anything. Can scientists control for every factor to determine whether chocolate is good or bad for you? Simply put, no. The same is true when understanding the effects of hydraulic fracturing for natural gas deep underground. Can it be proven beyond a reasonable doubt that displacing shale formations underground causes hazardous conditions above ground? No, probably not. Scientists can draw inferences and make educated predictions, but there are simply too many unknowns, and it takes a long time to draw definitive conclusions. Furthermore, time is something politicians and citizens alike generally do not extend to complex issues. Finally, critics can use ever-present scientific uncertainty to exploit the issue and argue against action.

Trade-offs between the Environment and the Economy

Related to the tensions regarding science, the complexities of scientific research, and our need for quick, digestible information is the ever-present, false trade-off between the economy and the natural environment. It is widely assumed that if an action is good for the environment, it must be bad for the economy. This presumption has been around for so long, it is difficult to trace its origins. Furthermore, it continues to persist because politicians on either side of environmental and energy issues perpetuate it when they argue in sound bites for or against some government action.

Consider the rhetoric surrounding the nation's domestic energy supplies and increasing renewable energy sources. Politicians would have us believe that increasing renewable sources of energy will kill jobs and hurt the middle class. At first glance, this seems logical. If the nation transitions to getting more of its energy from renewable sources, such as solar, would that not hurt the economy? But it is not so simple. Yes, energy companies that are solely focused on nonrenewable sources of energy, such as coal, would be hurt and those jobs might be in jeopardy. And it is going to cost money in research and development to scale-up renewable energy sources to replace dirtier, nonrenewable sources.

However, all the money that is spent to come up with new technologies creates jobs and stimulates the economy. If more manufacturing plants are needed to develop and build photovoltaic cells, then there is job creation and the growth of a new industry sector. Consumers may pay more in their energy bills, but they may not spend as much money on medicine and doctor visits because of poor air quality near coal mines and coal-fired power plants. The bottom line is there are economic considerations of all areas of public policy, but it is not as simple as something is good or bad for the environment; it is far more complicated than that.

The Commons

Underlying all of these challenges is the idea that the natural environment and its energy sources are held in common and property rights and ownership cannot be easily assigned to the air, for instance. Energy and environmental issues can be a bit harder for governments to grapple with because so much of society is based on property ownership to assign responsibility and liability, and it is hard to own schools of fish offshore, or mineral deposits miles underground, or the air we breathe. Further complicating matters is the fact that many of these resources also do not observe political boundaries. Garrett Hardin famously wrote about the "tragedy of the commons" in the 1960s, maintaining that because natural resources are held in **common**, they are susceptible to tragedy because no one is singularly responsible for them. For example, California has put in place (because of the federal system of government) some of the most stringent air pollution control laws in the nation. Having those laws does not mean California has some of the best air quality in the nation, however. Why? Because air from its neighboring states does not stop at the California state line.

These challenges are part of the reality of environmental and energy policy concerns for the future. How citizens and politicians grapple with these issues will define these policy areas for decades to come. There is a great deal of work to be done in these areas and plenty of ways for you to get involved, which our everyday citizen connection suggests below.

Everyday Citizen Connection

Think about it for a moment. You slept in a climate-controlled space that needed energy, probably coming from fossil fuels, to make sure you were not too hot or too cold last night. Some sort of alarm clock, powered by batteries or plugged into the wall, made sure you did not oversleep. The food you ate so far today was produced by the land, needed water, and then was manufactured and transported to the grocery store (or dining hall), where you purchased it and consumed it. That food, both in production and your eating of it, resulted in waste, and has to be disposed of. The book you are reading required energy to produce.

The point is, without thinking too hard, you are completely dependent on energy—whatever the source—and clean air and water to live. So while the discussions here and their policies were probably passed well before you were born, they affect you and will affect you for your entire life (unless, of course, you somehow manage to live completely off the grid, but you would still rely on the health of the natural environment). Thus, it should be clear why these topics matter to you. If you live in the Midwest, for example, the power grid that supplies energy to that region of the country is among the dirtiest in the nation, so while you may be the model of energy conservation in your apartment or house, you are contributing more pollution than a counterpart in the Pacific Northwest, which has one of the nation's cleanest grids, due largely to lots of hydroelectric power. If you live in the Northeast, you may pride yourself on taking mass transit and not even owning a car, but your counterpart in the Southeast, who may want to take public transit, has few practical options for it.

Accordingly, we are all interconnected when it comes to environmental and energy concerns. What happens at a nuclear power plant in Pennsylvania may have major consequences for neighboring states. With this intermingling, you might be wondering how to get involved in this policy area. Here, we offer a few ideas and invite you to spend time seeking others. First and foremost, you can get involved with these issues simply by being informed. Do you know where the energy you consume every day comes from? If you are in favor of developing more renewable sources of energy, have you investigated green energy credits you can purchase on your monthly utility bill? What kind of car do you want to drive? Where is it made, and what is its fuel economy? How does it rank in terms of greenhouse gas emissions? In terms of the political candidates you support, what are their viewpoints on environmental and energy challenges? Are those views aligned with your own? If you want to volunteer, there are local chapters of countless environmental organizations with which you can get involved. You can help educate your friends and neighbors about a particular environmental or energy topic that is particularly important to you. You can help with river sweeps and litter cleanups. There are also professional opportunities for you in these policy areas. Interest groups and government agencies are looking for the next generation of environmental and energy professionals. Even if you do not want to pursue these issues as part of your full-time career, what is your employer's policy on sustainability or energy consumption? Does your organization recycle or buy recycled products? As with all of the chapters, if your interest is piqued, start with some of the suggested resources at the end of the text and get involved.

Discovery Question:

For the next week, every time you throw something in the trash and (hopefully!) recycling bin, write it down. At the end of the week, take a look at your list. How many of those items could you make reusable or compost? Are there drink containers you recycled that could be replaced with a reusable water bottle?

CONCLUDING THOUGHTS

This chapter has sketched not only the important historical context of U.S. environmental and energy policy but current and future concerns as well. Most important, environmental and energy concerns will continue to play a significant role in government and society more generally, as we are dependent on the health of the natural environment and the sources of energy it offers us to support our lifestyles.

Through our review of the history and development of each of the policy areas, we can conclude that the United States has made a great deal of progress, yet much work remains. Pollution, and in particular nonpoint source pollution (which we tackle in the policy choices section), is a major issue along with efforts surrounding climate change. And it is the latter policy area that demonstrates the significant overlap that exists between environmental and energy issues. As we close the chapter, consider what approach or combination of approaches is necessary to tackle nonpoint source pollution in the United States.

POLICY CHOICES: NONPOINT SOURCE POLLUTION

Nonpoint source pollution refers to both water and air pollution from diffuse sources. Simply put, nonpoint source pollution is not traceable to a single point, such as a discharge pipe from a manufacturing plant or leakage from an abandoned mine. Examples of nonpoint source pollution include runoff from agricultural fields, parking lots, or even the tailpipes of our cars. Unlike pollution from sewage treatment plants or industrial businesses, nonpoint source pollution is discharged over a wide geography, not from one specific location. Nonpoint source pollution can be caused by rainfall or snowmelt moving over and through the ground. Nonpoint sources are one of the most significant single sources of water pollution in the United States. Yet we do not have legislation to determine what to do with nonpoint source pollution. In the meantime, we offer four plausible options for consideration.

POLICY CHOICES REFLECTION QUESTIONS

1. Which policy choice do you favor and why?

2. If the policy choice you favor were to be adopted, which stakeholders would be supportive of this approach? Which stakeholders would be critical of this approach? How might consensus be built between the supporters and critics?

Policy Choices: Nonpoint Source Water Pollution

Choice #1: Strengthen CWA	Choice #2: Create Economic Incentives	Choice #3: Require Liability and Mitigation Funding	Choice #4: Increase Education
Passed in 1972, the Clean Water Act's (CWA) enforceable provisions are primarily directed at point sources of pollutants. Nonpoint sources of pollution are primarily addressed through nonregulatory means, via the CWA. States, as a result, have adopted piecemeal NPS policy in the absence of enforceable federal regulation. As nonpoint sources become the largest source of water pollution in the United States, it is imperative that the CWA's regulatory mechanisms be strengthened to provide federal enforcement for clean water policy.	Relying on complex government regulation or the moral compass of business has failed to produce results. Businesses respond to market demands; therefore, providing economic incentives for the reduction of NPS pollution will effectively produce results. The CWA provides certain economic incentives designed to control NPS pollution. By expanding incentive-based tools to include performance incentives such as taxes on nonpoint sources; or design incentives, like subsidies on inputs and technology; or market-based approaches, like trading and abatement allowances, NPS pollution can be controlled through the marketplace.	The fundamental problem driving NPS pollution is the outsourcing of costs from businesses to local government. Too often, polluters pass the buck for cleanup or mitigation expense. Rather than shifting responsibility to citizens, businesses should be held liable for environmental damage. To ensure adequate capital investment and resources to mitigate any residual environmental impacts, liability requirements should direct polluters to insure their projects for the cost of any potential damage caused by their activities.	The environmental legislation of the 1960s and 1970s was largely influenced by citizen activism. A continued sense of citizen engagement is essential to design and enforce better NPS pollution regulation. There are already a number of mechanisms for citizen engagement in the development of federal policy, and the Environmental Protection Agency is required to share best management practices for NPS coastal pollution management between states. Increasing best management practice sharing across industry and government will inform educated activism and decision making to control NPS pollution.

GLOSSARY TERMS

common   262
conservationists   240
energy policy   245

environmental policy   237
focusing events   240
greenhouse gas emissions   243

preservationists   240

DISCUSSION QUESTIONS

1. What does the history and development of environmental and energy policy indicate for these policy arenas in the coming decade?

2. What would it take for the United States to focus on environmental and energy concerns and devise a coherent and comprehensive national strategy? Does the nation need to have a coherent and comprehensive national strategy? Why or why not?

3. Of the challenges associated with environmental and energy policy, which is the most debilitating and why? How might it be overcome?

4. Among your family and friends, what is the biggest misunderstanding about environmental and energy issues? What are the implications of that misunderstanding and what might be done to get beyond it?

SUGGESTED RESOURCES

Suggested Websites

Intergovernmental Panel on Climate Change, http://www.ipcc.ch

U.S. Energy Information Administration, http://www.eia.gov

U.S. Environmental Agency's Report on the Environment, http://cfpub.epa.gov/roe

Suggested Books or Articles

Andrews, Richard N. L. 2006. *Managing the Environment, Managing Ourselves: A History of American Environmental Policy.* 2nd ed. New Haven, CT: Yale University Press.

Geri, Laurance R., and David E. McNabb. 2011. *Energy Policy in the U.S.: Politics, Challenges, and Prospects for Change.* New York: CRC Press.

Hardin, Garrett. 1968. "The Tragedy of the Commons." *Science* 162, no. 3859 (December): 1243–48.

Klyza, Christopher McGrory, and David Sousa. 2013. *American Environmental Policy: Beyond Gridlock.* Revised and expanded ed. Cambridge, MA: The MIT Press.

Layzer, Judith A. 2014. *Open for Business: Conservatives' Opposition to Environmental Regulation.* Cambridge, MA: The MIT Press.

Rinfret, Sara R., and Michelle C. Pautz. 2014. *U.S. Environmental Policy in Action: Practice and Implementation.* New York: Palgrave.

Rosenbaum, Walter A. 2015. *American Energy: The Politics of 21st Century Policy.* Washington, DC: CQ Press.

Scheberle, Denise. 2004. *Federalism and Environmental Policy: Trust and the Politics of Implementation.* 2nd ed. revised and updated. Washington, DC: Georgetown University Press.

Suggested Films

Avatar, DVD, directed by James Cameron (2009: United States), http://www.imdb.com/title/tt0499549/

GasLand, DVD, directed by Josh Fox (2010: United Kingdom), http://www.imdb.com/title/tt1558250/?ref_=fn_al_tt_1

An Inconvenient Truth, DVD, directed by Davis Guggenheim, written by Al Gore (2006: United States), http://www.imdb.com/title/tt0497116/?ref_=nv_sr_1

An Inconvenient Sequel: Truth to Power, DVD, directed by Bonni Cohen, Jon Shenk, written by Al Gore (2017: United States), http://www.imdb.com/title/tt6322922/?ref_=nv_sr_2

Marathon for Justice, DVD, directed by Brian McDermott (2016: United States), https://www.empathyworksfilms.net/future-projects

Promised Land, DVD, directed by Gus Van Sant (2012: United States), http://www.imdb.com/title/tt2091473/

Sharpen your skills with SAGE edge at **http://edge.sagepub.com/rinfret. SAGE edge for students** provides a personalized approach to help you accomplish your coursework goals in an easy-to-use learning environment.

Conclusion
Public Policy: A Concise Introduction

LEARNING OBJECTIVES

Readers of this chapter will be able to:

1. Explain why the "doing side" of public policy is important for the study and practice of public policy

2. Articulate why involvement of citizens in public policy is important for today, tomorrow, and the future

3. Recognize and evaluate facts and misinformation in the public square to make informed policy choices

4. Understand why public policymaking is driven by consensus building

---
ON THE FRONT LINES

On the first Tuesday of each November, registered voters across the United States cast ballots for their chosen representatives and ballot initiatives. But do we ever stop to consider what it takes to organize an election so we can vote (e.g., training volunteers for polling places, mailing absentee ballots)? **Election administrators**, often the unsung heroes of U.S. elections, spend countless hours implementing state and federal election laws so we can exercise our right to vote. However, with increased political rhetoric of voter fraud, election administrators are alarmed with the lack of evidence used for such accusations. Consider an example from Montana.

In August 2017, Montana secretary of state Corey Stapleton announced he was going to rid the state of fraudulent voter practices. In Montana, as in most states, the **secretary of state** helps oversee elections, with the day-to-day implementation guided by election administrators at the county level. The August statement by the Montana secretary of state befuddled many election administrators. Voter fraud is something taken seriously by any election administrator, but it has not been prevalent in Montana or nationwide. Indeed, New York University School of Law's Brennan Center for Justice found in its research that the incident rate for voter fraud in the 2016 election was between .0003 and .0025 percent (Brennan Center for Justice 2017).

However, Stapleton suggested that in the March 2017 special congressional election, approximately 300 votes were fraudulent out of the 383,000 ballots cast—or 0.008 percent (Calvan 2017). This statement alarmed many Montana election administrators because of the lack of evidence to support the secretary of state's claim of fraudulent voting. Montana election administrators counted the ballots and asked the secretary of state to provide evidence of fraudulent practices. As of November 2017, evidence was not submitted (Calvan 2017).

In a response to the secretary of state, an election administrator from Madison County, Montana, lamented in a letter to Stapleton that election administrators "feel as though they have been kicked in the stomach by someone who is supposed to be the captain of their team" (Calvan 2017). Moreover, Montana's former secretary of state, Linda McCullough, suggested that voter fraud should be taken seriously, but the job of a secretary of state is to focus on increasing access for individuals to participate in voting. "Those things are incredibly important—as is voter fraud, if it existed, but it just doesn't exist" (Calvan 2017). Despite the challenges in Montana between Secretary Stapleton and election administrators, the state convenes an annual convention where county-level clerks, recorders, and election administrators meet to discuss how best to address any electoral issues.

As we conclude *Public Policy: A Concise Introduction,* the example of the Montana election administrator illuminates the interconnectedness of public policy in the United States, but from a different vantage point. Public policy is far greater than understanding how a bill becomes a law and is better understood through the lens of the **doers** of public policy. Recall that the doers of U.S. public policy are the individuals on the front lines of public policy implementation we have documented throughout this text. These individuals, like an election administrator, affect our daily lives because they ensure polices are carried out.

Most notably, these individuals can serve as consensus makers in an era of policy divisiveness. In this final chapter, we revisit how the doers of policy provide us, on a daily basis, important information to make informed decisions for our future. We begin our final chapter with a brief recap of how the substantive policy areas explored here truly connect because of the role of policy implementation. We conclude the chapter with the examination of three broader reflections for consideration: public policy can have multiple options; public policy is driven by facts; and public policy is a consensus-making process. These themes help us to identify our own policy future.

....

PUTTING THE PIECES TOGETHER

The expertise of policy doers is far-reaching and cuts across policy areas, from the clerk processing your license plate at the Department of Motor Vehicles to the U.S. Fish and Wildlife Service's biologist working on habitat recovery for the Salt Creek tiger beetle in Nebraska. Inevitably, the doers help you put a familiar face with public policy because they are your next-door neighbor, cousin, parent, or maybe your future coworkers. Figure C.1 lists perspectives from each chapter from this text. We begin with a brief reexamination of how each example is an interconnected piece of the public policy puzzle and produces outcomes for us.

Chapter 2 presented the stages heuristic model, a descriptive framework to understand how and why a public policy comes to fruition. As we have learned in this text, most issues begin as a focusing event that garners public support and news attention. However, not all focusing events reach congressional consideration. But for the policies that do make it onto the congressional agenda and become law, someone needs to maintain them.

FIGURE C.1

Pieces of the Policy Puzzle

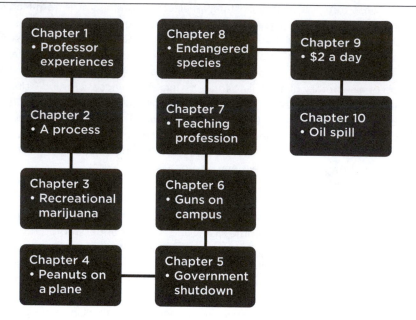

The maintenance—or, put more succinctly, the implementation—of policy is carried out by the doers of public policy, and their roles are illustrated in the subsequent chapters.

Nonetheless, in reviewing the examples listed in Figure C.1, let us pause and consider: What are the connections across recreational marijuana, regulating peanuts on a plane, an endangered jaguar, the standards to become a teacher, guns on college campuses, a federal government shutdown, living on $2 per day, and the management of an oil spill?

In each of these examples, an individual or team of individuals implements public policy at the local, state, and federal level. Experts within state and federal agencies play an instrumental role in this implementation of policy. Officials in the U.S. Department of Transportation (DOT) investigate the appropriateness of peanuts on a plane and their impact on individuals who might be allergic in Chapter 4. In Chapter 8, experts within the U.S. Fish and Wildlife Service research the implications of immigration policy on the survival of the jaguar. And in Chapter 10, environmental inspectors who work for the U.S. Environmental Protection Agency manage the cleanup of environmental disasters such as an oil spill. Moreover, individuals with financial expertise in Chapter 3 navigate how states can implement the proceeds of recreational marijuana in states such as Oregon or Colorado.

A Dynamic Enterprise

Although these examples are not exhaustive, the purpose is to remember that public policy is not possible without the implementation carried out by individuals who are experts across policy areas who navigate dynamic enterprise. As our subsequent chapters suggest, public policy is dynamic and has evolved over time, influenced by societal events, institutional and noninstitutional actors, and defined by our own preferences. Each chapter highlights issues and challenges that are informed by our policy preferences, past and present. The ever-changing nature of public policy should continue to engage us in discussions about why public policy matters and why we should stay involved.

WHY PUBLIC POLICY MATTERS

In Chapter 1, we demonstrated that public policy matters because experts use a systematic process to help communities address problems. This was illuminated throughout the text with a variety of policy examples. However, in order for the United States to continue addressing public problems, we need to reflect upon the following: Public problems should offer more than one solution; how do we determine fact from fiction, and what approaches offer consensus?

Public Problems and Solutions

From a young age, we are often taught the old adage: there are two sides to an argument. In our high school history classes, for instance, we participate in classroom debates not only to enhance our public speaking skills but also our ability to argue for or against an issue. Through instances like these, we become socialized to think our responses to an issue should be bimodal—pro or con.

These sentiments can become engrained in us and permeate the way in which elected officials design their campaign slogans and policy positions. For instance, during an election year, take a look at a candidate's campaign website. Political candidates usually have an issues tab on their website. The issues tab demonstrates their stance on a host of issues, from guns to abortion.

Policy perspectives from online campaign websites also carry over into other venues—television, radio, or print advertising. Again, the message from politicians is a clear stance: for or against an issue. In the 2017 special election for Montana's vacant congressional seat, Democrat Rob Quist and Republican Greg Gianforte had dueling television commercials about who had a stronger pro-gun stance. Once elected to office, these stances often persist out of fear that compromising with an opponent could mean the end of a political career. As a result, policy outcomes are affected—what issue makes the congressional policymaking agenda? If members of Congress are gridlocked there persists a lack of action.

The Doers and Policy Perspectives Yet what we forget is that public policy is much more than arguments for and against a particular issue. It is not this simple, and challenges our way of thinking. Consider what the reaction would be if a candidate running for the U.S. Senate stated, "Public policy is complex and it is often a shade of gray, instead of seeing an issue as black or white." Not everyone wants to know the policy wonk's guide to how best to tackle public policy issues.

Instead, the policy wonks reside within our bureaucracy, crafting multiple solutions to public problems. The variation of solutions is noted throughout this text in our substantive policy chapters broadly and in our policy choices sections more specifically. The policy choices challenge our preconceived notions that U.S. public policy issues only have two options (for or against). For instance, Chapter 8 explores immigration policy. In the final pages of Chapter 8, students are presented with policy choices surrounding how undocumented immigrants can obtain citizenship.

The purpose of our policy choices sections is to compel us to consider a variety of options when making policy recommendations. And individuals within agencies at local, state, and federal levels do just that. As we previously discussed in Chapter 5, consider the role that budget and economic analysts play in providing advice taxing and spending policies of the federal government such as the Federal Reserve.

Your Role and Policy Preferences Although the case can be made for why public policy has multiple solutions, and agency implementers can offer these choices, how do they affect you? You understand that the actions bureaucrats take can and do impact your daily life. However, what about your own personal policy preferences and actions? Do they matter?

This May, you could graduate from college with a degree in nonprofit administration and obtain employment with a local organization that focuses on the protection of nearby farmlands from a housing development. You are excited about this new job because you grew up in a farming community and get to protect farmers' rights. However, your best friend, a business major, obtains a position with a local development agency. Her new job is to locate vacant farmland for sale and purchase this land to build affordable housing complexes for single mothers with children. You strongly oppose development of any kind on vacant farmland, regardless of why it is being used. Conversely, your friend approaches you to listen to the value of developing vacant farmland. Because she is your friend, you begrudgingly attend a community forum with local farmers, the developer, and individuals seeking affordable housing to discuss what is best for the community. Exposure to multiple points of view changes your perspective, and you speak to the board of directors for your nonprofit organization about other ways to use vacant farmland. These experiences also link to your consideration to run for office at the local level.

Public policy can, and usually does, have multiple solutions to address a public problem. However, we need to understand that policy solutions need to be informed by fact.

Finding the Facts

Much like the recognition that public policy has a variety of plausible solutions, it is also based upon fact. A fact is defined as evidence of something that is indisputable. You know for a fact that you were born on September 12, 1998, because you have a birth certificate verifying this information. Your professors write a research article about how the use of laptops during class affects the ability of students to absorb information. This research uses numerous classes to compare test scores of students who use a laptop during class versus students who do not. The students who do not use a laptop during class have higher test scores. The information collected by your professors is written in a report and peer reviewed (other experts in the field review the study) before being published in a higher-education journal. This peer review process verifies the professor's research, and professors across the United States could adopt a no-laptop-during-class policy in order to enhance student performance.

Doers and Policy Facts Presumably, facts presented by experts inform public policy decisions more broadly. In Chapter 4, airlines grew concerned about the safety of their passengers with the distribution of peanuts on a plane. Therefore, experts who work for the U.S. DOT investigated the best approach moving forward for all passengers involved. Recall from Chapters 4 and 5 that local, state, and federal agencies are comprised of individuals who have cross-cutting expertise that range from biology, to economics, to political science, to entomology. These individuals are trained in their respective fields to implement the law. Individuals with backgrounds in law and air quality work to ensure factories have the correct scrubbers on their smokestacks so pollution does not endanger the public's health under the Clean Air Act.

By way of comparison, anyone can run for public office and, in turn, make decisions about which polices to adopt. Granted, congressional lawmakers have aides to provide assistance in policy areas with which they are unfamiliar. But it is up to us to determine if an elected official is making the most informed policy decisions through elections.

Although Congress creates policy and agencies provide expertise for implementation, due to technological advancement, are our own abilities impaired by our easy access to technology? If we, the public, primarily receive our information from online sources—which might not be based upon fact—then pressure lawmakers to make policy decisions based upon incorrect information, what happens?

Your Role and Policy Facts Figure C.2 demonstrates Pew Research Center data from 2016. The data present results from a nationwide survey that asked Americans where they receive information about issues. Individuals could select a variety of options to indicate where they get their information about issues: online, print (e.g., newspapers), television, or radio. Over half of individuals between the ages of eighteen and forty-nine receive their information online. Comparatively, 72 percent of fifty- to sixty-four-year-olds prefer television, and sixty-five years or older, print.

FIGURE C.2

Where We Get Our News, by Age, 2016 (in percentages)

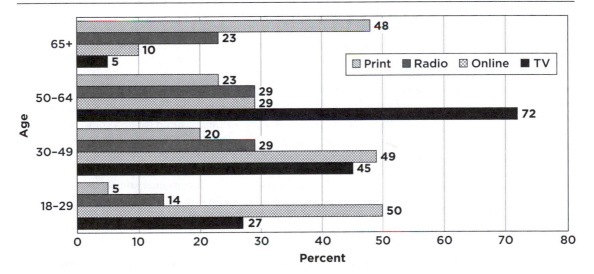

Source: "The Modern News Consumer." Pew Research Center, Washington, D.C. (July 7, 2016). http://www.journalism.org/2016/07/07/pathways-to-news/#.

Trudeau Promises Canadian Citizens A Wall. 'U.S. Will Pay'
#Election2016, #Wall

Trudeau Promises Canadian Citizens A Wall. 'U.S. Will Pay' - The Rochdale Herald

Canadian Premier Justin Trudeau reacted to the news of Donald Trump's election as US President by announcing plans for a wall to be built along the US/Cana -

THE ROCHDALE HERALD | BY SEBASTIAN WIESEL

👍 Like   💬 Comment   ➤ Share

PHOTO C.1
Sample of "fake news"

With the increased use of online formats to receive information, there is growing concern surrounding "**fake news**"—information published that appears to be from a reputable source but is not. For instance, Photo C.1 presents an image posted on the social media website Facebook. The image resembles a reputable news source and illustrates Canadian prime minister Justin Trudeau's desire to build a border wall along the U.S.–Canada border, but have the United States pay for its construction. This information is false, but what do we need to do as consumers of information to decipher fact from fiction?

National Public Radio's (NPR) Wynne Davis suggests that fake news has real-life implications. Davis (2016) uses the example of an armed man in Washington, D.C., who fired shots in a pizza restaurant because of a conspiracy theory he read of on the Internet, which was not true. In order for all of us (e.g., public, elected, and policy implementers) to ensure the accuracy of information we consume, Davis (2016) recommends the following tips:

1. **Examine the domain or URL.** Most major new sources use a .com, but we should be wary of entities that do not use .com—this is a red flag for misleading information.

2. **Do your research.** When examining a website, most have a tab "about us"—investigate the background of these individuals. Is this person an expert on the topic presented on the website? If not, be aware.

3. **Quotes.** Does the online source provide quotes, and by whom are these quotes made? If the quote is from an elected official, or public official more broadly, these are public record and you can examine the full transcript. Are the quotes evidence of academic research from a professor or researcher? If none of the above, the information is not reliable.

4. **Read the story, not the headlines.** Due to our consumeristic behaviors or our scan and skim culture, most individuals only read the headlines (see Figure C.2) and therefore are misguided because the text of the story can be different from the headlines.

5. **Right click.** In the era of gifs and memes, check your images. If an image is posted on Instagram or Facebook, right click the image for the source. Place this source in Google to trace the origins (Davis 2016).

Nonetheless, millions of Americans (e.g., public, elected officials, experts) receive their information from a multitude of sources, which are readily at our fingertips. If we do not take the time to fact-check the information we receive, inappropriate decisions or actions can result. Take our introductory story as a cautionary tale. Let's say the election administrators did not challenge Secretary Stapleton to verify evidence of voter fraud in Montana. Could the secretary, in turn, post personal information of registered voters on a website and, as a result, registered voters deactivate their voter registration for fear of their information being stolen? This example might seem extreme, but it demonstrates what could happen if we do not take time to fact-check information. Experts on the front lines of implementation play an instrumental role in providing facts to inform policy decisions.

Consensus and Public Policy

So far in this chapter and throughout this text, we have discussed the importance of the doers and our own role in addressing our public policy future through everyday citizen connections. The doers of public policy play an essential role in providing multiple solutions to tackle policy issues as well as evidence-based facts to inform our decision making. We, on the other hand, can decide whether or not to consider multiple perspectives for policy issues and take the time to determine the origins of information we read and see on a daily basis. The steps taken by doers and us can also lead to pathways of **consensus** around controversial policy areas, many of which we have covered in Chapters 5–10 of this text. But here we unpack what consensus can, and does, do for U.S. public policy.

The Consensus Makers Although we know congressional action is stymied by an inability to find consensus on controversial policy issues, there are alternative pathways. Consensus, or finding a middle ground in decision making, is something in which the doers of public policy are well versed. Here, we use the U.S. EPA as an example.

Over the course of several decades, personnel within the U.S. EPA have implemented environmental legislation that protects the air we breathe and the water we drink. However, this does not come easily because building collaborative relationships between environmental groups and industry is not an easy task (Rinfret 2011).

As we discussed in Chapter 4, agencies create policy through the rulemaking process. However, if an agency is going to propose a rule that it believes will engender controversy among groups, shuttle diplomacy is a consensus-building mechanism that has been adopted by specific programs within the U.S. EPA. For example, the EPA's Office of Transportation and Air Quality uses shuttle diplomacy as a tool for agency personnel to serve as a broker among stakeholder groups, remaining the authority for designing regulation. Agency rule-writers use the development phase of an agency rule to create an open dialogue between agency staff and affected groups of a particular rule. As a result, trust can build between the agency and stakeholder groups through the sharing of information. Simply put, stakeholder groups trust the process, because they help to create it (Rinfret 2011).

Nonetheless, the U.S. EPA is able to create consensus-building tools, such as shuttle diplomacy, to work with impacted groups during rule development. Although no particular group "wins," consensus is achieved because a variety of groups are part of the process to develop the language of a rule that is then published in the *Federal Register* for public comment. Moreover, consensus-building approaches invoke an atmosphere of open dialogue and a space where decisions can be informed by a variety of perspectives from industry to environmental organizations.

Your Role in Consensus Building The millennial generation (those individuals ages eighteen to thirty-five—presumably most of you reading this textbook) has an ability to compromise and forge consensus (Pew Research Center 2010). According to a Pew Research Center study conducted in 2010, millennials are the most open generation to change, and have a robust ability to accept others. In particular, millennials, counter to baby boomers (fifty-one to sixty-nine years of age), believe that immigration strengthens the United States and the pay gap between men and women should be addressed, to name a few (Pew Research Center 2010). Even so, building consensus is probably not at the top of your priority list; but should it be for the future of public policy in the United States?

How often have you had to complete the often-dreaded team project for a course? Maybe your professor required all the students in your class to conduct a classroom project to develop a public policy solution on how best to enhance recycling on your campus. You are not able to select your group and are assigned to work with complete strangers. Your team of five is comprised of you, who cares about the final grade; three individuals who cannot meet regularly due to their full-time work schedule; and another person who shouts loudly at the professor during class. Instead of working together to find a common meeting time, and to avoid the aggressive classmate, you just volunteer to complete the entire project because you do not want to receive a low grade. You opted to take this route because it was the easiest solution and took the least amount of effort.

Upon graduation, you become the volunteer coordinator for a political campaign and are tasked with organizing large canvassing teams to get out the vote for your candidate. You are uncertain about how best to organize the teams to canvas in neighborhoods because you are used to doing everything by yourself. Moreover, two of your student interns got into a yelling match with the opponent's campaign adviser during a county fair stop. Unclear of what course of action to take to reconcile a canvassing plan and how best to address intern conflict, you speak with the candidate directly for advice. The candidate asks why you do not know how to manage teams—isn't this something you learned how to do in college? Nonetheless, as painful as group projects can be during college, they play a broader role in your future profession and, more broadly, allow you to acquire consensus-building skills.

Without an ability to understand how to compromise and build consensus with others, the next generation of elected officials and policy implementers will fall short. The ability to work with a variety of groups and perspectives could help you to generate solid policies for the future. So how do you learn to build consensus around issues? Participating in team projects is a start, but what else can you do?

Pete Buttigieg, one of the country's youngest elected mayors (South Bend, Indiana), suggests starting with dinner table conversations (Groppe 2017). Like many of us, Buttigieg did not grow up in a politically active family, but family discussions revolved around current events. Not everyone has the luxury to have such talks with relatives, so other options could be to attend and participate in a local public hearing, or to join a student organization about an issue with which you are unfamiliar. The point is, being involved in something with which you are unfamiliar increases your capacity to listen to and become exposed to multiple perspectives. In turn, you can enhance your ability to listen to a variety of viewpoints. This can be helpful in any future career because an ability to reconcile differences not only makes policies stronger but is also beneficial to your next employer or your decision to run for office at the local, state, or federal level.

Inevitably, the outcome of consensus is that no one is necessarily happy with the end result, because there is not a specific winner or loser. Public policymaking is not perfect, but if the end result is informed by expertise and multiple pathways, then we can all benefit because it was collectively decided.

CONCLUDING THOUGHTS

Your public policy toolbox is now full of approaches, theories, stories, and lessons from everyday practitioners. Throughout this text you have learned about a variety of substantive policy areas and choices to tackle some of its dilemmas. So in the future, why should you continue to be a student of public policy? The study and practice of public policy matters because it helps our communities address problems, follows a systematic process to provide solutions, and is designed and implemented by countless practitioners whose expertise provides value-neutral options for us to benefit.

In the United States, most of us have the privilege to decide our future. Let's remember that public policy is much larger than being for or against a particular topic. Instead, public policy is a space where elected officials, media, the public, stakeholders, doers of policy implementation, and us can converge to collectively determine what public problems should be addressed.

GLOSSARY TERMS

consensus   275

doers   269

election administrators   268

"fake news"   274

secretary of state   268

DISCUSSION QUESTIONS

1. If you wanted to build consensus around a particular public policy issue, what steps would you take and why? If you are unsure, use this website from the University of Minnesota to get started: https://www.extension.umn.edu/community/civic-engagement/tip-sheets/consensus-decision-making/

2. You are assigned to work on a group project. What steps do you take to encourage active participation from all group members? What accountability measures do you use in case a teammate does not carry his or her own weight?

3. Your friend texts you a political image that links to a controversial public policy topic; this same friend posts the same image on Facebook. You right click on the image to determine it is fake news. What do you do as a result?

SUGGESTED RESOURCES

Suggested Websites

Candidate College, http://www.huffingtonpost.com/morgan-pehme/candidate-college-10-esse_b_1181763.html

EMILY's List (how to run for office), https://www.emilyslist.org/pages/entry/run-for-office

Pew Research Center, http://www.pewresearch.org/fact-tank/2015/05/11/millennials-surpass-gen-xers-as-the-largest-generation-in-u-s-labor-force/ft_15-05-11_millennialsdefined/

The Regulatory Review, https://www.theregreview.org/

University of Minnesota Consensus Building, https://www.extension.umn.edu/community/civic-engagement/tip-sheets/consensus-decision-making/

Suggested Books or Articles

Kraft, Michael, and Scott Furlong. 2017. *Public Policy.* Washington, DC: CQ Press.

Sabatier, Paul, and Christopher Weible. 2017. *Theories of Policy Process.* 4th ed. New York: Westview Press.

Stone, Deborah. 2012. *Policy Paradox: The Art of Political Decision Making.* New York: W. W. Norton Company.

Suggested Films

The Great Debaters, DVD, directed by Denzel Washington (2007: United States), http://www.imdb.com/title/tt0427309/

Hidden Figures, DVD, directed by Theodore Melfi (2016: United States), www.imdb.com/title/tt4846340/

Run Granny Run, DVD, directed by Marlo Poras (2007: United States), http://www.imdb.com/title/tt1087525

Sharpen your skills with SAGE edge at **http://edge.sagepub.com/rinfret. SAGE edge for students** provides a personalized approach to help you accomplish your coursework goals in an easy-to-use learning environment.

Glossary

Administrative Procedure Act (APA) of 1946: Legal parameters for federal agencies to create policy.

Alien and Sedition Acts: Acts that allowed the federal government to deport immigrants and also stated that immigrants could not vote until they lived in the United States for fourteen years.

broadcast: A type of news presented in the form of television.

bully pulpit: Speeches, radio addresses, Twitter, YouTube videos, or forums to engender public support for a position presented by popular presidents.

business interest group: Organization of individuals that represents business interest and persuades members of Congress to pass policies to benefit its interest.

capitalist economy: An economy in which the market largely determines the production and consumption of goods and services, but there is a role, albeit limited, for government involvement.

civil law: Law that deals with disputes between individuals or organizations.

civil liberties: Protections for citizens from the government.

civil rights: Protections for citizens by the government.

classical economic theory: Theory that draws on laissez-faire ideas whereby individuals act according to their own self-interests to make economic decisions.

command or centrally planned economy: An economy in which the government controls all aspects of the economy and owns everything.

commons: The resources that are available to all members of society and cannot be limited or privately owned in a way that excludes access and use by others; air and water are examples.

confederation or confederal system of government: A union of sovereign states, with the central government having only those powers delegated to it. States hold power over the central, or national government. The Articles of Confederation is an example.

consensus: The ability to bring individuals together to compromise on a policy issue.

conservationists: Those whose perspective embraces the idea that natural resources can and should be used in a responsible manner for human flourishing.

cooperative federalism: A type of federalism where national, state, and local governments interact to solve common problems, sharing responsibility and working together to address public needs. Also referred to as "marble cake" federalism, this concept was realized during the New Deal programs in the late 1930s.

crime rate: The ratio of crimes in an area, such as a city, state, or country, to the population. In the United States, the crime rate is typically defined as the number of offenses per 100,000 population.

criminal justice: Our law enforcement system, which includes three main components: police, courts, and corrections.

criminal law: Law that regulates the conduct of individuals.

criminology: The scientific study of crime, seeking to better understand the causes, management, and prevention of criminal behavior.

debt: The accumulation of government's deficits over years.

deficit: The gap that occurs when a government spends more money than it accrues in revenues each year. Put differently, it is the amount of overspending by a government.

deflation: The drop in the price of the same goods over time.

delegation of authority: Congress delegates its authority for public agencies to interpret and carry out legislation.

depression: The sustained, long-term negative growth of an economy.

deterrence: Strategies designed to prevent members of society from committing a crime.

discretionary spending: Government spending that is not automatic or optional each year or up to the decisions of government officials. Examples of program areas that are discretionary include education, agriculture, and the environment.

doers: The individuals on the front lines of public policy implementation.

doing side of policy: Individuals who implement public policy on a daily basis.

dual federalism: A type of federalism that suggests the national government is responsible for certain policy issues, such as the economy or national defense, while state governments are responsible for other policy areas. Thus, each government operates individually. Dual federalism is often used to describe the United States before the Great Depression.

economic policy: The umbrella term used to encapsulate any number of public policies related to the economy, including decisions about taxation, government spending, and subsidies for various industry sectors.

economy: The wealth and resources of a particular region or country; also included are the goods and services produced and consumed and the value ascribed to them and their management.

education policy: Substantive policy area to explain K–12 education in the United States.

election administrators: Individuals responsible for implementing U.S. election law at the local or county level.

elementary education: Education for Grades 1–8.

elitism: The idea that only a select few—the elite—have the power to influence policymaking.

energy policy: Policy referring to government action or inaction that deals with issues related to the production, distribution, transportation, and consumption of energy.

environmental policy: A broad, umbrella term that encompasses government action, or inaction, related to the natural environment.

executive order: Rule or order issued by the president that carries the same weight as a law.

"fake news": Information that is distorted and inaccurately presents the news.

federalism: Power divided between national government and the states.

federalism: A system of government that divides power among political units, where each unit retains sovereignty. In the United States, this power is divided among the national government and the state governments through the Constitution.

fiscal federalism: A term that describes the system of transferring funds from the national government to state or local governments in order to achieve public policy goals.

fiscal policy: The term for government decisions surrounding the revenues it takes in and how it spends that money.

focusing events: Significant episodes or experiences that catapult particular issues to prominence on the public's agenda.

free market or laissez-faire economy: An economy in which the goods and services are produced in the market as determined by the demand of consumers and supply of producers without any interference by government.

grants-in-aid: Grants of money from the national government to state or local governments as specified by law or program. Categorical grants, or federal aid for specific purposes, and block grants, or federal aid within a broad policy area, are the two types of grants-in-aid.

greenhouse gas emissions: Any of the gases that contribute to the greenhouse effect, including carbon dioxide, methane, and nitrous oxide.

gross domestic product (GDP): The nation's total production of goods and services for a single year.

horizontal federalism: A term used to define the relationships among state governments, especially those found in Article IV of the Constitution.

hyperinflation: A period of time in massive rises in inflation rates.

ICE: (U.S. Immigration and Customs Enforcement), a federal enforcement agency under the Department of Homeland Security.

immigration: When a person comes to live permanently in a country.

immigration policy: The guidelines used by a country for allowing individuals entry.

implementation: The phase after a law is created by Congress.

incarceration rate: Similar to the crime rate, the incarceration rate is the ratio of people who are in prison in a defined area. The U.S. incarceration rate is expressed as the number of people in prison per 100,000 population.

incrementalism: The idea from Charles Lindblom that governmental action is governed by small, gradual steps.

inflation: The rise in the cost of the same basket or assortment of goods over time; it is a measure of the purchasing power of a currency.

intention-based style: A flexible regulatory approach adopted by a regulator when working with organizations to ensure compliance with the law.

intergovernmental relations: The interactions among national, state, and local governments designed to implement public policy. This term is broader than federalism, in that it includes local governments of all types, and implies a more day-to-day, informal working relationship.

jurisdiction: The authority of a court or individual to hear and decide cases.

Keynesian economic theory: The economic perspective established by John Maynard Keynes that contends government intervention is necessary for a successful market.

lobbying: A profession that works for an organization to discuss or persuade members of Congress to create and pass policies for the benefit of their organization.

mandatory spending: Government spending that is mandated by law for particular programs or initiatives as determined by government. Examples of programs that are mandatory include Social Security, Medicare, and Medicaid.

means-tested: A term that describes the eligibility of an individual to receive public welfare or other kinds of social benefits. Many means-tested programs require that the recipient be low-income, living at, below, or near the poverty threshold or poverty guidelines. In short, benefits are given based on need.

Medicaid: A federal program that provides health care benefits to eligible low-income adults, children, pregnant women, elderly adults, and people with disabilities. Medicaid is administered by states, funded jointly by the federal and state governments, and is a means-tested program.

Medicare: A federal social insurance program created in 1965 and funded by a payroll tax. Medicare provides health care benefits for eligible persons over age sixty-five.

mix of enforcement styles: Term to describe a regulator that uses a combination of regulatory approaches to ensure organizations are in compliance with the law.

monetary policy: Deals with government decisions concerning the supply of a nation's currency.

Multiple Streams Framework: A theory to explain public policymaking that includes a policy stream, a problem stream, and a political stream flowing toward a policy window.

nonincrementalism: The idea that governmental action occurs with sweeping and perhaps sudden changes.

official actors: Those individuals and organizations in the policy process that have a constitutionally defined role in creating policy.

picket fence federalism: A type of federalism that involves national, state, and local government agencies working on public issues such as health care, transportation, poverty, or environmental protection. This contrasts with dual federalism, where state and national governments operate individually.

pluralism: The notion that we all have equal access to influence policymaking.

policy: A course of action adopted or created by the government.

policy entrepreneurs: Individuals who make it their professional objective to get the public and their policy-makers to address a particular public problem.

policy evaluators: Profession across disciplines that examines the effectiveness of a public policy.

policy subsystems: Sometimes called issue networks; refers to the networks of actors working to achieve policy goals.

politics: The process of who gets what, when, and why.

poverty guidelines: Another way of measuring poverty. Developed every year by the U.S. Department of Health and Human Services, the guidelines are based on the poverty thresholds, and are used administratively to set eligibility requirements for federal programs.

poverty thresholds: The main form of determining who is poor in America, based on a minimum amount of income needed to survive. Sometimes referred to as the poverty line, the U.S. Census Bureau updates these amounts annually by the size of family. For example, the poverty threshold for four people in one family was $24,257 in 2016.

power: The ability to alter or influence a course of action.

precision-based style: Term used to describe a regulator that goes by the book to implement a public policy.

preservationists: Those whose perspective is that nature has intrinsic value itself and should be protected for future generations.

print: Type of news that can be read in the form of newspaper articles.

professional interest groups: Professional organizations such as the American Bar Association that lobby to benefit their interest with members of Congress.

property tax: Tax on the value of property, often used to fund public schools.

public: Encompasses ordinary people or community.

public law: Deals with constitutional and administrative questions related to government actions.

public policy: A course of action adopted or created by the government in response to public problems.

public welfare programs: Cash assistance or other support provided by governments to people who are unable to support themselves.

Punctuated Equilibrium Theory: A theory to explain public policymaking that describes periods of relative stability augmented by periods of instability.

recession: Defined by economists as two or more quarters of negative economic growth, or declines in GDP.

recidivism: Occurs when a convict relapses back into criminal behavior. Criminologists study why people reoffend as a way of understanding how to reduce the recidivism rate.

regulation: Policy created by an agency to govern the activities of businesses or organizations.

reserved powers: Refers to the Tenth Amendment to the Constitution, which holds that all powers not given to the national government are reserved to the states, and to the people. These reserved powers became a part of the Bill of Rights in order to protect state sovereignty.

risk assessment: The process of determining whether the likelihood of an adverse situation or circumstance is worth the potential benefit.

rule: Agency policy that creates the same weight as a congressional law.

school choice: Options for individuals to obtain an education.

secondary education: Education for Grades 9–12.

secretary of state: Individual responsible for overseeing state election laws.

shift of responsibility: Congress shifts its lawmaking authority to experts within federal agencies to interpret the law.

single-payer health care system: A health care system where one entity, typically a central government, is responsible for paying all health care claims. *See* Universal health care for a closely related concept.

social insurance: A set of insurance programs administered by the government that provide benefits if an insured person becomes unemployed, reaches old age, or becomes disabled. People pay into the insurance program, typically through payroll taxes, with the expectation that benefits will be provided at some future time. Social Security and Medicare are two prominent examples.

Social Security: A federal social insurance program that provides monthly cash benefits to eligible persons upon their retirement. Eligibility is determined by a minimum amount of time in the workforce and by the amount of contributions made to the Social Security system through the payroll tax. Provisions for people who become disabled and families of deceased wage earners are part of Social Security benefits.

social welfare policy: This encompasses laws, programs, and rules designed to improve the lives of all people in a society.

sovereignty: The political system that exercises authority over its citizens. In the context of federalism, both the national government and the state governments have autonomous power granted by the Constitution.

stages heuristic approach: Term used to describe the steps in the public policymaking process.

statutory law: Legislation adopted by Congress.

Supplemental Poverty Measure (SPM): Used by the U.S. Census Bureau since 2011, the Supplemental Poverty Measure extends the official poverty thresholds by taking into account both additional benefits (such as food assistance) and additional expenses (such as transportation and child care) not in the official measure.

supply-side economic theory: Theory that reasons that capital investment and lowering barriers, such as tax rates and government regulations, lead to economic growth.

territorial dispossession: The idea that, historically, tribal people have had their land taken away from them due to their proximity to natural resources (e.g., uranium, tar sands).

"three strikes": Laws created by the federal government and many states that significantly increase prison sentences of previously convicted felons. For example, the U.S. Violent Crime Control and Law Enforcement Act of 1994 requires mandatory life imprisonment if a convicted felon has three "strikes" of serious violent felonies or serious drug offenses.

truth in sentencing: Policies and legislation that eliminate or reduce the ability of an individual convicted of a crime to seek an early release through parole.

undocumented workers or illegal immigrants: Individuals working in the United States without legal documentation.

unemployment rate: The percentage of people in an economy who are looking for work but do not have a job.

Uniform Crime Reporting Program: Administered by the FBI, the program collects and compiles data on crime from local, county, state, tribal, and federal law enforcement agencies. Crime statistics are released in the UCR, or Uniform Crime Reports. A second report is the National Crime Victimization Survey.

unitary system of government: The most common system of government in the world, a unitary system is one in which the central, or national, government holds the ultimate authority. The relationship between state and local governments is an example of a unitary system.

universal health care: A health care system where all people have access to the preventative, curative, rehabilitative, and palliative services that they need. This concept implies that health care should be available to all, not just those who can afford to pay for it, and is based on health care as a fundamental human right.

unofficial actors: The individuals and organizations in the policy process that do not have a constitutionally defined role in creating policy.

value-laden: Presents information with biases.

value-neutral: Presents information without biases.

voucher: Provides public money for students to attend the school of their choice.

References

Chapter 1

Anderson, James. 2003. *Public Policymaking*. 5th ed. New York: Houghton Mifflin.

Bachrach, Peter, and Morton S. Baratz. 1962. "Two Faces of Power." *The American Political Science Review* 56, no. 4: 947–52.

Bardach, Eugene S. 2005. *A Practical Guide for Policy Analysis: The Eightfold Path to More Effective Problem Solving*. 2nd ed. Washington, DC: CQ Press.

Dahl, Robert A. 1961. *Who Governs? Democracy and Power in an American City*. New Haven: Yale University Press.

Downs, Anthony. 1964. *Inside Bureaucracy*. Prospect Heights, IL: Waveland Press Inc.

Dunn, William N. 2008. *Public Policy Analysis: An Introduction*. 4th ed. Upper Saddle River, NJ: Pearson Prentice Hall.

Gallup. 2016. "Presidential Approval Ratings—Barack Obama." http://www.gallup.com/poll/116479/ barack-obama-presidential-job-approval.aspx. Accessed February 17, 2018.

Ginsberg, Benjamin, Theodore J. Lowi, Margaret Weir, and Caroline J. Tolbert. 2013. *We the People: An Introduction to American Politics*. 9th essentials ed. New York: W. W. Norton & Company.

Guber, Deborah Lynn, and Christopher J. Bosso. 2013. "High Hopes and Bitter Disappointment." In *Environmental Policy: New Directions for the 21st century*, edited by Michael E. Kraft and Norman J. Vig. Washington, DC: CQ Press.

Kraft, Michael, and Scott Furlong. 2015. *Public Policy: Politics, Analysis, and Alternatives*. Washington, DC: CQ Press.

Lasswell, Harold. 1958. *Politics: Who Gets What, When, How*. New York: Meridian Books.

Lunney, Kellie. 2016. "Obama again Urges Paid Parental Leave for Federal Employees." *Government Executive*, February 9, 2016. http://www.govexec.com/ pay-benefits/2016/02/obama-again-urges-paid-parental-leave-federal-employees/125812/. Accessed February 17, 2018.

Mayhew, David. 2004. *Congress: The Electoral Connection*. New Haven, CT: Yale University Press.

Mills, C. Wright. 1956. *The Power Elite*. London: Oxford University Press.

Niskanen, William A. 1971. *Bureaucracy and Representative Government*. London: Aldine Transaction.

Oyez. 2016. *IIT Chicago–Kent College of Law*. https:// www.oyez.org/. Accessed February 17, 2018.

Quade, Edward S. 1989. *Analysis for Public Decisions*. 3rd ed. New York: North Holland Publishing.

Schneider, Anne L., and Helen Ingram. 1997. *Policy Design for Democracy*. Lawrence: University Press of Kansas.

Stone, Deborah A. 2012. *Policy Paradox: The Art of Political Decision Making*. 3rd ed. New York: W. W. Norton & Company.

Theodoulou, Stella Z., and Chris Kofinis. 2004. *The Art of the Game: Understanding American Public Policy Making*. Belmont, CA: Wadsworth.

Truman, David B. 1951. *The Governmental Process*. New York: Knopf.

Weber, Max. 1947. *Capitalism, Bureaucracy and Religion*. London: Routledge.

Weimer, David L., and Aidan R. Vining. 2011. *Policy Analysis*. 5th ed. Boston: Longman Pearson Ltd.

Wilson, James Q. 1991. *Bureaucracy: What Government Agencies Do and Why They Do It*. New York: Basic Books.

Chapter 2

Baumgartner, Frank R., and Bryan D. Jones. 1993. *Agendas and Instability in American Politics*. Chicago, IL: University of Chicago Press.

Berger, Peter L., and Thomas Luckman. 1966. *The Social Construction of Reality: A Treatise in the Sociology of Knowledge*. New York: Anchor Books.

Birkland, Thomas A. 2016. *An Introduction to the Policy Process: Theories, Concepts, and Models of Public Policy Making*. 4th ed. New York: Routledge.

Gallup Poll. 2013. June 15–16. http://www.pollingreport.com/food.htm. Accessed July 17, 2017.

Google. "What Is a Theory?" https://www.google.com/#q=what+is+a+theory. Accessed April 26, 2017.

Kettl, Donald F. 2013. *System under Stress: The Challenge to 21st Century Governance*. 3rd ed. Washington, DC: CQ Press.

Kingdon, John. 1984. *Agendas, Alternatives, and Public Policies*. New York: Pearson.

_____. 2010. *Agendas, Alternatives, and Public Policies*. Updated 2nd ed. New York: Pearson.

Lasswell, Harold. 1951. "The Immediate Future of Research Policy and Method in Political Science." *American Political Science Review* 45: 133–42.

_____. 1956. "The Political Science of Science: An Inquiry into the Possible Reconciliation of Mastery and Freedom." *American Political Science Review* 50: 961–79.

Lindblom, Charles E. 1959. "The 'Science' of Muddling Through." *Public Administration Review* 19: 79–88.

Peters, B. Guy. 1999. *American Public Policy: Promise and Performance*. Chappaqua, NY: Chatham House.

Pressman, Jeffrey L., and Aaron Wildavsky. 1973. *Implementation: How Great Expectations in Washington Are Dashed in Oakland*. Oakland: University of California Press.

Sabatier, Paul A. 2007. "The Need for Better Theories." In *Theories of the Policy Process*, edited by Paul A. Sabatier. 2nd ed., 3–17. Boulder, CO: Westview Press.

Schneider, Anne L., and Helen Ingram. 1997. *Policy Design for Democracy*. Lawrence: University Press of Kansas.

Schulman, Paul R. 1975. "Nonincremental Policy Making." *American Political Science Review* 69: 1354–70.

Smith, Kevin B., and Christopher Larimer. 2009. *The Public Policy Primer*. Boulder, CO: Westview Press.

Stone, Deborah A. 2012. *Policy Paradox: The Art of Political Decision Making*. 3rd ed. New York: W. W. Norton & Company.

Chapter 3

Anton, Thomas J. 1989. *American Federalism and Public Policy: How the System Works*. New York: Random House.

Ballotpedia. 2018. *The Encyclopedia of American Politics*. "State Government Trifectas." https://ballotpedia.org/State_government_trifectas . Accessed April 16, 2018.

Benedict, Michael Les. 1988. "Abraham Lincoln and Federalism." *Journal of the Abraham Lincoln Association* 10, no. 1: 1–46. http://hdl.handle.net/2027/spo.2629860.0010.103. Accessed October 7, 2016.

Bowman, Ann O'M., and Richard C. Kearney. 1986. *The Resurgence of the States*. Englewood Cliffs, NJ: Prentice Hall.

Boyd, Eugene, and Michael K. Fauntroy. 2000. "American Federalism, 1776 to 2000: Significant Events." Congressional Research Service Report RL30772.

Chicago-Kent College of Law at Illinois Tech. "McCulloch v. Maryland." Oyez. https://www.oyez.org/cases/1789-1850/17us316. Accessed October 7, 2016.

Congressional Budget Office. 2013. "Federal Grants to State and Local Governments." U.S. Congress. https://www.cbo.gov/publication/43967. Accessed November 5, 2017.

Dilger, Robert J. 2015. "Federal Grants to State and Local Governments: A Historical Perspective on Contemporary Issues." Congressional Research Service Report R 40638, March 5, 2015.

Elazar, Daniel J. 1966. *American Federalism: A View from the States*. New York: Thomas Y. Crowell Co.

Environmental Council of the States. 2010. "Status of State Environmental Agency Budgets, 2009–2011." ECOS Green Report, August 2010. http://www.ecos.org/documents/ecos-green- report-status-of-state-environmental-agency-budgets-2009-2011/. Accessed October 11, 2016.

Fehr, Stephen C., and Mary Murphy. 2016. "Flint Water Crisis Could Spur Changes to Michigan's Emergency Manager Law." *Stateline,* March 23, 2016. Pew Charitable Trusts. http://pew.org/1pyStsP. Accessed October 12, 2016.

Frohlich, Thomas C., Michael B Sauter, and Samuel Stebbins. 2016. "America's Richest and Poorest States." 24/7 Wall St., September 9. http://247wallst.com/special-report/2016/09/15/americas-richest-and-poorest-states-4/2/. Accessed October 13, 2016.

Hanson, Jonathan K., and Rachael Sigman. 2011. "Leviathan's Latent Dimensions: Measuring State Capacity for Comparative Political Research." September 2011. Paper presented at the annual meeting of the American Political Science Association. Available at SSRN: http://ssrn.com/abstract=1899933

Kaiser Family Foundation. Undated. "Medicaid: A Timeline of Key Developments."

Krane, Dale. 1993. "American Federalism, State Governments, and Public Policy: Weaving Together Loose Theoretical Threads." *PS: Political Science and Politics* 26, no. 2 (June): 186–90.

Leckrone, J. Wesley. 2013. "State and Local Political Culture." The American Partnership. https://theamericanpartnership.com/tag/elazars-political-culture/. Accessed October 11, 2016.

Liebelson, Dana, and Amanda Terkel. 2015. "Supreme Court Legalizes Gay Marriage Nationwide." *Huffington Post,* June 26, 2015. http://www.huffingtonpost.com/2015/06/26/supreme-court-gay-marriage_n_7470036.html. Accessed October 13, 2016.

Maxwell, James A. 1952. "Brief History of Grants." National Bureau of Economic Research. http://www.nber.org/chapters/c4900.pdf

McCarthy, Justin. 2016. "Americans Still More Trusting in Local over State Government." Gallup, September 19, 2016. http://www.gallup.com/poll/195656/americans-trusting-local-state-government.aspx. Accessed October 13, 2016.

_____. 2017. "Record-High Support for Legalizing Marijuana Use in U.S." Gallup, October 25, 2017. http://news.gallup.com/poll/221018/record-high-support-legalizing-marijuana.aspx. Accessed November 6, 2017.

Milakovich, Michael E., and George J. Gordon. 2009. *Public Administration in America.* 10th ed. Boston: Wadsworth Publishing.

Miller Center of Public Affairs, University of Virginia. "Lyndon B. Johnson: Domestic Affairs." http://millercenter.org/president/biography/lbjohnson-domestic-affairs. Accessed October 9, 2016.

National Conference of State Legislatures. 2016. "State Partisan Composition." http://www.ncsl.org/research/about-state-legislatures/partisan-composition.aspx. Accessed October 12, 2016.

National League of Cities. 2016a. "Local Government Authority." http://www.nlc.org/build-skills-networks/resources/cities-101/local-government-authority. Accessed October 10, 2016.

_____. 2016b. "Influence Federal Policy." http://www.nlc.org/influence- federal-policy. Accessed October 13, 2016.

Posner, Paul L. 1998. *The Politics of Unfunded Mandates: Whither Federalism?* Washington, DC: Georgetown University Press.

Saad, Lydia. 2016. "Americans' Confidence in Government Takes Positive Turn." Gallup, September 19, 2016. http://www.gallup.com/poll/195635/americans-confidence-government-takes-positive-turn.aspx. Accessed October 13, 2016.

Scheberle, Denise. 2004. *Federalism and Environmental Policy: Trust and the Politics of Policy Implementation.* 2nd ed. Washington, DC: Georgetown University Press.

_____. 2005. "The Evolving Matrix of Environmental Federalism and Intergovernmental Relationships." *Publius: The Journal of Federalism* (Winter): 69–87.

State Policy Reports. 2016. "The 2016 Camelot Index" 34, no 7 (April): Federal Funds Information for States. Washington, DC.

United States Climate Alliance. 2017. Press release dated June 5. "U.S. Climate Alliance, Co-Chaired by Governors Cuomo, Brown and Inslee, Now Includes 13 Members." New York State Government Website. https://www.governor.ny.gov/news/united-states-climate-alliance-adds-10-new-members-coalition-committed-upholding-paris-accord. Accessed November 6, 2017.

United States General Accounting Office. 1994. "Federal Mandates: Unfunded Requirements Concern State and Local Officials." GAO/HEHS-94-110R. http://www.gao.gov/assets/90/83685.pdf. Accessed October 8, 2016.

_____. 2004. "Unfunded Mandates: Analysis of Reform Act Coverage," GAO-04-637. http://www.gao.gov/new.items/d04637.pdf. Accessed October 8, 2016.

United States Supreme Court. 1932. *New State Ice Co. v. Liebmann*, No. 463.

United States White House. Undated. "Special Topics: Aid to State and Local Governments." https://www.whitehouse.gov/sites/default/files/omb/budget/fy2017/assets/ap_15_state_an d_local.pdf. Accessed October 8, 2016.

Wildavsky, Aaron. 2018 reissue. *The Art and Craft of Policy Analysis: Reissued with a New Introduction by B. Guy Peters*. New York: Palgrave Macmillan.

Wright, Deil S. 1982. *Understanding Intergovernmental Relations*. 2nd ed. Monterey, CA: Brooks/Cole.

Chapter 4

Administrative Procedure Act. 1946. Public Law, 79–404.

Amy, Douglas J. 2007. "Government Is Good: An Unapologetic Defense of a Vital Institution." *Government Is Good*. http://www.governmentisgood.com/articles.php?aid=20&print=1. Accessed February 22, 2018.

Anjarwalla, Tas. 2010. "Should Peanuts Be Banned from Planes?" *CNN*, June 22, 2010. http://www.cnn.com/2010/TRAVEL/06/22/ban.peanuts.planes/index.html. Accessed February 22, 2018.

Bardach, Eugene, and Robert A. Kagan. 1982. *Going by the Book: The Problem of Regulatory Unreasonableness*. New Brunswick, NJ: Transaction Publishers.

_____. 2002. *Going by the Book: The Problem of Regulatory Unreasonableness*. New Brunswick, NJ: Transaction Publishers.

Coglianese, Cary. 2015. "The Regulatory Excellence Molecule." PPR News, October 22, 2015. http://www.regblog.org/2015/10/22/coglianese-regulatory-excellence-molecule/. Accessed February 22, 2018.

Cook, Jeffrey J., and, Sara R. Rinfret. 2013. "The EPA Regulates GHG Emissions: Is Anyone Paying Attention?" *Review of Policy Research* 30, no. 3: 263–80.

Copeland, Curtis W. 2013. "Length of Reviews by the Office of Information and Regulatory Affairs." Final Report for the Administrative Conference of the United States, October 7, 2013. https://www.acus.gov/sites/default/files/documents/Copeland%20Report%20CIRCULATED%20to%20Committees%20on%2010-21-13.pdf. Accessed February 22, 2018.

Davis, Kenneth Culp. 1969. *Discretionary Justice: A Preliminary Inquiry*. Baton Rouge, LA: Louisiana State University Press.

Eisner, Mark, Jeffrey Worsham, and Evan Ringquist. 2006. *Contemporary Regulatory Policy*. Boulder, CO: Lynn Rienner Press.

Federal News Staff Radio. 2010. "*Federal Register* Set to Unveil Extreme Makeover." *Federal News Radio*, July 16, 2010. http://federalnewsradio.com/budget/2010/07/federal-register-set-to-unveil-extreme-makeover/. Accessed February 22, 2018.

Federal Register. 2011. "Enhancing Airline Passenger Protections: 12. Peanut Allergies." https://www.federalregister.gov/articles/2011/04/25/2011-9736/enhancing-airline-passenger-protections#h-57. Accessed February 22, 2018.

Fiorina, Morris P. 1982. "Legislative Choice of Regulatory Forms: Legal Process or Administrative Process." *Public Choice* 39, no. 1: 33–66.

Giles, Cynthia. 2014. "American Ingenuity on Display at Next Gen Tech Demo Day." *EPA Connect* (blog), August 13, 2014. http://blog.epa.gov/blog/2014/08/american-ingenuity-on-display-at-next-gen-tech-demo-day/. Accessed February 22, 2018.

Gilliard, Andrea. 2015. "DOT Issues New Flight Safety Rule for E-Cigarettes." *Pipeline and Hazardous Materials Safety Administration*, October 26, 2015. http://www.phmsa.dot.gov/hazmat/dot-issues-new-flight-safety-rule-for-e-cigarettes. Accessed February 22, 2018.

Golden, Marissa Martino. 1998. "Interest Groups in the Rule-Making Process: Who Participates? Whose Voices Get Heard?" *Journal of Public Administration Research and Theory* 8, no. 2: 245–70.

Goodsell, Charles T. 2004. *A Case for Bureaucracy: A Public Administration Polemic*. Washington, DC: CQ Press.

GovPulse. http://www.govpulse.us/. Accessed February 22, 2018.

Hawkins, Keith. 1984. *Environment and Enforcement: Regulation and the Social Definition of Pollution.* Oxford: Clarendon Press.

Hoefer, R., and K. Ferguson. 2007. "Controlling the Levers of Power: How Advocacy Organizations Affect the Regulation Writing Process." *Journal of Sociology and Social Welfare* 34, no. 2: 83–108.

Hutter, Bridget M. 1988. *The Reasonable Arm of the Law? The Law Enforcement Procedures of Environmental Health Officers.* Oxford: Clarendon Press, 1988.

_____. 1989. "Variations in Regulatory Enforcement Styles." *Law & Policy* 11, no. 2 (April): 153–74.

_____. 1997. *Compliance: Regulation and Environment.* Oxford: Clarendon Press.

Kerwin, Cornelius, and Scott Furlong. 2011. *Rulemaking: How Government Agencies Write Law and Make Policy.* Washington, DC: CQ Press.

Lipowicz, Alice. 2011. "New E-Rulemaking Site Facilitates Participation." *FCW,* October 26, 2011. http://fcw.com/articles/2011/10/24/feat-erulemaking-lessons-learned-regulation-room.aspx?s=fcwdaily_271011. Accessed February 22, 2018.

Lipsky, Michael. 1980. *Street-Level Bureaucracy: Dilemmas of the Individual in Public Services.* New York: Russell Sage Foundation.

Marcus, Peter, Shane Benjamin, and Mary Shinn. 2015. "EPA Takes Blame for Animas River Contamination." *Durango Herald,* August 8, 2015. http://www.durangoherald.com/article/20150807/NEWS01/150809708/EPA-takes-blame-for-Animas-River-contamination. Accessed February 22, 2018.

May, Peter J., and Søren Winter. 2000. "Reconsidering Styles of Regulatory Enforcement: Patterns in Danish Agro-Environmental Inspection." *Law & Policy* 22, no. 2 (April): 143–73.

Maynard-Moody, Steven, and Michael Musheno. 2003. *Cops, Teachers, Counselors: Stories from the Front Lines of Public Service.* Ann Arbor: The University of Michigan Press.

Pautz, Michelle C., and Sara R. Rinfret. 2013. *The Lilliputians of Environmental Regulation: The Perspective of State Regulators.* New York: Routledge.

Regulation Room. n.d. "What Is Regulation Room?" http://regulationroom.org/learn/what-regulationroom. Accessed February 22, 2018.

Renfrow, Patty, and David Houston. 1987. "A Comparative Analysis of Rulemaking Provisions in State Administrative Procedure Acts." *Policy Studies Review* 6, no. 4: 657–65.

Riccucci, Norma M. 2005. *How Management Matters: Street-Level Bureaucrats and Welfare Reform.* Washington, DC: Georgetown University Press.

Rinfret, Sara R. 2011a. "Behind the Shadows: Interest Groups and the U.S. Fish and Wildlife Service." *Human Dimensions of Wildlife: An International Journal* 16, no. 1: 1–14.

_____. 2011b. "Frames of Influence: U.S. Environmental Rulemaking Case Studies." *Review of Policy Research* 28, no. 3: 231–46.

Rinfret, Sara R., and Scott Furlong. 2013. "Defining Environmental Rulemaking." In *Oxford Handbook of U.S. Environmental Policy,* edited by Michael E. Kraft and Sheldon Kamieniecki. Cambridge: Oxford.

Rinfret, Sara, and Michelle Pautz. 2014. *U.S. Environmental Policy in Action: Practice and Implementation.* New York: Palgrave.

Rodriguez, Ashlie. 2011. "Judge Rules Polar Bears Still 'Threatened.'" *Los Angeles Times,* June 30, 2011. http://latimesblogs.latimes.com/greenspace/2011/06/polar-bears-arctic-sea-melting-global-warming.html. Accessed February 22, 2018.

Skrzycki, Cindy. 2003. *The Regulators: Anonymous Power Brokers.* Lanham, MD: Rowman & Littlefield.

Thompson, Jonathan. 2015. "When Our River Turned Orange." *High Country News,* August 9, 2015. https://www.hcn.org/articles/when-our-river-turned-orange-animas-river-spill. Accessed February 22, 2018.

Tomkin, Shelley Lynne. 1998. *Inside OMB: Politics and Process in the President's Budget Office.* London: M. E. Sharpe.

United States Department of Labor. "Mine Safety and Health Administration—MSHA." http://www.msha.gov/REGS/FEDREG/FINAL/1996FINL/5453(1).htm. Accessed February 22, 2018.

United States Food and Drug Administration. 1998. www.fda.gov. Accessed February 22, 2018.

West, William F. 2009. "Inside the Black Box: The Development of Proposed Rules and the Limits of

Procedural Controls." *Administration and Society* 41, no. 5: 576–99.

Yackee, Susan Webb. 2012. "The Politics of Ex Parte Lobbying: Pre-Proposal Agenda Building and Blocking during Agency Rulemaking." *Journal of Public Administration Research and Theory* 22, no. 2: 373–93.

Chapter 5

ABC News/*Washington Post* Poll. 2015. January. http://www.pollingreport.com/consumer2.htm. Accessed April 27, 2016.

Carroll, Lauren. 2014. "Rand Paul Rightly Says the Government Shutdown Was More Expensive Than Keeping It Open." *Politifact*, August 7, 2014. http://www.politifact.com/truth-o-meter/statements/2014/aug/07/rand-paul/rand-paul-rightly-says-government-shutdown-was-mor/. Accessed August 23, 2016.

Center on Budget and Policy Priorities. 2016. "Introduction to the Federal Budget Process." http://www.cbpp.org/research/policy-basics-introduction-to-the-federal-budget-process. Accessed June 28, 2016.

Clemons, Steve. 2012. "GOP Presidents Have Been the Worst Contributors to the Federal Debt." *The Atlantic*, October 27, 2012. http://www.theatlantic.com/politics/archive/2012/10/gop-presidents-have-been-the-worst-contributors-to-the-federal-debt/264193/. Accessed April 27, 2016.

CNN/ORC Poll. 2016. February. http://www.pollingreport.com/budget.htm. Accessed April 27, 2016.

Congressional Budget Office. 2017. "The Federal Budget in 2016: An Infographic." February 8, 2017. https://www.cbo.gov/publication/52408. Accessed October 11, 2017.

Council of Economic Advisers. 2016. "About CEA." https://www.whitehouse.gov/administration/eop/cea/about. Accessed July 2, 2016.

Encyclopedia Britannica. 2016. "Bank of the United States." https://www.britannica.com/topic/Bank-of-the-United-States. Accessed July 7, 2016.

Federal Deposit and Insurance Corporation. 2016. "Mission, Vision, and Values." https://fdic.gov/about/strategic/strategic/mission.html. Accessed June 6, 2016.

Federal Trade Commission. 2016. "About the FTC." https://www.ftc.gov/about-ftc. Accessed July 2, 2016.

Gallup Poll. 2016. April. http://www.gallup.com/poll/190775/americans-say-upper-income-pay-little-taxes.aspx?g_source=Economy&g_medium=newsfeed&g_campaign=tiles. Accessed May 6, 2016.

Internal Revenue Service. 2014. "Revenue Procedure 2014–061." https://www.irs.gov/pub/irs-drop/rp-14-61.pdf. Accessed June 2, 2016.

———. 2016. "The Agency, Its Mission and Statutory Authority." https://www.irs.gov/uac/the-agency-its-mission-and-statutory-authority. Accessed June 6, 2016.

Irwin, Neil. 2015. "What Is Glass-Steagall? The 82-Year-Old Banking Law That Stirred the Debate." *New York Times*, October 14, 2015. http://www.nytimes.com/2015/10/15/upshot/what-is-glass-steagall-the-82-year-old-banking-law-that-stirred-the-debate.html. Accessed July 30, 2016.

Kopan, Tal, and Jennifer Agiesta. 2016. "Poll: Economic Outlook Best in 9 Years." CNN, September 9, 2016. http://www.cnn.com/2016/09/09/politics/poll-economy-obama-approval-rating/index.html. Accessed September 18, 2017.

McCraw, Thomas K. 2012. *The Founders and Finance: How Hamilton, Gallatin, and Other Immigrants Forged a New Economy*. New York: Belknap Press.

Mikesell, John L. 2014. *Fiscal Administration*. Boston: Wadsworth.

Office of Management and Budget. 2016a. "Historical Tables: Table 1.1." https://www.whitehouse.gov/omb/budget/Historicals. Accessed July 29, 2016.

———. 2016b. "The Mission and Structure of the Office of Management and Budget." https://www.whitehouse.gov/omb/organization_mission. Accessed July 2, 2016.

O'Keefe, Ed, and Paul Kane. 2013. "Sen. Cruz Ends Anti-Obamacare Talkathon after More Than 21 Hours." *Washington Post*, September 25, 2013. https://www.washingtonpost.com/politics/sen-cruz-continues-night-long-attack-on-obamacare/2013/09/25/5ea2f6ae-25ae-11e3-b75d-5b7f66349852_story.html. Accessed June 1, 2016.

Public Broadcasting Service. 2007. *Alexander Hamilton: The Dinner Table Bargain*. May 8, 2007. http://www.pbs.org/wgbh/amex/hamilton/peopleevents/e_dinner.html. Accessed July 7, 2016.

Struyk, Ryan, and Grace Hauk. 2017. "Five Poll Numbers That Should Make Democrats Uneasy." CNN. http://www.cnn.com/2017/07/22/politics/five-poll-numbers-democrats-uneasy/index.html. Accessed September 18, 2017.

Superville, Darlene. 2014. "Five Years Later, What Did the Stimulus Bill Accomplish?" *PBS NewsHour,* February 17, 2014. http://www.pbs.org/newshour/rundown/stimulus-bill-turns-5-years-old-still/. Accessed July 24, 2016.

Tax Policy Center. 2016. "Laws and Proposals." http://www.taxpolicycenter.org/laws-proposals/major-enacted-tax-legislation-2000-2009. Accessed July 16, 2016.

Tollestrup, Jessica. "The Congressional Appropriations Process: An Introduction." Congressional Research Service, November 14, 2014. http://www.fas.org/sgp/crs/misc/R42388.pdf. Accessed June 29, 2016.

U.S. Bureau of Economic Analysis. 2017. "Gross Domestic Product Percent Change from the Preceding Period." http://www.bea.gov/national/index.htm#gdp. Accessed October 10, 2017.

U.S. Bureau of Labor Statistics. 2016. "Consumer Price Index." http://www.bls.gov/cpi/cpifaq.htm#Question_7. Accessed June 1, 2016.

_____. 2017. "Labor Force Statistics from the Current Population Survey." http://www.bls.gov/cps/cpsaat01.htm. Accessed October 10, 2017.

U.S. Census Bureau. 2012. "Statistical Abstract of the United States." http://www.census.gov/library/publications/2011/compendia/statab/131ed.html. Accessed June 1, 2016.

U.S. Department of the Treasury. 2016. "About TARP." https://www.treasury.gov/initiatives/financial-stability/about-tarp/Pages/default.aspx. Accessed July 31, 2016.

U.S. Securities and Exchange Commission. 2016. "What We Do." https://www.sec.gov/about/whatwedo.shtml. Accessed July 24, 2016.

Chapter 6

Abner, Carrie. 2006. "Graying Prisons: States Face Challenges of an Aging Inmate Population." *State News,* November/December, 2006. Council of State Governments.

American Bar Association, Task Force on the Federalization of Criminal Law, Criminal Justice Section. 1998. "The Federalization of Criminal Law." James A. Strazzella, Reporter. Washington, DC: ABA.

American Civil Liberties Union. n.d. "Racial Profiling." https://www.aclu.org/issues/racial-justice/race-and-criminal-justice/racial-profiling. Accessed May 19, 2017.

Arter, Melanie. 2012. "NRA: Only Thing That Stops a Bad Guy with a Gun Is a Good Guy with a Gun." CNSnews.com, December 12, 2012. http://www.cnsnews.com/news/article/nra-only-thing-stops-bad-guy-gun-good-guy-gun. Accessed May 1, 2017.

Blumstein, Alfred. 1982. "On the Racial Disproportionality of United States' Prison Populations." *The Journal of Criminal Law and Criminology* 73: 1259–81.

Bonn, Scott. 2014. "5 Myths about Serial Killers and Why They Persist [Excerpt]." *Scientific American,* October 24, 2014. https://www.scientificamerican.com/article/5-myths-about-serial-killers-and-why-they-persist-excerpt/. Accessed May 15, 2017.

Campaign for Youth Justice. 2007. "Jailing Juveniles: The Dangers of Incarcerating Youth in Adult Jails in America." November 2007. http://www.campaignfor-youthjustice.org/documents/CFYJNR_JailingJuveniles.pdf. Accessed May 2, 2017.

Cannon, Ashley. 2016. "Aiming at Students: The College Gun Violence Epidemic." Citizens Crime Commission of New York City, October, 2016. http://www.nycrimecommission.org/pdfs/CCC-Aiming-At-Students-College-Shootings-Oct2016.pdf. Accessed February 22, 2017.

Carson, E. Ann. 2014. "Prisoners in 2013." Bureau of Justice Statistics. U.S. Department of Justice, September, 2014. Bulletin NCJ 247282. https://www.bjs.gov/content/pub/pdf/p13.pdf. Accessed May 22, 2017.

Centers for Disease Control and Prevention. 2017. "Understanding the Epidemic: Drug Overdose Deaths in the United States Continue to Increase in 2015." https://www.cdc.gov/drugoverdose/epidemic/index.html. Accessed November 16, 2017.

Chemerinsky, Erwin. 2003. "Cruel and Unusual: The Story of Leandro Andrade." *Drake Law Review* 52: 1–24.

Chicago Tribune. 2017. "Chicago Shooting Victims." Last updated April 28, 2017. http://crime.chicagotribune.com/chicago/shootings. Accessed April 28, 2017.

Coalition for Juvenile Justice. n.d. "Youth in Adult Prisons Fact Sheet." http://www.juvjustice.org/juvenile-justice-and-delinquency-prevention-act/adult-jail-and-lock-removal. Accessed May 18, 2017.

Davis, Alyssa. 2016. "In U.S., Concern about Crime Climbs to a 15-Year High." Gallup Poll, April 6, 2016. http://www.gallup.com/poll/190475/americans-concern-crime-climbs-year-high.aspx. Accessed April 29, 2017.

Death Penalty Information Center. 2017. "Introduction to the Death Penalty." https://deathpenaltyinfo.org/part-i-history-death-penalty. Accessed November 17, 2017.

_____. 2018. "Facts about the Death Penalty." February 23, 2018. https://deathpenaltyinfo.org/documents/FactSheet.pdf. Accessed March 5, 2018.

Dowler, Kenneth. 2003. "Media Consumption and Public Attitudes toward Crime and Justice: The Relationship between Fear of Crime, Punitive Attitudes, and Perceived Police Effectiveness." *Journal of Criminal Justice and Popular Culture* 10, no. 2: 109–26.

Durose, Matthew R., Alexia D. Cooper, and Howard N. Snyder. 2014. "Recidivism of Prisoners Released in 30 States in 2005: Patterns from 2005 to 2010." Bureau of Justice Statistics Special Report, NCJ 244205.

Equal Justice Initiative. 2016. "Cruel and Unusual: Sentencing 13- and 14-Year-Old Children to Die in Prison," Discussion Guide. https://eji.org/sites/default/files/discussion-guide-cruel-and-unusual.pdf. Accessed March 5, 2018.

Farrell, Graham, Nick Tilley, and Adromachi Tseloni. 2014. "Why the Crime Drop?" *Crime and Justice* 43, no. 1: 421–90. doi:10.1086/678081

Furdella, Julie, and Charles Puzzanchera. 2015. "Delinquency Cases in Juvenile Court, 2013. Fact Sheet (October)." Office of Juvenile Justice and Delinquency Programs, U.S. Department of Justice. https://www.ojjdp.gov/pubs/248899.pdf. Accessed May 18, 2017.

Gallup. n.d. "Crime, Historical Trends." http://news.gallup.com/poll/1603/crime.aspx. Accessed March 5, 2018.

Gerbner, George, Larry Gross, Michael Morgan, and Nancy Signorielli. 1980. "The Mainstreaming of America: Violence Profile No. 11." *Journal of Communications* 30:10–29. doi:10.1111/j.1460-2466.1980.tb01987.x

Grawert, Ames, and James Cullen. 2016. "Crime in 2015: A Final Analysis," The Brennan Center for Justice. New York: NYU School of Law. https://www.brennancenter.org/analysis/crime-2015-final-analysis. Accessed April 27, 2018.

The Guardian. 2018. "Mass Shootings in the U.S.: There Have Been 1,624 in 1,870 Days." February 15, 2018. https://www.theguardian.com/us-news/ng-interactive/2017/oct/02/america-mass-shootings-gun-violence. Accessed March 5, 2018.

Harris, Jo Ann. 1995. Offices of the U. S. Attorneys. "Sentencing Enhancement—'Three Strikes' Law." Memorandum for All United States Attorneys, March 13, 1995. https://www.justice.gov/usam/criminal-resource-manual-1032-sentencing-enhancement-three-strikes-law. Accessed May 17, 2017.

Hooley, Doug. 2010. "6 Evidence-Based Practices Proven to Lower Recidivism." Corrections One. https://www.correctionsone.com/re-entry-and-recidivism/articles/2030030-6-evidence-based-practices-proven-to-lower-recidivism/. Accessed May 24, 2017.

Horowitz, Jake. 2017. "States Take the Lead on Juvenile Justice Reform." Pew Charitable Trusts, May 11, 2017. http://pew.org/2poqpgy. Accessed May 18, 2017.

Ingraham, Christopher. 2016. "The States That Spend More Money on Prisoners than College Students." *Washington Post*, July 7, 2016. https://www.washingtonpost.com/news/wonk/wp/2016/07/07/the-states-that-spend-more-money-on-prisoners-than-college-students/. Accessed March 3, 2018.

Kolivoski, Karen M., and Jeffrey J. Shook. 2016. "Incarcerating Juveniles in Adult Prisons: Examining the Relationship between Age and Prison Behavior in Transferred Juveniles." *Criminal Justice and Behavior* 43, no 9: 1242–59. doi:10.1177/0093854816631793

Lopez, German. 2017. "America's Unique Gun Violence Problem, Explained in 17 Maps and Charts." *Vox,* November 5. https://www.vox.com/policy-and-politics/2017/10/2/16399418/us-gun-violence-statistics-maps-charts. Accessed November 17, 2017.

Martin, Michel. 2016. "Examining the Reasons for Chicago's Violence." *All Things Considered*. National Public Radio, September 3, 2016. https://n.pr/2ciGlGV. Accessed April 28, 2017.

MacArthur Foundation. 2015. *Juvenile Justice in a Developmental Framework: A 2015 Status Report*. http://www.modelsforchange.net/publications/787. Accessed April 27, 2018.

Masci, David. 2017. "Five Facts about the Death Penalty." Pew Research Center, April 24, 2017. http://www.pewresearch.org/fact-tank/2017/04/24/5-facts-about-the-death-penalty/. Accessed May 24, 2017.

Mauer, M. 2009. "The Changing Racial Dynamics of the War on Drugs." Washington, DC: The Sentencing Project.

Michaels, Samantha. 2016. "New Research Confirms Guns on College Campuses Are Dangerous." *Mother Jones,* November 2, 2016. http://www.motherjones.com/politics/2016/10/campus-carry-laws-guns-mass-shooters. Accessed February 24, 2017.

Miller v. Alabama. Oyez, https://www.oyez.org/cases/2011/10-9646. Accessed March 5, 2018.

Mydans, Seth. 1993. "Sympathetic Judge Gives Officers 2½ Years in Rodney King Beating." *New York Times,* August 5, 1993. https://nyti.ms/29InSBs. Accessed May 17, 2017.

National Association of State Budget Officers. 2016. "State Expenditure Report: Examining Fiscal 2014–2016 State Spending." Washington, DC: NASBO.

National Center for Victims of Crime. 2012. "Help for Crime Victims." http://victimsofcrime.org/help-for-crime-victims. Accessed November 17, 2017.

National Institute of Justice. n.d. "Recidivism." https://www.nij.gov/topics/corrections/recidivism/Pages/welcome.aspx. Accessed May 17, 2017.

_____. 2013. "Racial Profiling." https://www.nij.gov/topics/law-enforcement/legitimacy/Pages/racial-profiling.aspx. Accessed May 19, 2017.

Nellis, Ashley. 2016. "The Color of Justice: Racial and Ethnic Disparity in State Prisons." Washington, DC: The Sentencing Project.

Pew Center on the States. 2008. "One in 100: Behind Bars in America, 2008." Washington, DC: Pew Charitable Trust.

Public Opinion Strategies. 2010. "National Research of Public Attitudes on Crime and Punishment." Pew Center on the States, September 2010. http://www.pewtrusts.org/~/media/assets/2010/09/14/summarynationalresearchpublicattitudescrimepunishment2010.pdf. Accessed April 28, 2017.

Robertson, Lori. 2016. "Dueling Claims on Crime Trend." FactCheck.Org. Blog post dated July 13, 2016. http://www.factcheck.org/2016/07/dueling-claims-on-crime-trend/. Accessed April 25, 2017.

Roeder, Oliver, Lauren-Brooke Eisen, and Julia Bowling. 2015. "What Caused the Crime Decline?" The Brennan Center for Justice. New York: NYU School of Law.

Rosenberg-Douglas, Katherine, and Tony Briscoe. 2017. "2016 Ends with 762 Homicides; 2017 Opens with Fatal Uptown Gunfight." *Chicago Tribune,* January 2, 2017. http://fw.to/8gDvDqJ. Accessed April 28, 2017.

Roufa, Timothy. 2016. "What's the Difference between Criminology and Criminal Justice?" *The Balance,* September 23, 2016. https://www.thebalance.com/difference-between-criminology-and-criminal-justice-3975265. Accessed May 15, 2017.

Sabol, William J., Katherine Rosich, Kamala Mallik Kane, David Kirk, and Glenn Dubin. 2002. "Influences of Truth-in-Sentencing Reforms on Changes in States' Sentencing Practices and Prison Populations, Executive Summary." National Criminal Justice Reference Service, National Institute of Justice. https://www.ncjrs.gov/pdffiles1/nij/grants/195163.pdf. Accessed May 17, 2017.

The Sentencing Project. 2017. "Criminal Justice Facts." https://www.sentencingproject.org/criminal-justice-facts/. Accessed April 27, 2018.

Spohn, Cassia. 2015. "Race, Crime, and Punishment in the Twentieth and Twenty-First Centuries." *Crime and Justice* 44: 49–97. doi:10.1086/681550

U.S. Census Bureau. 2015. "Quick Facts." https://www.census.gov/quickfacts/table/PST045216/00. Accessed May 18, 2017.

U.S. Department of Justice. Bureau of Justice Statistics. 2015. "Victims of Identity Theft, 2014." Summary. NCJ 248991.

U.S. Department of Justice. Federal Bureau of Investigation, Criminal Justice Information Services Division. 2016. "Crime in the United States, 1996–2015"

Table 1. UCR Publication. https://ucr.fbi.gov/crime-in-the-u.s/2015/crime-in-the-u.s.-2015/tables/table-1/table_1_crime_in_the_united_states_by_volume_and_rate_per_100000_inhabitants_1996-2015.xls. Accessed May 8, 2017.

Wagner, Peter, and Bernadette Rabuy. 2017. "Following the Money of Mass Incarceration." Prison Policy Initiative, January 25, 2017. https://www.prisonpolicy.org/reports/money.html. Accessed May 23, 2017.

Webster, Daniel W., et al. 2016. *Firearms on College Campuses: Research Evidence and Policy Implications.* Johns Hopkins Bloomberg School of Public Health, October 15, 2016. http://www.jhsph.edu/research/centers-and-institutes/johns-hopkins-center-for-gun-policy-and-research/_pdfs/GunsOnCampus.pdf. Accessed February 24, 2017.

Wright, Valerie. 2010. "Deterrence in Criminal Justice: Evaluating Certainty vs. Severity of Punishment." The Sentencing Project. http://www.sentencingproject.org/wp-content/uploads/2016/01/Deterrence-in-Criminal-Justice.pdf. Accessed May 9, 2017.

Chapter 7

Adams, Caralee J. 2012. "K–12, Higher Education United to Align Learning." *Education Week,* December 11, 2012. http://www.edweek.org/ew/articles/2012/12/12/14minn.h32.html. Accessed March 4, 2018.

Center for Public Education. 2018. "Table: State Contributions to School Funding." http://www.centerforpubliceducation.org/Main-Menu/Policies/Money-matters-At-a-glance/Table-State-contributions-to-school-funding.html. Accessed March 4, 2018.

Chen, Grace. 2016. "Who Oversees Public Schools?" *Public School Review.* https://www.publicschoolreview.com/blog/who-oversees-public-schools. Accessed March 4, 2018.

Clemmitt, Marcia. 2013. "Digital Education." *CQ Researcher: Issues for Debate in American Public Policy.* Washington, DC: CQ Press.

Early Edge Montana. 2017. http://earlyedge.mt.gov/. Accessed March 4, 2018.

Education News. 2013. "American Public Education: An Origin Story." http://www.educationnews.org/education-policy-and-politics/american-public-education-an-origin-story/. Accessed March 4, 2018.

Gallup. 2015. "Education." http://www.gallup.com/poll/1612/education.aspx. Accessed March 4, 2018.

Kent, Lauren. 2015. "5 Facts about America's Students." Pew Research Center. http://www.pewresearch.org/fact-tank/2015/08/10/5-facts-about-americas-students/. Accessed March 4, 2018.

Kraft, Michael, and Scott Furlong. 2017. *Public Policy: Politics, Analysis, and Alternatives.* Washington, DC: CQ Press.

Ledermen, Doug, and Paul Fain. 2017. "The Higher Education President." *Inside Higher Ed.* https://www.insidehighered.com/news/2017/01/19/assessing-president-obamas-far-reaching-impact-higher-education. Accessed March 4, 2018.

Lemire, Jonathan. 2015. "Mayor de Blasio Outlines Education Policies for NYC Schools." *NBC New York.* http://www.nbcnewyork.com/news/local/Mayor-Bill-de-Blasio-Education-Agenda-New-York-City-Schools-327800751.html. Accessed March 4, 2018.

McGreevey, Patrick, and Chris Megerian. 2015. "California Mandates New High School Lessons to Prevent Sexual Assaults." *Los Angeles Times.* http://www.latimes.com/politics/la-me-pc-brown-high-school-sexual-assaults-20151001-story.html. Accessed March 4, 2018.

National Center for Education Statistics. 2017. "Fast Facts: Tuition Costs of Colleges and Universities." https://nces.ed.gov/fastfacts/display.asp?id=76. Accessed March 4, 2018.

Office of Civil Rights. 2017. "Know Your Rights." https://www2.ed.gov/about/offices/list/ocr/know.html?src=ft. Accessed March 4, 2018.

Reckhow, Sarah. 2013. *Follow the Money: How Foundation Dollars Change Public School Politics.* New York: Oxford University Press.

Richmond, Emily. 2013. "Teacher Job Satisfaction Hits 25-Year Low." *The Atlantic.* https://www.theatlantic.com/national/archive/2013/02/teacher-job-satisfaction-hits-25-year-low/273383/. Accessed March 4, 2018.

Rippner, Jennifer A. 2015. *American Education Policy Landscape.* Abingdon, UK: Routledge.

Sanchez, Claudio. 2013. "Is Pitbull 'Mr. Education'? Rapper Opens Charter School in Miami." NPR. http://www.npr.org/sections/codeswitch/2013/10/15/234683081/is-pitbull-mr-education-rapper-opens-charter-school-in-miami. Accessed March 4, 2018.

Smith, Ashley A. 2016. "Feds Act against DeVry." *Inside Higher Ed*. https://www.insidehighered.com/news/2016/01/28/ftc-and-education-department-take-action-against-devry-university. Accessed March 4, 2018.

Strauss, Valerie. 2013. "The Real 21st-Century Problem in Public Education." *Washington Post*. https://www.washingtonpost.com/news/answer-sheet/wp/2013/10/26/the-real-21st-century-problem-in-public-education/?noredirect=on&utm_term=.790651f28c9a. Accessed March 4, 2018.

Strauss, Valerie. 2016. "Diane Ravitch: Why All Parents Should Opt Their Kids out of High-Stakes Standardized Tests." *Washington Post*. https://www.washingtonpost.com/news/answer-sheet/wp/2016/04/03/diane-ravitch-why-all-parents-should-opt-their-kids-out-of-high-stakes-standardized-tests/?utm_term=.99c054df7b73. Accessed March 4, 2018.

Toppo, Greg. 2016. "GAO Study: Segregation Worsening in U.S. Schools." *USA Today*. https://www.usatoday.com/story/news/2016/05/17/gao-study-segregation-worsening-us-schools/84508438/. Accessed March 4, 2018.

Turner, Cory. 2016. *"Why America's Schools Have a Money Problem."* NPR. https://www.npr.org/2016/04/18/474256366/why-americas-schools-have-a-money-problem. Accessed March 4, 2018.

U.S. Department of Education. 2016. "Education Department Proposes New Regulations to Protect Students and Taxpayers from Predatory Institutions." https://www.ed.gov/news/press-releases/education-department-proposes-new-regulations-protect-students-and-taxpayers-predatory-institutions. Accessed March 4, 2018.

_____. 2017. "Every Student Succeeds." https://www.ed.gov/essa. Accessed March 4, 2018.

U.S. News & World Report. 2017. "School for the Talented and Gifted." https://www.usnews.com/education/best-high-schools/texas/districts/dallas-independent-school-district/school-for-the-talented-and-gifted-18937. Accessed March 4, 2018.

Washington Governor: Jay Inslee. 2017. http://www.governor.wa.gov/office-governor/office/policy-advisors. Accessed March 4, 2018.

WBUR. 2017. "To Ban Howard Zinn Books from Schools." http://www.wbur.org/hereandnow/2017/03/08/howard-zinn-books-ban-arkansas. Accessed March 4, 2018.

Westervelt, Eric. 2015. "Where Have All the Teachers Gone?" NPR. http://www.npr.org/sections/ed/2015/03/03/389282733/where-have-all-the-teachers-gone. Accessed March 4, 2018.

Chapter 8

American Association for University Women (AAUW). 2017. "The Simple Truth about the Gender Pay Gap." http://www.aauw.org/research/the-simple-truth-about-the-gender-pay-gap/. Accessed March 5, 2018.

American Civil Liberties Union (ACLU). 2017. "ACLU History." https://www.aclu.org/about/aclu-history. Accessed March 5, 2018.

American Immigration Council. 2016. "Fact Sheet: Public Education for Immigrant Students: Understanding *Plyler v. Doe*." https://www.americanimmigrationcouncil.org/research/plyler-v-doe-public-education-immigrant-students. Accessed March 5, 2018.

Bernal, Rafael. 2017. "Reports Find That Immigrants Commit Less Crime than U.S.-Born Citizens." http://thehill.com/latino/324607-reports-find-that-immigrants-commit-less-crime-than-us-born-citizens. Accessed March 5, 2018.

Blake, Aaron. 2016. "What Is an Executive Order? And How Do President Trump's Stack Up?" *Washington Post*. https://www.washingtonpost.com/news/the-fix/wp/2017/01/27/what-is-an-executive-order-and-how-do-president-trumps-stack-up/?utm_term=.dc34c009a612. Accessed March 5, 2018.

Butcher, Maddy. 2017. "Small Towns Are the Place to Challenge Immigration Policy." *High Country News*. http://www.hcn.org/articles/opinion-immigration-why-small-towns-are-the-place-to-challenge-trumps-immigration-policy/. Accessed March 5, 2018.

Davis, Kenneth C. 2010. "America's True History of Religious Tolerance." *Smithsonian*. http://www.

smithsonianmag.com/history/americas-true-history-of-religious-tolerance-61312684/. Accessed March 5, 2018.

Doherty, Carroll. 2013. "5 Facts about Republicans and Immigration." Pew Research Center. http://www.pewresearch.org/fact-tank/2013/07/08/5-facts-about-republicans-and-immigration/. Accessed March 5, 2018.

Duara, Nigel. 2016. "Arizona's Once-Feared Immigration Law, SB 1070, Loses Most of Its Power." *Los Angeles Times*. http://www.latimes.com/nation/la-na-arizona-law-20160915-snap-story.html. Accessed March 5, 2018.

Dwyer, Colin. 2017. "Gay Couple's Lawsuit against Kentucky Clerk Kim Davis Is Back on after Court Ruling." NPR. http://www.npr.org/sections/thetwo-way/2017/05/03/526615385/gay-couples-lawsuit-against-kentucky-clerk-is-back-on-after-appeals-court-ruling. Accessed March 5, 2018.

Emrick, Gail. 2017. "Trump's Wall Threatens Last Jaguars in U.S." *Daily Beast*. http://www.thedailybeast.com/trumps-wall-threatens-last-jaguars-in-the-us. Accessed March 5, 2018.

Federal Register. 2018. https://www.federalregister.gov/executive-orders. Accessed March 8, 2018.

Gallup. 2017. "Immigration." http://www.gallup.com/poll/1660/immigration.aspx. Accessed March 5, 2018.

Ginsberg, Benjamin, Theodore Lowi, Margaret Weir, and Robert J. Spitzer. 2011. *We the People: An Introduction to American Politics*. New York: W. W. Norton & Company.

Harvard University Library. 2017. "Chinese Exclusion Act (1882)." http://ocp.hul.harvard.edu/immigration/exclusion.html. Accessed March 5, 2018.

Hing, Bill. 2011. *Defining America: Through Immigration Policy*. Philadelphia, PA: Temple University Press.

History. "Ellis Island." 2017. http://www.history.com/topics/ellis-island. Accessed March 5, 2018.

Indianz.com. 2015. "Julian Brave NoiseCat: Sen. John McCain Sells Out on Sacred Sites." http://www.indianz.com/News/2015/09/28/julian-brave-noisecat-sen-john.asp. Accessed March 8, 2018.

Jost, Kenneth. 2012. "Immigration Conflict." In *Issues for Debate in American Public Policy*. 20th ed. Washington, DC: CQ Press.

Lind, Dara. 2017. "The Future of DACA Suddenly Looks Very Shaky." *Vox*. https://www.vox.com/policy-and-politics/2017/7/14/15966356/daca-dreamers-trump-amnesty. Accessed March 5, 2018.

Meyers, Jessica. 2013. "E-Verify Triggers Privacy Concerns." *Politico*. http://www.politico.com/story/2013/05/immigration-e-verify-triggers-privacy-cost-concerns-091092. Accessed March 5, 2018.

NBC News. 2006. "Posse Targets Illegal Immigrants in Arizona." http://www.nbcnews.com/id/12730462/ns/us_news-crime_and_courts/t/posse-targets-illegal-immigrants-arizona/#.WWlznU1OWM8. Accessed March 5, 2018.

Thomsen, Jacqueline. 2017. "Gender Pay Gap for White House Staff Triples under Trump." *The Hill*. http://thehill.com/blogs/blog-briefing-room/news-other-administration/340712-gender-pay-gap-for-white-house-staff. Accessed March 5, 2018.

Chapter 9

Brookings Institution. 2006. "Welfare Reform, Success or Failure?" *Policy and Practice* (March 2006): 10–12.

Centers for Disease Control and Prevention, National Center for Health Statistics. 2017. "Health Insurance Coverage." https://www.cdc.gov/nchs/fastats/health-insurance.htm. Accessed August 27, 2017.

Congressional Budget Office. 2015. *Temporary Assistance for Needy Families: Spending and Policy Options*, January 2015. Report 49887.

Dear, Ronald B. 1989. "What's Right with Welfare? The Other Face of AFDC." *The Journal of Sociology and Social Welfare* 16, no 2: 5–43.

Edin, Kathryn, and H. Luke Shaefer. 2015. "Living on $2 a Day in America." *Los Angeles Times*, September 3, 2015. http://www.latimes.com/opinion/op-ed/la-oe-0903-shaefer-edin-2-dollar-a-day-poverty-20150903-story.html. Accessed March 9, 2018.

Fang, Marina, 2013. "Poverty among College Students Increases the Overall Rate." *ThinkProgress*. https://thinkprogress.org/poverty-among-college-students-increases-the-overall-rate-ae283dcd3c47. Accessed November 21 2017.

Garfield, Rachel, Rachel Licata, and Katherine Young. 2014. "The Uninsured at the Starting Line: Findings from the 2013 Kaiser Survey of Low-Income Americans and the ACA." The Kaiser Family Foundation. http://www.kff.org/uninsured/report/the-uninsured-at-the-starting-line-findings-from-the-2013-kaiser-survey-of-low-income-americans-and-the-aca/. Accessed August 25, 2017.

Gramlich, John. 2017. "Few Americans Support Cuts to Most Government Programs, Including Medicaid. Pew Research Center." May 26, 2017. http://pewrsr.ch/2r3BfpM. Accessed June 14, 2017.

Hansan, John E. 2011a. "Origins of the Nation's First Department of Public Welfare, Established April 14, 1910." VCU Social Welfare History Project. http://socialwelfare.library.vcu.edu/public-welfare/public-welfare-the-first-department-of-public-welfare/. Accessed August 17, 2017.

_____. 2011b. "Social Security and the Old Age, Survivors Insurance Program (OASI)." VCU Social Welfare History Project. https://socialwelfare.library.vcu.edu/programs/social-security-old-age-survivors-insurance-programs/. Accessed March 8, 2018.

Institute for Research on Poverty. 2017. "What Are Poverty Thresholds and Poverty Guidelines? Frequently Asked Questions." University of Wisconsin–Madison. http://www.irp.wisc.edu/faqs/faq1.htm. Accessed August 12, 2017.

Institute for Women's Policy Research. 2016. "Poverty, Gender, and Public Policies." Briefing Paper (February). Washington DC: IWPR.

Johnson, Lyndon B. 1964. "Annual Message to the Congress on the State of the Union." January 8, 1964. http://www.presidency.ucsb.edu/ws/?pid=26787. Accessed March 8, 2018.

Journal of the American Medical Association. 1943. Editorial. "Wagner-Murray-Dingell Bill." *JAMA,* 123, no. 1: 36–37. doi:10.1001/jama.1943.02840360038011. http://jamanetwork.com/journals/jama/article-abstract/263579. Accessed August 21, 2017.

Kaiser Family Foundation. 2012. "Health Care Costs: A Primer." https://www.kff.org/report-section/health-care-costs-a-primer-2012-report/. Accessed November 27, 2017.

Kaiser Family Foundation. 2017. "Poverty Rate by Race/Ethnicity: 2016." https://www.kff.org/other/state-indicator/poverty-rate-by-raceethnicity/. Accessed March 8, 2018.

Kaiser Health Tracking Poll. 2013. March, 2013. http://www.kff.org/health-reform/poll-finding/march-2013-tracking-poll/. Accessed August 27, 2017.

Lauder, Thomas Suh, and David Lauter. 2016. "View on Poverty: 1985 and Today." *Los Angeles Times* and American Enterprise Institute Poll. http://www.latimes.com/projects/la-na-pol-poverty-poll-interactive/. Accessed August 10, 2017.

Marx, Jerry, D. 2011. "American Social Policy in the 1960's and 1970's." Social Welfare History Project. http://socialwelfare.library.vcu.edu/war-on-poverty/american-social-policy-in-the-60s-and-70s/. Accessed August 15, 2017.

Noah, Timothy. 2007. "A Short History of Health Care." *Slate,* March 13, 2007. http://www.slate.com/articles/news_and_politics/chatterbox/2007/03/a_short_history_of_health_care.html. Accessed August 2, 2017.

Page, Stephen B., and Mary B. Larner. 1997. "Introduction to the AFDC Program." *The Future of Children* 7, no. 1: 20–27.

Palmer, Karen S. 1999. "A Brief History: Universal Health Care Efforts in the U.S." Physicians for a National Health Program. http://www.pnhp.org/facts/a-brief-history-universal-health-care-efforts-in-the-us#.WZ3WZHUbgJA. Accessed August 23, 2017.

Pittsburgh Post-Gazette. 2014. "Poor Health: Poverty and Scarce Medical Resources in U.S. Cities," June 14, 2015. http://www.post-gazette.com/news/health/2014/06/15/Poor-Health-Poverty-and-scarce-medical-resource-in-U-S-cities/stories/201406150218. Accessed November 27, 2017.

"Poverty." 2001. *Encyclopedia of the United States in the Nineteenth Century,* edited by Paul Finkelman. Charles Scribner's Sons. U.S. History in Context. link.galegroup.com/apps/doc/BT2350040328/UHIC?u=oldt1017&xid=5bc61dcf. Accessed August 1, 2017.

Proctor, Bernadette D., Jessica L. Semega, and Melissa A. Kollar. 2016. "U.S. Census Bureau, Current Population Reports, P60–256(RV), Income and Poverty in the United States: 2015." Washington, DC: U.S. Government Printing Office.

Roosevelt, F. D. 1935. "Presidential Statement Signing the Social Security Act—1935." http://www.ssa.gov/history/fdrsignstate.html. Accessed August 19, 2017.

Rothman, Lily. 2016. "Why Bill Clinton Signed the Welfare Reform Bill, as Explained in 1996." *Time Magazine*. http://time.com/4446348/welfare-reform-20-years/. Accessed August 24, 2017.

Segal, Elizabeth A. 2016. *Social Welfare Policy and Social Programs: A Values Perspective*. 4th ed. Boston, MA: Cengage Learning.

Semega, Jessica L., Kayla R. Fontenot, and Melissa A. Kollar. 2017. "U.S. Census Bureau, Current Population Reports, P60-259, Income and Poverty in the United States: 2016." Washington, DC: U.S. Government Printing Office.

Shaefer, H. Luke, and Kathryn Edin. 2012. "Extreme Poverty in the United States, 1996 to 2011." National Poverty Center Policy Brief No. 28. University of Michigan: National Poverty Center.

Sommeiller, Estelle, Mark Price, and Ellis Wazeter. 2016. "Income Inequality in the U.S. by State, Metropolitan Area, and County." Economic Policy Institute. http://www.epi.org/publication/income-inequality-in-the-us/. Accessed August 28, 2017.

U.S. Census Bureau. 2014. "How Census Measures Poverty." January 2014. http://www.census.gov/library/visualizations/2014/demo/poverty_measure-how.html. Accessed July 25, 2017.

_____. 2016. "Historical Poverty Tables: People and Families, 1959–2015," Table 4. https://www.census.gov/data/tables/time-series/demo/income-poverty/historical-poverty-people.html. Accessed August 27, 2017.

U.S. Department of Agriculture. 2017. "Supplemental Nutrition Assistance Program: Fact Sheet on Resources, Income, and Benefits." https://www.fns.usda.gov/snap/fact-sheet-resources-income-and-benefits. Accessed August 21, 2017.

U.S. Department of Health and Human Services. n.d. "A Brief History of the AFDC Program." https://aspe.hhs.gov/system/files/pdf/167036/1history.pdf. Accessed August 21, 2017.

U.S. Department of Housing and Urban Development. 2016. "2016 PIT Estimate of Veteran Homelessness in the U.S." July 2016. https://www.hudexchange.info/resources/documents/2016-PIT-Estimate-of-Homeless-Veterans-by-State.pdf. Accessed November 21, 2017.

Virginia Commonwealth University, VCU Libraries Social Welfare History Project. 2017. "Proceedings of the National Conference of Charities and Correction at the Seventeenth Annual Session in Baltimore, Md., May 14–21, 1890." 73–81. A Report of the Committee by F. B. Sanborn, Chairman. https://socialwelfare.library.vcu.edu/issues/indoor-outdoor-relief-1890/. Accessed March 8, 2018.

World Bank. 2016. "Poverty Overview." http://www.worldbank.org/en/topic/poverty/overview. Accessed August 21, 2017.

Chapter 10

Adler, Jonathan H. 2011. "Heat Expands All Things: The Proliferation of Greenhouse Gas Regulation under the Obama Administration." *Harvard Journal of Law and Public Policy* 34, no. 2: 421–52.

Ansolabehere, Stephen, and David M. Konisky. 2014. *Cheap and Clean: How Americans Think about Energy in the Age of Global Warming*. Cambridge, MA: The MIT Press.

CBS News Poll. 2017. April 11–15. http://www.pollingreport.com/enviro.htm. Accessed September 20, 2017.

Dunlap, Riley E. 2002. "An Enduring Concern." *Public Perspective* 10–14 (September/October): n.p.

Gallup Poll. 2001. March 5–7. http://www.pollingreport.com/energy.htm. Accessed October 12, 2015.

_____. 2010. March 4–7. http://www.pollingreport.com/energy.htm. Accessed October 12, 2015.

_____. 2011. March 3–6. http://www.pollingreport.com/energy.htm. Accessed October 12, 2015.

_____. 2013. March 7–10. http://www.pollingreport.com/enviro.htm. Accessed September 29, 2015.

_____. 2014. March 6–9. http://www.pollingreport.com/enviro.htm. Accessed September 29, 2015.

Hardin, Garrett. 1968. "The Tragedy of the Commons." *Science* 162, no. 3859 (December): 1243–48.

Intergovernmental Panel on Climate Change. 2014. "Climate Change 2014: Synthesis Report Summary for Policymakers." http://www.ipcc.ch/. Accessed July 21, 2015.

Kraft, Michael E. 2015. *Environmental Policy and Politics.* 6th ed. New York: Pearson.

Layzer, Judith A. 2014. *Open for Business: Conservatives' Opposition to Environmental Regulation.* Cambridge, MA: The MIT Press.

Massachusetts v. EPA 549 U.S. 497 (2007). NPR/*PBS NewsHour*/Marist Poll. 2017. June 21–25. http://www.pollingreport.com/enviro.htm. Accessed September 20, 2017.

O'Leary, Rosemary. 1995. *Environmental Change: Federal Courts and the EPA.* Philadelphia: Temple University Press.

Pautz, Michelle C. 2016. "Regulating Greenhouse Gases: The Supreme Court, the Environmental Protection Agency, Madison's 'Auxiliary Precautions,' and Rohr's 'Balance Wheel.'" *Public Integrity* 18, no. 2 (Spring): 149–66.

Plumer, Brad. 2017. "Trump Is Making Promises on Coal Mining Jobs He Can't Possibly Keep." *Vox,* February 21, 2017. https://www.vox.com/energy-and-environment/2017/2/21/14671932/donald-trump-coal-mining-jobs. Accessed 20 September 20, 2017.

Puko, Timothy. 2017. "Hundreds of EPA Workers Leave in Recent Days." *Wall Street Journal,* September 5, 2017. https://www.wsj.com/articles/hundreds-of-epa-workers-leave-in-recent-days-1504660207. Accessed September 6, 2017.

Quinnipiac University. 2017a. March 30–April 3. http://www.pollingreport.com/energy.htm. Accessed September 20, 2017.

_____. 2017b. May 4–9. http://www.pollingreport.com/enviro.htm. Accessed September 20, 2017.

Rosenbaum, Walter A. 2015. *American Energy: The Politics of 21st Century Policy.* Washington, DC: CQ Press.

Shelbourne, Mallory. 2017. "Rick Perry Misunderstood Energy Secretary Job: Report." *The Hill,* January 18, 2017. http://thehill.com/policy/energy-environment/315005-rick-perry-misunderstood-energy-secretary-job-report. Accessed September 20, 2017.

U.S. Coast Guard. 2011. "On Scene Coordinator Report *Deepwater Horizon* Oil Spill." www.uscg.mil/foia/docs/DWH/FOSC_DWH_Report.pdf. Accessed December 18, 2015.

U.S. Department of Energy. 2015. "Fiscal Year 2016 Congressional Budget Request Budget in Brief." DOE/CF-0113.

U.S. Department of the Interior. 2015. "Fiscal Year 2016: The Interior Budget in Brief." February, 2015.

U.S. Energy Information Administration. 2015. "Monthly Energy Review, June 2015." www.eia.gov/mer. Accessed July 24, 2015.

U.S. Environmental Protection Agency. 2011. "National Hazardous Waste Biennial Report." http://www.epa.gov/wastes/inforesources/data/br11/index.htm. Accessed August 20, 2015.

_____. 2015a. "Air Quality Trends." AirTrends. http://www.epa.gov/aqtrends. Accessed August 20, 2015.

_____. 2015b. "EPA's Budget and Spending." http://www2.epa.gov/planandbudget/budget. Accessed July 24, 2015.

_____. 2015c. "Municipal Solid Waste." http://www.epa.gov/wastes/nonhaz/municipal/. Accessed August 20, 2015.

_____. 2015d. "Watershed Assessment, Tracking, and Environmental Results." Available at http://iaspub.epa.gov/waters10/attains_nation_cy.control. Accessed August 20, 2015.

_____. 2016. "Air Quality Trends." https://www.epa.gov/air-trends. Accessed September 19, 2017.

U.S. Nuclear Regulatory Commission. 2015. "Organizations and Functions." http://www.nrc.gov/about-nrc/organization.html. Accessed October 20, 2015.

Utility Air Regulatory Group v. Environmental Protection Agency 573 U.S. ___ (2014).

Vaughn, Jacqueline. 2007. *Environmental Politics: Domestic and Global Dimensions.* 5th ed. New York: Wadsworth.

Vaughn, Jacqueline, and Hanna J. Cortner. 2005. *George W. Bush's Healthy Forests: Reframing the Environmental Debate.* Boulder: University Press of Colorado.

Wong, Edward. 2016. "Trump Has Called Climate Change a Chinese Hoax. Beijing Says It Is Anything But." *New York Times,* November 18, 2016. https://www.nytimes.com/2016/11/19/world/asia/china-trump-climate-change.html?_r=0. Accessed October 9, 2017.

Conclusion

Brennan Center for Justice. 2017. "Debunking the Voter Fraud Myth." https://www.brennancenter.org/analysis/debunking-voter-fraud-myth. Accessed March 10, 2018.

Calvan, Bobby Caina. 2017. "Voter Fraud Allegations Roil Montana Elections Officials." *Independent Record,* August 7, 2017. http://helenair.com/news/politics/voter-fraud-allegations-roil-montana-elections-officials/article_9796773c-2d54-5cd1-91fe-358c6cbf6136.html. Accessed March 10, 2018.

Davis, Wynne. 2016. "Fake or Real? How to Self-Check the News and Get the Facts." NPR, December 5, 2016. http://www.npr.org/sections/alltechconsidered/2016/12/05/503581220/fake-or-real-how-to-self-check-the-news-and-get-the-facts. Accessed March 10, 2018.

Groppe, Maureen. 2017. "This 35-Year-Old Indiana Mayor Says He Can Revive Democratic Party." *USA Today,* February 19, 2017. https://www.usatoday.com/story/news/politics/2017/02/19/young-indiana-mayor-pete-buttigieg-democratic-party/98052850/. Accessed March 10, 2018.

Pew Research Center. 2010. "Millennials: Confident. Connected. Open to Change." http://www.pew-socialtrends.org/files/2010/10/millennials-confident-connected-open-to-change.pdf. Accessed March 10, 2018.

Rinfret, Sara. 2011. "Shuttle Diplomacy." *Environmental Practice* 13, no. 3 (August 17, 2011).

Index

Page numbers followed by b, f, p, t indicate boxes, figures, photos, and tables, respectively

AALL. *See* American Association of Labor Legislation (AALL)

AARP. *See* American Association of Retired Persons (AARP)

AAUW. *See* American Association for University Women (AAUW)

Abortion
in California, 65
Kansas banning of, 64

ACA. *See* Affordable Care Act (ACA)

Accountability
Congress and, 7f, 77–78
the president and, 78
U.S. Supreme Court and, 79

ACLU. *See* American Civil Liberties Union (ACLU)

Adams, John, 187

Administrative environment, 23–24

Administrative Procedure Act (APA) of 1946, 77

Adversarialism, as attribute to precision-based regulatory approach, 88

Advisory Commission on Intergovernmental Relations, 58

AFDC. *See* Aid to Families with Dependent Children (AFDC)

Affordable Care Act (ACA)
beyond and, 220
challenge by Hobby Lobby, 10
Cruz's efforts to undo, 95
as example of state initiatives, 61
key provisions of, 220, 222, 222t
repeal attempts under Trump, 22, 225
spending pertained to implementation of, 96
See also Obamacare

African Americans
incarceration of, 146–147
literacy test required by, 180f
in 1950s–1960s, 179
postwar devastation, 213
poverty and, 208
welfare queen, 218

AFT. *See* American Federation of Teachers (AFT)

Age discrimination, 179–180

Agency policymaking, 72

Agendas and Instability in American Politics, 40

Agenda setting, policymaking and, 5f, 6, 26, 26f, 28–30

Aid to Dependent Children under Title IV, 216

Aid to Families with Dependent Children (AFDC), 215–216, 218

AILA. *See* American Immigration Lawyers Association (AILA)

Airbags, 41

Airport security, 21

Alaska
amount received by poor family under AFDC, 216
medicinal marijuana laws, 46
opening government lands to drilling, 242
polar bear, 84, 85, 85p
Supplemental Poverty Measure, 208

Alien and sedition acts, 187

Alien Registration Act of 1940, 190

Almhouses, 213

Amazon.com, 23

American Association for University Women (AAUW), 179

American Association of Labor Legislation (AALL), 223

American Association of Retired Persons (AARP), 225, 228

American Association of State Colleges and Universities (AASCU), 168, 169t

American Bankers Association Political Action Committee (PAC), 2

American Bar Association, 10, 137, 138

American Civil Liberties Union (ACLU), 146, 197, 199

American Clean Energy and Security Act, 8

American dollar, 103

American Dream, 210, 216, 229

American economy, policy and, 22

American Enterprise Institute poll, 211

American Federation of Labor, 223

American Federation of Teachers (AFT), 168, 169t

American Immigration Council 2016, 194
American Immigration Lawyers Association (AILA), 197t
American Indians, as original inhabitants of, 178–179
American Medical Association, 10, 11, 224
American Recovery and Reinvestment Act of 2009, 110, 114, 116, 243, 250
Americans, and soda, 28
Americans with Disabilities Act of 1990, 57, 179
American Taxpayer Relief Act of 2012, 116
America's Natural Gas Alliance, 259
Amish politics, 1
Anderson, James, 4
Andrade, Leandro, 143
Animas River, Colorado, 89–90, 90p
Anti-soda drinking mascot, 32
Anton, Thomas, 68
ANWR. *See* Arctic National Wildlife Refuge (ANWR)
APA. *See* Administrative Procedure Act (APA) of 1946
APSCU. *See* Association of Private Sector Colleges and Universities (APSCU)
Arctic National Wildlife Refuge (ANWR), 242
Arkansas's Central High School, 179
AR-15 rifle, 128
Articles of Confederation, national policymaking under, 48–49
Asbestos Hazards and Emergency Response Act, 57
Assault rifle, ban on, 150–151
Assessing the stages model, 37–38
Association of Private Sector Colleges and Universities (APSCU), 169t
Assorted economic instruments, 32
Assumptions Bill, 111
ATF. *See* Bureau of Alcohol, Tobacco, Firearms, and Explosives (ATF)
Atomic Energy Commission, 248

Banking Act of 1933, 115
Banking system, basic operations of, 103–104
Bank of America, 115
Baumgartner, Frank, 40
Berger, Peter L., 28
Birkland, Thomas, 29
Black defendants, all-white juries and, 146
Black Lives Matter movement, 6
Black Tuesday, 111
Blended learning, in San Francisco, 161
BLM. *See* Bureau of Land Management's (BLM)
BLM's rule for the disclosure of chemicals, 90
Bloomberg, Michael, 27, 27p

BLS. *See* Bureau of Labor Statistics (BLS)
Blue Cross organizations, 224
Board of Public Welfare, 214
Body scanner at airports, 30
Books or articles
    on civil rights and immigration, 204
    on crime and public policy, 152
    on economic policy and public budgeting, 125
    on education policy, 176
    on environmental 268and energy policy, 266
    on federalism and intergovernmental relations, 70
    on policy process and theories, 43–44
    on public policy, 18, 278
    on rulemaking and regulations, 93
    on social welfare and health care policy, 233
Border Security and Immigration Enforcement Improvements, 193t
Bowman, Ann O'M, 60
Branches of government, 7–9
Brandeis, Louis, 61
Brennan Center for Justice, 127, 133, 268
Brexit, 122
British Petroleum (BP), 235
British thermal units (Btu), 246, 249
Broadcast media, 10
Broader Bolder Approach to Education, 171
Brookings Institution 2006, 218
Brown, Jerry, 61, 166
Brownback, Sam, 65
Brown v. Board of Education (1954), 160, 164, 179
Btu. *See* British thermal units (Btu)
Budget
    agency, 77
    cuts, public support for, 212f
    See also Federal budget
Budget and Accounting Act (1921), 115
Budget resolution, concurrent, 105
Bullock, Steve, 166
Bully pulpit, 8
Bundy, Ted, 139
Bureaucracy
    as actor in immigration policy, 195–196
    as actor in U.S. education policy, 165
    as defined by Wilson, 9
    federal, as actor in social welfare and health care policy, 227
    role in society, 10
    role within policymaking process, 8t
Bureaucrats, 9–10

Bureau of Alcohol, Tobacco, Firearms, and Explosives (ATF), 138
Bureau of Consumer and Financial Protection, 114
Bureau of Engraving and Printing, 117
Bureau of Immigration, 190
Bureau of Justice Statistics, 130, 132, 133, 135, 144, 146
Bureau of Labor Statistics (BLS), 99, 102b
Bureau of Land Management's (BLM), 80
Bureau of Prohibition, 138
Bureau of the Budget. *See* Office of Management and Budget
Burrell v. Hobby Lobby Stores, Inc., 9
Bush, George W., 110, 160, 189, 242, 250
Bush, George W., administration
    after 9/11, 189, 242
    bailing out the auto industry, 114
    ban on assault rifle, 150
    environmental initiatives, 242–243
    taking over Fannie Mae and Freddie Mac, 113
    tax credits and business investment incentives, 110
Business and industry, government regulation on, 73f
Business interest group, 10

CAFE. *See* Corporate average fuel economy (CAFE)
California
    abortion in, 65
    domestic partnership law, 68
    oil spills in, 240
    pollution control laws, 262
    state-level penalties in, 46
    U.S. Climate Alliance, 61
    workers' payroll payment, 231–232
Camelot Index
    for comparing states, 62–63
    top-and bottom-ranked states in, 64t
Campaign for Youth Justice 2007, 147, 148
Capitalist economy, 97
Capital punishment, 19, 143–144, 145f
Carson, Rachel, 240
Carter, Jimmy, 248
CBO. *See* Congressional Budget Office (CBO)
CBP. *See* U.S. Customs and Border Protection (CBP)
Census Bureau, 188
Center for Biological Diversity, 85
Center for Budget and Policy Priorities, 228
Center for Public Education 2018, 156, 157
Centers for Disease Control and Prevention, 139, 151, 219, 229
Centers for Medicare and Medicaid Services, 227

CEQ. *See* White House Council on Environmental Quality (CEQ)
CeRi (Cornell eRulemaking Initiative), 91
Charter schools, 161
CHEA. *See* Council for Higher Education Accreditation (CHEA)
Cheney, Dick, 250, 253
Chernobyl, Ukraine, 242
Chicago, murders and shooting victims in, 134
Chicago Police Department, CLEAR, 134
Chicago Tribune, 134
Children
    cash support to, 216
    poor, number of, 208, 209f
Children's Health Insurance Program (CHIP), 208, 219–220
Chin, Douglas S., 195
Chinese Exclusion Act of 1882, 187
Chinese immigrants, 187
Chinese Labor Exclusion Act of 1882, 189–190
CHIP. *See* Children's Health Insurance Program (CHIP),
Cho, Seung Hui, 126
Christian Coalition, 11
Chrysler, 114
Church in Sutherland Springs, Texas, mass shooting at, 148
Cigarette taxes, 31
CIS. *See* Citizenship and Immigration Services (CIS)
Citigroup, 114, 115
Citizen Law Enforcement Analysis and Reporting System (CLEAR), 134
Citizens
    making impact on U.S. public policymaking, 12
    role within policymaking process, 8t, 10–11
Citizens Crime Commission of New York City, 127
Citizenship and Immigration Services (CIS), 195
City of Clinton v. Cedar Rapids and Missouri River Railroad Co., 51
Civil cases, federal and state courts and, 141
Civilian Conservation Corps, 214
Civil law, 9
Civil liberties, 178
Civil rights
    amnesty, and enforcement, 188
    defined, 178
    discrimination, 181
    immigration and, 181–183
    overview of, 177–186
Civil Rights Act of 1964, 55, 66, 160, 181, 216
Civil War, 52, 146, 213

Classical economic theory, 97–98

Clean Air Act, 5, 10, 31, 34, 57, 74, 238, 240, 252, 259, 260, 273

Clean Air Act Amendments of 1990, 253

Clean Power Plan Rule, 79, 243

Clean Water Act (CWA), 31, 57, 78, 252, 265

CLEAR. *See* Citizen Law Enforcement Analysis and Reporting System (CLEAR)

Clemson University, 92

Climate change policy, 29, 61, 67, 242, 261

Climate Reality Project, 6

Clinton, Bill
  changes to AFDC, 218
  Defense of Marriage Act in 1996, 67
  Goals 2000, 163
  promise of shifting energy policy, 249
  support of environmental issues, 242
  Unfunded Mandates Reform Act, 57

Clinton administration, 110, 242, 249

CNN Money, 206

CNN/ORC poll, 100

Coalition for Juvenile Justice, 148

Cocaine, 45

Coercive federalism, 56

College campus, guns on, 126–127

College education, cost of, 159

College Navigator, 165, 165p

College Scorecard, 156, 157p, 164

College tuition, 120

Colonialism and Mann, U.S. education system and, 159–161

Colorado
  Animas River in, 89–90, 90p
  assault-style rifles in, 150
  legalizing marijuana for recreational use, 46
  money spent on K–12 education, 158
  spending on corrections, 137

Command or centrally planned economy, 97

Commerce and Labor Department, 190

Common, 262

Common School Movement, 159, 160

Community, public policy and, 13–14

Comprehensive Emergency Response, Compensation, and Liability Act of 1980, 253

CompStat, 133

Confederal system of government, 48

Confederation, 48

Congressional Budget and Impoundment Act of 1974, 115

Congressional Budget Office (CBO), 18, 54, 55, 105, 107, 109, 117, 218, 218, 225

Consensus
  building, 276
  doers and, 275
  makers, 275–276

Conservationists, 240

Consistency, as attribute to precision-based regulatory approach, 88

Consumer Price Index (CPI), 99, 104, 207

Contract Labor Law 1885, 190

Controlled substance, marijuana as, 47b

Controlled Substances Act (CSA), 45, 46

Cooperative federalism, 53–54

Cornell University's regulation room, 91, 92

Corporate average fuel economy (CAFE), 248, 249, 250, 253

Cost, of college education, 159

Cotton, Safiyyah, 206

Council for Global Immigration 2016, 197t

Council for Higher Education Accreditation (CHEA), 168, 169t

Council of Economic Advisers, role in policy arena, 118

Council of State Governments, 60

County Poorhouse Act of 1824, 213

Courts
  as actors in education policy, 164–165
  as actors in immigration policy, 194–195
  as actors in social welfare and health care policy, 227
  role within policymaking process, 8t
  system in the U.S., 8
  See also Federal courts; State courts

CPI. *See* Consumer Price Index (CPI)

Creative federalism, 54–55

Credits, 108

Crime, 128–137
  actors in criminal justice policy, 140–141
  capital punishment, 143–144, 145f
  crime and race, 146–147
  crime victims, 141–142
  criminal justice and crime policy statutes, 142–144
  defined, 128
  deterrence and recidivism, 144, 146
  federal and state courts and, 141
  federalizing crime, 137–138
  incarceration rate, 135–137, 136f
  inchoate, 128–129
  juvenile crime, 147–148
  mass shootings, 148–149
  media and crime, 139–140
  personal crime, 128

probation officers and parole officers, 142
property, 128
public attitudes about incidence of crime, 138–139
public perceptions, 134–135
punishable crimes, 128
rate of, 130, 131f, 132–134, 132f, 134f
security and, 200
statutory crime, 129
types of crime, 128–130
Crime in the United States (publication), 130
Crime policy statutes, criminal justice and, 142–144
Crime rate, 129–134, 131f, 132f
Criminal cases, 129, 141
Criminal justice and crime policy statutes, 142–144
Criminal justice policy, 20
Criminal justice system, 128, 142
Criminal law, 9
Criminology, 128
Cruz, Ted, 95
CSA. *See* Controlled Substances Act (CSA)
Cultural community, 14
Curriculum and technology, 171–172
Cuyahoga River in Ohio, 240
CWA. *See* Clean Water Act (CWA)

DACA program. *See* Deferred Action for Childhood
    Arrivals (DACA) program
Dallas's School for the Talented and Gifted, 161
DAPA. *See* Deferred Action for Parents of Americans
    and Lawful Permanent Residents (DAPA)
Davis, Kim, 68, 181
Davis, Wynne, 274
DEA. *See* Drug Enforcement Administration (DEA)
de-Americanization, 184–185
Dean, Howard, 3
Death penalty
    crime and, 133
    public support for, 145f
    states abolishment of, 143
Death Penalty Information Center 2017, 143
de Blasio, Bill, 167–168
Debt, 109–110, 119–120
Debt ceiling, challenges of, 120
Decision agenda, 29–30
Decision making, agency, 77, 83–84
"Decision process," Lasswell on, 26
Deepwater Horizon, 21, 235, 237p, 243, 254
Defense of Marriage Act in 1996 (DOMA), 49, 67–68, 74
Defense spending, 109

Deferred Action for Childhood Arrivals (DACA)
    program, 194
Deferred Action for Parents of Americans and Lawful
    Permanent Residents (DAPA), 202
Deficits, as economic policy challenge, 119–120
Deflation, 99
Delegation of authority, 76
Deloitte LLP, 231
Democracy
    federalism and safeguarding, 66
    laboratories of, 67
Democrats
    government assistance for unemployed, 213
    immigration policy and, 194
Depression, defined, 100
Deterrence, 144
Deterrence through enforcement actions, as attribute to
    precision-based regulatory approach, 88
DeVry University, 165
DHS. *See* U.S. Department of Homeland Security
    (DHS)
Digital revolution, schools and, 161–162
Dillon, John, 51
"Dillon's Rule," 51
Discrimination
    against individuals from Muslim nations, 182
    national origin, 181
    against religion, 181, 182f
Distance learning, 161
Distributive public policy, 4, 4f
Dodd-Frank Act, 114
DOEd. *See* U.S. Department of Education (DOEd)
DOEd's Office of Civil Rights, 156
Doers, 269, 271–273
Doing side of policy, 7
DOMA. *See* Defense of Marriage Act in 1996 (DOMA)
Down, Anthony, 9
DREAM Act, 189
Drinking water in Flint, Michigan, 65–66
Drug Enforcement Administration (DEA), 45, 46
Drug laws, 45
Dual federalism, 52–53
Duncan, Arne, 163

Early Edge Montana, 166
Earned Income Credit, 217
Earth Liberation Front. Businesses, 258
EAs. *See* Environmental assessments (EAs)
E-cigarettes, on a plane, 71–72, 92

Economic environment, as factor influencing policymaking, 22
Economic Growth and Tax Relief Reconciliation Act (2001), 115–116
Economic incentives, creating, 265
Economic instruments tool, 31
Economic Opportunity Act of 1964, 55, 112, 217
Economic Policy Institute, 228
Economic Report of the President, 118
Ecstasy, 45
Educational landscape, 161
Education Commission of the States, 166
Education for All Handicapped Children's Act of 1975, 163
Education funds, 156, 157, 158b, 163
Education News 2013, 159
Education of Handicapped Children Act of 1975 (Individuals with Disabilities Education Act [IDEA] of 1990), 162
"Education policy wonks," 166
Education standards, 61
Eighth Amendment, 136, 143, 144
Eisenhower, Dwight D., 23, 164, 179
Eisenhower administration, 110
Eisner, Mark, 74
EISs. *See* Environmental impact statements (EISs)
"Elastic clause," 49
Elazar, Daniel, 62
Elderly, poverty among, 208, 209f
Election administrators, 268
Elections, cycle of, 22
Electric vehicles, battery technology for, 237
Elementary and Secondary Education Act (ESEA) of 1965, 156, 160, 162, 217
Elementary education, 172
Elitism, 3
Ellis Island, 187, 188p
Elshikh, Ismail, 195
Emergency Banking Act, 112
Emergency Relief and Construction Act of 1932, 225
Employers, Family and Medical Leave Act and, 230–231
Employment, unlawful termination of, 179
Employment Act of 1946, 118
Endangered Species Act of 1973 (ESA), 10, 74, 85, 178, 196, 252
Energy Independence and Security Act of 2007, 253
Energy Policy Act of 2005, 250, 253
Energy Policy and Conservation Act of 1975, 253
Energy task force, 250

Environment, state regulators and, 86
Environmental assessments (EAs), 252
Environmental Council of the States 2010, 61
Environmental impact statements (EISs), 252
EPA. *See* U.S. Environmental Protection Agency (EPA)
EPA's Comprehensive Environmental Response, Compensation and Liability Act of 1980, 89
Equal Justice Initiative, 147–148
ESA. *See* Endangered Species Act of 1973 (ESA)
ESEA. *See* Elementary and Secondary Education Act (ESEA) of 1965
ESS. *See* Every Student Succeeds Act (ESS) of 2015
European countries, early efforts in health care, 223
European immigration, 182
Evaluation methods
    alternative, 174–175
    of education, 174–175
E-Verify state requirements, 186f, 196
E-Verify system, 188, 196
Everyday citizen connection
    on crime and public policy, 149
    factors affecting educational pathways, 173
    on family origin and immigration, 201
    impact of regulations, 92
    public policy, 67–68
    reliance on energy and health of natural environment, 263
    student loans, 120
    wages and poverty level income, 230
Every Student Succeeds Act (ESS) of 2015, 160–161, 163, 174–175
Excise taxes, 108
Executive action, environmental policy in 2010, 243–245
Executive agencies, as actors in environmental and energy policy, 257
Executive orders
    6757, 215
    12287, 249
    12291, 241
    13767, 202
    Kentucky governor, 181
    Nixon, 257
    presidents and, 78, 191, 192, 192t
    Trump, 194
Expenditures
    government, 108–109, 109f, 111–112
    per capita, health, 220, 221f
Experts, within state education department, 166–167
Exxon Valdez oil spill in 1989, 2, 11, 11p, 65, 235, 237, 242, 254

Fake news, 274
Family and Medical Leave Act of 1993 (FMLA), 226, 231–232
Family Educational Rights and Privacy Act (FERPA) of 1974, 162
Fannie Mae, 113
FBI. *See* Federal Bureau of Investigation (FBI)
FDA. *See* Food and Drug Administration (FDA)
FDIC. *See* Federal Deposit Insurance Corporation (FDIC)
Federal agencies
  in education, 169t
  role in education, 165
Federal budget, 104–110
  debt and deficit, 109–110
  forces creating obstacles, 106–107
  government expenditures, 108–109, 109f
  government revenues, 107–108, 107f
  Obama White House and, 95
  process, 105, 106f
Federal Bureau of Investigation (FBI), 130
Federal Coal Mine Health and Safety Act of 1969, 86
Federal courts
  as actors in environmental and energy policy, 256–257
  crime and, 141
  hearing of criminal and civil cases, 129
Federal Deposit Insurance Corporation (FDIC), 112, 119
Federal Emergency Relief Administration, 214
Federal employees, 96
Federal Energy Regulatory Commission (FERC), 258
Federal funds, sanctuary cities and, 200
Federal government
  providing block grant to state governments, 210
  role in U.S. education, 156, 156t
  support for assistance, 212, 212f
  support needy children, 216
Federal government shutdown, 95–96, 105, 106
Federal income tax brackets, 2016, 108t
Federal Insurance Contributions Act of 1939 (FICA), 207, 210, 226
Federal Insurance Deposit Insurance Corporation (FDIC), 129
Federalism
  American, Krane on, 68
  constitutional foundation of, 49–50
  cooperative, 53–54
  creative, 54–55
  defined, 48, 50
  dual, 52–53

evolvement of, 51–66
fiscal, 54
horizontal, 49–50
intergovernmental relations and, 56–65
picket fence, 58–59, 59f
system of, 3
virtues of, 66–67
Federalism and the Making of America (Robertson), 66
Federalist no. 51, 66
The Federalist Papers in 1787, 66
Federalizing crime, 137–138
Federal Land Policy and Management Act of 1976, 240
Federal law enforcement agencies, 140
Federal laws, 9
Federal Mine Safety and Health Administration (MSHA) regulators, 86
Federal News Staff Radio 2010, 91
Federal Open Market Committee (FOMC), 118
Federal Poverty Guideline, 230
Federal Register, 71, 72, 79–80, 80p, 82f, 84, 91, 92, 192
Federal regulators, 86
Federal Reserve Act (1913), 115
Federal Reserve Bank, 112, 113
Federal Reserve System (Fed)
  Federal Reserve Act and, 115
  as first bank of the United States, 111
  role in policy arena, 118
  role of, 103, 104
Federal rulemaking process, stages, 79f
Federal Stability Oversight Council, 114
Federal system, 3–4, 4f
Federal tax policy, policy choices, 123
Federal tax system, 122
Federal Trade Commission (FTC), role in policy arena, 118, 165
Federal Violent Crime Control and Law Enforcement Act of 1994, Title XI of, 150
Federal Water Pollution Control Act Amendments of 1972, 252
Federal work-study program, 217
FERC. *See* Federal Energy Regulatory Commission (FERC)
Ferguson, Bob, 194
FERPA. *See* Family Educational Rights and Privacy Act (FERPA) of 1974
Ferriero, David S., 91
FICA. *See* Federal Insurance Contributions Act of 1939 (FICA)
Fifth Amendment, 194

Fillibuster, 95
Films
 on civil rights and immigration, 204
 on crime and public policy, 152
 on economic policy and public budgeting, 125
 on education policy, 176
 on environmental and energy policy, 267
 on federalism and intergovernmental relations, 70
 on policy process and theories, 44
 on public policy, 18, 278
 on rulemaking and regulations, 93
 on social welfare and health care policy, 233–234
Final rule, in federal rulemaking, 79, 79f
Fiscal federalism, 54, 55, 57
Fiscal policy, 101, 103–104
Flex School, San Francisco, 161
FMLA. *See* Family and Medical Leave Act of 1993
 (FMLA)
Focusing events, 6, 21, 29, 240
FOMC. *See* Federal Open Market Committee
 (FOMC)
Food and Drug Administration (FDA), 72, 78
Food Stamp Act, 217
Food stamps. *See* Supplemental Nutrition Assistance
 Program (SNAP)
Force of events, 65
Formal proposed rulemaking, in rulemaking process,
 81–82
Fossil fuels, 245–246
Fox, Vincente, 189
Fraudulent voting, 268–269
Freddie Mac, 113
Free-market, 97
Front-line workers, 86
FTC. *See* Federal Trade Commission(FTC)
Furman v. Georgia, 144

Gallup, 8, 47b, 60, 183, 184, 186f, 251
Gallup Poll, 28, 47b, 100, 138, 162, 182,
 185b, 244, 251
GAO. *See* U.S. Accountability Office (GAO)
"Gay Marriage State by State: From a Few States to the
 Whole Nation" (Park), 68
Gay rights, 62
GDP. *See* Gross domestic product (GDP); Gross
 domestic product (GDP)
Gender, poverty rates by, 208, 209f
Gender discrimination, protections for, 160
General Motors, 114

GEPs. *See* Gubernational education policy advisers (GEPs)
Gianforte, Greg, 271
Gift tax rate, 116
Glass, Carter, 115
Glass-Steagall, or the Banking Act (1933), 115
Glazer, Nathan, 189
Global markets and free trade, 120
Goals 2000: Educate America Act of 1994, 163
Golden, Marissa, 84
Gold King Mine, 89–90
Goldman Sachs, 114
Gold Rush, 187
Goodsell, Charles, 74
Google, 25
Gore, Al, 6, 242
Government
 bailout, 112
 debt and deficit, 109–110
 expenditures, 108–109, 109f, 111–112
 focusing events and, 21
 great recession and response of, 113–114
 intervention surrounding soda consumption, 33
 outlays, 1980-2016, 113, 113f, 114f
 outlays 1914-1978, 112, 113f
 policies, 20, 121–122
 regulations, Kasich and, 73
 revenues, 107–108, 107f
 role in society, 249
 steps in health insurance 1960-2017, 224
 unitary system of, 52
 See also Federal government; Local government;
  National government; State government
Government Accounting Office. *See* U.S. Accountability
 Office (GAO)
Government agencies, as actors in economic policy,
 117–119
Government antipoverty efforts, 213
Government assistance, 205
Government Finance Officers Association, 104
Government-funded health care system, 223
Government-run insurance programs. *See* Children's
 Health Insurance Program (CHIP); Medicaid;
 Medicare
Governors, as actors in U.S. education policy, 166
GovPulse.US, 91
Graham-Cassidy bill, 19
Grammar schools, colonies funding, 159
Gramm-Leach-Bliley Act, 115
Grants, 55, 56f

Grants-in-aid, 53, 57, 58, 69
Great Depression
  economic contraction and, 100
  enormity of, 53
  federalism and IGR and, 54
  health reform efforts after, 223–224
  immigration policy and, 181
  people in poverty during, 214, 214p
  policy in Roosevelt's administration and, 20, 22
  punctuation after, 40
  stock market crash on 1929, 111, 113
  unemployment rate during, 99
Great Recession, 110, 113–114
Great Society
  connecting health care to social welfare, 216–217
  Johnson's effort to build, 54, 224
  policies, 55
  programs, 112, 219
Green Eggs and Ham (Dr. Seuss), 95
Greenhouse gas emissions, 243
Greenhouse gas (GHG) emissions regulation, 250, 259
Green houses, as actors in environmental and energy
      policy, 259–260
Gregg v Georgia, 144
Grodzins, Morton, 53
Gross domestic product (GDP), 55, 98, 99, 110
The Guardian, 148
Gubernational education policy advisers (GEPs), 166
Gubernatorial educational initiatives, 166
Gun control advocates, 149
"Gun-free zones," 127–128
Gun-restricted zones, 128
Gun violence, on college campus, 126–127, 126p

Hamilton, Alexander, 110, 111
Hanson, Jonathan K., 60
Hardin, Garrett, 262
Harrison, Benjamin, 163
Harvard University Library 2017, 187
Hate Crime Statistics, 130
Hawaii Supreme Court, same-sex marriage, 67
Hawaii v. Trump, 195
Hayes Lucy, 164
Head Start program, 55, 112, 217
Healthcare.gov, 23, 24f
Health insurance, 219
Health Insurance Marketplace, 227
Health Maintenance Organizations (HMOs), 224
Health reform, after Great Depression, 223–224

Healthy capacity, in state and local governments, 60
Healthy Forests Restoration Act, 2003, 242
Heroin, 45
High Country News, 200
Higher education, connecting K-12 with, 172
High schools shooting, 127
Highway Safety Act was passed, 42
Hispanic Americans, poverty and, 208
Hispanic population. See "sleeping giant" of electoral politics
HMOs. See Health Maintenance Organizations (HMOs)
Hobby Lobby, 9
Holder, Eric, 46, 68
Homeland Security Act of 2002, 191
Homeless, 205p, 206
Homicide, 133f, 134, 139
Hoover, Herbert, 112
Horizontal federalism, 49–50
House and Senate appropriations subcommittees, 105
House of Representatives, committees in, 116
Housing prices, 113
"How a bill becomes a law," 6, 8
HRSA. See Human Resources and Services
      Administration (HRSA)
Human Resources and Services Administration
      (HRSA), 10
Hunter, Duncan, 177
Hurricane Katrina, 110
Hurricane Sandy, 27
Hyperinflation, 99

ICE (U.S. Immigration and Customs Enforcement), 192,
      195
IDEA. See Education of Handicapped Children Act of
      1975 (Individuals with Disabilities Education Act
      [IDEA] of 1990)
Ideological groups, 11
IGR. See Intergovernmental relations (IGR)
Illegal Immigration Reform and Immigrant
      Responsibility Act of 1996, 188, 191, 193t, 202
Immigrant Quota Act of 1921, 187
Immigrants, undocumented, 188
Immigration Act
  Chinese immigrants under, 187
  of 1882, 187, 190
  of 1917, 190
  of 1924, 190
  of 1965, 188
  of 1990, 191
  See also Immigration and Nationality Act (INA)

Immigration and Customs Enforcement (ICE), 202
Immigration and Nationality Act (INA), 193t
    of 1952, 191
    of 1965, 191
Immigration and Naturalization Service (INS), 188
Immigration Equality, 197t
Immigration posse, and ACLU, 199
Immigration quota, 196
Immigration Reform and Control Act 1986 (IRCA), 181,
    188, 191, 202
implementation, 2, 10, 67, 85–86
Implementers, 9–10
Improved data acquisition methods/stealth assessments, 174
Improving America's Schools Act of 1994, 162
INA. *See* Immigration and Nationality Act (INA)
Incarceration, 130, 135–137, 136f, 149
Incentives, financial, 57
Inchoate crimes, 128–129
Income, states with highest, 64
Income inequality, 228–229
Income tax, 108, 108t
An Inconvenient Truth (film), 6
incrementalism, 40
Index of State Economic Momentum, 63
Indian Citizen Act of 1924, 179–180
Individualistic cultures, states with, 62, 63t
Individual responsibility, 210, 211
Individual rights, federalism and safeguarding, 66
Individuals with disabilities, 179
Industrialization, 239–240
Inflation, 99
Innovation, federalism and stimulating, 67
INS. *See* Immigration and Naturalization Service (INS)
Inside Bureaucracy (Downs), 9–10
Inslee, Jay, 166
Institute for Research on Poverty, 208, 208b
Institutional actors, 7–10, 8t
Institutional agenda, 29
Intention-based enforcement style, 88f, 89
Interest groups
    as actors in education policy, 168, 169t
    as actors in environmental and energy policy, 258–259
    agency decision making and, 82–83
    public, 10
    role within policymaking process, 8t, 10–11
Intergovernmental lobbying, 60
Intergovernmental relations (IGR), 50–51
    evolvement of, 51–66
    federalism and, 56–65

Internal agency review, in rulemaking process, 81
Internal Revenue Service (IRS), 108, 117–118
IRCA. *See* Immigration Reform and Control Act 1986
    (IRCA)
Issue networks. *See* Policy subsystems

Jackson, Andrew, 117
Jackson, Reverend Jesse, 135
Jackson v. Hobbs, 147
Jack the Ripper, 139
Jefferson, Thomas, 111, 187
Job Creation Act of 2010, 116
Jobs Corps, 217
Johns Hopkins University, 127
Johnson, Eddie, 135, 146
Johnson, Lyndon B.
    changes in domestic policies, 55
    "creative federalism," 54
    on education, 164
    Elementary and Secondary Education Act, 160
    goals of eliminating poverty, 112, 216, 217, 219,
        224, 227
    shaking the hand of an Appalachian, 217p
Johnson administration, 112, 219
Jones, Bryan, 40
Journal of the American Medical Association 1943, 224
JPMorgan Chase, 114, 115
Jurisdiction, 129
Just Say No to Drugs program, 164
Juvenile crime, 147–148
Juvenile Justice and Delinquency Prevention Act of
    1974, 147

K–12
    actors involved in students lunch, 170, 170f
    connecting with higher education, 172
    educational initiatives, 164
    education interest groups for, 168
    public education/schools, 159, 168
    school breakfasts or lunches, 170
    students, tax credits for, 164
Kaiser Family Foundation, 55, 210, 220, 228
Kansas, as Republican trifecta state, 64–65
Kasich, John, 73
Kearney, Richard, 60
Kennedy, John F., 54, 112, 188, 192, 216
Kentucky, marriage license to gay couples, 68
Keynes, John Maynard, 98
Keynesian economic theory, 97, 98

Keystone XL pipeline, 243
King, Rodney, 138
Kingdon, John, 38
Know-Nothing Political Party formed, 182
Kofinis, Chris, 14
Kraft 2015, 249, 250
Krane, Dale, 68
Krueger, Freddy, 139
Kyoto Protocol, 242

Laboratories of democracy, 67
Laissez-faire economy, 97
LaPierre, Wayne, 135
Lasswell, Harold, 3, 26
Lasswell, Harold, 26
Las Vegas Strip, mass shooting of, 148
La Tuna Canyon brush fire, California, 61p
Lau decision, 194
Lau v. Nichols, 164, 179
Law Enforcement Officers Killed and Assaulted, 130
Laws
    drug, 45
    federal or state rule and, 85–86
    passing, 49
    as response to mass shooting, 150
    state and federal, 129
    "three strikes," 142, 143
    truth in sentencing, 142
    in the U.S., 8–9
    See also Federal laws
Laws tool, 31
Lecter, Hannibal, 139
Legislation, on Great Recession, 114
Literacy test, for immigrants, 187
Litigation, impact of final rule, 84–85
Lobbying, 11, 12t, 60
Lobbyists, 11, 258–259
Local dry cleaner, regulating, 86–87, 92
Local government
    citizens and trust in, 66
    federal grants 1980-2010, 56f
    increasing capacity of, 60–62
    policy in, 50–51
    in public policymaking, 62
    role in education, 156t
Lockyer v. Andrade., 143
Los Angeles Times, 205, 211
LSD, 45
Luckman, Thomas, 28

Lunney, Kellie, 8
Lynch, Loretta, 78

MacArthur Foundation, 148
Madison, James, 66, 111
Magnet school, 161
Mandates, underfunded and unfunded, 56–59
Mandatory and *discretionary spending,* 108
Mandatory spending, 108–109
Mann, Horace, 159, 160, 172
Marijuana
    federal and state policy, 45–46
    legalizing, 46, 47b
    medicinal laws, 46
    use of, 67
Marjory Stoneman Douglas High School, Parkland,
        Florida, 21, 29, 134
Marshall, John, 52
Maryland
    crime in, 134
    national bank in, 52
    political cultures as described by Elazar, 1966, 63t
    poverty rates, 208
    as richest state, 63
Massachusetts Supreme Court, legalizing same-sex
        marriage, 68
Mass shootings
    definition and history in America, 148–149, 150
    events, 126–128
    in schools, public perception about, 134–135
Mayhew, David, 8
Mayors, as actors in U.S. education policy, 167–168
McCarran-Walter Act 1952, 188
McCulloch v. Maryland, 52
McCullough, Linda, 269
Means-tested, 210
Media
    crime and, 139–140
    role within policymaking process, 8t, 10–11
    teachers and, 154–155
Medicaid, 217, 219
Medical marijuana dispensaries, in California, 46
Medicare, 217, 219
Men, poverty rates of, 208, 209f
Mexican-American War, 181
Michigan, abolishment of death penalty, 143
Migrant Labor Agreement in 1951, 190–191
Mill, John Stuart, 98
Miller Center, 54, 55

Miller v. Alabama, 147, 148

Minerals Management Service, 243

Minnesota, same-sex couple case, 67

Mississippi

    health-related policies, 64

    poverty rate, 63

Mix of enforcement styles, 88f, 89–90

Model States Administrative Procedure Act, 81

Modern Environmental Movement, birth of, 240–241

MomsRising, 168

Monetary policy, 101, 103–104

Money, for government policy implementation, 121

Money tool, 31

Moniz, Ernest, 250

Montana, support for education, 166

Moralistic cultures, states with, 62, 63t

Morgan Stanley, 114

Morning-after bill. *See* Plan B

Morphine, 45

Morrill Act of 1862, 159, 162

Motor Vehicle theft crimes, 132, 133f

MSF. *See* Multiple Streams Framework (MSF)

MSHA regulators. *See* Federal Mine Safety and Health
    Administration (MSHA) regulators

Muir, John, 240

Multiple Streams Framework (MSF), 38–40, 38f, 41

Murder rate, in US 1960-2014, 31f

NAS. *See* National Academy of Sciences (NAS)

Nathan, Richard, 67

National Academy of Sciences (NAS), 13

National Aeronautics and Space Administration, 40

National Association of State Boards of Education
    (NASBE), 169t

National Association of State Budget Officers, 137

National Bureau of Economic Research, 127–128

National Center for Education Statistics 2017, 159

National Center for Victims of Crime 2012, 142

National Conference of Charities and Corrections,
    214

National Conference of State Legislatures, 166

National courts, prosecuted crime at the founding of the
    country, 137

National Crime Victimization Survey (NCVS), 130

National Education Association (NEA), 168, 169t

National Energy Act of 1978, 248, 253

National environmental laws, 61

National Environmental Policy Act of 1969 (NEPA),
    240, 252

National government

    citizens and trust in, 66

    grants to states, 53–54

    prosecution of criminal cases, 129

National Governors Association, 60

National Health Act, 223

National health insurance

    Roosevelt and, 223

    Truman and, 224

National Highway Traffic Safety Administration, 42

National Incident-Based Reporting System, 130

National Institute of Justice, 144, 146

National League of Cities, 51, 60

National Manufacturers Association, 259

National origin quotas, immigration and, 187–188

National Parent Teacher Association (PTA), 168, 169t, 170

National Prohibition Act. *See* Volstead Act

National Public Radio (NPR), 158, 158b, 274

National Rifle Association (NRA), 13, 135, 148

National School Boards Association (NSBA), 168, 169t

National School Lunch Program, 208, 211

National security, energy and, 250–251

"National supremacy clause," 49

"National Unfunded Mandates Day," 57

Naturalization Act 1906, 190

Natural Resources Defense Council, 258

NBC News 2006, 199

NCLB. *See* No Child Left Behind Act (NCLB) of 2002

NCVS. *See* National Crime Victimization Survey
    (NCVS)

NEA. *See* National Education Association (NEA)

NELS. *See* No Extra-Large Sodas (NELS)

NEPA. *See* National Environmental Policy Act of 1969
    (NEPA)

Ness, Eliot, 138

#NeverAgain movement, 66

New Deal

    Great Society programs and, 69

    program, 98, 112

    Roosevelt's, 50, 113, 227

    Social Security and, 214–215

    social welfare programs, 227

New Mexico, crime rate in, 64

News

    fake, 274

    received by age, 2016, 273f

New State Ice v. Liebmann 1932, 61

New York, rulemaking process, 81

New York's Society for the Prevention of Pauperism, 213

New York State Register, 81, 82, 83p
New York Times, 68
9/11 terrorist attack (2001), 21, 110, 189, 195, 242
Ninth Circuit U.S. Court of Appeals, 143
Niskanen, William, 9
Nixon, Richard, 51, 217, 241, 252
No Child Left Behind Act (NCLB) of 2002, 160, 161,
    162, 163, 167, 174–175
No Extra-Large Sodas (NELS), 34, 37
Nondefense spending, 109
Nonincrementalism, 40
Noninstitutional actors, 7, 10–11
Nonpoint source (NPS) pollution, 264, 265
Nonrenewable sources, 246
Norton, Gale, 241
Notice of proposed rulemaking (NPRM), 79, 79f, 81,
    85
NPRM. *See* Notice of proposed rulemaking (NPRM)
NRA. *See* National Rifle Association (NRA); National
    Rifle Association (NRA)
NRC. *See* Nuclear Regulatory Commission (NRC)
NSBA. *See* National School Boards Association (NSBA)
Nuclear power, 246f
Nuclear Regulatory Commission (NRC), 248, 258

Obama, Barack
    Americans opinions about economy under, 100
    approval ratings in 2016, 8
    clemency to federal prisoners, 136
    Deferred Action for Childhood Arrivals (DACA)
        program, 194
    environmental issues in agenda, 243
    Every Student Succeeds Act of 2015, 160
    executive orders, 192
    Great Recession legislation, 114
    health care crisis and, 220
    on higher education, 164
    immigration policy under, 192
    support for same-sex marriage, 68
    on use of marijuana, 78
Obama, Michelle, 164
Obama administration
    Affordable Care and Patient Protection Act, 243
    DOMA and, 68
    on drug policies for low level, 136
    federal penalties against creational marijuana users,
        46
    government transparency, 91
    immigration policy under, 189

Obamacare, 19, 20
    in 2010, 36
    efforts to replace, 40–41
    website, 23, 35
    See also Affordable Care Act (ACA)
Obama White House, federal budget and, 95
Obergefell v. Hodges, 68, 181
Obesity
    childhood, Michelle Obama on, 164
    rates of, 28
OECD. *See* Organization for Economic Co-operation
    and Development (OECD)
Office of Civil Rights 2017, 156
Office of Credit Ratings, 114
Office of Economic Opportunity, 217
Office of Immigration, 190
Office of Information and Regulatory Affairs (OIRA),
    78, 256
Office of Management and Budget (OMB), 105, 115,
    118, 200, 256
Official actors, 41
Oil Pollution Act of 1990, 65, 236, 242
OIRA. *See* Office of Information and Regulatory Affairs
    (OIRA)
Old Age, Survivors Insurance Program, 215
OMB. *See* Office of Management and Budget (OMB)
115th Congress, repeal and replace Obamacare, 19
OPEC. *See* Organization of the Petroleum Exporting
    Countries (OPEC)
Opioid use, 27
Oregon, medicinal marijuana laws in, 46
Organization for Economic Co-operation and
    Development (OECD), 231–232
Organization of the Petroleum Exporting Countries
    (OPEC), 248
Orshansky, Mollie, 207

Paid parental leave for parents, 8
Palmer, Mitchell, 199
Paper currency, 103
Paris Climate Accord, 61
Paris Climate Agreement in 2016, 243, 244p, 245
Park, Haeyoun, 68
Parkland High School shooting, 128
Parole officers, crime and, 142
Passenger cars safety features, 41
Patient Protection and Affordable Care Act of 2010, 226
    See also Affordable Care Act (ACA); Obamacare
Pautz, Michelle, 2, 10, 14

Paycheck Fairness Act of 1963, 179
Peanut-free buffer zone, 72
Peanuts, on a plane, 71–72
Pell Grants, 116
Pelosi, Nancy, 220
A People's History of the United States (Zinn), 166
Perkins, Frances, 215
Perry, Rick, 251, 257
Personal crime, 128
Personal Responsibility and Work Opportunity
    Reconciliation Act of 1996, 218, 226
Persons of color, prosecution of, 146
PET. *See* Punctuated equilibrium theory (PET)
Peters, B. Guy, 31, 32
Pew Center, 146
Pew Center on the States, 138
Pew Center on the States study, 146
Pew Research Center, 183, 211, 273, 276
Pew Research poll, 232
Picket fence federalism, 58, 59p
Pipeline and Hazardous Safety Administration, 72
Pittsburgh Post-Gazette 2014, 229
Plan B, 9
Plessy v. Ferguson, 160
Pluralism, 3
Plyler v. Doe, 194
PNC Financial Services, 114
Policy
    choices, federal tax system, 122
    choices of, 19
    defined, 2, 20
    focusing events and change in, 21
    force of events and change of, 65–66
    Great Society, 55
    implementation, 67
    national, state, and local, 50–51
    perspectives from chapters, 270f
    state-national, 61
    tools, 31
    see also Public policy
    See also Public policy making; Regulatory policy;
        Teaching policy
Policy actors
    in criminal justice, 140–141
    in economics, 116–119
    in environment and energy, 254–260
    in immigration, 192–196
    institutional and noninstitutional, 7–12
    policymaking process, 8f, 41–42

Policy analysis, 12–13
Policy choices
    federal tax policy, 123
    gun control, 150—151
    immigration reform, 202–203
    nonpoint source pollution, 264, 265
    social and welfare policy, family leave, 231–232
    student evaluation, 174–175
Policy debates, role of science in, 261
Policy doers, 269
Policy entrepreneurs, 6, 29
Policy evaluation
    as phase of policymaking process, 5f, 7
    policy analysts and program evaluators and, 13
    in public policy making, 26, 26f, 35–37
Policy evaluators, 7
Policy facts, 272–273
Policy formulation, policymaking and, 5f, 6, 26,
    26f, 30–32
Policy implementation
    according to Theodoulou and Kofinis, 10
    as phase of policymaking process, 5f, 6–7
    in public policy making, 26, 26f, 33–35
Policy legitimation, policymaking and, 5f, 6, 26, 26f, 33
Policymakers, about imprisonment of criminals, 143
Policymaking, national, Articles of Confederation under,
    48–49
"Policy primeval soup," 38f, 39
Policy stream, of Multiple Streams Framework, 38f, 39
Policy subsystems, 40
Policy wonks, 271–272
Political community, 14
Political culture, as defined by Elazar, 62
Political environment, as factor influencing
    policymaking, 21–22
Political polarization, 119, 122
Political subculture, in American states, 62
Politicians, 154–155, 261
Politicization, social welfare and energy policy and, 261
Politics, as described by Lasswell, 3
Politics stream, of Multiple Streams Framework, 38f, 39
Poor houses and "outdoor relief," 213–214
Posner, Paul, 56–57
Poverty
    AFDC and, 218
    Civil War and, 213
    defining, 207–208, 210
    economy after World War II and, 216
    during the Great Depression, 214, 214p

guidelines, 208
health and, 229
Johnson war on poverty, 217, 217p
line, 207
rate through the Great Society programs, 217
thresholds, 207
in the U.S., 206
U.S. poverty rates in 1968, 1990, by age and racial
group, 209f
Poverty Bill, 217
Power, 3
Precision-based regulatory approach, 88, 88f
Pre-rule stage, in federal rulemaking, 79f, 84
Preservationists, 240
President
accountability and, 78
as actor in economic policy, 117
as actor in environmental and energy policy, 254, 256
as actor in immigration policy, 192–194
as actor in social welfare and health care policy, 227
as actor in U.S. education policy, 163–164
U.S. public policymaking and, 7, 8, 8t
Presidential election of 2016, 22
Pressman, Jeffrey, 34
Primary education, 155–156
Print, 10
Prison Policy Initiative, 137
Private insurance companies, 223
Probation officers, crime and, 142
Problem identification and definition
as phase of policymaking process, 5, 5f
in public policy making, 26, 26f, 27–28
Problem stream, of Multiple Streams Framework, 38f, 39
Professional interest groups, 10, 11
Prohibition era, 137
Property crime, 128
Property tax, 157, 159
Prosecutors, use of three strikes, 143
Protecting the Nation from Foreign Terrorist Entry into
the United States, 193t
Protecting the Nation from Foreign Terrorist Entry into
the United States-Revised, 193t
Pruitt, Scott, 244
PSAs. See Public service announcements (PSAs)
PTA. See National Parent Teacher Association (PTA)
Public, 2
Publications, on crime, 130
Public attitudes, about incidence of crime, 138–139
Public Broadcasting Service 2007, 111

Public comments, in rulemaking, 82–83
Public education
changes in, 159
state and local government and, 156
Public interest groups, 10
Public law, 9
Public opinion, regarding environmental issues, 245
Public Opinion Strategies 2010, 138
Public perceptions, 73f
Public policy
about, 20
actors in policy process, 41–42
alternative process models, 38041
categories of, 4–5, 4f
community and, 13–14
consensus and, 275–277
context of, 21–24
defined, 3
development and implementation, 59
evolution over time, 270
as profession, 14
public problems and solutions, 271–275
shaping, 11
solutions and, 14
theories, 24–26
toward same-sex marriage, 67
See also Public policymaking
Public policymaking
factors influencing, 21–24
politics as part, 3
process, 5–7, 5f, 14, 26–38, 26f
stages heuristic model of, 26–37
steps of making, 26
time spans in, 25
Public problems, 20, 25
Public school system, Americans and, 162
Public service announcements (PSAs), 32
Public support
for legalizing marijuana (1969-2017), 47f
for social welfare programs, 211–213, 211t
Public welfare programs, 210
Public Works Administration, 112
Pulse nightclub, Florida, 21, 150
Punctuated equilibrium theory (PET), 40–41, 227
Punctuations, periods of, 40–41
Punishment, severity of, 143

"Quality of life," 100, 240
Quist, Rob, 271

Racial profiling, by law enforcement, 146
RCRA. *See* Resource Conservation and Recovery Act of 1976 (RCRA)
Reagan, Nancy, 164
Reagan, Ronald, 60, 78, 98, 218, 241, 249
Reagan administration, 241, 249
Recession, 99–100
Recidivism, 144–145
Redistributive public policy, 4f, 5
Refugees, sanctuary cities and, 200
Regulating, local dry cleaner, 86–87, 92
Regulation Room, 91
Regulations, 73
    as defined by Meier, 74
    populations involved in, 85–86
Regulations.gov, 80p, 82, 83, 91, 92
Regulator processes, 79–83
Regulators
    enforcement style use by, 88f
    rulemaking, 86
Regulatory committee members, 86
"Regulatory excellence molecule," 92
"Regulatory Impact Analysis of proposals for new regulations as well as for final regulations", 78
Regulatory policy, 4f, 5, 74, 76, 90–91
Regulatory processes, state ruling, 81–83
RegX, 92
Religious discrimination, 181, 182f
Renewable sources of energy, 246, 246f, 247, 262, 263
Republicans
    control of Congress, 41
    government assistance for unemployed, 213
    immigration policy and, 194
    leaders in Congress, Obamacare and, 22
    opposition of Obama, 96
    primary debate, 74
    trifecta, 64, 65f
Reserved powers, 50
Resource Conservation and Recovery Act of 1976 (RCRA), 240, 253
Responsibility
    promoting, federalism and, 66
    shift of, 76
Revenue
    forecasting methods, 107
    government, 107–108, 107f, 108t
Revolutionary War, 110, 111
Rhode Island, abolishment of death penalty, 143
Rinfret, Sara, 1, 14

Ringquist, Evan, 74
Risk assessment, 36
Robertson, David B., 66
Roosevelt, Franklin Delano
    dual federalism and, 52–53
    executive orders, 192
    national campaign for health insurance, 223
    New Deal program, 50, 77, 98, 214
    unemployment insurance and AFDC, 215–216
    on use of natural resources, 240
Roosevelt administration
    policies under New Deal, 22
    public policy, 20
Route 91 Harvest Festival, Nevada, 21
Rule, 77
Rulemaking, 34, 72, 75, 84f
    See also Agency policymaking
Rules orientation, as attribute to precision-based regulatory approach, 88

Sabatier, Paul, 25
Sabido, Rosa, 200
Safe Drinking Water Act, 57, 86
Safe Drinking Water Act of 1974, 57, 86, 252
Same-sex marriage
    American public policy toward, 67
    states legalizing, 68
San Carlos Apache Nation, Arizona, 179
Sanctuary cities, refugees and, 200
Sanders, Bernie, 221
Sandy Hook Elementary School, Connecticut, 21, 127, 148
San Francisco Flex School, 161
Scalia, Antonin, 259
Scheberle, Denise, 1–2, 14
Schedule 1 drug, 45
Schedule 2 substances, 45
School Breakfast Program, 211
Schools
    choice, 161, 163
    choice and technology, 161–162
SDWA. *See* Safe Drinking Water Act of 1974
Seagal, Steven, 199
Seat belts, 41, 42
SEC. *See* Securities and Exchange Commission (SEC)
Second Amendment, 148
Secondary education, 156
Secure Fence Act of 2006, 191–192, 193t
Securities and Exchange Commission (SEC), 117, 118

Security
  campus, universities and colleges, 127
  crime and, 200
Senate and House Budget Committees, 105
Senate committees, 116–117
Sentencing Project 2017, 135, 136, 146, 147, 200
Services tool, 31
Sessions, Jeff, 45, 136
Shift of responsibility, 76
Sierra Club, 11, 240, 258
Sigman, Rachael, 60
Silent Spring (Carson), 240
Single-payer health care system, 229
SIPs. *See* State implementation plans (SIPs)
"Sleeping giant" of electoral politics, 194
Small town USA, 200
Smith, Adam, 98
Smith, Joseph, 182
SNAP. *See* Supplemental Nutrition Assistance Program
  (SNAP)
Snyder, Rick, 65
Social, or collective responsibility, 210
Social and cultural environment, as factor influencing
  policymaking, 23
Social insurance, 210
Social insurance programs, 210, 219
Social Security
  defined, 215
  New Deal and, 214–215
  as social insurance, 210
  See also U.S. social welfare policy
Social Security Act of 1935, 215, 219, 223, 225, 227
Social Security Act of 1935. Title II, 215
Social Security Administration, 210, 217, 227
Social Security Amendments of 1965, 224, 226
Social Security Program, 210
Social Security Trust Fund, 215
Soda, 27, 28, 30, 32, 33, 37
Sonoma Technology, 92
South Dakota v. Dole, 54
Sovereignty, 49
Spending, government, 109–110, 109f, 111–112
SPM. *See* Supplemental Poverty Measure (SPM)
Sports Leadership and Management Academy, 161
SPR. *See* Strategic petroleum reserve (SPR)
Spurlock, Morgan, 30
Stages heuristic approach, 5–7, 5f
Stages heuristic model of public policymaking, 26–38
Standardized testing/status quo, 174

Stapleton, Corey, 268, 269
State administrative capacity, 61
State Administrative Procedure Act (SAPA), 81
State agencies, examples of, 75t
State and local law enforcement agencies, 140
State courts, 9
  crime and, 141
  hearing of criminal and civil cases, 129, 129f
State education departments, 167p
State expertise, as actors in education policy, 166–167
State funds, for paid family leave, 231–232
State government
  as actor in social welfare and health care policy, 228
  citizens and trust in, 66
  federal grants (1980-2010), 56f
  increasing capacity of, 60–62
  prosecution of criminal cases, 129
  in public policymaking, 62, 69
  role in education, 156t
State implementation plans (SIPs), 252
State legislators, as actors in education policy, 166
State-national policy, 61
State Policy Reports 2016, 62
State regulators, 86
State ruling, 81–83, 82f
State University (Virginia Tech), 126, 126p
Statutory crime, 129
Statutory law, 74
Steagall, Henry, 115
"Stimulus." *See* American Recovery and Reinvestment
  Act of 2009
Stock market crisis, 113
Stone, Deborah A., 13, 14, 31
Stoneman Douglas High School, Parkland, Florida, 21,
  29, 66, 148, 151
Strategic petroleum reserve (SPR), 253
Street-level bureaucrats, 86
Student loans, 32, 120–121
Suasion tool, 31
Subsidies, 32
Sugary drinks, 27, 30, 32, 34
Sugary Drinks Portion Cap Rule, 27, 28
Sullivan, Emmett, 85
"Superfund," 240
Superintendents, as actors in U.S. education policy,
  167–168
Super Size Me (film), 30
Supplemental Nutrition Assistance Program (SNAP), 31,
  77, 208, 209–210, 227

Supplemental Poverty Measure (SPM), 207–208
Supplemental Security Income, 210
Supply-side economic theory, 98

TANF Program. *See* Temporary Assistance to
    Needy Families (TANF) Program
TARP. *See* Troubled Asset Relief Program (TARP)
Taxes tool, 31
Tax Policy Center 2016, 116
Tax Relief, 115
Teachers, as actors in education policy, 167–168
Teaching as career, 154–155
Teaching policy
    education policy and, 155
    structure of U.S. education, 155–159
Technology and curriculum, 171–172
Temporary Assistance to Needy Families (TANF)
    Program, 210, 218, 228
Tennessee Valley Authority, 112
Tenth Amendment, 155
Territorial dispossession, 179
Terrorism, threat of, 21
Teslas, 237
Theodoulou, Stella, Z., 14
Theoretical underpinnings, 28
Theory, as defined by Google, 25
Three Mile Island nuclear plant, 248p
"Three strikes," 142, 143, 147
Thrifty Food Budget, 207
Title I program, 217
Title I schools, 160
Title IX, passage of, 160
Tough enforcement, as attribute to precision-based
    regulatory approach, 88
Traditionalistic cultures, states with, 62, 63t
Transatlantic Trade and Investment Partnership
    (TTIP), 120
TransCanada, 243
Transocean, 235
Treasury Department, 111, 116, 190
Treaty of Guadalupe Hidalgo, 1848, 181
"Trickle-down" economic policies, 97, 98
Trifectas, 64, 65f
Troubled Asset Relief Program (TARP), 113–114,
    116, 227
Trudeau, Justin, 274p
Truman, Harry, 110, 188, 192, 224
Truman administration, 110

Trump, Donald
    changes to environmental issues, 243
    Deferred Action for Childhood Arrivals (DACA)
        program and, 194
    energy policy and, 250
    executive orders, 192, 192t, 194
    on illegal immigration, 189
    on immigration reform, 200
    on replacing and repealing ACA, 19, 22, 41, 225, 227
    on ridding major cities of crime, 134
    salient issues for, 22
    stance toward immigration, 192
    state-national policy diversion and, 61
    on U.S. Mexican border, 184, 192
Trump administration
    Americans opinion about handling economy, 100
    on environmental policy, 245
    federal prohibitions against marijuana use, 46
    list of sanctuary cities, 200
    policy priority, 22
Trust
    in local, state, and national governments, 66
    in sentencing, 142
TSA. *See* U.S. Transportation Security Administration
    (TSA)
TTIP. *See* Transatlantic Trade and Investment
    Partnership (TTIP)
Tubman, Harriet, 117
Turner, Cory, 158
Twenty-first century
    education, 171, 172
    immigration, 200
24/7 Wall St., 63

UCR. *See* Uniform Crime Reporting Program (UCR)
UK's National Health Service, 229
Underfunded mandates, 56–59
Undocumented immigrants, 188, 192, 200
Undocumented workers, 181
Unemployment
    in 1933, 214
    insurance, 210, 215–216
    rate, 98–99, 99t
Unemployment Insurance Reauthorization, 116
Unfunded mandates, 56–59
Unfunded Mandates Reform Act, 57
Uniform Crime Reporting Program (UCR), 130
Union Carbide, 242

Unitary system of government, 52
United States' energy supply, 245–246
United States General Accounting Office 2004, 57, 58
Universal health care, 229
University of Michigan's National Poverty Center, 206
University of Pennsylvania (UPenn), 92
Unofficial actors, 42
    in immigration policy, 196–197, 197t
    in social welfare and health care policy, 228
Urban Institute, 197
U.S. Accountability Office (GAO), 164
USA Patriot Act, 189
U.S. attorney general, 140–141
U.S. Border Patrol, 196
U.S. Bureau of Economic Analysis, 2017, 98
U.S. Bureau of Fisheries, 240
U.S. Census Bureau, 63, 99, 146, 206, 207, 208, 227
U.S. Census Report, 51
U.S. Chamber of Commerce, 259
U.S. Climate Alliance, 61, 62
U.S. Coast Guard 2011, 235
U.S. Conference of Mayors, 60
U.S. Congress, 136
    accountability and, 77–78, 77f
    as actor in economic policy, 116–117
    as actor in education policy, 164
    as actor in environmental and energy policy, 254, 255–256t
    as actor in immigration policy, 194
    as actor in social welfare and health care policy, 227
    approval of federal payment, 216
    crime and, 136
    delegation of authority in, 76
    Department of Homeland Security and, 195
    Elementary and Secondary Education Act in 1965
        and, 156
    energy policy and Energy Policy Act, 249, 250
    EPA and, 259
    financial contribution to, 11, 12t
    Immigration Reform and Control Act (IRCA), 181
    McCarran-Walter Act 1952, 188
    Morrill Act, 159
    passes bill, 33
    pass of the budget by, 96
    Poverty Bill, 217
    public policymaking and, 7, 8, 8t
    Republican control of, 41
    USA Patriot Act, 189
U.S. Constitution
    Article I, Section 7, 108
    Article I, Section 8, 49
    Article IV of, 49–50
    Article VI, Section II, of, 49
    Congress as lawmaking authority, 7
    racial profiling, 146
    Tenth Amendment to, 50
U.S. Constitution and Immigration and Nationality
    Act, 195
U.S. court of appeals, 9
U.S. credit rating, 119
U.S. currency, 103
U.S. Customs and Border Protection (CBP), 140, 195t,
    196
U.S. Declaration of Independence, 178
U.S. Department of Agriculture, 207, 211, 227
U.S. Department of Agriculture's MyPlate, 20
U.S. Department of Education (DOEd), 156, 160, 165
    fined Virginia Tech, 127
    formation and responsibility, 165
U.S. Department of Energy, 248, 249, 250, 257
U.S. Department of Health and Human Services (HHS),
    208, 216, 227
U.S. Department of Homeland Security (DHS), 189,
    192, 194, 195, 195t, 202
U.S. Department of Housing and Urban Development, 206
U.S. Department of Justice (DOJ), 46, 130, 140
U.S. Department of Labor, 86
U.S. Department of State, Bureau of Population,
    Refugees, and Migration, 195t
U.S. Department of the Interior, 257–258
U.S. Department of Transportation (DOT), 71, 72, 249,
    270, 272
U.S. Department of Transportation's peanut rule, 91
U.S. Department of Treasury
    role in policy arena, 117
    taking over Fannie Mae and Freddie Mac, 113
U.S. district court, 9
U.S. economic and national security policy, 245
U.S. economic policy, 101, 103–104
    actors in, 116–119
    economic policy defined, 97
    economic theories, 97–98
    energy policy and, 250
    history and development of, 110114
    issues and challenges of, 119–120
    statutes, 115–116
U.S. economy
    after the 2008 recession, 206
    after World War II, 216

data, exploring regional, 102b
definition of, 96–97
global, policy and, 22
growth and contraction in 1930-2016, 101f
public opinion and, 100–101
Republicans on legal citizenship and, 194
size and scope of, 98–104, 99t, 100t
states with strong economy, 64
types of economies, 97
See also U.S. economic policy
U.S. education policy, 20, 21
  actors in, 163–165
  governors and state legislators as actors in, 166
  history and development of U.S. education system, 159–163
  issues and challenges, 171–172
  major education policy statutes, 162–163
  teaching as career, 154–155
U.S. education system
  colonialism and Mann, 159–161
  European model and, 172
  structure of, 155–159
U.S. Energy Information Administration 2017, 246
U.S. Energy Information Agency, 246
U.S. energy policy
  actors in, 254–260
  the commons, 262
  energy and national security concerns in 2000s, 250–251
  energy policy defined, 245
  history and development of, 248–251
  issues and challenges, 260–262
  lack of coherent and cohesive policy, 260–261
  overview of, 237–239
  politicization and, 261
  role of science in policy debates, 261
  statutes, 251–254
  trade-off between economy and natural environment, 262
  U.S. energy consumption 1950-2014, 247, 247f
  U.S. energy production 2016, 246f
  understanding, 245–248
U.S. environmental policy
  actors and environment disaster, 235–237
  actors in, 254–260
  the commons, 262
  history and development of, 239–245
  issues and challenges, 260–262
  lack of coherent and cohesive policy, 260–261
  overview of, 237–239
  politicization and, 261
  role of science in policy debates, 261
  statutes, 251–254
  trade-off between economy and natural environment, 262
U.S. Environmental Protection Agency (EPA), 7, 10, 34, 58, 78, 96, 148, 239, 241, 257, 275–276
U.S. EPA Air Quality Trends 2016, 238, 239b
U.S. EPA 2015 Municipal Solid Waste, 239
U.S. EPA Watershed Assessment 2015, 238
U.S. Federal Agencies, 75t
U.S. Fish and Wildlife Service (USFWS), 7, 10, 85, 85f, 196, 252
U.S. Forest Service's campaign, 20
USFWS. *See* U.S. Fish and Wildlife Service (USFWS)
U.S. Government Accountability Office (GAO), 13, 115
U.S. health care policy, 19, 21
  actors in, 226–228
  after the 2008 recession, 206
  connecting to social welfare, 216–217
  history and development of, 222–225
  immigration policy and, 196
  Medicaid and Medicare as component of, 217
  overview of, 218–222
  poor people and, 229
  role of government in, 25
  social welfare policy and, 206
  statutes, 225–226
  universal health care coverage and single-payer health care, 229–230
U.S. households living on $2 a day, 205–206
U.S. House of Representatives, 6, 7, 78, 164
U.S. immigration/immigration policy
  actors in immigration policy, 192–196
  civil rights and, 181–183, 182f
  history and development of, 187–189
  immigration defined, 181
  immigration patterns, 177–178
  immigration policy defined, 21, 181
  immigration posse and the ACLU, 199
  immigration sentiments, 184–185, 185b
  issues and challenges, 199–201
  national origin quotas, 187–188
  public opinion research, 184
  reform, 22, 188
  statutes, 189–192
  trends, 183, 185b
  unofficial actors in, 196–197, 197t
  See also U.S. immigration reform

U.S. immigration reform
in 2016, 189
Democrats and Republicans concern about, 194
U.S. Immigration Reform PAC (USIRPAC), 197t
USIRPAC. *See* U.S. Immigration Reform PAC
(USIRPAC)
U.S. justice system, 139
U.S. Mexico border, 184, 189, 196, 199, 200
U.S. Mint, 103
U.S. National Guard, 179
U.S. News & World Report 2017, 161
U.S. public policymaking, 7
U.S. regulations, context of, 73–79
U.S. Senate, 6, 7, 8
U.S. Senate Appropriations Committee, 77
U.S. social welfare policy
actors in, 226–228
economy after the 2008 recession and, 206
health care policy and, 206
history and development of, 213–218
income inequality, 228–229
opinions about welfare responsibility, 211t
U.S. states
AFDC and, 216
background checks and mass shooting, 150
with highest income, 64
immigration policy and, 197, 198f, 199
with individualistic cultures, 62, 63t
with moralistic cultures, 62, 63t
paid family leaves and, 232
per capita basis of, 62–63
policy innovation and, 67
political cultures of, 62
poverty levels by state, 209b
poverty rates among, 208
state actors in education policy, 166–170
top and bottom-ranked states in Camelot Index, 64t
with traditionalistic cultures, 62, 63t
U.S. Supreme Court, 50p, 146
accountability and, 78
education cases, 160
environmental and energy policy and, 256
Hawaii v. Trump, 195
implication for U.S. education, 164
legalizing same-sex marriage, 68
same-sex marriage case, 67
on school choice, 161
on segregating schools social issues, 165
U.S. public policymaking and, 7, 8–9
See also Massachusetts supreme court
U.S. Transportation Security Administration (TSA), 21p,
30, 71
U.S. voters, perceptions on crime, 200
*Utility Air Regulatory Group v. Environmental Protection
Agency* 573 U.S., 259

value-laden, 2
value-neutral, 2
Vargas, Jose Antonio, 189
Vermont, domestic partnership law, 68
"Vertical functional autocracies," 58
Veterans, 206
Victims, crime, 141–142
Violent Crime Control and Law Enforcement Act, 142
Violent crimes, 130, 131f, 133f
Virginia, Jamestown Colony of, first execution in, 143
Virginia Commonwealth University's Social Welfare
History Project, 2017, 214
Virginia Polytechnic Institute, 126
VISTA. *See* Volunteers in Service to America (VISTA);
Volunteers in Service to America (VISTA)
VISTA program, 217
Volstead Act, 137–138
Volunteering, in environmental organizations, 263
Volunteers in Service to America (VISTA), 55, 112
Voting, 268–269
voting rights, 178
Voting Rights Act, 55
Voucher, 161

Wagner-Murray-Dingell Bill, 223
"War on Drugs," 136
"War on Poverty," Johnson's, 217, 217p
Wartime economic growth, 112
Washington, medicinal marijuana laws, 46
Washington Post poll, 100
Washington v. Trump, 194
Wastewater treatment plants (WWTPs), 252
Watt, James, 241
Waxman-Markey bill, 243
Waxman-Markey legislation, 8
WBUR 2017, 166
The Wealth of Nations (Smith), 98
Weber, Max, 9

Websites
    on civil rights and immigration, 204
    on crime and public policy, 152
    on economic policy and public budgeting, 124
    on education policy, 176
    on environmental and energy policy, 266
    on federalism and intergovernmental relations, 70
    on policy process and theories, 43
    on public policy, 18, 278
    on rulemaking actions of federal agencies, 80
    on rulemaking and regulations, 93
    on social welfare and health care policy, 233
Webster, Daniel, 52
Weiss, Elaine, 171
welfare policy
    poverty defined, 207–208, 210
    public support for budget cuts, 2017, 212f
    public support for social welfare programs, 211–213
    public values and types of social welfare programs,
        210–211
    social welfare policy defined, 207
    statutes, 225–226
    U.S. households living on $2 a day, 205–206
Welfare queen, 218
Welfare reform, 61, 218
Wells Fargo, 114
WestEd Interactive, 91
White House Council on Environmental Quality
    (CEQ), 252
White House Office of Information and Regulatory
    Affairs (OIRA), 241

White House Office of Management and Budget, 117
WIC. *See* Women, Infants, and Children (WIC)
Wildavsky, Aaron, 34, 67
Wilson, James Q., 9
Wilson, Woodrow, 192
Wisconsin, abolishment of death penalty, 143
Women
    African American, welfare queen to stigmatize, 218
    poverty rates, 208, 209f
Women, Infants, and Children (WIC), 211
Women-infant-Children programs, 96
Wool Growers Association, 2, 10–11
Worker's compensation, 210
Workhouses, 213
Work Projects Administration (WPA), 53p
Works Progress Administration, 112, 214
World Bank, 205, 206
World Health Organization, 229
World War I, 112
World War II, 110, 112, 223
Worsham, Jeffrey, 74
WPA. *See* Work Projects Administration (WPA)
Wright, Deil S., 51, 53
WWTPs. *See* Wastewater treatment plants
    (WWTPs)
Wyoming, distance learning in, 161

YouTube, 206

Zinke, Ryan, 258
Zinn, Howard, 166